Knowledge in action

Knowledge in action

The search for collaborative research for sustainable landscape development

edited by:
Annemarie van Paassen
Jolanda van den Berg
Eveliene Steingröver
Renate Werkman
Bas Pedroli

Mansholt publication series - Volume 11

Wageningen Academic Publishers

ISBN: 978-90-8686-167-5
e-ISBN: 978-90-8686-724-0
DOI: 10.3920/978-90-8686-724-0

ISSN: 1871-9309

Cover photography:
George Kroon, Ben Kamphuis, Andre de Jager, Jessica Milgroom and Willemien Geertsema

First published, 2011

©**Wageningen Academic Publishers**
The Netherlands, 2011

This work is subject to copyright. All rights are reserved, whether the whole or part of the material is concerned. Nothing from this publication may be translated, reproduced, stored in a computerised system or published in any form or in any manner, including electronic, mechanical, reprographic or photographic, without prior written permission from the publisher:
Wageningen Academic Publishers
P.O. Box 220
6700 AE Wageningen
the Netherlands
www.WageningenAcademic.com
copyright@WageningenAcademic.com

The individual contributions in this publication and any liabilities arising from them remain the responsibility of the authors.

The publisher is not responsible for possible damages, which could be a result of content derived from this publication.

Mansholt Publication Series

The Mansholt Publication Series (MPS) contains peer-reviewed publications on social changes, transformations and control processes in rural areas and (agri)food chains as well as on their institutional contexts. MPS provides a platform for researchers and educators who wish to increase the quality, status and international exposure of their scholarly work.

The Series is named after Sicco Mansholt (1908-1995), who was Minister of Agriculture in The Netherlands from 1945 until 1958. In addition he was the European's Commissioner of Agriculture and Vice-President of the European Commission from 1958 until 1972.

MPS is supported by the Wageningen School of Social Sciences (WASS), the merger of former Mansholt Graduate School of Social Sciences and CERES Research School for Resource Studies for Development. The quality and contents of the Series is monitored by an interdisciplinary editorial board. All submitted manuscripts are reviewed by at least two independent reviewers before being considered for publication. MPS is published and marketed internationally by Wageningen Academic Publishers.

The Mansholt Publication Series editors are:

Prof. Wim Heijman
Prof. Leontine Visser
Prof. Ekko van Ierland
Prof. Arjen Wals

Acknowledgements

Many people contributed to the joint learning process and actual writing and editing of this book. Our first thanks go to the colleagues from Wageningen UR who participated in the Community of Practice on collaborative research for sustainable landscape development that was active in 2007-2008, and which formed the basis of this book. We want to thank the facilitators, presenters and discussion partners for sharing experiences and insights, which contributed to the joint learning process. Their experiences led to the initial idea of a scientific publication, and various participants of the Community of Practice have actually contributed to the implementation by (co-)writing a case chapter in this book. We would also like to acknowledge the financial support given by the former Dutch Ministry of Agriculture, Nature and Food Quality, through its strategic research programme 'Sustainable spatial development of ecosystems, landscapes, seas and regions' which is run by Wageningen UR. Special thanks go to Paul Opdam, Cees Leeuwis, Gert-Jan Noij, Judith Klostermann, Floor Geerling-Eijff and Barbara Sterk from the former working group of this programme on landscape development for their early support and guidance.

In preparing this book, many others are to be thanked as well. Special thanks go to Marion Bogers who persevered long and hard to support the editor and author meetings, kept the shared files updated and helped to co-ordinate final production. Thanks also to Dana Kamphorst, who assisted with the final editing of the chapters. We also want to thank the members of the scientific advisory group of the research theme 'Knowledge use and knowledge co-production' for their valuable input. We are particularly grateful to those who have contributed comments and suggestions to the chapter texts. A special mention in this regard goes to Ken Giller from the Plant Production Systems group and Bas Arts from the Forest and Nature Conservation Policy group of Wageningen University who reviewed the book manuscript.

And most of all, thanks to the authors of the case chapters, their partners and the participants in the collaborative research processes in the Netherlands, Africa and Asia. Through your careful reflection on these experiences, we all continue to learn to make collaborative research for sustainable landscape development work.

Jolanda van den Berg, for the editors

October 2010

Preface

This book is an important, tangible outcome of the research theme 'Knowledge use and knowledge co-production' which started in 2006 and is part of the strategic research programme 'Sustainable spatial development of ecosystems, landscapes, seas and regions' run by Wageningen UR. In this research theme we assembled a group of technical and social scientists working for Wageningen UR in a Community of Practice to share and critically reflect upon their collaborative research experiences in the field of sustainable landscape development. The meetings and discussions were exciting and rich in their learning. For many participants, it was one of the first opportunities to share their concerns and experiences and to learn from and with colleagues from other backgrounds and methodological approaches. This was the reason why it was deemed important for the Community of Practice not only to document and cross-analyse the gamut of the collaborative landscape research experiences Wageningen UR was engaged in, but also to broaden our scope towards other experiences in and outside Wageningen UR. We first asked Annemarie van Paassen (Communication and Innovation Studies) and Renate Werkman (Public Administration and Policy) and later Bas Pedroli (Alterra Landscape Center) to develop a book together. The book would link collaborative landscape research theories, related methodologies and their context-specific implementation.

The purpose of this book is to present a variety of collaborative landscape research approaches in their specific context and to provide more insight into: (a) the fit of the collaborative research approach with the practical and institutional needs of the stakeholders and (b) the adequacy of the theories and methodologies used to attain the desired societal outcome. The case chapters in this book aim to unravel collaborative research processes in order to identify generic lessons on the future perspective of landscape research. In this way we hope to contribute to the theoretical and methodological development of collaborative landscape science.

This book challenges researchers to go beyond knowledge production and the facilitation of learning, and also to reflect on how to organise collaborative research to enhance societal action for sustainable and equitable landscape development and governance.

We hope that this book will inspire students and researchers from different backgrounds to engage in collaborative research in enhancing sustainable landscape development and governance. And equally important: the joint work and reflection on the actual link between collaborative landscape research experiences, theories and societal outcomes has enriched all involved in developing this book.

Jolanda van den Berg and Eveliene Steingröver
Coordinators of the Knowledge use and knowledge co-production research theme,
LEI and Alterra, part of Wageningen UR

The Hague and Wageningen, October 2010

Contents

Acknowledgements   7

Preface   9
   Jolanda van den Berg and Eveliene Steingröver

1. Landscape science and societal action   17
   Annemarie van Paassen, Paul Opdam, Eveliene Steingröver and Jolanda van den Berg
      Abstract   17
      1.1 Introduction   17
      1.2 Sustainable development as the challenge for landscape research   18
      1.3 What concerns sustainable, equitable landscape development?   21
      1.4 Research perspectives aimed at sustainable landscape development   24
      1.5 The role of researchers in enhancing sustainable landscape development   30
      References   34

2. What is collaborative landscape research about?   41
   Renate Werkman, Jolanda van den Berg, Annemarie van Paassen and Bette Harms
      Abstract   41
      2.1 Introduction   41
      2.2 Key dimensions of collaborative research   43
      2.3 Collaborative landscape development research: a typology   45
      2.4 Getting the picture: two major challenges for collaborative landscape research   49
      2.5 Introducing the case studies   51
      2.6 Structure of the book   52
      References   54

3. Collaborative research to improve the water management in two polders in the Red River Delta in Vietnam   57
   Henk Ritzema, Le Quang Anh and Bui Thi Kim
      Abstract   57
      3.1 Introduction   57
      3.2 Participatory study approach   59
      3.3 Selection of study areas   64

3.4 Problem analysis and stakeholders' preferences	66
3.5 Participatory pre-drainage investigations and monitoring programme	68
3.6 Model simulations	73
3.7 PLA workshops to prioritise improvement options	75
3.8 Discussion	77
3.9 Lessons learned	79
3.10 Conclusions	80
Acknowledgements	81
References	82

4. Development and application of a landscape design method in the Frisian Lakes area — 85
Willemien Geertsema, Arianne de Blaeij and Martijn van der Heide

Abstract	85
4.1 Introduction	85
4.2 Theoretical background	87
4.3 The RITAM method	91
4.4 Implementation	92
4.5 Conclusions and lessons learned	105
Acknowledgements	108
References	108

5. Linking training, research and policy advice: capacity building for adaptation to climate change in East Africa — 113
Catharien Terwisscha van Scheltinga and Jouwert van Geene

Abstract	113
5.1 Introduction	113
5.2 Guiding climate change adaptation in agriculture and NRM in East Africa	117
5.3 Outcomes and observations	127
5.4 Lessons learned	130
Acknowledgements	131
References	131

6. Action research in a regional development setting: students as boundary workers in a learning multi-actor network — 133
Jifke Sol, Pieter Jelle Beers, Simon Oosting and Floor Geerling-Eiff

Abstract	133
6.1 Introduction	133
6.2. Approach	136
6.3. Process and implementation	140

6.4. Lessons learned	145
6.5. Conclusions and recommendations	149
Acknowledgements	151
References	151

7. The soil-plant-animal system as a boundary object for collaborative knowledge development — 153
Marian Stuiver

Abstract	153
7.1 Introduction	153
7.2 Nutrient Management Project of VEL and VANLA	154
7.3 The Nutrient Management Project as boundary work	158
7.4 Conflicts about the soil plant animal system	161
7.5 Lessons learned	163
Acknowledgements	165
References	166

8. Learning from learning: the experiences with implementing adaptive collaborative forest management in Zimbabwe — 169
Tendayi Mutimukuru-Maravanyika and Conny Almekinders

Abstract	169
8.1 Introduction	169
8.2 The ACM approach	171
8.3 Implementing the ACM approach in practice	174
8.4 Reflection on the experiences of the CIFOR team	181
8.5 Outcomes of the ACM project and follow-up study	183
8.6 Why the positive outcomes were not sustained	184
8.7 Concluding remarks	186
Acknowledgements	187
References	187

9. Northern Thailand case: gaming and simulation for co-learning and collective action; companion modelling for collaborative landscape management between herders and foresters — 191
Pongchai Dumrongrojwatthana and Guy Trébuil

Abstract	191
9.1 Context and changing role of collaborative landscape research in Northern Thailand	191
9.2 Collaborative companion modelling for landscape management: theoretical perspectives and applied research methodology	193
9.3 The companion modelling process in Doi Tiew village	204

    9.4 Research results and outcomes of the collaborative landscape research
        process   207
    9.5 Discussion   213
    9.6 Conclusion   217
    Acknowledgements   217
    References   217

10. Reflexivity in action research: two spatial planning cases   221
Marcel Pleijte, Marc Schut and Roel During
    Abstract   221
    10.1. Introduction   221
    10.2 Action research as a scientific practice   223
    10.3 On reflexivity in action research   225
    10.4 On performativity in action research   225
    10.5. Case 1. The Dutch Flood Mitigation project: Noordwaard   226
    10.6. Case 2. The demonstration project of area development:
        Wieringerrandmeer   232
    10.7 Discussion and conclusions   240
    Acknowledgements   243
    References   243

11. Limpopo case: the role of research in conflict over natural resources; informing resettlement negotiations in Limpopo National Park, Mozambique   247
Jessica Milgroom, Cees Leeuwis and Janice Jiggins
    Abstract   247
    11.1 Introduction   247
    11.2 The Competing Claims perspective on the role of science in societal
        negotiation   249
    11.3 The research context: competition for resources and resettlement in
        Limpopo National Park   253
    11.4 The research process as it unfolded, from the field researcher's
        perspective   254
    11.5 Discussion and reflections   269
    11.6 Conclusion   274
    Acknowledgements   274
    References   275

12. Conclusion: from knowledge for action to knowledge in action 277
Annemarie van Paassen, Renate Werkdam, Bas Pedroli, Jolanda van den Berg,
Eveliene Steingröver and Cees Leeuwis
    Abstract 277
    12.1 Introduction 277
    12.2 The cases revisited 278
    12.3 The role of collaborative research 284
    12.4 Practical recommendations for the future 296
    12.5 Epilogue: collaborative research: belief, science or art? 299
    References 300

About the authors 305

Keyword index 313

1. Landscape science and societal action

Annemarie van Paassen, Paul Opdam, Eveliene Steingröver and Jolanda van den Berg

Abstract

This book takes up the challenge of contemporary landscape research. Continued poverty and progressing environmental degradation and climate change show us that landscape development is complex and unpredictable. Landscapes consist of nested biophysical and social systems, which are multi-dimensional and highly dynamic, and simultaneously interact at various system levels. This leads to complex, non-linear, divergent processes and the emergence of new landscape arrangements. Scientists have to acknowledge that they cannot predict or control landscape dynamics but need the local specific knowledge and experimentation of local stakeholders. Collaborative research-for-action and research-in-action together with societal stakeholders are needed. Many scientists accept this challenge. Based on different types of system thinking, they develop theoretical frameworks and methodologies to integrate scientific and local knowledge and/or enhance learning between them and societal stakeholders for sustainable landscape development and governance. Landscape researchers, inspired by these theoretical frameworks and the perceived issue-at-stake, start defining the orientation of the research and change process in interaction with policy makers and stakeholders. The question is whether and how the different types of research contribute to ecologically sustainable, socially equitable development and governance, valued by or at least acceptable for the variety of stakeholders, organisations and institutions involved.

1.1 Introduction

Sustainable landscape development and governance is a complex matter, as it has to deal with a high interdependency of nested biophysical and social systems, a high uncertainty, a variety of stakeholder perspectives and interests, power differences and institutional constraints. For researchers, it is a challenge to assist societal actors in finding an informed, ethical and locally-valued balance between ecological resilience and societal pursuits, and build the capacity for co-ordinated adaptive management of the involved stakeholders and governance institutions. In this book landscape researchers present and reflect upon critical issues of their collaborative research experiences. The purpose is not to develop a blue print for collaborative research, but to document and review these efforts, and see what lessons can be learnt. It focuses, above all, on how to enhance learning, fair negotiation and action for sustainable, equitable landscape development and governance. The book presents different collaborative research approaches in their specific context to provide natural and social scientists and students in the field of landscape and rural development with more insight into: (1) the fit of the collaborative research approach with the practical and institutional needs of the stakeholders and (2) the adequacy of the theories and methodologies used to

A. van Paassen, P. Opdam, E. Steingröver and J. van den Berg

attain the desired outcome. In this way we hope to contribute to theoretical and methodical development of collaborative landscape science, and inspire students and researchers to engage in collaborative research.

This first chapter provides a historical background of landscape science, and outlines its theoretical backgrounds. We first define the issue of landscape and sustainable landscape development, and then elaborate on various types of system thinking and their contribution to landscape research and the role of research in enhancing sustainable landscape development and governance. The purpose of the chapter is to raise issues and to identify questions emerging in the field of collaborative research for landscape development.

1.2 Sustainable development as the challenge for landscape research

The term landscape has its roots in the Latin term for 'region', which in the German language evolved into *Landschaft*, meaning land that was shaped by similar human land-use (Kienast *et al*., 2009). Alexander von Humboldt (1840) was the first to define the concept landscape as '*der Totalcharakter einer Erdgegend*', emphasising the holistic experiential character. Contemporary landscape scientists (e.g. Antrop, 2006; Naveh, 2000; Stephenson, 2008) also consider landscape as a synthetic and integrating concept including a material-physical reality, human economic activity, and immaterial existential values and symbols of which the landscape is a signifier. People have and always will use, manage and change the landscape in which they live and depend on for a wide range of reasons. The physical appearance of a landscape and its functioning and values are thus the result of a long-term interaction between humans and the physical systems providing them with physical and mental goods and benefits. Land-owners and users develop landscapes; they cause physical transformations that are supposed to better ensure the provision of landscape services, either because of evolving perceptions of value or to prevent loss of value due to changing external conditions, e.g. climate change. Private as well as public interests are involved, so most countries have developed some form of government-led regulation and planning.

In Europe, the elite first owned and managed large estates and agricultural production, but slowly land was privatised and the political authorities resumed responsibility for the overall regulation of land use. Land-use planning has its origins in agricultural development, town planning and nature conservation. For example, in the Netherlands the awareness that the development of land needed some co-ordination and protection rules emerged in the first half of the 20th century as a result of intense urban development. The government had faith in and promoted science-based rational use and management of resources in agriculture as well as in nature areas. Ecologists who studied the 'pure wilderness' to unravel the self-organisation and self-directedness of nature, developed criteria for the selection of conservation areas and the subsequent management of these areas. Governments used these criteria to select conservation areas, elaborate conservation measures, and compensate land-owners and users for the production loss (Johnston and Soulsby, 2006). However, local stakeholders started to question this procedure as modest human intervention in park reserves did not seem to threaten the biodiversity (Johnston and Soulsby, 2006), and many people valued historical agricultural landscapes for identity, aesthetic or recreational reasons (Nohl, 2001). This made landscape development and governance a more complex matter.

In the developing countries, most traditional societies also had clear rules for allocation and use of land, with procedures for monitoring, sanctions and jurisprudence to attain sustainable governance (Ostrom, 1990; Anderies *et al.*, 2004; Van den Berg *et al.*, 2007). People's livelihoods depended on natural resources. Local authorities and stakeholders had frequent face-to-face contact; members cared for each other, understood the agreed-upon rules and trusted the authorities. And if not, compliance was enforced by informal social control, cultural taboos, local jurisprudence and sanctions (Folke *et al.*, 1998). Local community-based institutions were quite robust, resilient and adaptive: as most disturbances were still slow and moderate, people easily adapted through ongoing field-experiments and minor organisational changes (Folke *et al.*, 1998). The situation changed with the arrival of the colonial powers. At first, the colonial authorities were primarily interested in the harvest of precious natural resources, commercial agriculture and the labour potential (Toulmin, 1992), but at the end of the eighteenth century they became alarmed by the progressing forest and land degradation in densely populated areas. The concern for environmental degradation legitimised increasing appropriation and regulation of land-use rights by colonial authorities (Leach and Mearns, 1996). These rules often neglected the traditional management rules and the critical role natural resources played in the livelihood of the rural population, who felt threatened. As a consequence, local authorities alternatively applied formal or traditional law, but in the end tenure rights were insecure and the natural resources became an open-access resource, apt to overexploitation and degradation (Hardin, 1968; Feeny *et al.*, 1990; Ostrom *et al.*, 1999; Van den Berg and Biesbrouck, 2005).

In the 1960s, most developing countries gained independence but also experienced severe droughts and famines. Various countries in the developed world initiated foreign aid programmes to fight hunger and extreme poverty. Inspired by the idea of modernisation these countries invested in agricultural research, land-use plans and technology development, and assumed the adoption of these techniques would enhance agricultural production and erase hunger crises. In practice, this Transfer of Technology model only succeeded in Asia (Chambers and Jiggins, 1985; Kline and Rosenberg, 1986), where strong farmer organisations and/or governments created favourable farm conditions (the provision of advice, credit, inputs, market infrastructure) (Van Huis *et al.*, 2007; Röling 2009). In Africa most farmers still have to deal with highly variable rainfall levels, low soil fertility, vagaries of transport and monopolistic traders, and cheap food imports (Van Huis *et al.*, 2007). To cope, they diversify their livelihood-, farm- and cropping strategies (e.g. Reij and Waters-Bayer, 2001). In the '80-90s, governments and researchers increasingly recognised the variety in conditions and the small windows of opportunity for rural households. They embarked

A. van Paassen, P. Opdam, E. Steingröver and J. van den Berg

on participatory research approaches to develop farm practices and governance plans fit for the local situation.

By the end of the 20th century, landscape development and governance approaches changed. Widespread modernisation led to unforeseen problems such as the ongoing treadmill of technological innovation, which led to the entrepreneurial success and expansion of the early adopters and the bankruptcy and eviction of the smaller firms in less favourable conditions (Röling, 2009). Ignorance of social and environmental costs in technical-economic oriented development plans led to growing distrust and revolt among local stakeholders involved. Events such as the Chernobyl disaster, the BSE catastrophe fed a growing public distrust of science and science-based governance (Beck, 1992). In the Western knowledge society, highly educated citizens now openly defy general science-based rules and regulations, when ill-suited to local circumstances (Nowotny *et al.*, 2001). To reverse this civil distrust and revolt, most governments and other regulatory institutions nowadays try to regain trust and embrace the discourse of decentralisation and democratic deliberation (Pellizzoni, 2003). They call upon scientists to include local knowledge and consider stakeholder, citizen and public values and interests in their landscape assessments. Scientists have had to rethink their epistemology, research methods and role in society.

In 1972 the report 'Limits to growth' of the Club of Rome triggered the first worldwide concern about ongoing developments: rapid population growth, food production, industrialisation and exhaustion of non-renewable natural resources. Due to the oil-crisis, politicians took the warnings seriously and in 1983 the United Nations Assembly convened a World Commission on Environment and Development (WCED) to address growing concerns 'about the accelerating deterioration of the human environment, the natural resources and the consequences of that deterioration for economic and social development'. The Brundtland commission had the task (UN, 1983) of proposing long-term environmental strategies for achieving sustainable development by the year 2000 and beyond, and recommended ways in which concern for the environment may be translated into greater co-operation among developing countries and between countries at different stages of economic and social development. The Brundtland Commission's 1987 report 'Our common future' popularised the concept of sustainable development by stating that its 'aim is to meet the needs of the present without compromising the ability of future generations to meet their own needs'. It focused attention on finding strategies to promote economic and social development in ways that avoid environmental degradation, over-exploitation or pollution, and sidelined less productive debates about whether to prioritise development or the environment. Nowadays development and business plans are increasingly assessed on the PPP dimensions: People (social), Planet (environmental) and Profit (economic). Slowly, development is starting to include climate mitigation and adaptation measures. In September 2000 the UN launched 8 Millennium Goals, which at the World Summit of 2005 were endorsed by 170 heads of state. These goals include the reduction of extreme poverty and integrating principles of sustainable development in state policies.

1. Landscape science and societal action

The Brundtland report not only promoted the vision of environmental friendly development, but also made the case for research to take a leading role. It prompted scientific institutions in the 1980s to engage in Sustainability Science, to give the broad-based support for sustainable development a stronger analytical and scientific underpinning. Sustainable development science was defined as problem- and action-oriented research (Kates *et al.*, 2001; Clark, 2003; 2007). Scientists from various disciplines engaged themselves in integrating and restructuring knowledge to attain a problem-oriented comprehensive view on sustainable development issues which are complex and interconnected. To link knowledge with action, scientists now try different kinds of collaboration with societal partners. This is especially the case for landscape- and agricultural researchers: previously developed land-use plans and technologies did not bring the socio-economic and environmental development hoped for; hence they were one of the first to adopt a more problem-oriented approach, start interdisciplinary research and involve local stakeholders (so-called trans-disciplinary research) (Fry *et al.*, 2007).

We underscore the importance of sustainable development, and we hope to make a relevant contribution. To date, many researchers have engaged in collaborative research for sustainable landscape development (for a conceptual clarification of collaborative research, see Chapter 2). In the book, we present and analyse these experiences for the purpose of improving them for the future. Equitable, sustainable development is used as the context for this analysis, considering it as a globally accepted challenge.

1.3 What concerns sustainable, equitable landscape development?

Landscape development has become a complex issue. Progressing climate change, pollution and tropical deforestation have made scientists aware that they can no longer assume it is possible to explain, predict and control these events. Increasing population, migration, urbanisation, international trade and globalisation make our society highly connected and interdependent (Dietz *et al.*, 2003; Kates and Parris, 2003). In line with the ideas of Naveh (2000), Tress and Tress (2001), Antrop (2006) and Stephenson (2008), we take landscape as a synthetic and integrating concept including a biophysical reality, human land-use activity, and immaterial existential values and symbols of which the landscape is a signifier. Landscapes in our perception consist of nested biophysical and social systems, which are multi-dimensional, highly dynamic and simultaneously interact at various system levels. This leads to complex, non-linear, divergent processes and the emergence of new phenomena (Gunderson and Holling, 2001). Hence, landscape as a complex system is highly variable in biophysical, socio-economic, cultural and political properties, and these may be very locality- and time-specific. What makes it even more complex is the fact that many more societal stakeholders and institutions have become involved, directly or indirectly at different scales. Whilst landscape development and governance were previously the domain of farmers, fishermen, land boards, water boards, forest committees, and (local) government authorities, nowadays organisation and institutions such as agricultural markets, international trade, nature conservation groups, international tourist industry and the IMF exert their influence on landscapes. And they all have their own specific interests, perspectives, norms and values. Hence, integrated approaches are needed which value ecological, social and economic interests equally.

The biophysical systems of a landscape are composed of ecosystems and human habitations, spatially arranged in a mosaic pattern, composed for example of fields for growing crops and intertwining elements like ditches and field verges, roads and embankments, hedgerows and remnants of more natural ecosystems. Other landscapes mosaics may consist of ecosystems where natural processes predominate. The physical structure of the landscape supports landscape functions. These functions turn into ecological services if perceived and valued by social actors (Termorshuizen and Opdam, 2009). Social actors, or so-called social systems, refer to stakeholder groups, organisations and institutions such as land-owners, farmers, citizens, nature managers, entrepreneurs and visitors, NGOs and pressure groups at the local level as well as markets and formal regulatory bodies at the higher systems levels. A landscape provides a wide variety of ecological services to social actors such as foods and fibres, water regulation services, aesthetic, experiences related to recreational and cultural identity, biodiversity-related services and cultural services, depending on the temporal physical characteristics and the socio-economic values. The provision of ecological services, the value different social actors attach to these material and mental services, and the concrete activities social actors undertake in the landscape connect the biophysical and social systems. Hence, the landscape is a co-production of the material and human world. Social actors may cause physical transformations that are supposed to better ensure the provision of landscape services, either because of evolving ideas of landscape values or to prevent loss of value due to changing external conditions, e.g. climate change. Sustainable landscape development for us means that within social systems we should find an informed, ethical and locally-valued balance between ecological resilience and societal pursuits.

In the book, we recognise that landscape systems are inherently dynamic. We also note that landscape development is initiated by the actors and institutions, which may have either economic (production of food and fibres, green landscapes for office parks), social (cultural assets, health, recreation) and/or ecological (conservation of rare plants and animals, regulation of water cycle) motives. Hence, landscape development is about retaining or gaining values. However, the landscape is a living dynamic system in a hierarchy of spatial and organisational scales, and its potential to provide services is not only relevant for present users in the area, but also for stakeholders elsewhere and for future generations. Based on the work of Tress and Tress (2001), Lebel *et al.* (2006), Termorshuizen and Opdam (2009 and Musacchia (2009), we identify the following principles for sustainable, equitable landscape development:
- added value of ecological services, as perceived by the stakeholders involved;
- just distribution and proportional equivalence between benefits and costs of the stakeholders involved;

- incorporation of the prospected provision of landscape services for the long term;
- incorporation of impacts and values at higher levels of spatial scale.

This implies that decisions about landscape development demand a thorough understanding of the landscape as a complex socio-ecological system and the legitimate perspectives, interests and values of the stakeholders involved, notably those of the marginalised. Because valuation varies between cultures, between areas and between moments in time, what makes a landscape change sustainable depends on the actual physical, economic, legal and institutional and cultural circumstances in the area; hence there is no one-solution-fits-all concept. For example, in poverty-stricken rural areas of developing countries, people try to cope and primarily value resources enabling them to produce food and shelter. In peri-urban areas, there is fierce competition for services; hence productivity and equity become the main issues of concern, and people might value 'wilderness' and the historical cultural landscape.

To attain sustainable equitable landscape development, we need adaptive but robust governance (Anderies *et al.*, 2004; Dietz *et al.*, 2003):
- Organisations and institutions inclined to innovate and adapt to changing societal or biophysical situation: there is regular interaction and exchange of knowledge, close monitoring of socio-ecological changes, exploration of and experimentation with new resource use practices.
- Collective choice arrangements, ensuring informed, inclusive decision-making about landscape use and protection within a changing world.
- Co-ordinated action amongst the various institutions that influence and regulate landscape design, use and governance.
- Graduated sanctions for those who violate the agreed-upon rules.
- Low cost conflict resolution mechanisms to resolve conflict among users or between users and institutions.

Sustainable landscape development requires robust multilayered polycentric governance. In this section we argued that all major stakeholders should be informed, have an effective voice and in one way or another participate in the decision-making process. The recognition of multiple scales, multiple perspectives, and the dynamic character of socio-ecological systems as well as the actors and institutions makes governance a complex issue (Cash *et al.*, 2006). Various organisation and institutions intentionally or unintentionally influence landscape use, and they have different levels of awareness, legitimacy and power to participate in landscape decision-making processes (Ramirez, 2001). Robust governance of sustainable landscape development requires informed, concerted action by a network of multilayered polycentric organisations and institutions (Dietz *et al.*, 2003; Tompkins and Adger, 2004; Cash *et al.*, 2006; Lebel *et al.*, 2006):

- *Nesting*. Simple one-level strategies based on markets or centralised-command-and-control have failed so institutional arrangements must be complex, nested in many layers and redundant.
- *Institutional variety*. Different institutional forms such as community self-governance and markets tend to complement each other's strengths and weaknesses. Governance should employ mixtures of institutional types with a variety of decision rules to change incentives, increase information, monitor use and induce compliance (Dietz, 2003; Newman and Dale, 2005).
- *Concerted action*. A type of co-ordination is needed to ensure maximum efficacy: institutions should not work against each other (Lambin, 2005) but with each other, delegating the authority-to-act to those institutions that cover the system level at which the perceived issue-at-stake occurs (Dietz *et al.*, 2003). At times, government regulators mobilise information and resources from cross-level interactions to reinforce their authority, disempowering lower level institutions and stakeholders (Adger *et al.*, 2006). Congruence, or so-called structural coupling, of the human organisation with ecological conditions is needed and can be obtained through collective or distributed cognition and decision-making (Gigerenzer *et al.*, 1999; Röling, 2002).

Now what does this entail for scientists: what role do they have to play?

1.4 Research perspectives aimed at sustainable landscape development

Society increasingly expects landscapes to fulfil many and often conflicting – economic, social, ecological – functions and to incorporate different values in relation to their physical and spatial structures (Termorshuizen and Opdam, 2009). As a result of these conflicting functions and values, complex societal problems have arisen. Landscape changes affect the interest of various stakeholders, of which some have a vested interest in maintaining the status quo (Giller *et al.*, 2008). In this context, the acceptance of research results is affected by dynamics of conflict, power and political strife and societal outcomes are shaped by unequal opportunities to take part, mobilise resources and exert influence (Long and Long, 1992; Leeuwis, 2000; Edmunds and Wollenberg, 2001a,b). To contribute to sustainable equitable development, landscape scientist need to study landscape dynamics in their whole complexity and think about what role to play in the ongoing societal debate and negotiation. Hence, a new field of science and new research paradigms have emerged that we propose to call landscape science.

Landscape science bears on distinctive collaborative science approaches, based on different epistemologies, assumptions about governance and change (Leach *et al.*, 2007), and the role of science in society (Hoppe, 2005). Landscape science is a loose collection of different scientific disciplines which converge towards interdisciplinary and trans-disciplinary research methods. In this inter- or trans-disciplinary collaboration, researchers develop a common conceptual framework and language, often based on system thinking, to transcend their original discipline. Systems theories emerged around the 1970s and view 'problems' as parts of an overall system, rather than focusing on a specific part. In the following sections, we discuss the various types of system thinking and their contribution to landscape science.

1.4.1 Hard system thinking

At first, most landscape researchers employed positivist epistemology, a causal logic focused on biophysical aspects and technical designs. This was called hard-system thinking as it referred to conceivable 'real' or 'hard systems', that one could discover by experimental and statistical analysis. Scientists from geography (spatial explicit focus), ecology (functional view on natural systems) and agronomy (functional view on soil, plant and animal systems) and economy integrated knowledge to better understand biophysical dynamics, and explore/design ecological sustainable and economic productive options. First it was assumed ecological systems had built-in goals or optimum states (homeostasis): hence sustainable land use aimed not to surpass the 'carrying capacity', beyond which ecological services to human society could not be maintained. Nowadays, hard system thinking has recognised the multi-scale dynamic interaction between biophysical and human systems, leading to complex, divergent and non-linear dynamics. Scientists cannot rely on general scientific knowledge but need locally specific knowledge about biophysical and human dynamics. However, at the heart of the approach remains 'the basic concept of central control and planning', which characterises functionalist approaches (Snowden, 2005: 5). Functionalist research approaches aim to develop universally generic theories and serve as a knowledge basis for advice to policy makers (Van Kerkhoff and Lebel, 2006).

Examples of hard system approaches in landscape science:
- *Nature conservation* mainly focussed on the conservation of natural landscapes and biodiversity with little or no anthropogenic influence, or focussed on the conservation of historical landscape assets. Here human use and development is usually restricted by regulations. The exclusive focus on nature conservation is increasingly questioned by conservation and development professionals as it ignores the critical importance of the natural resources for the livelihood of the local population (Colchester, 1994; Pimbert, 1995).
- *Land-use analysis*. The aim of land-use analysis is to optimise technical-economical use of the land-related resources to ensure vital life-support services, notably economic welfare. It started with land evaluation, which involved the multidisciplinary assessment of the capability of land for different uses (FAO, 1976). In the 1960-70s, land-use suitability maps provided rough indications of the agronomic potential of different types of soil and landscape. To improve the utility for agricultural decision-makers, land-use plans had to be more precise and indicate the 'best' land-use option. This required the use of quantitative data on yield prospects, labour requirements, economic returns, etc. (Fresco *et al.*, 1992). With the use of bio-economic modelling, scientists were able to

integrate knowledge of soil sciences, plant sciences, animal sciences and economics in an explorative model that is able to show trade-offs between competing development goals.
- *Landscape ecology* emerged in the last decades of the 20th century as a melt of geography (spatially explicit multi-scale focus) and ecology (contributing the functional view on natural systems). Many early landscape ecologists visualised the landscape as a mosaic of land units. The main paradigm is that landscapes evolve from an interaction between this physical pattern and the processes and between the units (Turner, 1989). While landscape ecology was initially dominated by descriptive and analytical approaches mainly within environmental disciplines, with an important role played by geostatistics, nowadays interdisciplinary and design-oriented approaches are being advocated (Nassauer and Opdam, 2008). Landscape ecology especially contributes knowledge about the relationship between the physical mosaic of the landscape and its functions, with an emphasis on the horizontal processes which functionally link land units into a coherent land mosaic.

1.4.2 Soft system thinking

In 1981, Checkland highlighted the importance of constructivism and soft systems (imaginary constructs of ideas and reason) for landscape research. The constructivist epistemology recognises that all knowledge, scientific knowledge included, is socially constructed. The 'constructions' evolve selectively; they are historically culturally embedded and continuously recreated through experimentation and communication (Knorr-Cetina, 1981). Scientists who embrace the constructivist epistemology note that, like all knowledge, scientific knowledge is partial and conditioned by the history of the scientific institutions, their rules of good scientific practice and rigour in research methods. Science is not 'a purely objective, value-free activity of discovery', but a creative process in which social and individual values interfere with observation, analysis and interpretation (Van Asselt and Rotmans, 2002). For instance, knowledge generated by agricultural scientists differs from knowledge of farmers who live, work and experience the landscape on a day-to-day basis, and whose livelihoods and identities are closely related to agricultural practices (Wynne, 1996). Hence, when dealing with complex issues such as landscape development, it is crucial to acknowledge the 'black spots' (ignorance) of scientific analysis and integrate other types of knowledge and values to get 'a rich picture' or 'socially robust knowledge' (Nowotny *et al.*, 2001). Furthermore, it is ethically more sound to involve users in the landscape debate, as they have high stakes in the proposed solutions (Funtowicz and Ravetz 1993, 1994; Probst *et al.*, 2003).

Examples of soft system thinking in landscape science:
- *Valuation of landscape services.* For a long time the environmental sciences have been struggling with the valuation of natural systems (Constanza *et al.*, 1997). The underlying idea was that nature, being the basis for human life, had to be protected against ongoing development and that expressing its value in the same way as the value of economic

activities could provide a powerful way of balancing nature protection against economic development. The emerging paradigm of sustainability stimulated methods to balance ecological, social and economic functions (Fry, 2001). The concept of ecosystem services (Daily, 1997) provides a means to link ecological systems to human society. The physical structure of the landscape supports landscape functions. These functions turn into landscape services if valued by humans. In this value-oriented approach, the landscape consists of (Thermoshuizen and Opdam, 2009):
- The multi-scale biophysical components.
- The human practices subtracting ecological services, with an impact on the biophysical component.
- The valuation of ecological services by the societal component, including foods and fibres, water regulation services, aesthetic experiences related to recreational and cultural identity, biodiversity related services and cultural services.

- Landscape development aims to create 'added value' for the stakeholders at different scale levels. At times scientists determine the 'added value' by using money as the common denominator for the valuation and comparison. In other cases they use scenario analysis: various stakeholders explore various (computer-generated) landscape scenarios and the respective ecological services they provide. After these explorations, stakeholders negotiate and agree upon a landscape design they consider to have the best 'added value'.

- *Adaptive management.* Proponents of 'adaptive management' not only recognise the complexity and uncertainty of sustainability issues, but they also acknowledge the partiality and conditionality of scientific knowledge (Jiggins and Röling, 2000; Anderson, 2001). Adaptive management (or -governance) therefore problematises the issue of social learning. Social learning aims to create mutual understanding between social groups, for instance between scientists, policy makers and various types of nature resource users. Social learning exchange of knowledge, opinions and interest, but also exquisite inquiry into each other's underlying beliefs, norms and values (Argyris and Schön, 1996; Leeuwis and Pyburn, 2002; Röling, 2002). This allows actors to get a new, broader perspective on landscape issues (a so-called 'rich picture') and subsequently identify shared goals (common ground) for future landscape development. The latter step is often executed with so-called soft-system methodologies such as Future Search (Weisbord and Janoff, 2000) and Search Conference (Emery and Purser, 1996), in which stakeholders are invited to envision the desired future, define common ground and elaborate an action plan via back-casting. Many scientists and policy makers consider the latter methodologies too qualitative and open to guide future action; hence they try the so-called 'third way' and use participatory GIS applications, participatory computer simulations to integrate local-specific landscape characteristics, functions and legal requirements in the explorations (Hessel *et al.*, 2009; Runhaar *et al.*, 2009).

Adaptive management is about social learning, but also requires experiential learning. Experiential learning is 'learning from experience' to develop concrete technical and organisational solutions: it concerns continuous observation of, sharing knowledge about, and concrete experimentation within the landscape to better understand the dynamics of the biophysical system, the impact of various types of human practices on this system and the ecological services it provides. Through experiential learning stakeholders adapt to smaller changes in the landscape.

1.4.3 Critical system thinking

Critical system thinking emerged in reaction to the failure of hard and soft system thinking to deal with coercive situations and to address power imbalances among stakeholders (Ulrich, 2003). Critical system researchers aim to develop a theory about issues of dominance, suppression and empowerment. They feel a responsibility to analyse decision-making processes, power dynamics and raise awareness about their implications. Their main interest is in social interrelations, in particular the societal structures and patterns of thought that reinforce power relations and hinder change. Core commitments in critical system thinking include (Jackson, 2000):
- Critical awareness: a never-ending attempt to uncover hidden assumptions.
- Social awareness and human emancipation: to prevent coercion and exercise of power from distorting communication to promote a more equitable distribution of power.
- Complementarity: the acknowledgement that various systems approaches tend to provide different rationalities, which complement each other. For instance, research can comprise of hard system methodologies complemented with critical system thinking.

Within the field of landscape science, political ecology explicitly examines political dynamics surrounding material and discursive struggles over the environment. They note politics should be 'put first' in the attempt to understand human-environment interaction (Blaikie, 1985; Bryant, 1998). Political ecology focuses primarily on third world countries, because colonial systems of political and economic control often led to the marginalisation of the local poor. Today the colonial legacy is still alive in many parts where the political and economic elite accumulate wealth and power based on tenure arrangements and governance practices inherited from the colonial authorities (Bryant, 1998). The fashionable 'devolution of natural resource management' reflects more political rhetoric than reality: governments use contractual agreements and regulations as instruments for devolution, which allows officials to impose their perspective on the issue (Shackleton *et al.*, 2002). The conservation of natural resources still occurs at the expense of resource use for the livelihood of the poor. And in the cases where the decision-making power is delegated to local platforms, local elites tend to dominate the discussion and take all the benefits (Cooke and Kothari, 2001; Edmunds and Wollenberg, 2001a; Ribot, 2003). Involvement in negotiation poses considerable risks for the disadvantaged (Edmunds and Wollenberg, 2001b).

Critical system thinkers therefore call upon landscape researchers to make multilevel stakeholder analyses, identifying interests, power relations, perceived responsibilities and rights, ties of collaboration and conflict. To identify space for change in favour of the marginalised, it is important to examine (Gaventa, 2006):

- The situation in different domains and at different scale levels, as changes in one sphere or scale level might spill over and create opportunities in other levels.
- Whether decision-making spaces are closed or key players consider the situation of the poor and invite participation; and whether the local stakeholders are able to mobilise themselves to claim their right. It is important to work on both sides: create space for inclusive decision-making at higher levels, while also working on capacity-building to enable marginal groups to claim and use this space, thus creating new decision-making routines.
- Whether power is invisible (people are not aware of their disadvantaged position, so awareness-raising is needed); hidden (others tend to set the agenda so the marginalised need to organise themselves); and/or visible in formal rules and procedures (the marginalised need to organise themselves for advocacy, claiming citizens' rights).

Researchers who choose to support the marginalised in the societal negotiation and power play, have two options: to focus on the decision-making level, putting the issue on the political agenda, informing higher-level decision-makers about the situation and interests of the marginalised, advocating new more inclusive decision-making procedures, or to focus on the local level creating awareness by the marginalised themselves so as to organise them for advocacy. The positioning of the research (goal, intended user, participants and methodology) depends on the political context, the capability the researcher and funding possibilities.

1.4.4 Institutional theory/innovation system thinking

Like critical system thinking, researchers inspired by institutional theory and innovation system thinking emphasise structural and systemic processes. Many landscape scientists concluded that local development perspectives remain limited, when research does not address constraints imposed by existing institutions. Institutions are cultural-cognitive beliefs, norms and values, rules and routines that provide stability and meaning to social life in groups and organisations (Scott 2001: 48). 'Together, these elements frame reality for a social system, explaining what is and what is not, what can be acted upon and what cannot' (Hoffman, 1999: 351). For robust governance, social systems need institutions that provide order and stability, but they also need norms, value, routines that keep them alert and ready to adapt to ongoing external changes.

Past experiences show that linear approaches to sustainable development had limited potential to trigger innovations. This led to the emergence of the concept of innovation systems. Apparently, innovation is not science-led change but an interactive, evolutionary phenomenon, whereby networks of organisations together with institutions and policies that affect their innovative behaviour and performance, bring new products and processes into economic and social use (Freeman, 1987; Lundvall, 1992; Hall, 2005). The innovation concept calls for research and action to be linked, while at the same time dealing with the

A. van Paassen, P. Opdam, E. Steingröver and J. van den Berg

governance of change (World Bank, 2006). Successful innovation systems are characterised by (Hall *et al.*, 2003; 222): continuous evolutionary cycles of learning and innovation; combinations of technical and institutional innovation; interaction of diverse research and non-research actors; shifting roles for information producers, users and transfers of knowledge on a needs basis; an institutional context that supports interactions, learning and knowledge flows between actors. In this sense, it represents a new pathway of science for impact that includes but supersedes earlier conceptions of such pathways, such as technology-supply-push and participatory bottom-up approaches (Röling, 2009).

The adoption of the innovation system perspective enables researchers to address institutional constraints to local development; it encourages researchers to engage in networking and knowledge-sharing at multiple levels, and to identify new institutional arrangements that contribute to sustainable development (cf. Jiggins and Röling, 2000).

Figure 1.1 shows our conceptualisation of landscape as a complex system and the four associated types of system thinking in contemporary landscape development research. When designing their research approach, landscape researchers decide which of the above considerations and types of system thinking they take on board. Inclusion of certain issues has implications for the research goal, inclusion of stakeholders and methodology. Collective learning or collective action, for example, requires more intensive collaboration than knowledge production for policy advice (cf. Vernooy and McDougall, 2003). It also has implications for the methods and tools that researchers employ to generate knowledge and stimulate learning and action; and for the co-operation between natural and social researchers.

1.5 The role of researchers in enhancing sustainable landscape development

To assess and enhance sustainability, we need to know and act upon global issues and simultaneously care for the sensitivity and resilience of the ecological and social systems in a specific locality (Gunderson and Holling, 2002). What does this mean for researchers? First of all, in developing countries, but often also in the industrial countries, scientists do not have reliable, detailed historical data of specific localities. They need to include local stakeholders in their knowledge-sharing and experiential learning about sustainable landscape development as they possess valuable contextual knowledge about the biophysical landscape dynamics as well as the socio-organisational context and farmer behaviour (Funtowicz and Ravetz, 1994). Secondly, scientists tend to disagree about the 'key' dimensions to measure, judge and enhance sustainability. Should ecological elements predominate in the judgements, the social, or the economic? In fact, the interpretation of what is valued sustainable landscape development differs among scientists as well as the societal stakeholders. Sustainable landscape development issues are so-called 'unstructured problems' (Hisschemöller *et al.*, 2001; Michaels, 2009): uncertainties are big and knowledge is controversial. The question

1. Landscape science and societal action

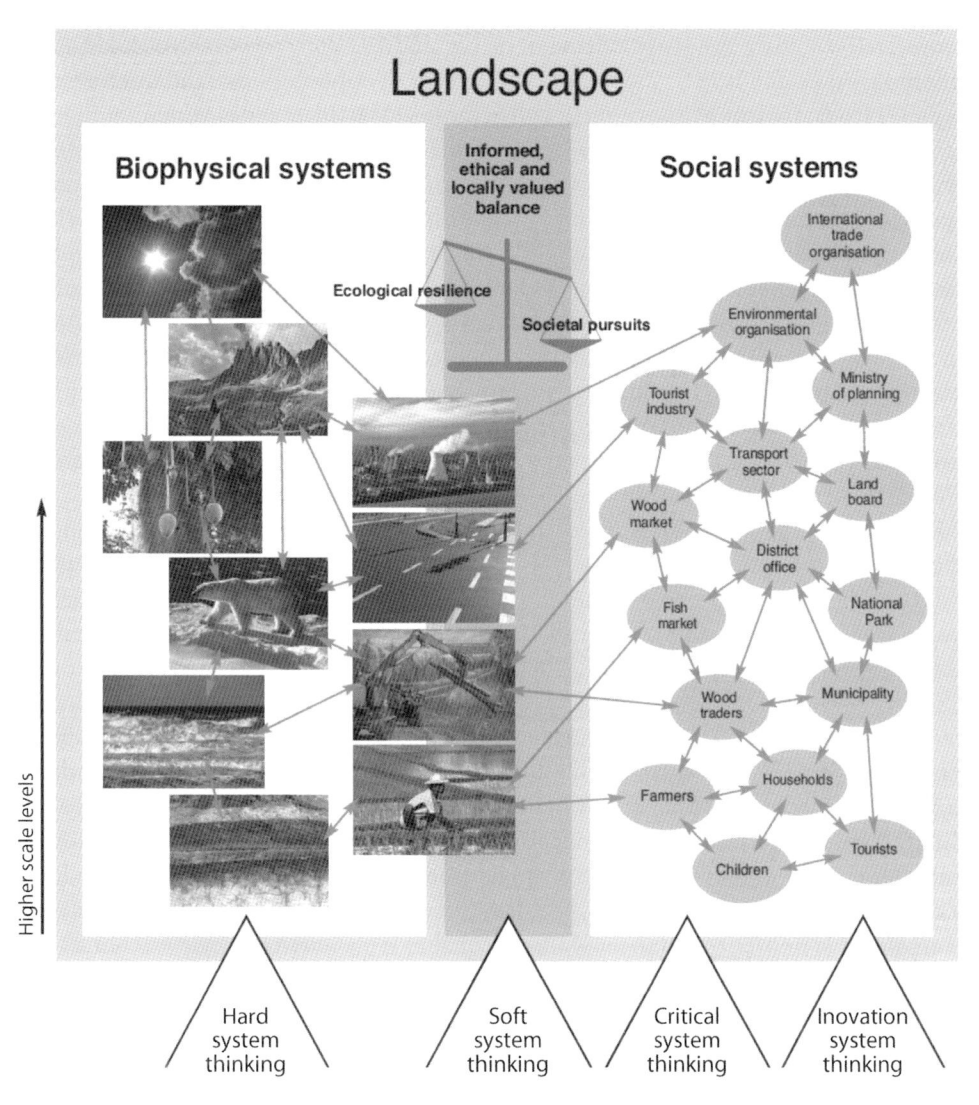

Figure 1.1. The landscape as complex system and four associated types of system thinking.

is: what perspective and values should prevail? A creative solution to this issue would be to opt for a problem-oriented approach and involve relevant stakeholders as they bear the consequences of the decisions made (Funtowicz and Ravetz, 1994; Pearson, 2003).

Most researchers are used to consulting authorities and policy makers, who are often the research funders (In 't Veld, 2009), to find out and produce the knowledge the latter consider credible, salient and legitimate. They often refer to the insights of Cash *et al.* (2003) who noted research results are likely to have a societal effect to the extent that key actors perceive the information as *credible* (scientific adequacy of the technical evidence and arguments), *salient* (relevant to the needs of the decision-maker) and *legitimate* (respectful of stakeholder's diverging values and beliefs, and fair in its treatment of opposing views and interests). But for most landscape issues this is not enough because stakeholders and governing authorities at the various spatial levels, time frames and domains perceive problems differently (Cash *et al.*, 2006). This means researchers cannot just reorganise knowledge according to the (perceived or imagined) interest of one key actor, but they have to create knowledge that is credible, salient and legitimate across levels, time frames and domains. Local stakeholders and governing authorities need to be included in all phases of the research (the problem exploration, goal setting and search for solutions), to enable them to get a rich picture of the issue-at-stake; to better understand the concerns, underlying values and interest of the various stakeholders and institutions concerning the issue-at-stake and possible solutions; and to negotiate, agree upon, and support the implementation of certain measures. In other words, a social learning approach provides the opportunity to create mutual understanding, trust and partnerships for multilevel co-ordinated landscape development (Lebel, 2004; 2006; Cash *et al.*, 2006; Van Kerkhof and Lebel, 2006). In line with these ideas, policy makers and authorities nowadays ask for new ways to integrate the concerns, norms and values of the various stakeholders and institutions in the landscape research and planning process (Van Mansfelt, 2003). They call for trans-disciplinary research to solve societal and environmental problems (Tress *et al.*, 2005).

However, landscape researchers struggle with the issue of trans-disciplinarity. There are two interpretations. Theorists like Gibbons *et al.* (1994) and Nowotny *et al.* (2001) define trans-disciplinarity as 'Mode 2' research: Mode 2 science differs from the conventional disciplinary Mode 1 science as it concerns knowledge production that is institutionally distributed, produced in the context of application, integrating (often tacit) knowledge of local stakeholders and practitioners, problem-driven and action-oriented. Mode 2 science is accountable to science and society, and the quality is measured on a wider set of criteria than the quality and number of peer-reviewed articles (Gibbons *et al.*, 1994; Nowotny *et al.*, 2001). However, a review of articles about actual landscape research reveals another interpretation of trans-disciplinarity. In most articles landscape researchers aim at knowledge integration, but do not elaborate on how they operationalised this integration. They use the term trans-disciplinary to express an intensified form of inter-disciplinarity; it requires a theoretical framework that transcends the different research paradigms (Regeer and Bunders, 2007; Tress *et al.*, 2004). Research funders, on their part, are ambiguous: they want researchers to solve societal and environmental problems, but prefer peer-reviewed scientific articles rather than research reports. At this moment landscape researchers perceive the lack of common operational understanding (the diversity in theoretical frameworks, research goals and methodologies) as a problem, but do not arrive at a common terminology (Tress *et al.*, 2005).

From our perspective it is not very fruitful to aim at the development of one transcending research paradigm and methodology. The choice of a research goal and methodology is value-laden and normative (Wesselink, 2008). The perspective and position of the research initiator, funder and researchers are often paramount to the overall research goal. For instance, researchers need a different research approach (theoretical perspective and related methodology) when a water board invites them to start an interactive learning process about appropriate irrigation measures, than when being approached by a marginalised group that claims to be ignored by local forest governance procedures. But there is another important consideration to take on board. Landscape research is part and parcel of a landscape planning and development process, and to be effective it should more or less fit in the discourse and surrounding societal arrangements (Fischer, 1995). Comparative studies on regulatory systems show each country has a certain way of framing risks, norms and practices in policy advice and the kinds of scientific evidence that predominate in political deliberations, and these differences reflect back on the scientific institutions (Miller, 2001). It is easier and more effective to start an intense collaborative research in countries where government authorities experiment with interactive planning approaches, than in countries with a hierarchic policy culture where authorities feel threatened by democratic learning and decision-making processes with uncertain outcomes (Arghiros, 2001; Hoppe, 2002).

The socio-political context not only defines what is an acceptable research and innovation approach, but also the role that different actors, such as the researcher, government officers, NGOs, private actors need to take. Through their discourse and practices, researchers, policy makers and other actors continuously maintain, withdraw and redefine the boundaries between their professions, and define their role vis-à-vis the other (Gieryn, 1983; Jasanof (1987; 1990). The demarcation of science from other non-scientific intellectual or technical activities is essential for scientists' pursuit of professional goals, claiming intellectual authority and resources (Gieryn, 1983). Through boundary work scientists usually keep non-scientists from interfering or challenging their scientific 'truth claim' to ensure science is able to remain 'disinterested', 'objective' and 'sceptical' (Jasanoff 1987; Turnhout 2007). Governing authorities also define their activities to discern them from others, and emphasise it is their responsibility and authority to interpret research results, deliberate, make value-judgements and decide upon action. Boundary work enables actors from different professional domains and social worlds to negotiate and demarcate their specific role, and those of others to attain cross-domain orchestration of action. In this way, they also determine more or less what form the role of actors and collaboration between actors takes in a collaborative research and innovation process aimed at landscape development. Depending on the availability of actors and their legitimate roles, researchers might contribute knowledge to societal learning processes; organise societal learning processes; or even go beyond the border of their profession and perform tasks such as advocacy, mobilisation, conflict management, etc., to enforce decision-making and societal action. In this way they may contribute to knowledge integration for problem-solving, to capacity-building for learning and decision-making, and simultaneously create new knowledge exchange and governance institutions.

A. van Paassen, P. Opdam, E. Steingröver and J. van den Berg

Sustainable landscape development means researchers have to engage in collaborative research, to find an informed, ethical and local-valued balance between ecological resilience and societal pursuits and enhance the co-ordinated adaptive development capacity of the involved stakeholders and governance institutions. In ideal terms the design of the research process should be problem-driven; the (often tacit) perspective and concerns of the stakeholders and governing institutions should be leading. In practice, the positioning of the research depends on the visibility, urgency, scale and irreversibility of the emerging problem (Dovers, 2005), the (theoretical) perspective of the research funding policy makers and the research team start from, and the boundary work in which societal partners define the problem definition and the legitimate roles of different actors in the research and innovation process (In 't Veld, 2009; Hoppe, 2010). In the research implementation natural scientists tend to focus on content (what physical landscape development is required), while social scientists tend to focus on the social learning, engagement and negotiation process. They are used to different research methods, but both are needed to attain good results (problem-solving plus capacity-building). The question is whether and how scientists from different backgrounds are able to successfully integrate their theoretical framework and research methods, to design a research methodology that effectively contributes to sustainable, equitable development in a specific context.

References

Adger, W.N., K. Brown and E. Tompkins, 2006. The political economy of cross-scale networks in resource co-management. Ecology and Society 10 (2): 9. Available at: www.ecologyandsociety.org/vol10/iss2/art9/.

Anderson, J., 2001. On the edge of chaos: Crafting adaptive collaborative management for biological diversity conservation in a pluralistic world. In: L. Buck, C. Geisler, J. Schelhas and E. Wollenberg (eds.), Biological diversity: Balancing interests through adaptive collaborative management, CRC Press, Boca Raton, FL, USA, pp. 171-186.

Anderies, J.M., M.A. Janssen and E. Ostrom, 2004. A framework to analyse the robustness of socio-ecological systems from an institutional perspective. Ecology and Society 9 (1): 18. Available at: www.ecologyandsociety.org/vol9/iss1/art18/.

Antrop, M., 2006. Sustainable landscapes: contradiction, fiction or utopia? Landscape and Urban Planning 75: 187-197.

Arghiros, D., 2001. Democracy, Development and Decentralization in Provincial Thailand. Curzon and Nordic Institute of Asian Studies, Richmond, Surry, UK.

Argyris, C. and D.A. Schön, 1996. Organisational Learning II. Theory, method and practice. Addison-Wesley Publishing, Reading, UK.

Beck, U., 1992. Risk society: towards a new modernity. Sage, London, UK.

Blaikie, P., 1985. The political economy of soil erosion in developing countries. Longman Development Series, No.1, Longman, London, UK. Reprinted in 2000 by Pearson Education, Harlow, UK.

Bryant, R.L., 1998. Power, knowledge and political ecology in the third world: a review. Progress in Physical Geography 22: 79-94.

Cash, D.W., W.N. Adger, F. Berkes, P. Garden, L. Lebel, P. Olsson, L. Pritchard and O. Young, 2006. Scale and cross-scale dynamics: governance and information in a multi-level world. Ecology Society 11 (2): 8 Available at: www.ecologyandsociety.org/vol11/iss2/art8/.

Cash, D.W., W.C. Clark, F. Alcock, N.M. Dickson, N. Eckley, D.H. Guston, J. Jäger and R.B. Mitchell, 2003. Knowledge systems for sustainable development. Proceedings of the National Academy of Sciences of the USA 100: 8086-8091.

Chambers, R. and J. Jiggins, 1985. Agricultural Research for Resource-Poor Farmers: a Parsimonious Paradigm. Manuscript for discussion. Institute for Development Studies, Sussex, UK.

Clark, W.C., 2007. Sustainability science: a room of its own. Proceedings of the National Academy of Sciences of the USA 104: 1737-1738.

Clark, W.C., 2003. Research systems for a transition towards sustainability. In: W. Steffen, J. Jäger, D.J. Carson and C. Bradshaw (eds.), Challenges of a changing earth. Proceedings of the global open science conference. Springer-Verlag, Berlin, Germany, pp. 197-199.

Colchester, M., 1994. Salvaging mature: indigenous peoples, protected areas and biodiversity conservation. Discussion Paper No 55, UNRISD, Geneva, Switzerland.

Constanza, R. and R. Arge (eds.), 1997. The value of the worlds ecosystem services and natural capital. Nature 387: 253-260.

Cooke, B. and U. Kothari, 2001. The Case for Participation as Tyranny. In: B. Cooke and U. Kothari (eds.), Participation: The New Tyranny? Zed Books, London. UK.

Daily, G.C. (ed.), 1997. Nature's services: Societal dependence on natural ecosystems. Island Press, Washington, DC, USA.

Dietz, T., E. Ostrom and P.C. Stern, 2003. Review: The struggle to govern the Commons. Science 302: 1907-1912.

Dovers, S., 2005. Environment and sustainability policy: creation, implementation, evaluation. Federation Press, Annandale, Australia.

Edmunds, D., and E. Wollenberg, 2001a. Historical perspectives on forest policy change in Asia; an introduction. Environmental Histrory 2001. Available at: www.foresthistry.org.

Edmunds, D., and E. Wollenberg, 2001b. A strategic approach to multi-stakeholder negotiations. Development and Change 32: 231-253.

Emery, M. and R.E. Purser, 1996. The Search Conference. A powerful method for planning organizational change and community action. Jossey-Bass Publishers, San Francisco, CA, USA.

FAO (Food and Agriculture Organization), 1976. A framework for land evaluation. FAO Soils Bulletin, 32. FAO, Rome, Italy.

Folke C., F. Berkes and J. Colding, 1998. Ecological practices and social mechinsms for building resilience and sustainability. In: F. Berkes, C. Folke and J. Colding (eds.), Linking social and ecological systems; management practices and social mechanisms for building resilience. Cambridge University Press, Cambridge, UK, pp. 414-436.

Feeny, D., F. Berkes, B.J. McCay and J.M. Acheson, 1990. The tragedy of the commons: Twenty-two years later. Human Ecology 18:1: 1-19.

Fischer, F., 1995. Evaluating public policy. Nelson-Hall Publishers, Chicago, IL, USA.

Freeman, C., 1987. Technology and Economic Performance: Lessons from Japan. Pinter, London, UK.

Fresco, L.O., H. Huizing, H. Van Keulen, H.A. Luning and R.A. Schipper (eds.), 1992. Land evaluation and farming systems analysis for land use planning. FAO working document. Rome, Italy.

Fry, G., 2001. Multifunctional landscapes; towards transdisicplinary research. Landscape and Urban Planning 57: 159-168.

Fry, G., B. Tress and G. Tress, 2007. Integrative landscape research: facts and challenges. In: J. Wu and R. Hobbs (eds.), Key topics in landscape ecology. Cambridge University Press, Cambridge, UK, pp. 246-268.

Funtowicz, S.O. and J.R. Ravetz, 1993. Science for the post-normal age. Futures 25: 739-755.

Funtowicz, S.O. and J.R. Ravetz, 1994. The worth of a songbird: ecological economics and post-normal science. Ecological Economics 10: 197-2007.

Gaventa, J., 2006. Finding the spaces for change: a power analysis. IDS bulletin 37: 23-33.

Gigerenzer G., P.M. Todd and ABC research group, 1999. Simple heuristics that make use smart. Oxford University Press, Oxford, UK.

Gibbons, M., C. Limoges, H. Novotny, S. Schwartzman, P. Scott and M. Trow, 1994. The New Production of Knowledge. Sage, London, UK.

Gieryn, T.F., 1983. Boundary-work and the demarcation of science from non-science: strains and interests in professional ideologies of scientists. American Sociological Review 48: 781-795.

Giller, K.E., C. Leeuwis, J.A. Andersson, W. Andriesse, A. Brouwer, P. Frost, P. Hebinck, I. Heitkönig, M.K. Van Ittersum, N. Koning, R. Ruben, M. Slingerland, H. Udo, T. Veldkamp, C. Van de Vijver, M.T. Van Wijk and P. Windmeijer, 2008. Competing claims on natural resources: what role for science? Ecology and Society 13(2): 34. Available at: www.ecologyandsociety.org/vol13/iss2/art34/.

Gunderson, L. and C.S. Holling, 2001. Panarchy; understanding transformations in systems of humans and nature. Island Press, Washington, DC, USA.

Hall, A., 2005. Capacity development for agricultural biotechnology in developing countries: an innovation systems view of what it is and how to develop it. Journal of International Development 17: 611-630.

Hall, A., V.R. Sulaiman, N. Clark and B. Yoganand, 2003. From measuring impact to learning institutional lessons: an innovation system perspective on improving the management of international agricultural research. Agricultural Systems 78: 213-241.

Hardin, G., 1968. The tragedy of the Commons. Science 162: 1243-1248.

Hessel, R., J. Van den Berg, O. Kaboré, A. Van Kekem, S. Verzandvoort, J.-M. Dipama and B. Diallo, 2009. Linking participatory and GIS-based land use planning methods: A case study from Burkina Faso. Land Use Policy 26: 1162-1172.

Hisschemöller, M., R. Hoppe, P. Groenewegen and C. Midden, 2001. Knowledge use and political choice in Dutch environmental policy: a problem structuring perspective on real life experiments in extended peer review. In: M. Hisschemöller, R. Hoppe, W.N. Dunn and J.R. Ravetz (eds.), Knowledge, power and participation in environmental policy analysis and risk assessments. Transaction Publishers, New Brunswick, NJ, USA, pp. 437-470.

Hoffman, A.J., 1999. Institutional evolution and change: Environmentalism and the U.S. Chemical Industry, Academy of Management Journal 42: 451-371.

Hoppe, R., 2002. Cultures of public policy problems. Journal of Comparative Policy Analysis: Research and Practice 4: 305-326.

Hoppe, R., 2005. Rethinking the science-policy nexus: from knowledge utilisation and science technology studies to types of boundary arrangements. Poiesis Prax 3: 199-215.

Hoppe, R., 2010. From knowledge use towards 'boundary work': a sketch of an emerging new agenda for inquiry into science-policy interaction. In: R.J. In 't Veld (ed.), Knowledge democracy: Consequences for science, politics and media. Springer-Verlag, Berlin, Germany, pp. 169-186.

In 't Veld, R.J., 2009. Willingly and Knowingly; The roles of knowledge about nature and the environment in policy processes. RMNO series preliminary studies and background studies nr. V15e. RMNO, the Hague, the Netherlands.

Jackson, M.C., 2000. Systems approaches to management. Kluwer Academic/Plenum publishers, New York, NY, USA.

Jasanoff, S., 1990. The fifth branch: science-advisors as policymakers. Harvard University Press, Cambridge, MA, USA.

Jasanoff, S.S., 1987. Contested boundaries in policy-relevant science. Social Studies of Science 17: 195-230.

Jiggins, J. and N. Röling, 2000. Adaptive management: potential and limitations for ecological governance. International Journal of Agricultural Resources, Governance and Ecology 1: 28-42.

Johnston, E. and S. Soulsby, 2006. The role of science in environmental policy: an examination of the local context. Land Use Policy 23: 161-169.

Kates R.W. and T.M. Parris, 2003. Long term trends and a sustainability transition. Proceedings of the National Academy of Sciences of the USA 1000: 8062-8067.

Kates, R.W., W.C. Clark, R. Corell, J.M. Hall, C.C. Jaeger, I. Lowe and J.J. Mc Carthy, 2001. Sustainability Science. Science 292: 641-642.

Kienast, F., O. Wildi and S. Ghosh, 2009. Change and transfarmation: a synthesis. In: F. Kienast, O. Wildi and S. Ghosh (eds.), A changing world; challenges for landscape research. Springer, Dordrecht, the Netherland, pp 1-4.

Kline, S. and N. Rosenberg, 1986. An overview of the process of innovation. In: G. Landau and N. Rosenberg (eds.), The Positive Sum Strategy: Harnessing Technology for Economic Growth. National Academy Press, Washington, DC, USA, pp. 275-306.

Knorr-Cetina, K., 1981. The manufacture of knowledge: An essay on the constructivist and contextual nature of science. Pergamon, Oxford, UK.

Lambin, E.F., 2005. Conditions for sustainability of human-environmental systems: information, motivation and capacity. Global Environmental Change 15: 177-180.

Leach, M. and R. Mearns, 1996. Environmental change and Policy. In: M. Leach and R. Mearns (eds.), The Lie of the land. Challenging received wisdom on the African environment. The International African Institute, London, UK, pp. 1-33.

Lebel, L., 2004. The politics of scale in environmental assessment. USER Working Paper WP-2004-07. Unit for Social and Environmental Research, Chiang Mai University, Chiang Mai, Thailand.

Lebel, L., Anderies, J.M., Campbell, B., Folke, C., Hatfield-Dodds, S., Hughes, T.P. and J. Wilson, 2006. Governance and the capacity to manage resilience in regional socio-ecological systems. Ecology and Society 11 (1): 19. Available at: www.ecologyandsociety.org/vol11/iss1/art19/.

Leeuwis, C., 2000. Re-conceptualizing participation for sustainable rural development: towards a negotiation approach. Development and Change 31(5): 931-959.

Leeuwis, C. and R. Pyburn, 2002. Introduction to the book. In: C. Leeuwis and R. Pyburn (eds.), Wheelbarrows full of frogs: social learning in rural research management. Koninklijke Van Gorcum, Assen, the Netherlands, pp. 11-24.

Long, N., and A. Long (eds.), 1992. Battlefields of knowledge: the interlocking of social theory and practice in research and development. Routledge, New York, NY, USA.

Lundvall, B.A. (ed.), 1992. National Systems of Innovation and Interactive Learning. Pinter, London, UK.

Michaels, S., 2009. Matching knowledge brokering strategies to environmental policy problems and setting. Environmental Science & Policy 12: 994-1011.

Miller, C., 2001. Hybrid management: boundary organizations, science policy, and environmental governance in the climate regime. Science, Technology and Human Values 26 (4): 478-500.

Musacchia, L.R., 2009. The scientific basis for the design of landscape sustainability: a conceptual framework for translational landscape research and practice of designed landscapes and the six Es of landscape sustainability. Landscape Ecology 24: 993-1013.

Nassauer, J. and P. Opdam, 2008. Design in science: extending the landscape ecology paradigm. Landscape Ecology 23: 633-644.

Naveh, Z., 2000. What is holistic ecology? A conceptual introduction. Landscape and Urban Planning 50: 7-26.

Newman, L. and A. Dale, 2005. Network structure, diversity and proactive resilience building: a response to Tompkins and Adger. Ecology and Society 10 (1): 2. Available at: www.ecologyandsociety.org/vol10/iss1/resp2/.

Nohl, W., 2001. Sustainable landscape use and aesthetic perception-preliminary reflections on future landscape aesthetics. Landscape Urban Planning 54: 223-237.

Nowotny, H., P. Scott and M. Gibbons, 2001. Re-thinking science; knowledge and the public in the age of uncertainty. Blackwell Publishers, Oxford, UK.

Ostrom, E., 1990. Governing the commons. The evolution of institutions for collective action. Cambridge University Press, New York, NY, USA.

Ostrom, E., J. Burger, C.B. Field, R.B. Norgaard and D. Policansky, 1999. Revisiting the Commons: lessons learned, global challenges. Science 284: 278-282.

Pearson, C.J., 2003. Sustainability: Perceptions of problems and progress of the paradigm. International Journal of Agricultural Sustainability 1 (1): 3-13.

Pellizzoni, L., 2003. Uncertainty and participatory democracy. Environmental Values 12: 195-224.

Pimbert, M.P., 1995. Parks, people and professionals: Putting 'participation into protected area management'. Discussion paper No 57, UNRISD, Geneva, Switzerland.

Probst, K. and J. Hagmann, with contributions from M. Fernandez and J.A. Ashby, 2003. Understanding Participatory Research in the Context of Natural Resource Management: Paradigms, Approaches and Typologies. ODI-AGREN Network Paper No. 130.

Ramirez, R., 2001. Understanding the approaches for accommodating multiple stakeholders' interests. International Journal of Agricultural Resources, Governance and Ecology 1 (3/4): 264-285.

Reij, C. and A. Waters-Bayer, 2001. Farmer innovation in Africa: a source of inspiration for agricultural development. Earthscan, London, UK.

Ribot, J.C., 2003. Democratic decentralisation of natural resources: institutional choice and discretionary power transfers in sub-Saharan Africa. Public Administration and Development 23: 53-65.

Regeer, B.J. and J.F.G. Bunders, 2007. Kenniscocreatie: samenspel tussen wetenschap en praktijk. Complexe, maatschappelijke vraagstukken transdisciplinair benaderd. Athena Instituut, Vrije Universiteit Amsterdam, Amsterdam, the Netherlands.

Röling, N., 2002. Beyond the aggregation of individual preferences; moving from multiple to distributed cognition in resource dilemmas. In: Leeuwis, C. and R. Pyburn (eds.), Wheelbarrows full of frogs; social learning in rural resource management. Konklijke van Gorcum, Assen, the Netherlands, pp. 25-48.

Röling, N., 2009. Pathways for impact: Scientist's different perspective on agricultural innovation. International Journal of Agricultural Sustainability 7(2): 83-94.

Runhaar, H.A.C., P.P.J. Driessen and L. Soer, 2009. Sustainable urban development and the challenge of policy integration: an assessment of planning tools for integrating spatial and environmental planning in the Netherlands. Environmental and Planning B: Planning and Design 36(3): 417-431.

Scott, W.R., 2001. Institutions and Organizations. Sage, Thousand Oaks, CA, USA.

Shackleton, S, B. Campbell, E. Wollenberg and D. Edmunds, 2002. Devolution and community-based natural resource management: Creating space for local people to participate and benefit? ODI Natural Resource Perspectives 76: 1-6.

Snowden, D.J., 2005. Multi-ontology sense making: a new simplicity in decision making. Available at: http://www.cognitive-edge.com/ceresources/articles/40_Multi-ontology_sense_makingv2_May05.pdf.

Stephenson, J., 2008. The cultural values model: an integrated approach to values in landscapes. Landscape and Urban Planning 84: 127-139.

Termorshuizen, J.W. and P. Opdam, 2009. Landscape service as bridge between landscape ecology and sustainable development. Landscape Ecology 24: 1037-1052.

Tompkins, E. and N. Adger, 2004. Does adaptive management of natural resource enhance resilience to climate change? Ecology and Society 9 (2): 10. Available at: www.ecologyandsociety.org/vol9/iss2/art10.

Toulmin, C., 1992. Cattle, women and wells: managing household survival in the Sahel. Clarendon, Oxford, UK.

Tress, B. and G. Tress, 2001. Capitalising on multiplicity: a transdisciplinary systems approach to landscape research. Landscape and urban Planning 57: 143-157.

Tress, B., G. Tress and G. Fry, 2005. Integrative studies on rural landscapes: policy expectations and research practice. Landscape and Urban Planning 70: 177-191.

Tress, G., B. Tress and G. Fry, 2004. Clarifying integrative research concepts in landscape ecology. Landscape Ecology 20: 479-491.

Turner, M.G., 1989. Landscape Ecology: The Effect of Pattern and Process. Annual Review of Ecological System 20: 171-197.

Turnhout, E., 2007. The effectiveness of boundary objects: the case of ecological indicators. Science and Public Policy 36(5): 403-412.

Ulrich, W. 2000. Reflective practice in the civil society: the contribution of critically systemic thinking. Reflective Practice 1 (2): 247-268.

Ulrich, W., 2003. Beyond methodology choice: critical systems thinking as critically systemic discourse. Journal of the Operational Research Society 54: 325-342.

United Nations, 1983. Process of preparation of the Environmental Perspective to the Year 2000 and Beyond. General Assembly Resolution 38/161, 19 December 1983. Available at: http://www.un.org/documents/ga/res/38/a38r161.htm.

Van Asselt, M.B.A. and M. Rotmans, 2002. Uncertainty in integrated assessment modelling; from positivism to pluralism. Climate Change 54: 75-105.

Van den Berg, J. and K. Biesbrouck, 2005. Dealing with power imbalances in forest management: reconciling multiple legal systems in South Cameroon. In: Ros-Tonen, M.A.F. and T. Dietz (eds.), African forests between nature and livelihood resource: Interdisciplinary studies in conservation and forest management. African Studies 81, The Edwin Mellen Press, Lewiston, New York, NY, USA, pp. 221-254.

Van den Berg, J., H. Van Dijk and K.F. Wiersum, 2007. The role and dynamics of community institutions in the management of NTFP resources. Forest, Trees and Livelihoods 17: 183-197.

Van Huis, A., J. Jiggins, D. Kossou, C. Leeuwis, N. Röling, O. Sakyi-Dawson, P.C. Struik and R.C. Tossou, 2007. Can convergence of agricultural sciences support innovation by resource-poor farmers in Africa? The cases of Benin and Ghana. International Journal of Agricultural Sustainability 5 (2-3): 91-108.

Van Kerkhoff, L. and L. Lebel, 2006. Linking knowledge with action for sustainable development. Annual Review of Environment and Resources 31: 1-33.

Van Mansfelt, M., 2003. The need for knowledge brokers. In: B. Tress, G. Tress, A. van der Valk and G. Fry (eds.). Interdisciplinary and transdisciplinary landscape studies: Potential and limitations. Delta Series 2, Wageningen University and Research Centre, Wageningen, the Netherlands, pp. 33-38.

Vernooy, R. and C. McDougall, 2003. Principles for Good Practice in Participatory Research: Reflecting on Lessons from the Field. In: B. Pound, S. Snapp, C. McDougall and A. Braun (eds.). Managing Natural Resources for Sustainable Livelihoods: Uniting Science and Participation. Earthscan, London, UK, pp. 113-141.

Wesselink, A., 2008. Interdisciplinarity, problem focused research and normativity. Sustainable Research Institute Papers no. 11. Sustainable Research Institute, University of Leeds, Leeds, UK.

Weisbord, M. and S. Janoff, 2000. Future search; an action guide to finding common ground in organisaions and communities. Second edition, updated and expanded. Berrett-Koehler Publishers, San Francisco, CA, USA.

World Bank, 2006. Enhancing agricultural innovation: how to go beyond the strengthening of agricultural research. World bank, Washington, DC, USA.

Wynne, B., 1996. Misunderstood misunderstandings: social identities and public uptake of science. In: A. Irwin and B. Wynne (eds.), Misunderstanding science? The public reconstruction of science and technology. Cambridge University Press, Cambridge, UK, pp. 19-46.

2. What is collaborative landscape research about?

Renate Werkman, Jolanda van den Berg, Annemarie van Paassen and Bette Harms

Abstract

Many different landscape research approaches involve some form of collaboration between researchers with different disciplinary backgrounds or between these researchers and societal actors. Often, however, the underlying theoretical assumptions behind these approaches and corresponding research goals and intended societal outcomes are not made explicit. These goals and intended outcomes do however require different forms of stakeholder participation, representing various degrees of sharing responsibilities and powers concerning the collaborative research process between researchers and societal stakeholders. Taking the theoretical perspectives, aims and goals and types of stakeholder participation into account, we distinguish between four general types of collaborative research approaches in landscape research. These types reflect the increasing engagement of researchers in processes of societal and institutional change. The case chapters in this book reflect this gamut of collaborative research types. In each of them, the authors describe and reflect on the theories and methods they used, the contribution to societal development they intended to achieve, the challenges or difficulties they encountered, the actual outcomes they achieved and the lessons they learned. The cases thus provide a valuable knowledge base for a comparative analysis of the collaborative practices and research roles employed and of the adequacy of the theories and methodologies practiced. The insights derived are used in the last chapter for the formulation of practical recommendations for those who want to engage in collaborative research for landscape development and governance.

2.1 Introduction

In the previous chapter we addressed the complexity of landscape management and the global concerns for sustainable landscape development (Van Paassen *et al.*, 2011). We highlighted the importance of collaborative research approaches and the role researchers may play in addressing concrete landscape problems, social learning and institutional change. The challenge for contemporary landscape researchers is to link science with policy and practice; hence, defying the scientific boundaries for integrating different types of knowledge. Researchers should integrate the different theories and methods belonging to their scientific disciplines, and find meaningful ways to integrate knowledge of local stakeholders in their perspectives and approaches. In order to effectively address the complexities of landscape development, researchers, policy makers and local stakeholders should work together towards an approach that is adapted to the requirements of the local context of landscape development. This may be a prospect worth pursuing, but practice is often unruly and stubborn. Therefore, in this chapter, we aim to set the scene for understanding the practice of collaborative research. What theories do landscape researchers use? What goals or societal impacts do they envision and what role does collaboration play in them? What does this mean for the researchers' role vis-à-vis societal partners?

From the 1970s onwards, landscape researchers engaged in a wide variety of research approaches that are characterised by some form of collaboration between researchers with different disciplinary backgrounds or between these researchers and societal actors. In this book, we refer to these approaches as collaborative research. Collaborative research includes approaches such as (participatory) action research, action learning, community-based research, participatory rural appraisal, farmer field schools research, and participatory learning and action, to mention just a few. These approaches emerged in response to the limitations of researcher-driven (top-down models of) knowledge production and subsequently provided rich descriptions of how collaborative research should be practised (cf. Wadsworth, 1998; Allen, 2001). They described case study research, provided toolkits and addressed best practices (Nyden and Wiewel, 1992; Sutherland, 1998; McNiff *et al.*, 2003). Research has shown that the resulting diversity in collaborative research is a consequence of researchers employing different philosophical assumptions and combining different types of participation (cf. Lilja *et al.*, 2001, cited in: Ashby, 2003; Cassell and Johnson, 2006). But notwithstanding the relevance of such collaborative studies for societal stakeholders, many of them do not explicitly address the ontological and epistemological assumptions and corresponding theories and methods of their research approach. Also, and as a consequence of this, many research efforts on sustainable landscape development do not feed back the lessons they have learned in their practical application of collaborative research to enrich landscape development theories. The articles that do address philosophical backgrounds and the corresponding theories and methods (cf. Eden and Huxham, 1996; Narayan, 1996; Gustavsen, 2003; Greenwood and Levin, 2007; Kindon *et al.*, 2007), often do so on a higher level of abstraction and do not relate their insights to the practical choices to be made with regard to collaboration. In this book we try to bridge the gap between the theory and practice of collaborative research. We invited landscape researchers from a large variety of collaborative research projects related to Wageningen UR to present and reflect on their intentions, theoretical inspirations, the actual research practices and outcomes and lessons learned.

In this chapter, we first describe the results of a literature review and an exploratory survey that we performed among collaborative research projects related to Wageningen UR in order to get a better idea of the diversity of collaborative research theories and approaches employed in practice (Harms *et al.*, 2009). In this section, we first introduce the key dimensions we derived from literature that represent choices to be made in collaborative research: the theoretical inspirations and contribution to societal development, the roles of researchers and type of stakeholder participation. We then describe four different collaborative research types we derived from our exploratory survey. These types represent the gamut of approaches that can be found among collaborative research projects in Wageningen UR. From that, we elaborate on two specific challenges for collaborative landscape research, as an epilogue for the case studies in the subsequent chapters of this book. In the final chapter we will come back to these challenges and identify the lessons learned on the basis of a comparative review of the cases presented in this book. We will then introduce and classify the cases. The chapter ends with a short explanation of the structure of the remainder of the book.

2.2 Key dimensions of collaborative research

Collaborative research approaches take varying positions on dimensions that reflect: (1) the theoretical inspirations and intended contribution to societal development; (2) the role of the researchers vis-à-vis the role of the stakeholders, responsibilities and control; and (3) how knowledge is generated and integrated with societal stakeholders, aimed at problem-solving or capacity-building for adaptive innovation.

2.2.1 Theoretical inspirations and intended contribution to societal development

In Chapter 1, we discussed four different types of system thinking that underpin research for landscape development in the 21st century: hard system thinking, soft system thinking, critical system thinking and institutional theory/innovation thinking. Researchers who embrace positivist research methods and hard system thinking, tend to focus on knowledge integration and concrete landscape development. Researchers who embrace soft system thinking focus more on (local or multilevel) social learning and capacity-building for landscape development and governance. Critical system thinkers strive for more equitable landscape development and/or a more inclusive, democratic knowledge exchange and governance structure. They may incite stakeholders to reflect upon and change institutional power dynamics, but when the situation is politically sensitive and threatening, researchers tend to use critical system in an oblique way: they try to guide the knowledge integration and/or social learning process in such a way that stakeholders cannot ignore the needs of the marginalised (Flood and Romm, 1995). So the role of a researcher who embraces critical system thinking may be limited to strategic knowledge exchange for equitable landscape development, or expand towards capacity-building for empowerment of the marginalised and the creation of more inclusive knowledge exchange and governance structures. Researchers who approach landscape development from a multilevel institutional perspective do not focus on concrete landscape development. They may act as individual knowledge broker, and consult, inform and match knowledge of stakeholders at various system levels to enhance knowledge exchange for action, or opt for capacity-building, and enable stakeholders to reflect upon and tackle institutional bottlenecks for learning, communication and change. And last but not least, researchers may also decide to cross the border of science and engage in innovation process management tasks such as advocacy, mobilising people and funding, managing conflicts, and enforcing alignment, which are all needed to link learning with concrete action and change.

There is a thin line between a researcher engaged in collaborative research and a researcher engaged in an interactive innovation process. The majority of the collaborative researchers primarily see themselves as knowledge brokers, who support landscape development and governance by producing and recombining knowledge. Others take a broader perspective. For them, knowledge brokerage involves exploiting the preconditions for innovation that reside within a larger social structure by bridging multiple domains, learning about the resources within those domains, linking the people and their knowledge to new situations, and building networks and institutional routines around the innovations that emerge from the process (Hargadon, 2002). Devaux *et al.* (2010) call this 'first level brokerage', and various research institutes currently experiment with this approach. First level brokerage focuses on a certain issue (substance) as well as the interactive search process and innovation capacity-building. It is difficult to find research institutions who are involved in second level or systemic brokerage. Systemic brokers primarily aim for innovation capacity-building, by strengthening linkages, information flows, learning and co-operation amongst public and private actors (Klerkx and Leeuwis, 2009; Devaux, 2010).

2.2.2 Roles of researchers

In conclusion, there is large variety of roles and tasks that researchers and other actors can perform to enhance sustainable landscape development and governance:
- Networking, which concerns the scanning, scoping, filtering and matchmaking of possible research and innovation partners involved in the use and governance of the landscape.
- Mobilising and sharing knowledge and opinions with stakeholders about the problem situation in order to come to an integrated perspective on the problem.
- Mobilising and sharing knowledge, and experimenting with possible development options (biophysical development, use and/or governance) together with stakeholders.
- Innovation process management, which concerns the facilitation of engagement, negotiation, conflict resolution, alignment of actors and mobilisation of resources to realise the envisaged biophysical landscape development, but also establishing congruent norms, values and reward systems to support co-ordinated action and governance (adapted from Klerkx *et al.*, 2009).

The concrete focus and role of the researcher depends on the type of system thinking the research initiator, funder and scientists start from; the problem situation and the surrounding socio-political context; and the boundary work in which researchers and other actors demarcate responsibilities and powers concerning the learning and innovation process. As a result of this boundary work, a researcher may act as a detached scientist who contributes knowledge to a learning and innovation process or gets engaged and actively influences the multi-stakeholder learning and change process via facilitation and mediation (Pohl, 2008). And in line with the definition of the role of the researcher, the type of stakeholder participation, the research goals and intended contribution to societal development of the research are defined. Social learning and institutional change, for example, require different forms of collaboration between scientific disciplines and between researchers and societal actors than knowledge production for policy advice (cf. Vernooy and McDougal, 2003).

2.2.3 Type of stakeholder participation

In literature, collaboration is defined as 'the mutual engagement of (scientific and non-scientific) participants in a coordinated effort to solve the problem together' (Roschelle and Teasley, 1995). But in practice, the actual involvement of non-scientific, societal actors varies strongly and is more or less congruent with the role of the researchers and the amount of control that they exercise. The different gradations of collaboration that can be distinguished are (Biggs, 1989; Probst and Hagmann, 2003):

- Contractual participation: one social actor has sole decision-making power over most decisions and can be considered owner of the research process. Other stakeholders are formally or informally contracted to provide services or support.
- Consultative participation: most decisions are kept with one stakeholder group, but the emphasis is put on consultation and gathering information from others, especially for identifying constraints and opportunities, priority-setting and/or evaluation. The aim is to produce locally specific, socially robust knowledge for societal decision-making.
- Collaborative participation: different actors collaborate on a more equal footing, emphasising linkages through and exchange of knowledge and sharing decision-making power. The role of researchers is to contribute to contextual knowledge production and learning; the final negotiation and decision-making remains the responsibility of the societal actors.
- Collegiate participation: different actors work together as partners. Ownership is equally distributed and decisions are made by agreement or consensus. Apart from the contextual knowledge production and learning, researchers commit themselves to the development process. Together with other stakeholders they act, monitor, reflect and re-act upon the unfolding process of knowledge production, learning/empowerment, decision-making and action.

2.3 Collaborative landscape development research: a typology

The field of collaborative research for sustainable landscape development has spiralled into an enormous diversity of approaches and an equally large diversity in practices (Lilja *et al.*, 2001, cited in: Ashby 2003). In the literature, there is much debate on what collaborative research is about; how to apply it; the validity and objectivity of the research results; and the effectiveness in terms of knowledge production, social learning and action (cf. Gustavsen, 1992; McNiff, 1988; Kock, 2004). Collaborative landscape researchers, however, tend not to scrutinise and compare the theoretical assumptions and methodologies that they use and the societal impact of the collaborative research they carry out. Instead, they tend to smooth over differences between approaches, remarking that collaborative research is context-specific and highly applied in nature (Cassell and Johnson, 2006; Greenwood and Levin, 2007).

To get a grip on the large diversity of collaborative research approaches, we did a literature study to better understand: (1) the theories used in landscape development research; (2) different aims and goals of landscape development research; (3) types of stakeholder participation. We translated these elements into measurable items in a questionnaire, which was subsequently distributed among collaborative landscape researchers working for Wageningen UR[1]. Data analysis, exploration of a selection of case studies and reference back to theory yielded four collaborative research types in landscape research. These approaches are characterized by a different combination of theoretical perspective, type of knowledge production, intended contribution to societal development and the type of stakeholder involvement. The collaborative research types are presented in Table 2.1. They reflect a pattern of increased involvement of landscape researchers in enhancing social learning and negotiation in different societal networks and at different levels for institutional change, and hence from the production of scientific knowledge that is relevant for solving complex societal problems to co-production of knowledge in interaction with societal stakeholders in practice.

In the first type, *research for problem-solving,* researchers try to generate 'hard' scientific evidence to produce credible knowledge and solutions, using scientific methods. Networking is perceived as part of the research process, to inform and consult societal actors. Researchers consult local actors to generate detailed knowledge about the particular context or ask them to participate in experiments, the insights from which are subsequently used to optimise solutions. However, they do not actively involve local actors in the interpretation of research results. Using this approach, researchers try to create credible and salient knowledge to influence policy-makers' decision-making processes. Landscape development researchers address particular biophysical and social issues in landscape development, either in multi-disciplinary or interdisciplinary research teams. The main challenge is to translate complexity and uncertainty inherent to biophysical and human dynamics into relevant policy advice to guide future actions. Researchers do not consider innovation process management part of a researcher's responsibilities.

The second type is *research for social learning*. Here, researchers try to enhance social learning for change in a mutual collaboration and learning process with local stakeholders, and, sometimes, civil society organisations and/or governmental actors. Learning often starts with local actors. Depending on the contacts that researchers have with governmental actors, different levels of governmental actors might be included. This type is inspired by soft system thinking, which departs from the assumption that researchers and stakeholders should construct shared visions about the issue being studied and the developments pursued. Its

---

[1] An online questionnaire was sent to 161 researchers working for Wageningen University or an applied research institute of Wageningen UR. The response rate was 33% (a total of 48 completed questionnaires).

Table 2.1. Four types of collaborative research approaches in landscape research. The engagement of researchers in processes of societal and institutional change increases from left to right.

Attributes	Research for problem-solving	Research for social learning	Research for balanced negotiations	Research for institutional change
Theoretical perspective	hard system thinking	soft system thinking	critical system thinking	institutional theory/ innovation system thinking
Intended contribution to societal development	research for producing knowledge, methods, solutions	research for social learning for change	research for balanced, integrative negotiations	research for multilevel institutional change
Networking	yes	yes	yes	yes
Exploring perspectives and articulating problem definition	consultative participation at most	collaborative or collegiate participation	consultative, collaborative or collegiate participation	consultative, collaborative or collegiate. may be task researcher, but may also be performed by network members.
Research for problem-solving	consultative participation at most	collaborative or collegiate participation	consultative, collaborative or collegiate participation	consultative, collaborative or collegiate participation
Process management for alignment and execution (e.g. engagement, conflict management)	no	sometimes, marginally	dependent on situation	yes

main aim is to construct a rich picture of reality, which takes into consideration the various perspectives on the issue. The next step is to create mutual understanding of the form of sustainable development to pursue. Researchers and stakeholders then together engage in a process of knowledge-sharing and experimenting with possible solutions, which is assumed to generate a learning process. Researchers, however, do not engage in strategic negotiation to come to agreement, as in the third type.

The third type is *research for balanced negotiations*. Inspired by critical theory, researchers focus on substantive problems of which they believe power differences play an important role. Therefore, they engage in joint learning and negotiation, but simultaneously study the power dynamics of the socio-political system and use the derived insights to strategically influence the learning and negotiation process in order to create a context in which balanced negotiations can take place. Researchers consider networking and knowledge sharing essential to ensure balanced and equitable outcomes. They influence negotiations through strategic knowledge exchange and may also engage in innovation management process tasks such as mediation and conflict management. Researchers may take an outsider position and provide information to strategically influence the negotiation process, or they may join a (marginalised) coalition of stakeholders and start a collaborative or collegiate research process.

Finally, in the fourth type, *research for institutional change,* researchers are inspired by institutional theory and innovation system thinking. They aim to change constraining institutional contexts and governance arrangements that hinder learning and change towards a more sustainable landscape management. Research is characterised by collegiate forms of collaboration in which different scientific disciplines and societal stakeholders are included, in partnerships. Networking, producing and sharing knowledge are core activities in research efforts, and researchers often fulfil roles in mobilising stakeholders and managing conflicts if necessary to achieve the desired goals.

We found in our study that the choice for a particular type of collaborative research approach is among others influenced by the conditions posed by the commissioner of the research, the position of the researcher, the network within which researchers work and the institutional restrictions of his or her research institute (see also Regeer and Bunders, 2009). This may even imply that researchers use different collaborative research approaches in different stages of the research process, that different members of a research team employ different approaches, or that different approaches are being used in different projects. This makes it all the more important to learn from and about collaborative research experiences and enrich theories and methodologies in order to create more creative and effective solutions for collaborative research.

2.4 Getting the picture: two major challenges for collaborative landscape research

Within the broad framework of collaborative landscape research, the authors of the case chapters of this book reflect upon two important research challenges, as set out below.

2.4.1 The need for a better understanding of collaboration and broker roles of landscape researchers

In Chapter one, we argued that there is an urgent call for landscape researchers to make their work more societally relevant. They are challenged to broaden their traditional role as knowledge brokers; integrate and recombine knowledge for change. In the new broader definition, knowledge brokers are supposed to collaborate more closely with societal networks enhancing communication, translation, learning, mediation and action (e.g. Hargadon, 2002; Cash *et al.*, 2003; Devaux *et al.*, 2010).

However, both researchers from different disciplines and societal stakeholders tend to have different perspectives and sometimes conflicting expectations of what research is, what a researcher should do and what results research should yield, i.e. concerning the *type* of research applied. More specific, three factors in particular may constrain the envisaged research collaboration (Carlile, 2002):

- The syntactic problem: actors from different social worlds do not share a syntax or language to transfer knowledge to one another.
- The semantic problem: actors from different social worlds give different interpretations and meaning to words and issues, as they have a different historical background, norms, values and interests.
- The pragmatic problem: actors from different social worlds have invested in knowledge production and practice. They are used to and value these practices, which have always been beneficial, so they find it hard to change and adopt practices with uncertain outcomes.

An effective way of dealing with different research perspectives and involve stakeholders with their variety of perspectives in knowledge-sharing and action is the use of boundary (spanning) concepts, objects and processes. Sometimes multidimensionality is captured in the design of a new concept, for instance that of 'ecological indicator for water ecosystems at the Wadden Sea' (Turnhout, 2007), or 'ecological services' (Mollinga, 2008). The latter concept allowed ecologists, economists, sociologists and other professionals to create a shared language about the usefulness of ecosystems for human society, to express the functions and meanings different professionals and users attribute to landscapes, and to negotiate and agree upon core functions they wanted the landscape to fulfil.

While boundary concepts help to solve the syntactic and semantic problem, boundary objects also enable practical problem-solving (Carlile, 2002). Star and Griesemer (1989) defined boundary objects as objects that are plastic enough to adapt to the needs and constraints of the several parties that employ them, yet robust enough to maintain identity. Boundary objects such as simple theoretical frameworks, simulation models, role playing games and visual designs incite individual participants to express and add their (often tacit) knowledge about the issue-at-stake, and how the issue and possible solutions affects them. By focussing on learning (experiential learning about substantive issues plus social learning) and negotiation processes, researchers build the adaptive management capacity of individual participants as well as the collective, while simultaneously creating new knowledge exchange procedures and routines. This might affect the existing knowledge exchange and governance structure, enhancing communication and co-ordinate adaptive management.

The authors of the case chapters in this book looked at their collaborative practices and broker roles, enhancing open integrated knowledge production for action; enhancing trust and alignment for co-ordinated action; building the capacity for learning and landscape governance. What type of stakeholder participation and collaboration occurred in the different research phases, and how were the process and outcome communicated with outsider stakeholders? How could we characterise the boundary process? What boundary (spanning) concepts and -objects did researchers use and what broker roles did they perform? What (institutional and other) barriers did they encounter and how did they deal with those barriers? What did they aim for and consider critical for good performance?

2.4.2 The need for further theoretical development of collaborative landscape research

Collaborative forms of research are often referred to as Mode 2 knowledge production (Gibbons *et al.*, 1994, Nowotny *et al.*, 2001) or transdisciplinary research (Fry, 2001; Gibbons and Nowotny, 2001; Regeer and Bunders, 2009). In the field of landscape science, collaborative research is credited among other things with the advantages of: providing context specific knowledge about biophysical and human dynamics, and emerging (landscape) problems and opportunities (Funtowicz and Ravetz, 1993; Irwin, 1995; Ashby, 2003); enabling joint exploration of future development options, valued or at least acceptable to the local stakeholders involved (ibid); stimulating equality and a level playing field, thus empowering the stakeholders involved (Sohng, 1995; Berardi, 2002; Ashby, 2003), and directly contributing to social change (Berardi, 2002). It allows for negotiation about the division of costs and benefits (Ostrom, 1999); stimulates agreement on research outcomes and recommendations (Ostrom, 1990); and generates research outcomes that are more grounded in the perspectives and interests of the stakeholders concerned than in traditional research approaches (Reason and Bradbury, 2006), and is therefore more relevant than linear research models (Berardi, 2002). Moreover, it provides opportunities for easier regulation of resource use and capacity-building for ecological and social resilience (Ostrom, 1990; Ashby, 2003).

The results of our exploratory survey on collaborative research theories and approaches showed that researchers are inspired by different kinds of theories and assumptions about governance and change. The choice that researchers make for certain research outcomes and related research goals is associated with their theoretical perspectives and this more or less determines the type of stakeholder collaboration envisaged. To enhance good quality, effective landscape science, they need an inspiring, binding and guiding theoretical framework that:
- helps researchers to look further than their disciplinary focus, communicate and collaborate with other disciplines and societal actors, develop knowledge about the issue-at-stake and possible solutions that the variety of stakeholders involved perceive as credible, salient and legitimate;
- enables researchers and societal stakeholders to position and operationalise the landscape research in such a way that it more or less fits with the problem situation and the societal arrangements, enhancing societal uptake of lessons learned leading to sustainable equitable landscape development and/or governance.

The authors of the case studies of this book reflected on the landscape development theories and methodologies they employed. What initial insights did they have, and what challenges did they face that led them to choose a specific theoretical perspective as a starting point? What were the aims and goals to achieve; what were the concrete methods and tools they used; and what was the outcome (plus appreciation of researchers and societal actors)? What was missing or misconceived in the initial theories and methodologies they used? How can these experiences contribute to the future perspective of landscape science?

2.5 Introducing the case studies

This book contains a collection of 9 case studies. The authors of these case chapters describe the processes of collaborative research that they engaged in. They describe the theories and methods they used, the contribution to societal development they intended to achieve, the challenges or difficulties they encountered, the actual outcomes they achieved and the lessons they learned. By doing so, they provide us with valuable insights into the unruly practice of collaborative research. Only if we understand the actual practices they engage in and understand the barriers and challenges that they face, the questions that arise, the doubts that they have, will we be able to recognise the challenges ahead and reflect on the way forward.

2.5.1 Selecting the cases

The editors of this book sent a call for papers to the participants of a scientific Community of Practice on action research for sustainable landscape development that was active within Wageningen UR in 2007 and 2008. From the submitted abstracts, the editors then selected a series of case studies that together represented the gamut of different research types found in their previous study of the field of collaborative research. Another selection criterion was that the research team would incorporate both natural and social scientists. The underlying idea was to address the differences between the different approaches and between research 'worlds' in the concluding chapter. Finally, we wanted both Dutch and foreign cases to be included.

Most cases are indeed described by an interdisciplinary team of social and natural researchers from renowned research institutes, in close consultation with the participating civil society organisations and governmental organisations. The case studies reflect a wide range of collaborative landscape approaches, that cut across different sectors, from water management, land-use planning and regional development to forest management and climate adaptation. Table 2.2 summarises the different cases and shows that, in addition to the Netherlands, the geographical focus of the cases is on Southeast Asia and Africa.

We selected the case studies on the basis of the intended contribution to societal development, ranging from the uptake of scientific knowledge by policy makers to institutional change. Figure 2.1 shows the variation in the intended contribution to societal development, in relation to the type of participation. The figure shows that with the increasing complexity of the societal process the researchers were involved in, the type of participation also changes from dedicated stakeholder consultation, via collaborative participation to collegiate participation. In practice, the type of participation may shift during the project. However, the general observation of this relationship remains valid.

2.6 Structure of the book

In Chapters 3 to 11, our authors reflect on critical issues in collaborative research for landscape development and governance they engaged in. Together, the case chapters reflect a wide range of collaborative research approaches that each describe the theory and methods they used, the contribution to societal development they intended to achieve, the challenges or difficulties they encountered, the actual outcomes they achieved and the lessons they learned. In the final Chapter 12, we review, analyse and compare the cases presented in this book highlighting the type of boundary processes pursued, the associated type of collaboration with societal stakeholders and the results attained and lessons learned. With respect to the lessons learned we focus on the two challenges as elaborated in this chapter: the collaborative practices and researcher roles employed, and adequacy of the applied theory and methodology. This enables us to recognise the challenges ahead and reflect the way forward.

2. What is collaborative landscape research about?

Table 2.2. Overview of the cases described in the book (+: types of collaborative research most applicable).

Title case (chapter, reference name)	Region	Sector	Research for policy making	Research for social learning	Research for balanced negotiations	Research for institutional change
Collaborative research to improve the water management in two polders in the Red River Delta in Vietnam (Chapter 3, Red River case)	Vietnam	Water management	+	+		
Development and application of a landscape design method in the Frisian Lakes area (Chapter 4, Frisian Lakes case)	Netherlands	Landscape planning	+			
Linking training, research and policy advice: capacity-building for adaptation to climate change in East Africa (Chapter 5, East Africa case)	East Africa	Climate change adaptation		+		
Action research in a regional development setting. Students as boundary workers in a learning multi-actor network (Chapter 6, Westerkwartier case)	Netherlands	Regional development			+	
The soil-plant-animal system as a boundary object for collaborative knowledge (Chapter 7, Frisian Woodlands case)	Netherlands	Soil nitrogen management		+		
Learning from learning: the experiences with implementing adaptive collaborative forest management in Zimbabwe development (Chapter 8, Mafungautsi case)	Zimbabwe	Forest management				+
Gaming and simulation for co-learning and collective action: Companion modelling for collaborative landscape management between herders and foresters (Chapter 9, Thailand case)	Thailand	Land-use management			+	
Dutch spatial planning cases: performance and reflexivity in action research (Chapter 10, Reflexivity in action research, two spatial planning cases.)	Netherlands	Climate change mitigation			+	
The role of research in conflict over natural resources. Informing resettlement negotiations in Limpopo National Park, Mozambique (Chapter 11, Limpopo case)	Mozambique	Protected areas and village relocation			+	

	Stakeholder consultation	Collaborative participation	Collegiate participation
Multilevel institutional change			Friesian Woodlands Case
Integrative societal negotiations			Dutch Spatial Planning Cases / Limpopo Case
Networking and social learning		East Africa Case / Mafungantsi Case / Northern Thailand Case	Westerkwartier Case
Uptake of scientific knowledge	Red River Delta Case / Frisian Lakes Case		

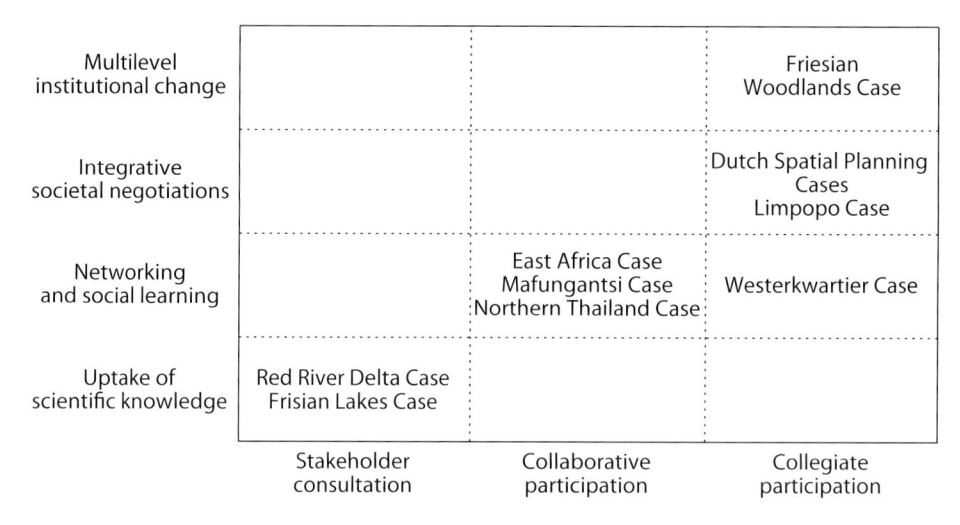

Figure 2.1. Cases ordered according to intended contribution to societal development and type of participation.

References

Allen, W.J., 2001. Working together for environmental management: the role of information sharing and collaborative learning. PhD (Development Studies), Massey University, New Zealand.

Ashby, J., 2003. Uniting science and participation in the process of innovation – research for development. In: Pound, B., S.S. Snapp, C. McDougall and A. Braun (eds.), Managing Natural Resources for Sustainable Livelihoods: Uniting Science and Participation. Earthscan, London, UK, pp. 1-19.

Berardi, G., 2002. Commentary on the Challenge to Change: Participatory Research and Professional Realities. Society and Natural Resources 15: 847-852.

Biggs, S.D., 1989. Resource-poor Farmer Participation in Research: A Synthesis of Experiences from Nine Agricultural Research Systems. OFCOR Comparative Study Paper No 3, ISNAR.

Carlile, P.R., 2002. Transferring, translating and transforming: An integrative framework for managing knowledge at boundaries. Massachusetts Institute of Technology, Cambridge, MA, USA.

Cash, D.W., W.C. Clark, F. Alcock, N.M. Dickson, N. Eckley, D.H. Guston, J. Jäger and R.B. Mitchell, 2003. Knowledge systems for sustainable development. Proceedings of the National Academy of Sciences of the USA 100 (14): 8086-8091.

Cassell, C. and P. Johnson, 2006. Action research: Explaining the diversity. Human Relations 59: 783-814.

Eden, C. and C. Huxham, 1996. Action research for the study of Organizations. In: S. Clegg, C. Hardy and W. Nord (eds.), The handbook of Organization Studies. Sage, Beverly Hills, CA, USA, pp. 526-542.

Flood, R.L. and N.R.A. Romm, 1995. Enhancing te process of methodology choice in Total Systems Intervention (TSA) and improving chances for tackling coercion. Systems Practice 8 (4): 377-408.

Fry, G., 2001. Multifunctional landscapes-towards transdisciplinary research. Landscape and Urban Planning 57: 159-168.

Funtowicz, S.O. and J.R. Ravetz, 1993. Science for the Post-Normal Age. Futures 25: 739-755.

Gibbons, M. and H. Nowotny, 2001. The potential of transdisciplinarity. In: J.T. Klein, W. Grossenbacher-Masuy, R. Haberli, A. Bill, R.W. Scholz and M. Welti (eds.), Transdisciplinarity: joint problem solving among science, technology and society. An effective way for managing complexity. Birkhäuser Verlag, Basel, Switzerland, pp. 67-80.

Gibbons, M., C. Limoges, H. Nowotny, S. Schwartzman, P. Scott and M. Trow, 1994. The New Production of Knowledge: The Dynamics of Science and Research in Contemporary Societies. Sage, London, UK.

Greenwood, D. and M. Levin, 2007. Introduction to action research: social research for social change. Sage, Thousand Oaks, CA, USA.

Gustavsen, B., 1992. Dialogue and development. Van Gorcum, Assen, the Netherlands.

Gustavsen, B., 2003. New forms of knowledge production and the role of action research. Action Research 1: 153-164.

Harms, B., J. Van den Berg, A. Van Paassen and R.A. Werkman, 2009. The state of the art of collaborative research in landscape development: examples from the Netherlands. Paper prepared for the International conference 'Towards Knowledge Democracy', Leiden, the Netherlands, August 25-27.

Irwin, A., 1995. Citizen Science: A Study of People, Expertise, and Sustainable Development. Routledge, New York, NY, USA.

Kindon, S., R. Pain and M. Kesby (eds.), 2007. Participatory Action Research Approaches and Methods: Connecting People, Participation and Place. Routledge, London, UK.

Klerkx, L. and C. Leeuwis, 2009. Establishment and embedding of innovation brokers at different innovation system levels: Insights from the Dutch agricultural sector. Technological Forecasting and Social Change 76: 849-860.

Klerkx, L., A. Hall and C. Leeuwis, 2009. Strengthening agricultural innovation capacity: are innovation brokers the answer? International Journal of Agricultural Resources, Governance and Ecology 8 (5/6): 409438.

Kock, N., 2004. The three threats of action research: a discussion of methodological antidotes in the context of an information systems study. Decision Support Systems 37: 265-286.

McNiff, J., 1988. Action research: principles and practices. MacMillan, London, UK.

McNiff, J., P. Lomax and J. Whitehead, 2003. You and your action research project. Routledge, New York, NY, USA.

Mollinga, P.P., 2008. The rational organization of dissent; boundary concepts, boundary objects and boundary settings in the interdisciplinarity study of natural resources management. ZEF (Center for Development Research), Bonn, Germany.

Nowotny, H., P. Scott and M. Gibbons, 2001. Re-thinking science: Knowledge and the public in an age of uncertainty. Blackwell, Malden, MA, USA.

Narayan, D., 1996. What is participatory research? In: D. Narayan (ed.), Toward Participatory Research. World Bank, Washington, DC, USA, pp. 17-30.

Nyden, P. and W. Wiewel, 1992. Collaborative research: harnessing the tensions between researcher and practitioner. American Sociologist 23 (4): 43-55.

Ostrom, E., 1990. Governing the Commons: The Evolution of Institutions for Collective Action. Cambridge University Press, New York, NY, USA.

Ostrom, E., 1999. Coping with tragedies of the commons. Annual Review of Political Science 2: 493-535.

Pohl, C., 2008. From science to policy through transdisciplinary research. Environmental Science and Policy 11: 46-53.

Probst, K. and J. Hagmann, with contributions from M. Fernandez and J.A. Ashby, 2003. Understanding Participatory Research in the Context of Natural Resource Management: Paradigms, Approaches and Typologies. ODI-AGREN Network Paper No. 130.

Reason, P. and H. Bradbury, 2006. Introduction: Inquiry and participation in search of a world worthy of human aspiration. In: P. Reason and H. Bradbury (eds.), Handbook of action research: participative inquiry and practice. Sage, London, UK, pp. 1-14.

Regeer, B.J., 2009. Making the invisible visible: Analysing the development of strategies and changes in knowledge production to deal with persistent problems in sustainable development. PhD Thesis Free University, Amsterdam, the Netherlands.

Regeer, B.J. and J.F.G. Bunders, 2009. Knowledge co-creation: Interaction between science and society, A transdisciplinary approach to complex societal issues. RMNO-series Preliminary studies and background studies, Preliminary study nr V.16. DeltaHage BV, The Hague, the Netherlands.

Roschelle, J. and S. Teasley, 1995. The construction of shared knowledge in collaborative problem solving. In: O'Malley, C.E., (ed.), Computer Supported Collaborative Learning, Springer-Verlag, Heidelberg, Germany, pp. 69-97.

Star, S.L. and J.R. Griesemer, 1989. Institutional ecology, 'translations' and boundary objects; amateurs and professionals in Berkeley's museum for Vertebrate Zoology. Social Studies of Science 19 (3): 387-420.

Sutherland, A., 1998. Participatory research in natural resources. Socioeconomic methodologies. Best practice guidelines. Natural Resources Institute, Chatham, UK.

Sohng, S., 1995. Participatory Action Research and Community Organizing. Paper presented at The New Social Movement and Community Organizing Conference, University of Washington, Seattle, WA, USA, November 1-3.

Turnhout, E., M. Hisschemoller and H. Eijsackers, 2007. Ecological indicators: between the two fires of science and policy. Ecological Indicators 7 (2): 215-228.

Van Paassen, A., P.F.M. Opdam, E. Steingröver and J. van den Berg, 2011. Landscape science and societal action. In: A. van Paassen, J. van den Berg, R.A. Werkman, E. Steingröver and B. Pedroli (eds.). Knowledge in action: The search for collaborative research for sustainable landscape development. Mansholt Publication Series 11, Wageningen Academic Publishers, Wageningen, the Netherlands, pp. 17-40.

Vernooy, R. and C. McDougall, 2003. Principles for Good Practice in Participatory Research: Reflecting on Lessons from the Field. In: B. Pound, S. Snapp, C. McDougall and A. Braun (eds.). Managing Natural Resources for Sustainable Livelihoods: Uniting Science and Participation. Earthscan, London, UK, pp. 113-141.

Wadsworth, Y., 1998. What is participatory action research? Action Research International, Paper 2. Available at: www.scu.edu.au/schools/gcm/ar/ari/p-ywadsworth98.html.

3. Collaborative research to improve the water management in two polders in the Red River Delta in Vietnam

Henk Ritzema, Le Quang Anh and Bui Thi Kim

Abstract

A collaborative research study on the effectiveness of the water management systems was conducted in two polder areas in the Red River Delta in Vietnam. The project adopted the participatory learning and action approach. The main objective of the study was to match the tacit knowledge of the various local stakeholders (groups) with the explicit scientific knowledge of the researchers in order to: (1) overcome the shortcomings of traditionally validated simulation models; (2) improve the mutual understanding of the complexity of the existing irrigation and drainage system; and (3) reach agreement on the outlines for an integrated action plan. The study started with a series of workshops in which (representatives of) farmers, communes, local government, unions, NGOs and scientists assessed the problems they face and identified and prioritised their preferences. The workshops were followed up by a participatory pre-investigation to identify and quantify the constraints in the functioning of the water management systems. Next, the drainage system was modelled and computer simulations were used to develop conceptual designs to improve the functioning of these systems. In concluding workshops with the stakeholders recommendations to improve the institutional capacity of the drainage system management were formulated and prioritised. In addition to technical innovations, recommendations to reform the complex institutional setting were formulated. The collaborative modelling approach proved to be a useful tool for tackling the hydrological and social complexity, overcoming the lack of long-term data records and getting a consensus among the stakeholders on the outline of an integrated approach.

3.1 Introduction

The implementation of national water policies at the local level is a major struggle. Organisational complexity and involving stakeholders are important constraints and at the same time important conditions for success. Collaborative or participatory research and social learning have become buzz words to tackle these issues. The concept of social (or collaborative) learning refers to learning processes among a group of people who seek to improve a common situation and take action collectively. It is also 'learning-by-doing'. Over the past decades progress has been made both on the social and technical aspects, but there is still a large gap between the views of the social and more biophysical oriented scientists. Based on a collaborative research project to improve the water management in two rice polders in the Red River Delta in Vietnam, the lessons on learning to narrow this gap are discussed.

Henk Ritzema, Le Quang Anh and Bui Thi Kim

The Red River Delta (1.7 Mha), located in the north of Vietnam, is one of the most densely populated areas in the world supporting about 1000 people per km². An extensive centuries-old system of more than 3,000 km of river dikes and 1,500 km of sea dikes reduces the vulnerability to flooding (Pilarczyk and Nuoi, 2005). Agriculture accounts for about 35% of the gross domestic product, compared to 24% for industry and 41% for services (Bakker *et al.*, 2003). The Red River Delta is the cradle of the wet rice cultivation in Vietnam, producing about 20% of Vietnam's annual rice production. Rice is planted twice a year and followed by winter crops if possible. Farm holdings are small, on average about 0.3 ha per household. The irrigation and drainage systems were designed and constructed in the 1950s and '60s and serve virtually all agricultural land in the Delta. Many of these systems are complex, using dual-purpose canals and pumped irrigation and drainage.

In the period 1995 to 2001, the irrigation and drainage infrastructure was rehabilitated and upgraded under the Red River Delta Water Resources Sector Project (Bakker *et al.*, 2003). A review of the project showed that improvements in the irrigation system performed reasonably well, but the improvements in the drainage systems performed less than anticipated (Asian Development Bank, 2001). The reasons for this inadequate functioning of the drainage systems are diverse and complicated. Firstly, in the Red River Delta, with its low elevations, drainage rather than irrigation is often the limiting factor affecting agricultural production (Water Resources Consulting Services, 2000). The average rainfall varies between 1,600 and 1,800 mm, of which 80-85% falls in the rainy season from May to October. The rains that cause waterlogging always occur in July-August and coincide with the occurrence of storms, floods and floodtide. Secondly, the drainage systems have not been designed and constructed in an integrated, comprehensive way, but have gradually expanded over the last 30-40 years. Consequently, the capacity of the pumping stations does not always match the capacity of the main canal and field drainage systems (Capacity Building in the Water Resources Sector Project, 1999). Thirdly, given the dynamic situation, the official research and extension system does not always effectively respond to farmers' needs (Linh, 2001). Fourthly, maintenance, repairs and upgrading practices are poor, resulting in a continuous deterioration of the systems (Vietnam Institute for Water Resources Research, 2003). Fifthly, water storage in the agricultural fields has also decreased due to changes in cropping patterns, i.e. introduction of high-yield rice varieties and 'dry-foot' crops. On top of this there is a gradual change in land use: urbanisation and non-agricultural use has rapidly increased over the last decades. These changes have increased the burden on the drainage systems as the non-rice areas have on average less storage capacity and higher run-off intensities (Water Resources Consulting Services, 2000). Finally, the organisation of the water management is complicated and fragmented. The management transfer from government authorities to farmers, initiated in the 1980s, has not yet brought the expected benefits. The management of the drainage system is shared by several organisations, a clear overall responsibility is lacking, staff are poorly trained and service facilities and funding are insufficient (Fontenelle, 1999, 2000a). To overcome these constraints the Second Red River Basin Sector Project was initiated in 2002. The project promotes integrated water resources management and stakeholder participation at local and basin level. Within the framework of this project, a participatory research study was conducted in two polders in the Red River Delta. The main objectives were to match the tacit and local-specific knowledge of the various stakeholders with the explicit knowledge of the researchers in order (1) to identify and quantify the major constraints in the functioning of drainage systems, and (2) to develop guidelines to improve the functioning of these systems in other polder areas of the delta (Ritzema *et al.*, 2008a). The study was implemented by the Vietnam Institute for Water Resources Research (VIWRR) and the Center for Promoting Development for Women and Children (DWC), both based in Hanoi, Vietnam. VIWRR is Vietnam's leading institute in the field of water resources, engaged in research, technology transfer, consultancies, construction and post-graduate training. DWC is a community-based organisation focusing on the rights of women and children especially in relation to participation and grassroots democracy. With the community-based and the rights-based approach DWC works at district and communal levels to bring about change in the policy and attitude of local authorities towards disadvantaged groups and to promote implementation of the Grassroots Democracy Decree (issued in 1998) and of the Grassroots Democracy Ordinance (issued in 2007) in Vietnam. Technical assistance was provided by Alterra, Wageningen University and Research Centre, the Netherlands.

3.2 Participatory study approach

A major challenge in planning improvements in the land and water management systems in countries like Vietnam is the general lack of (reliable) data sets, especially of long-term data records. In the Red River polders the many, frequently conflicting land use functions, made the problems even more complicated. The urgent need to improve the functioning of the drainage systems made it unfeasible to spend too much time and effort on the collection of additional data on this hydrological and societal complex ecosystem. To deal with this type of complexity, d'Aquino *et al.* (2002) advise making the decision-making process incremental, iterative and continuous. Focusing on dynamics instead of results and focusing on wide-ranging analysis instead of quantitative data is a way to enable progress in complex, conflict-laden negotiations. According to Voinov and Bousquet (2010) participatory modelling has emerged as a powerful tool that can (1) enhance the stakeholder's knowledge and understanding of a system and its dynamics under various conditions, as in collaborative learning, and (2) identify and clarify the impacts of solutions to a given problem, usually related to supporting decision making, policy, regulation or management. The participatory research approach adopted for the study in Vietnam is based on a combination of the principles of integrated water resource management (IWRM), participatory learning and action (PLA) and experiences with participatory modelling from Europe and the USA.

IWRM is emerging as an alternative to the top-down approach that was central to water resources management in the 20th century (Castelletti and Soncini-Sessa, 2006). IWRM is a process that promotes the co-ordinated development and management of water, land and related resources, in order to maximise economic and social welfare in an equitable manner without compromising the sustainability of vital ecosystems (Global Water Partnership, 2003). Operationally, IWRM approaches involve the application of knowledge from various disciplines as well as the insights from diverse stakeholders to devise and implement efficient, equitable and sustainable solutions to water and development problems. An IWRM approach is an open, flexible process that brings stakeholders together to make sound, balanced decisions in response to specific water-related challenges. Thanks to the participatory approach in IWRM local people feel more attached to the project they have created. They will therefore manage and maintain the drainage systems better. Since projects resulting from PLA are based on priorities and solutions identified and analysed by community groups, they tend to be more sustainable than those formulated exclusively by people from outside (Lueder Cammann *et al.*, 2004).

PLA is an approach for joint learning and planning with communities (Goss, 2004; Thomas, 2002). PLA is a bottom-up, community and stakeholder driven investigation. It entails a set of participatory tools and visual methods such as mapping, making time lines, transect walks, constructing problem trees, ranking activities and making Venn diagrams (Van der Schans and Lempérière, 2006). PLA goes beyond mere consultation and promotes the active participation of communities in the issues and interventions that shape their lives. It enables local people to share their perceptions and identity, and prioritise and appraise issues from their knowledge of local conditions. By combining the sharing of insights with analysis, PLA provides a catalyst for the community to act on what is uncovered. PLA builds local people's confidence, capacities, skills and ability to co-operate. This enables them to tackle other challenges both individually and collectively. The process of working together and achieving things together creates a sense of community and of belonging together (Lueder Cammann *et al.*, 2004). This fits in one of the principles of IWRM: social learning, i.e. learning processes that occur between different social groups, notably scientists and stakeholders (Van Paassen *et al.*, unpublished data).

In such a 'knowledge creating process', the capacity development process can be divided into four phases (Figure 3.1) (Nonaka and Takeuchi, 1995):
- *socialisation* or the process of creating new tacit knowledge out of existing (tacit) knowledge by sharing experiences;
- *externalisation* or the process of converting this tacit knowledge in explicit knowledge;
- *combination* or the process to convert explicit knowledge into more complex and systematic sets of knowledge;
- *internalisation* or the process of turning this explicit knowledge into tacit knowledge.

Tacit knowledge supports explicit knowledge and becomes a synonym for 'capacity to act' or competence to solve problems (Luijendijk and Mejia-Velez, 2005). The success of participative planning strongly depends on the commitment of those institutions, businesses and communities that are closely involved, and the interventions that are appropriate to local circumstances and needs (Jeffrey and Russell, 2007). Thus capacity development is

3. Collaborative research to improve water management in the Red River Delta

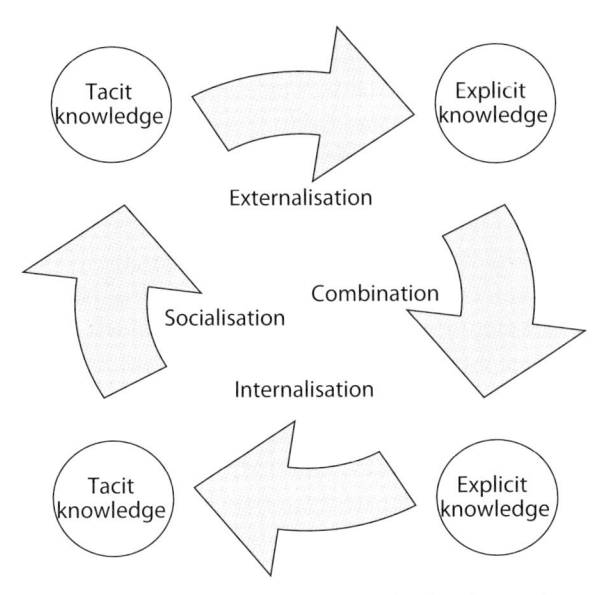

Figure 3.1. The knowledge creating process (after Nonaka and Takeuchi, 1995).

an essential element to achieve improved irrigation and drainage practices (Ritzema *et al.*, 2008b). Capacity development aims to develop institutions, their managerial systems, and their human resources to make the sector more effective in delivery of services (UNESCO-IHE, 2007). Within the framework of IWRM, capacity development has to focus on three elements (Global Water Partnership, 2003):
- creating an enabling environment with appropriate policy and legal frameworks;
- institutional development, including community participation;
- human resources development and strengthening of management systems.

Thus capacity development addresses three levels: the individual, the institution and the enabling environment. Each level has different goals, activities and outputs (Van Hofwegen, 2004). In this respect, capacity development is as much a process as a product (Kay and Terwisscha van Scheltinga, 2004). In this process, the more concrete or explicit aspects of capacity development such as training and institutional strengthening have to be linked with the local or tacit knowledge and aspects of ownership. Luijendijk and Mejia-Velez (2005) define explicit knowledge as the knowledge that 'can be expressed in facts and numbers and can be easily communicated and shared in the form of hard data, scientific formulae, codified procedures, or universal principles' and tacit knowledge as 'highly personalized and hard to formalize, subjective insights, intuitions and hunches'. Boon (Luijendijk and Lincklean Arriëns, 2007) estimated that this tacit or undocumented (local) knowledge accounts for 75 to 95% of the total organisational knowledge. Thus, to increase the impact of capacity development activities, the challenge is to link tacit with explicit knowledge and to update it continuously.

Participatory modelling is a way of linking this tacit and explicit knowledge by incorporating stakeholders, including the public, and decision makers into an otherwise purely analytical modelling process (Voinov and Brown Gaddis, 2008). Models are useful to get a better understanding of complex water management problems with many stakeholders and limited data records. Furthermore, experiences with environmental planning to rehabilitate an in-lake ecosystem in India show that participatory modelling is a useful tool for finding a balance between top-down control and bottom-up collaborative planning (Ritzema et al., 2010). Simulating alternative solutions is a method to encourage stakeholders to negotiate alternative solutions (La Grusse et al., 2006). Simulation models can be used to elucidate interrelationships between interventions and to suggest solutions that are acceptable to all stakeholders. Examples are *Waterwise*, a bio-economic model developed in the Netherlands for spatial planning of lowland basins (Van Walsum et al., 2008) and *Aquastress*, an EU-integrated project to develop participative approached in water stress management (Máñez et al., 2007). Similar initiatives with participatory modelling were initiated in the United States, where the Institute for Water Resources of the US Army Corps of Engineers, developed the Shared Vision Planning Method (SVP). The SVP method integrates planning principles, modelling and collaboration into a practical forum for making water resources management decisions (Institute for Water Resources, 2009). A participatory modelling approach that involves local stakeholders with their (tacit) knowledge of the local conditions and circumstances allows researchers to concentrate on the modelling process, rather than on the often time-consuming data collection (Argent and Grayson, 2003). Participatory modelling can help to achieve a common understanding or vision of how water resource systems function and how they can be managed in a sustainable way (Loucks, 2006). Even for complicated situations, simple, easy-to-understand models designed in collaboration with the stakeholders are useful tools to assist in planning (Berkhoff, 2007).

The basic principles of collaborative modelling were introduced a while ago and have gradually evolved over time. Voinov and Bousquet (2010) in their position paper on collaborative modelling show that in far too many cases the model developers have merely paid lip service to the stakeholders and that the engagement of the latter group has consequentially been quite nominal. They show that participatory modelling is still a top-down approach orchestrated by the model developers. We have tried to overcome these constraints by linking our modelling activities with participatory learning and action activities. For the study, a step-wise participatory approach was developed (Figure 3.2):

Step 1: Selection of study areas.
Step 2: PLA workshops to verify the initial problem analysis and to identify the stakeholders' priorities.
Step 3: Participatory pre-drainage investigations.
Step 4: Participatory monitoring programme.
Step 5: Model simulations.
Step 6: PLA workshops to prioritise improvement options.

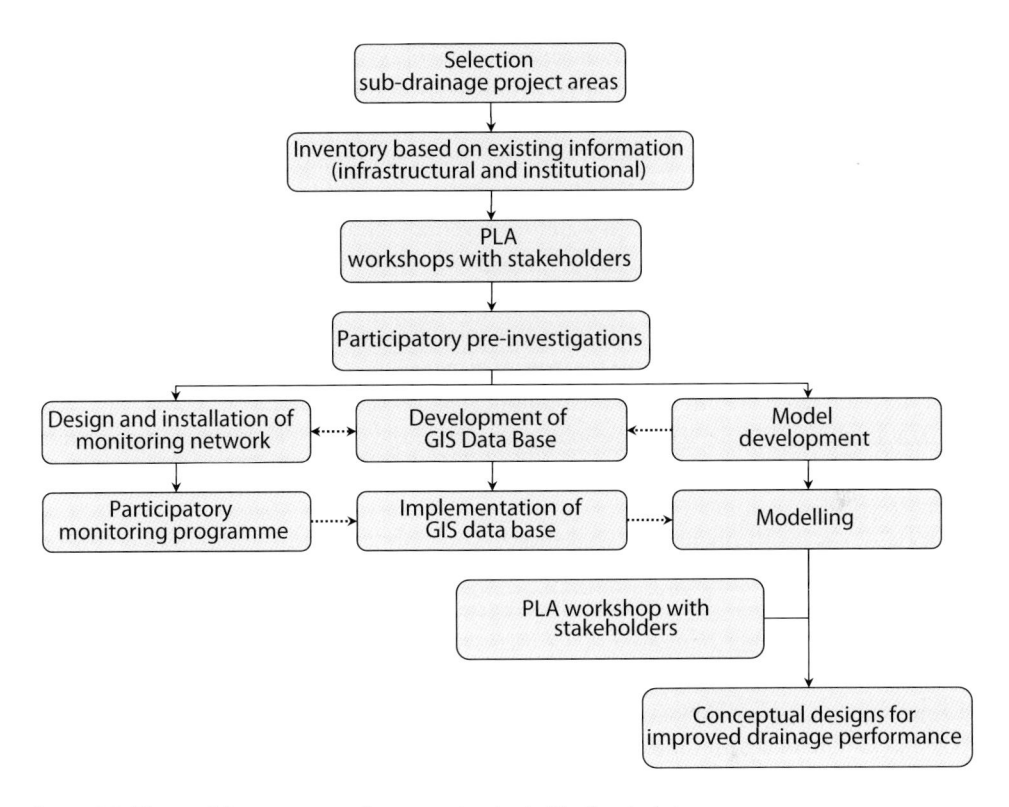

3. Collaborative research to improve water management in the Red River Delta

```
Selection sub-drainage project areas
        ↓
Inventory based on existing information
(infrastructural and institutional)
        ↓
PLA workshops with stakeholders
        ↓
Participatory pre-investigations
        ↓
┌─────────────────────┬─────────────────────┬─────────────────────┐
Design and installation   Development of       Model
of monitoring network ←   GIS Data Base   ←    development
        ↓                       ↓                   ↓
Participatory           Implementation of         Modelling
monitoring programme →  GIS data base      →
                                ↓
                        PLA workshop with
                        stakeholders
                                ↓
                        Conceptual designs for
                        improved drainage performance
```

Figure 3.2. The participatory research approach adopted by the study team.

VIWRR was the leading partner; their staff were responsible for the initial problem analysis, the monitoring programme, the model simulations and the development of the conceptual designs. DWC was the link between the researchers and the stakeholders and responsible for the organisation of the participatory activities and building capacity of local people on organising participatory events. Alterra provided technical assistance and provided training on participatory modelling activities. Because of the language, VIWRR and DWC communicated and exchanged information and knowledge with the stakeholders; Alterra had no role in this.

The (groups of) stakeholders were diverse; they represented local, district and provincial public organisations as well as individual farmers and interest groups. The stakeholders were representatives (both male and female) of the following organisations:
- *At provincial level*: provincial department of agriculture and rural development (DARD) and people's committees in the affected districts. Vietnamese provinces are governed by a people's council, elected by the inhabitants. This council appoints a people's committee, which acts as the executive arm of the provincial government.

- *At district level*: irrigation and drainage management committees (IDMC) and irrigation groups in the affected areas. The IDMC is responsible for water allocation and for the operation and maintenance (O&M) of the pumping stations and gravity outlets (Fontenelle, 2000b). Under the IDMC are district companies (IDMSC), established on the basis of district administrative boundaries. The IDMSCs obtain water from the IDMC, which they pay for with water fee revenues. They are responsible for irrigation and drainage. Each IDMSC has an associated set of about ten irrigation groups or teams, each responsible for around 1000 hectares. Irrigation groups, in turn, work with agricultural co-operatives to manage water, maintain facilities and collect the water fee. Irrigation groups are responsible for irrigation management, for maintenance and repairs of the main canal system (from the pumping station to the tertiary offtakes).
- *At commune level*: leaders of the people's committees and women and farmers' associations.
- *At village level*: heads of villages, irrigation and drainage teams and farmers.

To formalise the involvement of the stakeholders, sub-project drainage committees (SDCs) were formed in the two study areas. Members were elected from farmers, irrigation staff of communes, villages and co-operatives, agricultural extension associations, women organisations. The functions and tasks of the SDCs, including the required qualifications to be eligible, the membership ratio male/female, etc., were agreed upon during the start-up PLA workshops and laid down in regulations. The elected members are experienced farmers, both male and female. They have prestige, responsibility and show willingness to represent the farmers of the project areas. The stakeholders were involved in the problem analysis, the pre-drainage investigations, the monitoring programme and the PLA workshops. The various steps of the research programme are further elaborated in the following sections.

3.3 Selection of study areas

For the study, the research team was looking for two polders that represent the prevailing conditions in the Red River Delta polders. The study team decided to focus on relatively small polders with clearly defined boundary conditions, e.g. no open connections with neighbouring polders. This was done to avoid too much time and effort being spent on understanding the often complex interaction in water management between polders. The study areas were selected by the study team and based on the following criteria: (1) economic re-evaluation; (2) major constraints in agricultural production; and (3) opinion of local stakeholders, including the farmers on the functioning of the drainage system.

3.3.1 Economic re-evaluation

In 2001, upon the completion of the Red River Delta Water Resources Sector project, the internal rates of return (EIRR) of all rehabilitated polders were calculated (Asian Development Bank, 2001). The EIRR is the rate of return that would be achieved on all project resource costs, where all benefits and costs are measured in economic prices (Asian

3. Collaborative research to improve water management in the Red River Delta

Development Bank, 2010). For two of these polders, i.e. Trieu Dong and Phan Dong, the EIRRs, respectively 6.1% and 4.3%, were much lower than the 12% anticipated during the project formulation. The re-calculation done by the research team and based on the latest available data, confirmed these findings, with EIRRs of 7.9% for Trieu Duong and 7.3% for Phan Dong.

3.3.2 Major constraints in agricultural production

For the Second Red River Basin Sector project, a preliminary appraisal based on a participatory diagnostic survey, was conducted (Asian Development Bank, 2004). This survey indicated that the capacity of the existing drainage systems (including the pumping stations) in both Trieu Dong and Phan Dong is inadequate. Waterlogging and flooding still happens, on average in about 8 to 12% of the cropped areas, resulting in reduced agricultural productivity (Table 3.1).

3.3.3 Opinion of farmers on the functioning of the drainage system

During the above-mentioned participatory diagnostic survey, the farmers of Trieu Duong and Phan Dong told the project team that they were not really satisfied because, since the upgrading of the pumping stations, partial water-logging and flooding still occurred. They also felt that their yields were still below the expected yield level. They expressed their willingness to co-operate with researchers to investigate and tackle these problems.

Based on these criteria two areas were selected (Figure 3.3):
- Phan Dong area (1,956 ha), located in the upper reach of the Red River Delta in the Yen Phuong district, Bac Ninh Province (21° 13' N - 106° 04' E). Phan Dong has a relatively high elevation (about 2 to 4 m $^{+}$MSL) and is mainly used for agriculture. The population is 35,155, divided over 4 communes and 7,723 households.
- Trieu Duong area (4,051 ha), located in the middle reach of the Red River Delta in the Tien Lu District, Hung Yen Province (20° 38' N - 106° 07' E). Trieu Duong area has a

Table 3.1. Results of the participatory diagnostic survey: major agricultural constraints in Trieu Duong and Phan Dong areas.

Name of project	Trieu Duong B	Phan Dong
Area prone to flooding (average 1997-2004) (ha)	329 (8%)	234 (12%)
Summer rice yield (t/ha):		
area prone to flooding	4.6-5.1	3.3-4.6
total area	5.0-6.1	3.7-5.2

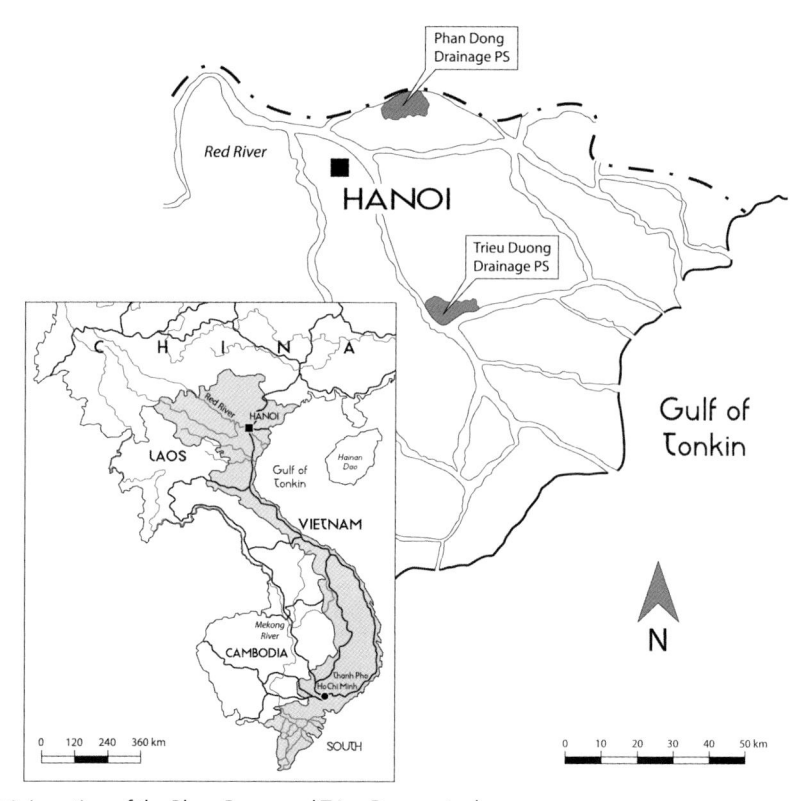

Figure 3.3. Location of the Phan Dong and Trieu Duong study areas.

lower elevation (1.3 to 3.0 $^+$MSL) with hardly any gradient. Although predominantly used for agriculture, urbanisation is increasing rapidly due to the proximity of Hung Yen town. The population is 62,729, divided over 22,736 households and 10 communes.

3.4 Problem analysis and stakeholders' preferences

To verify the initial problem analysis and to identify the stakeholders' priorities several PLA workshops were organised. The selection of stakeholders was based on the participatory diagnostic surveys conducted by the Second Red River Basin Sector project (Asian Development Bank, 2004). The workshops at the start of the project were used to establish Sub-drainage committees (SDCs), to verify the problem analysis and to make an inventory and ranking of the stakeholders' priorities. The workshops at the end of the project were organised to review and prioritise the conceptual design options to improve the functioning of the drainage systems. There were similar approaches, objectives and participants in the workshops for the two study areas. Technical as well as institutional (non-technical in terms society and management) aspects were taken into consideration.

3. Collaborative research to improve water management in the Red River Delta

The stakeholders identified the following priorities and preferences:
- to improve the functioning of the drainage system and to reduce risks of waterlogging and flooding;
- to increase crop productivity;
- to improve the economy within the framework of the policy and overall development plans of the local government.

The ranking of the problems as assessed by the stakeholders shows that, next to technical constraints in the infrastructure, institutional constraints are equally recognised (Table 3.2). It is interesting to note that farmers not only blame the authorities but also realise that their own attitude could be improved. The stakeholders also agreed to participate and co-operate in the pre-drainage investigations and the monitoring programmes.

Table 3.2. Ranking of the problems encountered in drainage as assessed by the stakeholders in the two sub-drainage areas.

Trieu Duong		Phan Dong	
Rank no.	Problem	Rank no.	Problem
1	Lack of culvert gates and valves	1	Some drains are too small
2	Lack of regulators	2	Inadequate regulations for violation(s)
3	IDMC is not active due to lack of funding	3	Regulators are operated improperly
4	It is not possible to regulate water levels in sub-areas	4	Budget to dredge the drainage canals is insufficient
5	Drainage outlets to the rivers are too small	5	Operation in (some) sub-areas hampers the functioning of the main system
6	Investments are not made systematically	6	Monitoring by local authorities is not done in time
7	Instructions from leadership are inadequate	7	Monitoring of IDMC is not done in time and is careless
8	Awareness of farmers is insufficient	8	Supervision, assessment, reports are unrealistic
9		9	Awareness of farmer is limited
10		10	Propaganda on canal protection is limited/has constraints
11		11	Pumping station is the main source of the problems

3.5 Participatory pre-drainage investigations and monitoring programme

The outcomes of the initial workshops were used to develop and conduct participatory pre-investigation and monitoring programmes. The pre-drainage investigation was based on the participatory diagnostic survey approach that was developed by the Second Red River Basin Sector Project (Asian Development Bank, 2004). Participation was obtained at various levels.

At district level, DARD and the IDMCs helped to collect data on the catchment area boundaries, topography, land use, design criteria, layouts of irrigation and drainage systems, social-economic and environmental parameters. To understand the institutional set-up, additional data were collected on the organisation of the water management, including funding and O&M practices. The IDMCs also participated in monitoring the performance of the pumping stations. Their staff collected data on running hours, water levels and O&M.

At field level, farmers, irrigation and drainage teams, PCs and women and farmers co-operatives participated. The participatory pre-investigations was based on the participatory rapid diagnosis and action planning approach for irrigated agricultural system (Van der Schans and Lempérière, 2006). The following tools were used: village profile, village diagram, cropping calendar, economic classification at household level and Venn diagram (Goss, 2004). These tools were used to collect data on the functioning of the drainage system (for the main and tertiary systems), the effectiveness of the drainage system (frequency and location of flooding, crop yields, etc.); the O&M of the canal system (type of maintenance, repairs, etc.) and; rules and regulations (e.g. measures to protect the canal system against unauthorised use). The tacit knowledge of the stakeholders was used to quantify the problem mentioned in Table 3.2. Simultaneously, the gaps in knowledge to quantify these problems were made explicit.

The findings of the pre-drainage investigations were used to develop and implement a participatory monitoring programme that was conducted during the rainy season of 2005 (May to October). The main objective of the programme was to collect sufficient data to model the drainage canal systems. The following data were collected: rainfall, evaporation, water levels in rice fields and in the main canal systems, pumping hours of the main pumping stations, operation practices of the pumping stations and the control structures in the canal system, water quality parameters, land use and crop yield, and cost of production. Under the overall guidance of the study team, the following stakeholders were involved in the monitoring programme: the irrigation department (monitoring the pumping station), the IDMCs (monitoring water levels in the main and secondary canals), the hydraulic groups and irrigation team (monitoring water levels in the fields) and famers' associations (monitoring land use and crop yields). Through the monitoring programme the drainage problems were quantified. The results are presented in the following paragraphs.

3. Collaborative research to improve water management in the Red River Delta

3.5.1 Drainage pumping stations

The results of the discharge measurements show that the actual discharge capacity of the pumping stations is less than the design capacities; respectively 92 and 80% for Phan Dong and Trieu Duong. The main reasons for these lower capacities are:
- Designs are based on assumptions, i.e. roughness and resistance coefficients, that are never 100% correct.
- For practical reasons, e.g. the availability of materials and construction equipment, etc., actual dimensions and capacities of pumps, gates, and pipes slightly differ from the design dimensions.

Next, the design capacity of the pumping stations had been underestimated because the design is based on the drainage requirements for rice crops only. In reality, only 52 to 68% of the land is used for rice cultivation. The rest of the land is used for the cultivation of other crops (mainly maize, vegetables and tree crops) and non-agricultural uses (i.e. roads, villages, town, etc.). These non-rice uses have significant lower in-field storage capacity and thus need a higher drainage capacity. Furthermore, land use has changed over the last 10 years. It is estimated that these land use changes require a discharge capacity that is higher than the design capacity: 12 to 18% for respectively Phan Dong and Trieu-Duong.

Finally, the effective pumping time is shorter than expected because the suction basins of the pumping stations are frequently blocked by floating debris. During periods of peak drainage demand, pumping has to be stopped for two to three hours per day to remove the debris.

The poor functioning of the pumping stations results in higher water levels in the sub-drainage areas and increases the risk of flooding. This risk of flooding is even greater because the functioning of the main drainage system is also below expectation.

3.5.2 Main drainage system

The main and secondary drains have higher bed levels and wider cross-sections than the design values. Fortunately, these two effects more or less neutralise each other. Thus, the hydraulic capacity of the main drainage canals is in general in balance with the capacity of the pumping stations. The overall capacity of the drainage systems, however, is below the design capacity. The main reason is that at various locations, the canal cross-sections, culverts and regulation structures are too small, especially where the drainage canals pass through villages. Drainage canals are also frequently blocked (without authorisation) by individual farmers or group of farmers, e.g. to irrigate fields with higher elevations or to store water for aquaculture. This results in an increase in upstream water levels.

Water levels in the drainage canal systems are also higher because some canal sections are (mis-)used for fishing (nets are installed across the drains) and used to dump farm and other waste products. The resulting huge amounts of floating debris restrict the flow and block culverts or other structures.

3.5.3 Tertiary and on-field drainage systems

The capacity of the tertiary and on-field drainage systems is low because these systems were not properly designed and/or constructed. Most on-farm outlets and field drains are missing, broken or damaged. It is almost impossible to regulate the water levels in the fields and/or the discharge to the main drainage system. The farmers decide among themselves when and how long each of them can irrigate and drain.

3.5.4 Institutional set-up

The following institutional constraints that hamper the functioning of the drainage system, were identified:

- *Complex ownership*: the boundaries of the sub-drainage areas and the underlying sub-division in secondary and tertiary units do not coincide with the boundaries of villages, communes. This complicates the organisation of the water management.
- *Many organisations*: many organisations are involved (Figure 3.4) and their responsibilities are not always clear, transparent and specific (Figure 3.5).
- *Poor coordination*: the coordination between the organisations is not adequate. The government does not put much emphasis on a participatory approach in O&M. Policy mechanism and specific guidance on participation are lacking. As a consequence the farmers look after their own benefits and not to the benefits of the commune, village or sub-drainage area.
- *Unbalanced investments*: the Government only invests in the main pumping stations and primary canals. Farmers are responsible for the tertiary and on-farm infrastructure.
- *Lack of funds*: drainage rates are included in the water fees. These fees, however, are insufficient: at present water fees cover only about 10-18% of the O&M costs. Consequently not all tasks as specified in Figure 3.5 are executed.
- *Inadequate monitoring network*: an adequate monitoring system is lacking. Only a few staff gauges have been installed and are monitored, mainly at the main pumping stations. Thus, because it is not known how much water is flowing through the system, operating the gates and sluices is partly a guessing game.
- *Limited capacity to control drainage*: there are not enough structures to regulate the flow in the drainage systems, and if there are structures the dimensions and levels are often incorrect. Furthermore, water regulation is based on local-specific preferences often obstructing upstream water management practices.
- *Low confidence*: the majority of the farmers and households lack confidence in drainage management (Table 3.2).

3. Collaborative research to improve water management in the Red River Delta

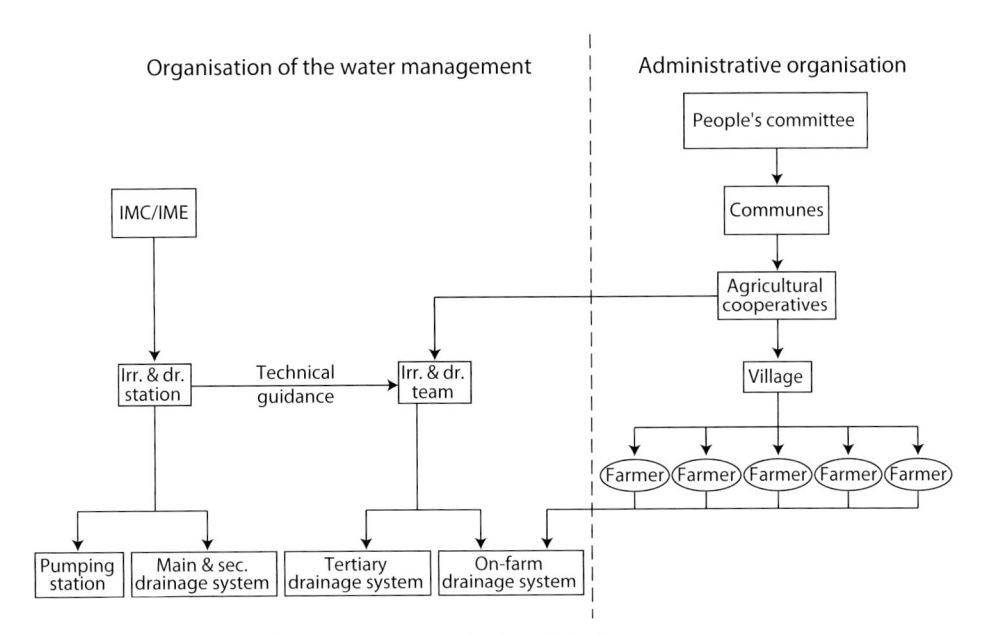

Figure 3.4. Organisation of water management in the sub-drainage areas.

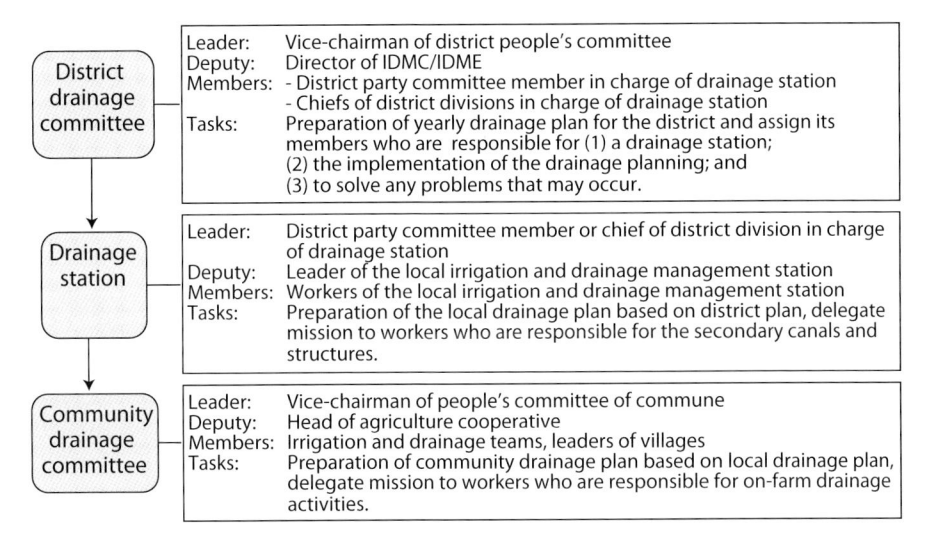

District drainage committee
- Leader: Vice-chairman of district people's committee
- Deputy: Director of IDMC/IDME
- Members: - District party committee member in charge of drainage station
  - Chiefs of district divisions in charge of drainage station
- Tasks: Preparation of yearly drainage plan for the district and assign its members who are responsible for (1) a drainage station; (2) the implementation of the drainage planning; and (3) to solve any problems that may occur.

Drainage station
- Leader: District party committee member or chief of district division in charge of drainage station
- Deputy: Leader of the local irrigation and drainage management station
- Members: Workers of the local irrigation and drainage management station
- Tasks: Preparation of the local drainage plan based on district plan, delegate mission to workers who are responsible for the secondary canals and structures.

Community drainage committee
- Leader: Vice-chairman of people's committee of commune
- Deputy: Head of agriculture cooperative
- Members: Irrigation and drainage teams, leaders of villages
- Tasks: Preparation of community drainage plan based on local drainage plan, delegate mission to workers who are responsible for on-farm drainage activities.

Figure 3.5. Each year, prior to the rainy season the management tasks of the various organisations are agreed upon.

Knowledge in action

The infrastructural and non-infrastructural constraints in the functioning of the drainage systems have major repercussions. Every year, parts of the areas suffer from waterlogging and flooding, on average 12 and 8% of respectively Phan Dong and Trieu Duong. This flooding is not so much related to the topography but more to:
- *Location*: in rice fields adjacent to the main drains, the depth of the standing water is always lower than 6 cm, even after heavy rainfall (Figure 3.6). This is well within the safe limits for rice cultivation. However, in fields further away from the drains or in upstream sections, the depth of the standing water may rise to 45 cm, well above the maximum allowable level. This indicates that the drainage systems at field and tertiary level are inadequate.
- *Land use*: flooding occurs upstream of fields used for aqua-culture and canal sections where farmers block drains to irrigate lands with slightly higher elevation.

As a result of the poor functioning of the drainage systems, rice yields in the flood-prone areas are 10 to 14% (Phan Dong) and 8 to 23% (Trieu Duong) below the overall average rice yields in the areas. Thus, it is not surprising that the actual economic internal rates of return, i.e. 7.3% for Phan Dong and 7.9% for Trieu Duong, are well below the anticipated 12%.

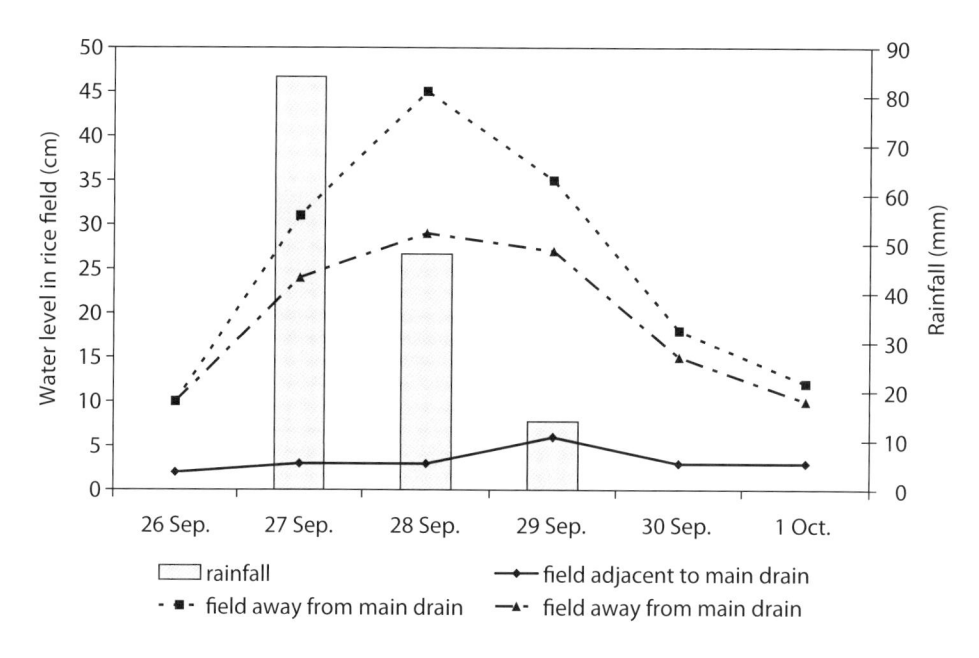

Figure 3.6. Water levels in rice fields near the main drains are lower compared to water levels in fields away from the drain (data from Phan Dong area).

3.6 Model simulations

A simulation model was used to get a better understanding of the hydraulic functioning of the drainage system and to simulate the improvement options that were proposed by the stakeholders in the start-up PLA workshops. DUFLOW, a one-dimensional, non-steady state model for water movement and water quality was selected because it has a user-friendly graphical interface. A scenario manager allows you to calculate various scenarios and to compare the results. Duflow is commercially available at a reasonable price and supported by an online helpdesk (Duflow Modelling Studio, 2010). An eight-day tailor-made course was organised to train VIWRR staff in the use of the Duflow and in the setup and implementation of the model in the two selected areas. The hydraulic functioning of the drainage system was simulated to get a better understanding of the complex relationship and interaction between the various elements of the system, i.e. drainage canal sections, structures connecting these sections (culverts, siphons, etc), regulation structures (gates, etc) and the pumping station(s) (Figure 3.7).

The DUFLOW model was calibrated with the data collected during the participatory monitoring programme. The calibration was done as follows: design water levels and discharges calculated based on the actual dimensions of the drains and related structures

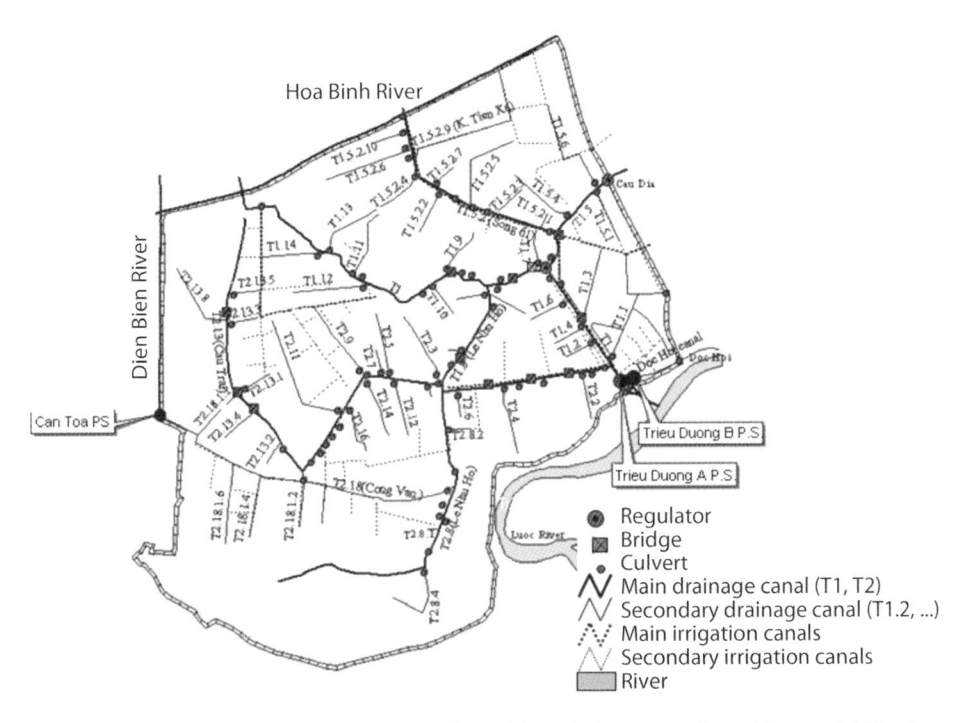

Figure 3.7. The lay-out of drainage systems in the Red River Delta is complicated (example Trieu Duong area).

were matched with the measured water levels at various locations in the drainage system during days with heavy rainfall and the corresponding discharges of the pumping stations (Figure 3.8). The resistance in the drainage system (roughness) was used to match the measured and simulated water levels.

After calibration, the model was used to simulate several conditions, i.e.:
- *Design situation*: to verify whether the design capacity of the pumping stations is in line with the design capacity of the canal system.
- *Actual situation*: to assess the capacities of the existing canal sections and associated structures and to check whether the installed pumping capacity is sufficient during 'normal' operation conditions (Figure 3.9).
- *Extreme conditions*: to assess the functioning of the system during extreme rainfall events that were recorded over the past 5 to 10 years.
- *Improvement options*: to get a better match between the capacity of the drainage canals (with related structures) and the pumping station.

The improvement options were formulated based on the pre-drainage investigations, the stakeholders' assessment of the problems (Table 3.2) and the results of the monitoring problem and included, among others:
- installation of trash racks, not only at the intake of the pumping stations, but also at specific locations in the main drainage system;
- re-dimensioning of the main drains;
- installation of more culverts and regulators, and;
- alternatives for the operation of the pumping stations and regulators.

The purpose of simulating the improvement options was not to optimise the technical design of these interventions but to show the stakeholders the effect of these improvements.

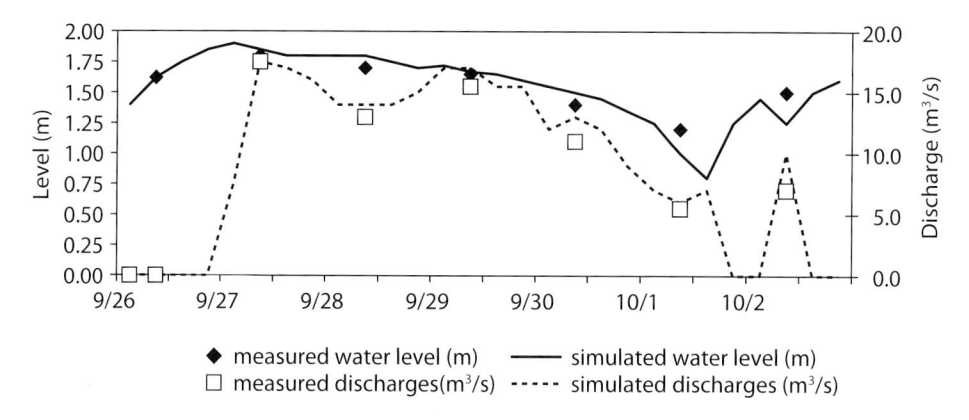

Figure 3.8. Example of the model calibration: measured (dots) and simulated (lines) upstream water levels and discharges at Trieu Duong B pumping station.

3. Collaborative research to improve water management in the Red River Delta

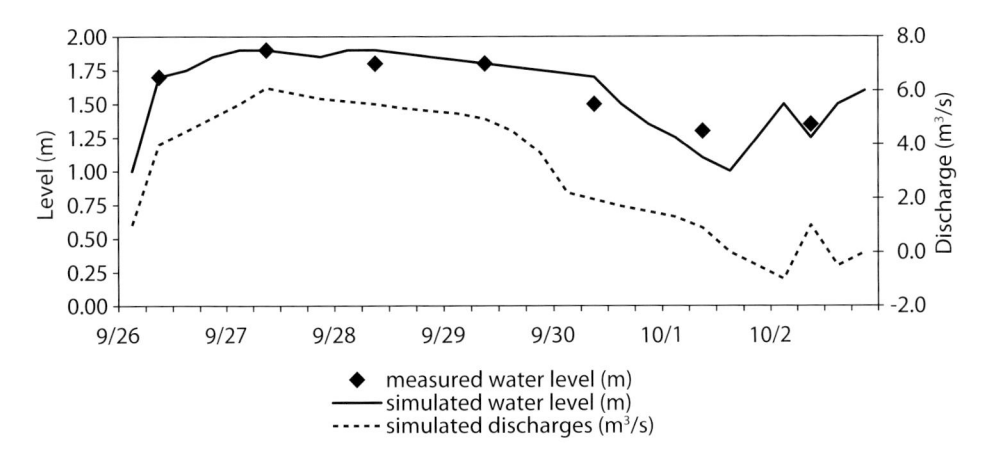

Figure 3.9. Measured (dots) and simulated (lines) upstream water levels and discharge through a road culvert in Canal T1 in Trieu Duong sub-drainage area.

3.7 PLA workshops to prioritise improvement options

During the final PLA workshops, that were attended by those stakeholders that were at the start-up workshops, the participants discussed and prioritised the improvement options. The outcome of these consultations was not merely a concrete set of measures, but a link of thinking that should form the basis for future investments and activities, i.e.:
- Increase the capacity of the pumping stations by the installation of trash racks, equipped with automatic debris removal devices. This measure will increase the total pumping time by 2 to 3 hours per day. It will also reduce the head loss over the pumping station and thus increase the discharge capacity.
- Improvement options should be based on a drainage design rate that is not based on rice cultivation only, but takes into account the percentage of land used for non-rice crops (maize, vegetables and fruit trees) and non-agricultural use (villages, town, road, graveyards, etc.).
- Step by step the functioning of the main drainage system can be improved. At present, structures are often too small compared to the capacity of the main canals. Furthermore, these structures should be designed and operated as control structures. This will allow farmers or farmers' groups to irrigate fields with higher elevations or to store water for aquaculture without hampering the functioning of the drainage in the upstream areas. Trash racks should be installed to avoid rubbish or debris ending up in the downstream parts of the system.
- The tertiary and on-farm drainage systems need to be rehabilitated based on the drainage requirements for the various types of land use, i.e. agriculture (rice crops, vegetables, fruit trees, etc.), aquaculture, etc.

The study team estimates that, if these prioritised improvement options are implemented, the EIRR will increase from 7.9 to 14.5% and from 7.3 to 13.0% for respectively Trieu Duong and Phan Dong. It should be realised that this increase is not only the result of improved drainage, but also of ongoing land-use changes, i.e. the decrease in rice cultivation in favour of the cultivation of more high-value crops and non-agriculture land use. Furthermore, some of the low-lying areas cannot be drained economically: 329 ha and 232 ha in respectively Trieu Duong and Phan Dong. In the simulations, these low-lying areas have been converted from rice paddies into aquaculture sites.

Next to these physical options to improve the functioning of the drainage systems, the participants discussed and formulated guidelines to improve the complex institutional setting, i.e.:

- *Clear and transparent responsibilities*: give organisations responsibility for a well-defined part of the drainage system and avoid overlap between organisations.
- *Responsibility at the lowest possible level*: at farm level, the farmers, being the main beneficiaries, have to be made responsible for the operation and maintenance of the on-farm drainage system. At tertiary level, the farmers' organisations (such as water-use co-operatives, water-use groups, agricultural co-operatives serving in irrigation and drainage) should be responsible.
- *Include all stakeholders*: the drainage system not only serves agricultural land, but also villages, sometimes even small towns, industrial sites, etc. All these non-agricultural stakeholders or users should be included in the existing organisations.
- *Charge all stakeholders*: water fees should not only be collected from the farmers, but from all stakeholders based on the benefits they receive.
- *Need for monitoring*: for proper operation of the pumping stations and the control structures in the drainage system, an adequate monitoring system is required. Water level gauges at various locations have to be installed and monitored. Stakeholders, including farmers, have expressed their willingness to participate in such a monitoring programme.
- *Need for capacity building*: drainage management in these flat polder areas is complicated and management practices at various levels are very much interrelated. All stakeholders, from the individual farmer to the operator of the pumping station, requested training and guidance in these complex drainage management practices.

Based on these recommendations, the study team prepared an 'implementation manual' (Vietnam Institute for Water Resources, 2006). The manual presents a method for a participatory diagnostic process to identify and qualify constraints in the functioning of drainage systems. The manual can then be used to prepare conceptual design options to improve the functioning of these systems. Technical and non-technical (institutional) improvement measures can be developed based on the prevailing socio-economic and environmental conditions. Based on a PLA approach, stakeholders can discuss, select and agree upon measures to improve the functioning of the drainage systems. The manual is now used to apply the participatory research approach in other areas in the Red River

3. Collaborative research to improve water management in the Red River Delta

Delta that have been rehabilitated under the Second Red River Basin Sector Project. The establishment of SDCs in each polder has been made compulsory to guarantee the stakeholder involvement.

3.8 Discussion

The challenges of the study were to match the implicit (or tacit) knowledge of the stakeholders with the explicit knowledge of the researchers in order to validate the problem analysis and the model simulations and to come to an integrated approach for the improvement of the irrigation and drainage systems in polders that were rehabilitated under the Second Red River Basin Sector Project. A wide range of studies have addressed the role of stakeholders in research on sustainable development. In this discussion we will focus on the role of participatory modelling. We aimed to make the modelling more a process than a product. Probst *et al.* (2003) suggest three prototypical approaches via this type of research, i.e. the 'transfer of technology approach', farmers first and participatory learning and action research. This project falls into the 3rd category: the research focus was on developing approaches for organisation and institution innovations through a mutual learning process. The role of the actors was clearly defined: VIWRR staff were responsible for the project implementation and the technical input, DWC for the interaction with the stakeholders and Alterra for guidance and advice. The procedures followed an iterative loop of action and reflection. DWC, as a community-based organisation, performed an important advocacy role working with the farmers (both men and women) to add their voices and views to the decision-making process, the problem analysis, the proposed simulation options and finally the prioritisation of the improvement options. DWC assisted the VIWRR team with the pre-drainage investigations and participatory monitoring programme by promoting and guiding the stakeholders' participation. The stakeholders, who represented individual farmers, other interest groups like women and agricultural organisations and public organisations at local, district and provincial level, were engaged from the beginning and had a final say in the problem analysis and the prioritisation of the improvement options. Some flexibility was built into the programme by planning the monitoring and modelling as parallel activities. As VIWRR staff were engaged in both activities, fine-tuning between these two activities was relatively easy. Due to limited funding, Alterra could only provide backstopping periodically. Communication via the internet, however, proved to be a powerful method for overcoming these shortcomings. (Potential) conflicts occur at many levels, e.g. between rice and non-rice farmers, between upstream and downstream farmers, between farmers and village (built-up areas), between farmers and fishermen, between farmers and operators of structures, gates, pumping stations, etc. Based on experiences from a similar study conducted in India (Ritzema *et al.*, 2010), the project staff realised that in such (potential) conflict-loaded situations, it was important that next to their role as a provider of scientific knowledge their role should be neutral, in the first place not looking for solutions but more in the role of a mediator.

The capacity to mobilise and use scientific knowledge is an essential component to promote sustainable development (Cash *et al.*, 2003). A participatory modelling approach was selected for two reasons. Firstly, simulation models are a useful tool for increasing and sharing knowledge and understanding complex irrigation and drainage systems as found in the Red River Delta. Secondly, simulation can be used to predict the impacts of improvement options. The selection of the model was based on the initial problem analysis and the proposed intervention options. We selected a model that is commercially available at a reasonable cost. A tailor-made course was organised to familiarise the VIWRR staff with the model and the participatory research approach. The course was set up on the principles of learning by doing; after a one-day introduction of the model, the remaining time was spent by the participants setting up the model for the two study areas. After the course, the participants were able to assess the type of input data needed for the calibrations. In a follow-up mission, the next steps in the modelling process, i.e. simulation of improvement options, were tackled.

The levels of participation can be assessed by using the IAP2 Spectrum method of Public Participation (International Association for Public Participation, 2007). The IAP2 spectrum recognises five levels of public participation, from level 1 *inform*, via level 2 *consult*, level 3 *involve* and level 4 *collaborate* to level 5 *empower*. Although, this research project has characteristics of all levels, the focus was on level 4. Stakeholders collaborated in the problem analysis, the pre-drainage investigations, the monitoring programme and the prioritisation of the improvement options, but they had no authority to make the final decisions: the end-product had to be approved by the Second Red River Basin Sector Project.

The capacity development approach is very similar to the knowledge-creating process of Nonaka (Figure 3.1). The pre-drainage investigations and tailor-made course addressed the internalisation or learning phase. The applied research activities were in the socialisation or sharing knowledge phase. The use of the newly developed knowledge to develop improvement options has characteristics of the externalisation or knowledge-encoding phase, and the dissemination of this new/updated knowledge through the development of guidelines was in the combination or synthesis phase. A strict distinction between the activities and the phases is not possible as the knowledge-creating process is in principle a never-ending loop. For example, pre-drainage investigations and the applied research activities in farmers' fields also include elements of internalisation, externalisation and combination. The PLA workshops had elements of internalisation and socialisation as they link tacit and explicit knowledge. For the researchers they were an effective tool for updating their knowledge of the drainage systems in the study areas. There are some essential elements to make this capacity development process successful. Bringing stakeholders and scientists with different backgrounds together and discussing tentative results of the research activities proved to be an effective tool to integrate explicit and tacit knowledge. A prerequisite is that the participants are stimulated to bring in their own experiences (tacit knowledge) and that the researchers are capable of linking this knowledge to the explicit knowledge they present and to their own tacit knowledge. DWC played a crucial role by stimulating the process of working together; they created a sense of community and mutual trust.

In the step-wise approach, all three elements of capacity development that form the based of IWRM were addressed. VIWRR staff were not only trained in model activities but also in the other aspects of collaborative research. The PLA workshops were a good example of 'learning by doing': under the guidance of DWC staff, the participants improved their ability to communicate and exchange information and knowledge in a participatory way, moving from 'teaching' to 'facilitating' in development issues. The participation of stakeholders in the problem analysis, pre-drainage investigation and prioritisation of the improvement options can be considered a major step in the institutional development. Finally, the guidelines prepared by the project and endorsed by the stakeholders helped to create an enabling environment. That this approach was appreciated could be seen at the end of the project, when the stakeholders, including the staff of the Second Red River Basin Sector project, asked for additional workshops to learn how to use and implement the 'implementation manual'.

3.9 Lessons learned

In this study we have used collaborative research theories to develop (physical and institutional) improvement options for the drainage systems in two rice polders in the Red River Delta in Vietnam. There are three categories of lessons that we can draw from this study: lessons related to the theoretical perspective, lessons on the role of the various actors and lessons on the effectiveness of the applied methodology. The main lessons learned can be summarised as follows:

- Theoretical perspective:
  - Collaborate research should be treated as a process. The step-wise approach as formulated in the guidelines probably needs adjustments when it is used in other polders in the Delta, each with its own specific technical and social-economic conditions. According to Voinov and Brown Gaddis (2008) there is a clear similarity with the open source paradigm in computer science, when software is a product of joint efforts of a distributed group of players. Ideally the process should continue, as it is a valuable asset for future decisions and conflict resolutions.
  - In such complex systems as found in the Red River Delta model, results can have a certain degree of uncertainty. To deal with this uncertainty, the research process should be flexible: there should be the possibility of making adjustments after consultation with the stakeholders.
  - The stakeholders know best which scenarios can be selected to address a certain problem. Local people are invariably the best source of knowledge and wisdom about their surroundings (Lueder Cammann *et al.*, 2004). Many of them have prestige, responsibilities and/or influence in the community. Engaging the stakeholders in

the selection of simulation options will lead to the development of more innovative solutions.
- Role of actors
  - The role of the research team is important in the social process, although they are the provider of the scientific knowledge, they should realise that their role as scientists is as a neutral mediator.
  - The selection of stakeholders is crucial. In this case, it was based on the participatory diagnostic surveys conducted by the Second Red River Basin Sector project. The establishment of the SDCs and the election of the members formalised the input of the stakeholders.
  - The level of confidence stakeholders have in modelling results is not so much related to the level of detail but much more whether they recognise the (simulated) effects of certain interventions. By discussing the effects of past events, i.e. extreme rainfall events or the effects of closing certain gates or sluices, stakeholders gained confidence in the model because the simulations matched their experiences and observations. By discussing these events, the stakeholders started to realise that isolated interventions only benefit some of the stakeholders and have negative repercussions on others.
  - The planners benefit because they can use the location-specific knowledge of the stakeholders to develop their models.
  - Both the planners and stakeholders acquire a better understanding of the location-specific problems (both physical and institutional) and their interrelated complexity.
- Research methodology
  - Selection of the model should be based on the knowledge, available data and priorities of the stakeholders and not on the preferences of the research team.
  - Lack of long-term data records that may seriously limit the usefulness of simulation models can be complemented by linking the tacit and location-specific knowledge of the stakeholders to the explicit knowledge of the researchers.
  - Discussing model simulations of the existing conditions with stakeholders and matching the results with the stakeholder's views and experiences proved to be a useful tool (1) to validate the model; (2) to create mutual understanding of complex problems; (3) to show that each intervention has its beneficiaries and victims, and; (4) to achieve consensus on the need for an integrated approach.
  - Collaborative research tools such as participatory modelling and participatory monitoring programmes are excellent ways of creating new knowledge from existing knowledge by sharing experiences (the so-called socialisation phase in the knowledge creating process).

3.10 Conclusions

A collaborative research study was conducted to gain a better understanding of the complex irrigation and drainage systems in the polders in the Red River Delta in Vietnam, to assess the effects of various improvement measures and to come to an agreement with the stakeholders on the outlines of an integrated approach. The challenges were to tackle the hydrological and social complexity, i.e. the large variety of hydrological functions, the many interests of different stakeholders and the lack of long-term data records. To achieve these goals, an approach was adopted that contained elements of participatory modelling, IWRM and PLA. The advantage of this approach is that, without an expensive and time-consuming data collection programme, a shared vision building and acting on emerging environmental issues could be initiated. Based upon existing data, stakeholder consultations and a quick reconnaissance survey for additional data, a hydrological model was built of the irrigation and drainage system. The model was calibrated using data collected during the participatory monitoring programme. This data was a mix of explicit information (maps, records etc.) and local specific knowledge of the stakeholders. For validation, simulations of the existing system were matched with the stakeholders' experiences. After calibration, the model was used to simulate the effects of proposed improvement measures as formulated by the stakeholders. Discussing model simulations with the stakeholders proved helpful in overcoming potential conflicts between stakeholders. Furthermore, by discussing the simulations the stakeholders started to realise that interventions would not necessarily satisfy all parties: each intervention has its beneficiaries and victims.

The obtained results and observations support the following hypothesis: a situation in which 'researchers know that model input is partly based on assumptions, and stakeholders understand that their own knowledge is an important contribution', is more productive for environmental planning than a situation in which 'researchers exactly understand the model input, but stakeholders do not believe that their own knowledge has been taken seriously'.

The study has shown that the current collaborative research theories can be effectively used in practice. It should be realised, however, that the theory should only provide the framework; flexibility is needed to allow for local-specific conditions both with respect to the physical environment and the social-economic setting. Only by applying existing theories, can the adequacy of the theoretical perspective be enhanced. We recommend that future research in this area should focus on the reduction of quantitative uncertainties in simulation results by including tacit knowledge in the process of input data compilation and plausibility checks. However, further research should also quantify whether the presented approach, despite the uncertainties, will give the same results compared with a traditional model validation and scenario-building process.

Acknowledgements

These research activities were conducted in the framework of the project Research on the Effectiveness of Drainage (VIWRR 2006). The project was implemented by the Vietnam Institute for Water Resources Research and the NGO Center for Promoting Development for Women and Children, both from Hanoi, Vietnam. Scientific support was provided by Alterra-ILRI, Wageningen University and Research Centre, the Netherlands. The project was financed through a loan from the Asian Development Bank and the support of the Dutch Ministry of Agriculture, Nature and Food Quality. This paper could not have been written without the data and support provided by this project.

References

Argent, R.M. and R.B. Grayson, 2003. A modelling shell for participatory assessment and management of natural resources. Environmental Modelling & Software 18: 541-551.

Asian Development Bank, 2001. Project completion report on the Red River delta water resources sector project (loan no. 1344-VIE(SF)) in Vietnam. Ministry of Agriculture and Rural Development, Hanoi, Vietnam.

Asian Development Bank, 2004. Bac Nam Ha irrgation and drainage system, sub-project praparation and appraisal, participatory diagnostic survey. Second Red River Basin Sector Project, part A: Water Resources Management. Ministry of Agriculture and Rural Development, Hanoi, Vietnam.

Asian Development Bank, 2010. Guidelines for the Economic Analysis of Projects - Glossary of Terms. Ministry of Agriculture and Rural Development, Hanoi, Vietnam. Available at: http://www.adb.org/documents/guidelines/Eco_Analysis/glossary.asp.

Bakker, N., Chu Tuan Dat, P. Smidt and C. Steley, 2003. Developing a basin framework for prioritizing investments in water resources infrastructure in Vietnam's Red River Basin. In: Proceedings 9th International Drainage Workshop, Wageningen, the Netherlands, p. 11.

Berkhoff, K., 2007. Groundwater vulnerability assessment to assist the measurement planning of the water framework directive - a practical approach with stakeholders. Hydrology and Earth System Sciences Discussions 4: 1133-1151.

Capacity Building in the Water Resources Sector Project, 1999. Review of design process, criteria and standards in the water sector of Vietnam. Hanoi, Vietnam.

Cash, D.W., W.C. Clark, F. Alcock, N.M. Dickson, N. Eckley, D.H. Guston, J. Jäger and R.B. Mitchell, 2003. Knowledge systems for sustainable development. Proceedings of the National Academy of Sciences of the USA 100: 8086-8091.

Castelletti, R. and R. Soncini-Sessa, 2006. A procedural approach to strengthening integration and participation in water resources planning. Environmental Modelling & Software 21: 1455-1470.

D'Aquino, P., C. Le Page, F. Bousquet and A. Bah, 2002. A novel mediating participatory modelling: the 'self-design' process to *accompany* collective decision making. International Journal of Agricultural Resources 2: 59-74.

Duflow Modelling Studio, 2010. Duflow modelling studio. Available at: http://www.mx-groep.nl/duflow/.

Fontenelle, J.P., 1999. The response of farmers to political change: decentralization of irrigation in the Red River Delta, Vietnam. International Institute for Land Reclamation and Improvement, Wageningen, the Netherlands.

Fontenelle, J.P., 2000a. Local institutional innovation in Red River delta irrigation management. Irrigation and Water Engineering, Wageningen University Wageningen, the Netherlands.

Fontenelle, J.P., 2000b. Water management decentralization in the Red River delta, Vietnam An uncompleted transition process toward local governance. Eighth Biennial IASCP Conference, Bloomington, IN, USA.

Global Water Partnership, 2003. Sharing knowledge for equitable, efficient and sustainable water resources. Global Water Partnership, Stockholm, Sweden.

Goss, D., 2004. Fieldbook for participatory learning and action. DWC and InWENT, Hanoi Department of Culture and Information, Hanoi, Vietnam.

Institute for Water Resources, 2009. Shared Vision Planning. US Army Corps of Engineers. Available at: www.svp.iwr.usace.army.mil, http://www.svp.iwr.usace.army.mil.

International Association for Public Participation, 2007. IAP2 Spectrum of Public Participation. Available at: http://www.iap2.org.

Jeffrey, P. and S. Russell, 2007. Participative planning for water reuse projects, a handbook of principles, tools & guidance. Aquarec project. Available at: http://www.aquarec.org/.

Kay, M. and C. Terwisscha van Scheltinga, 2004. Towards sustainable irrigation and drainage through capacity building. 9th International Drainage Workshop, September 10-13, 2003, Utrecht, the Netherlands, p. 16.

La Grusse, P., H. Belhouchette, M. Le Bars, G. Carmona and J.M. Attonaty, 2006. Participative modelling to help collective decision-making in water allocation and nitrogen pollution: application to the case of the Aveyron-Lère Basin. International Journal of Agricultural Resources, Governance and Ecology 5(2/3): 247-271.

Linh, N.V., 2001. Agricultural innovation: multi ground for technology policies in the Red River delta of Vietnam. Wageningen University, Wageningen, the Netherlands.

Loucks, D.P., 2006. Modeling and managing the interactions between hydrology, ecology and economics. Journal of Hydrology 328: 408-416.

Lueder Cammann, Bui Thi Kim and Ha, D.S., 2004. Fieldbook for Participatory Learning and Action (PLA). Feldafing, Germany and Hanoi,Vietnam.

Luijendijk, J. and W. Lincklean Arriëns, 2007. Water knowledge networking: partnering for better results. In: Proceedings Water for a changing world - enhancing local knowledge and capacity, Delft, the Netherlands, June 13-15, p. 25.

Luijendijk, J. and D. Mejia-Velez, 2005. Knowledge networks for capacity building: a tool for achieving MDGs? Design and Implementation of Capacity Development Strategies, Beijing, China, 14 September 2005, pp. 113-131.

Máñez, M., J. Froebrich, N. Ferrand and A. Siva, 2007. Participatory dam systems modelling: a case study of transboundary Guadianan River in the Iberian Peninsula. Water Science & Technology 56(4): 145-156.

Nonaka, I. and H. Takeuchi, 1995. The knowledge-creating company; how Japanese companies create the dynamics of innovation. Oxford University Press, New York, NY, USA.

Pilarczyk, K.W. and N.S. Nuoi, 2005. Experience and practices on flood control in Vietnam. Water International 30(1): 114-122.

Probst, K., J. Hagmann and with contributions from M. Ferandez and J.A. Ashby, 2003. Understanding participatory reseach in the context of natural resource management. Paradigms, approached and typologies. Agricultural Research & Extension Network, Agren-Network Paper no. 130.

Ritzema, H., J. Froebrich, R. Raju, C. Sreenivas and R. Kselik, 2010. Using participatory modelling to compensate for data scarcity in environmental planning: a case study from India. Environmental Modelling & Software 25: 145-1458.

Ritzema, H.P., L.D. Thinh, L.Q. Anh, D.N. Hanh, N.V. Chien, T.N. Lan, R.A.L. Kselik and B.T. Kim, 2008a. Participatory research on the effectiveness of drainage in the Red River Delta, Vietnam. Irrigation and Drainage Systems 22: 19-34.

Ritzema, H.P., W. Wolters and C.T.H.M. Terwisscha van Scheltinga, 2008b. Lessons learned with an integrated approach for capacity development in agricultural land drainage. Irrigation and Drainage 57: 354-365.

Thomas, S., 2002. What is participatory learning and action: an introduction. Centre for International Development and Training, Wolverhampton, UK.

UNESCO-IHE, 2007. Draft conclusions and recommendations. In: Water for a changing world: enhance local knowledge and capacity, Delft, the Netherlands.

Van der Schans, M.L. and P. Lempérière, 2006. Manual - Participatory rapid diagnosis and action planning for irrigated agricultural systems. International Programme for Technology and Research in Irrigation and Drainage, International Water Management Institute and Food and Agriculture Organization of the United Nations, Rome, Italy.

Van Hofwegen, P., 2004. Capacity-building for water and irrigation sector management with application in Indonesia. Capacity Development in Irrigation and Drainage Issues. Challenges and the Way Ahead. FAO Water Report, 26, Food and Agriculture Organization of the United Nations, Rome, Italy.

Van Walsum, P., J. Helming, L. Stuyt, E. Schouwenberg and P. Groenendijk, 2008. Spatial planning for lowland-stream basins using a bioeconomic model. Environmental Modelling & Software 23(5): 569-578.

Vietnam Institute for Water Resources, 2006. A participatory approach for the formulation and design of future drainage projects - Implementation manual (draft). Vietnam Institute for Water Resources, Hanoi, Vietnam.

Vietnam Institute for Water Resources Research, 2003. Final report on benefit monitoring and evaluation system 1999-2002. Red River Delta Water Resources Sector Project (Loan no. 1344 – VIE(SF)). Vietnam Institute for Water Resources Research, Hanoi, Vietnam.

Voinov, A. and F. Bousquet, 2010. Modelling with stakeholders. Environmental Modeling & Software 25: 1268-1281.

Voinov, A. and E.J. Brown Gaddis, 2008. Lessons for successful participatory watershed modeling: A perspective from modeling practitioners. Ecological Modelling 216: 197-207.

Water Resources Consulting Services, 2000. Final report on management study on land use and water management. Red River Basin Water Resources Management Project, Asian Development Bank, Hanoi, Vietnam.

4. Development and application of a landscape design method in the Frisian Lakes area

Willemien Geertsema, Arianne de Blaeij and Martijn van der Heide

Abstract

The 'Friese Merenproject' is a project initiated by the provincial government to increase the economic and ecological value of wetlands in the Frisian Lakes area in the north of the Netherlands. This chapter reports the development and application of a landscape design method (RITAM) in co-operation with stakeholders. Researchers from landscape ecology and environmental economy initiated the research project in which RITAM was developed. The theories that form the basis of RITAM are metapopulation theory, planning theory, welfare theory and knowledge about stated preferences. The application of a choice experiment is a central feature of RITAM. In the choice experiment conducted for this research, stakeholders expressed their preference for different landscape scenarios. The input for variation between the scenarios was provided by the stakeholders in a workshop, and the landscape scenarios were subsequently designed by the researchers. The landscape scenarios had a price tag, to determine 'willingness to pay'. The preferences for the development of the study area were derived from the results of the choice experiment. The preferences of stakeholders representing economic (recreation, agriculture) interests and those representing ecological interests showed some small, but remarkable, differences. We evaluated the RITAM with stakeholders to reflect on its credibility, salience and legitimacy. Several points for improvement became apparent from this evaluation. The development and application of RITAM paralleled the process of the Friese Merenproject. This had some advantages, but also a number of drawbacks, such as the low degree of participation in the choice experiment. The implications of working with representatives of different interest groups instead of with individual citizens is discussed. We conclude that we succeeded in developing and applying RITAM for the first time in the Frisian Lakes area. Ecological and economic values of the area were integrated in the design of landscape scenarios and in the preferences of stakeholders.

4.1 Introduction

This chapter presents a collaborative research project initiated by ecologists and economists with the aim of developing a method to integrate ecological and economic values in landscape development processes. By ecological values, we mean the presence of nature areas and biodiversity. By economic values, we mean the value represented by landscapes, either in terms of economic activities, or monetary and non-monetary values that people attach to landscapes. The economic value of a landscape (or a specific landscape characteristic) can be measured by making trade-offs: how much is a desired landscape (or characteristic) worth relative to other objects or conditions? Landscape means an area whose physical appearance and functioning is the result of the action and interaction of natural and human factors and as perceived by people (after Council of Europe, 2000).

The economic valuation of a landscape is partly based on ecosystem services provided by natural or semi-natural landscape elements, such as forests, lakes, grasslands, streams, hedgerows, etc. (De Groot *et al.*, 2002). Together, these landscape elements make up a 'green-blue network'. Examples of ecosystem services are pollination, natural pest control, water purification or landscape beauty. According to the definition of ecosystem services, biodiversity itself is not an ecosystem service; it is related but not the same (Benayas *et al.*, 2009; Naidoo *et al.*, 2008; Turner *et al.*, 2007). Therefore, it is mentioned separately in this research.

The project was initiated by the Netherlands Organisation for Scientific Research as one of the final projects in a biodiversity research programme. The aims of the final projects were firstly to make fundamental scientific knowledge about biodiversity applicable to society (in particular to policy makers and practitioners) and secondly to integrate the knowledge about nature conservation from gamma and beta sciences. Because of those two aims, we (the authors) worked together as scientists with backgrounds in landscape ecology, environmental economy and land-use planning.

The aim of our project was to develop a landscape design method integrating the ecological and economic value of landscapes. One of the underlying motives for this aim was the frequent conflict between economic development and conservation of biodiversity in landscape development programmes. Our ambition was to make relevant ecological and economic scientific knowledge applicable through this new method. We reckoned that a landscape design method would be suitable to make scientific knowledge applicable to actors in an area because it would more or less force us as scientists to translate our knowledge into simple relations between (variation in) spatial structures and the resulting ecological or economic value. The concepts of ecological value and economic value would also have to be made applicable to actors in the region. Knowledge from beta sciences about the relationship between the spatial structure of the landscape and ecological values as well as knowledge from gamma sciences about ways to determine the economic value of environmental goods, such as landscapes, was essential. The goal of the landscape design method was to design the composition and spatial configuration of the landscape, aiming at increasing the ecological and economic values of the landscape simultaneously, rather than emphasising the conflict between these two values. The method was meant to be applied not only in the case-study area as described in this chapter, but also in other areas later on. Because of this intended real-world application, we developed the method in close co-operation with stakeholders. We named the method that we developed 'RITAM', a Dutch acronym (*Ruimtelijk, Interactieve, Transdisciplinaire Afwegingsmethode*). For a description of the basic characteristics of the method see Section 4.3.

4. Development and application of a landscape design method

Most existing methods for the design or evaluation of landscapes are often not spatially explicit (Bonnieux and Le Goffe, 1997; Sayadi *et al.*, 2009); do not involve stakeholders (Brosi *et al.*, 2008; Higgins *et al.*, 2008); or are monodisciplinary in nature and focus, for instance, solely on the development of ecological value by biodiversity conservation (Giordano and Riedel, 2008; Paar *et al.*, 2008). RITAM departs from these existing methods in the sense that it integrates the economic and ecological value of green-blue networks, strives for a spatially explicit network design and involves stakeholders from the planning area of interest.

We chose to take two scientific knowledge issues as basic elements of the RITAM method, together making the structure-function-value chain, as described by Termorshuizen and Opdam (2009). The first issue is the relationship between the spatial structure of the landscape and its constituent elements and the provision of biodiversity and ecosystem service. The planning and design of landscapes concerns, among other things, the spatial structure of green-blue networks: the shapes and sizes and the location of the constituent landscape elements. The spatial structure is one of the determinants of the level of ecosystem services provided (Goldman *et al.*, 2007) (e.g. effectiveness of natural pest control, volume of water storage, amount of carbon sequestration). The second issue is the relationship between the landscape characteristics and the value they represent. The value represented by landscapes depends on the ecosystem services they provide, in the context of the specific region. Some of the ecosystem services have real market value, such as reed or wood, but most of them are not captured in market transactions and thus their values must be assessed in non-market terms. In this study, the value of the landscape is based on the preferences of stakeholders. We use 'willingness to pay' (WTP) as a proxy for the economic value stakeholders attribute to different spatial alternatives for the landscape (Garrod and Willis, 1999; Hanley and Barbier, 2009).

In this chapter, we first discuss the theoretical background of the project. Next, we present the basic characteristics of RITAM. After that, we reflect on the development and application of RITAM in the case-study area: the Frisian Lakes area (province of Friesland, the Netherlands). Issues to be discussed include the selection of the case-study area and the identification of stakeholders. When describing the different phases of the application of RITAM, we give special attention to the roles of the scientists and the stakeholders. We end with the conclusions and lessons learned.

4.2 Theoretical background

Figure 4.1 illustrates the coherence between the different theories that form the basis of this project: metapopulation theory, planning theory, welfare theory and knowledge about stated preferences.

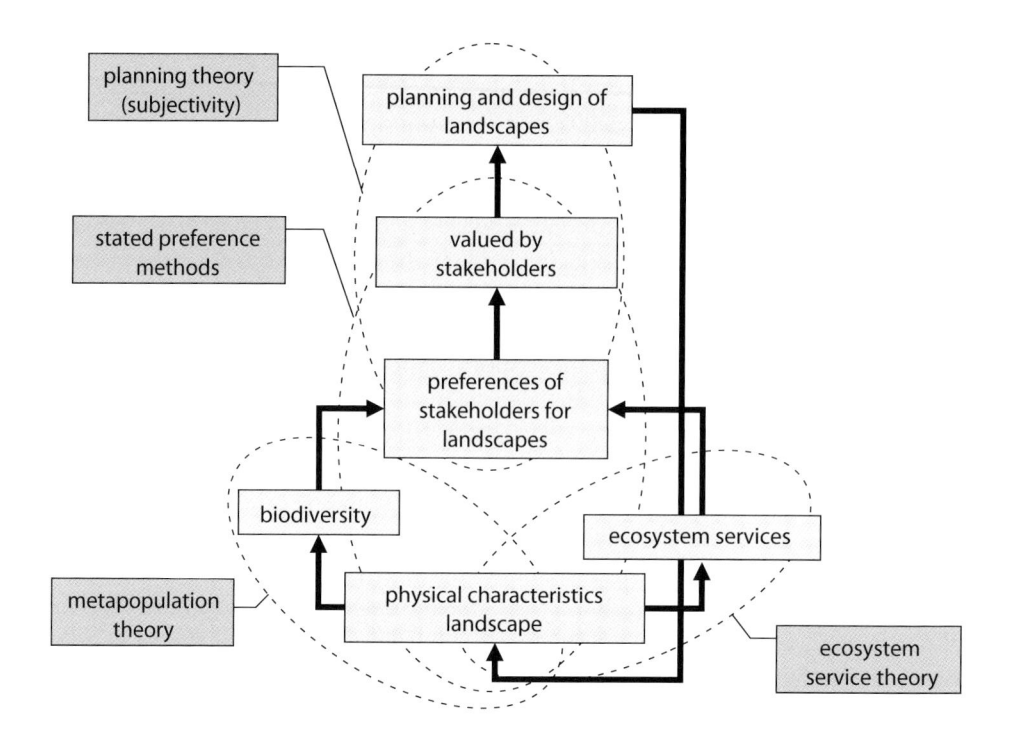

Willemien Geertsema, Arianne de Blaeij and Martijn van der Heide

Figure 4.1. Relationship between landscapes, stakeholders, planning process and theories.

Metapopulation theory relates the fragmentation of natural areas to the survival probability of species (Hanski, 1985; Verboom *et al.*, 1993). Different areas can make up a network of habitat patches for species. The population of a species that lives in such a network of habitat patches is called a metapopulation: a population of local populations. Smaller habitat patches and patches that are isolated from each other threaten the survival of metapopulations. These characteristics can be influenced by spatial planning. Simple guidelines have been developed (Opdam *et al.*, 2008) that relate these characteristics to the design of ecological networks for different species (in an ecological network, habitat networks of different species can be found). So, metapopulation theory is relevant for spatial planning processes. Spatial norms for the design of landscapes (e.g. patch area, distance between patches) can be derived from metapopulation research. Depending on the species, different possible spatial alternatives (e.g. several small patches or a few large) can enable the survival of target species in the habitat network.

The theory of a landscape as a structure that provides ecosystem services explains the benefits human society can derive from the network. The value of ecosystem goods and services was first studied mostly at the global scale (e.g. Millennium Ecosystem Assessment 2005). However, studies of ecosystem services at the regional scale are increasing in number (e.g.

Barkmann *et al.*, 2008; Feld *et al.*, 2009). The level to which these ecosystem services are realised in a landscape depends on the spatial structure of the landscape (Goldman *et al.*, 2007; Steingröver *et al.*, 2010). Green-blue networks are important providers of ecosystem services. Human-dominated parts of the landscape, such as agricultural areas or forests, are also considered providers of ecosystem services, e.g. food and timber production (Harrison *et al.*, 2010).

Welfare theory is the central theoretical framework adopted for RITAM from economics. It is assumed that utility is achieved through the satisfaction of human needs, or preferences, and utility maximisation is the main goal for any individual. Within this theory, a landscape can be seen as a 'good' that can satisfy human needs. Consequently, the landscape has a value, but not a market value because, in general, it is not possible to go to a market to buy (part of) a landscape, or to sell (part of) a landscape. The absence of a market price does not mean that landscape has no economic or monetary value. To measure the monetary value of landscapes, several monetary valuation methods exist (see, for example, Garrod and Willis, 1999; Perrings, 1995; Van der Heide *et al.*, 2003).

We chose to make use of the choice experiment (CE) method (see Box 4.1), which is grounded within economic theory. A choice experiment is, like the well-known contingent valuation method (CVM), a stated preference method that is capable of measuring the total economic value of an environmental good, and not just the so-called 'use part' of this value. The use value refers to the actual use of an environmental good in consumption and production activities. However, there are also 'non-use values', which involve no tangible interaction between the environmental good and the people who use it for production or consumption. Examples of non-use values are aesthetic value and feelings of identity. Because non-use values are closely linked to ethical concerns and altruistic motives, they are more amenable to debate than use values.

In the field of monetary valuation, the choice experiment is being increasingly applied as an alternative to CVM. The main reason for this is that a choice experiment is capable of measuring consumer preferences of multi-attribute commodities – such as landscapes. Unlike CVM, which tends to provide a single value for an expected (spatial or environmental) quality change, a CE enables estimation of the value of the change as a whole as well as the implicit values of its (spatial) attributes. Thus, the basic premise underlying the choice experiment is that a particular good (in our study, a rural landscape) has a value because of its attributes (in our study, for example, total area of natural grassland, the length of watercourses, water quality and the number of camp sites in nature areas). The inclusion of a monetary attribute (price tag as cost per household) allows for the derivation of implicit prices for each of the other attributes. The choices of the respondents determine the WTP, which indicates the value of the landscape characteristics and the importance of each of the characteristics (Hensher *et al.*, 2005). The WTP serves as the common denominator for comparing the values people attach to different kinds of goods, such as landscapes.

> **Box 4.1. Choice experiment.**
>
> A choice experiment can be used to investigate what the 'ideal' landscape looks like for different groups of people and what it is worth to them. The objective of this method is to estimate the economic values of a divisible set of characteristics of a good – in this case, the landscape. By varying the levels of the characteristics, decision-makers in the landscape development process will have detailed information about preferences for multiple landscape designs. This information consists of the 'ideal' landscape for groups of participants and information about the preferred landscape characteristics, even in monetary terms.
>
> A choice experiment investigates people's preferences for landscapes by letting them choose a number of times (e.g. 10 times) between two (or more) alternative landscape designs. Each time, the characteristics of the alternative designs change. In the choice experiment conducted in this research, the alternatives between which respondents were asked to choose were constructed by systematically varying the attribute levels (e.g. 10, 100, 200 ha of natural grassland or 10, 25, 50 km cycling routes, etc). To determine the economic value, one of the characteristics in the choice experiment is a monetary amount, a price tag. The idea is that people's preferences for an alternative landscape are influenced by the price tag: a higher price decreases the preference.
>
> Specifically in the RITAM choice experiment, we gave the respondents extra information about the alternatives by indicating the ecological value of each landscape using a picture of the animal species that can survive given the spatial composition of the habitat of the species (wetlands and grassland in the case of the Frisian Lakes area). The relevant literatures about choice experiments in landscape decision-making could be found in van der Heide *et al.* (2008).

From planning science we used the theory about the subjectivity of planning processes. Traditionally, landscape professionals and experts have developed 'objective' principles and practices for landscape planning and design. In planning processes, the people involved regard their knowledge as objective and neutral, meaning that their knowledge provides an objective basis for developing landscape composition and structure. Although the knowledge of these experts and professionals is indisputable, the assumption of objectivity has been questioned, or at least has been subjected to critical reflection in recent years. Nowadays it is acknowledged that in society there is a large variety of ideas about, and appreciation of, sustainable landscape development. After all, spatial planning and design is highly subjective – beauty is in the eye of the beholder (Kerkstra, 1998). If several individuals are asked how to design a landscape, they will probably give several different answers, depending on their personal goals, motives and social and economic background. In the Netherlands, a (centralistic) top-down landscape planning approach is being increasingly replaced by a bottom-up governance approach in which interest groups and stakeholder organisations participate, sharing their knowledge about the landscape and expressing their ideas and appreciations.

4. Development and application of a landscape design method

The importance and necessity of including subjective perspectives in the planning and design of landscapes has encouraged the development of a range of collaborative approaches and methodologies, all based on some kind of citizen involvement. These approaches are referred to as deliberative valuation, stakeholder-oriented approaches, group-based approaches or participatory decision-making (for example, Macmillan *et al.*, 2002; Howarth and Wilson, 2006; Lynam *et al.*, 2007; O'Neill, 2007). Although these methodologies and approaches have been described in the scientific literature on valuation and participatory decision-making, and have been applied to various problems in practice, less has been written about how to use collaborative tools to gauge people's willingness to pay for changes in the structure and characteristics of landscapes. That is, the process of citizen involvement in landscape planning and design is often based on discourse and negotiation (and on achieving consensus), without any explicit reference to people's willingness to pay or without including the spatially explicit conditions for the realisation of ecosystem services. There are only a few landscape studies in which the estimation of individual willingness to pay is combined with an overall participatory planning process (for example Hanley *et al.*, 1998; Johnston *et al.*, 2002; Campbell, 2007). And, to our knowledge, none of these existing methods explicitly takes into account knowledge about the relationship between spatial characteristics of landscapes and the survival probability of species.

4.3 The RITAM method

In this section, we describe the most important characteristics of RITAM. We assume that these characteristics will help in the design of landscapes in co-operation with stakeholders, and in integrating ecological and economic scientific knowledge. The most important characteristics of the RITAM design method are that it is spatially explicit, interactive, applying both ecological and economic science and that a valuation method is incorporated. In later sections, we reflect on the further development and application of the method in a specific case; this section is about its basic, generic characteristics.

4.3.1 Spatially explicit

Investing in landscapes requires spatially explicit choices: decisions have to be taken about what to do where: which landscape measures should be taken where in the landscape. In RITAM, spatial alternatives for landscape design are developed. Each alternative represents a combination of spatial characteristics. The alternatives differ in the level of the specified landscape characteristics. The spatial alternatives are visualised through geographical maps of the planning area. Visualisation is an important tool in the communication between science and practice.

4.3.2 Interactive

The interaction between science and practice is an important aspect of RITAM. Scientific knowledge about the relationship between spatial characteristics of a landscape and biodiversity and ecosystem services is used in workshops and in the choice experiment described and further elaborated in Section 4.4. The role of local stakeholders ('practice') involves setting targets for the planning area, and delivering detailed knowledge about the area and structures and processes present, but also involves issues that determine the preferences for future development (power, implicit knowledge, knowledge about social structures, etc.). Different stakeholders from an area participate in the application of RITAM. The participation of stakeholders and their role in different phases of the method is described in Section 4.4.3.

4.3.3 Transdisciplinary

RITAM is transdisciplinary, as it is both interdisciplinary (combining scientific disciplines) and interacts with stakeholders. It is based on close co-operation across the boundaries of the scientific disciplines. The major sources of scientific knowledge included in the method are landscape ecological knowledge about the relationship between spatial characteristics and biodiversity and ecosystem services, economic knowledge about stated preferences, monetary valuation methods and spatial planning knowledge about planning processes.

4.3.4 Valuation method

Stakeholders' monetary valuation of spatial alternatives is explicitly included in RITAM. We expect that this will help develop economically viable plans, because it elucidates stakeholders' subjective preference for spatial alternatives. The results of RITAM can be used as input for cost-benefit analyses. As already mentioned, RITAM uses the choice experiment approach in which the WTP is included to denote the monetary value that stakeholders attribute to different spatial landscape characteristics.

4.4 Implementation

4.4.1 Selection of the case-study area

The aim of the research project was to develop a landscape design method together with stakeholders involved in landscape planning. In this way, we expected to develop an applicable method. To develop and apply the method, we looked for a case-study area with an ongoing landscape planning process. We wanted both the researchers and the stakeholders to benefit from the project: the research team would develop an applicable and tested method and the stakeholders would gain insight into how to design the landscape to improve both ecological and economic values; this insight could be used in the ongoing planning process.

4. Development and application of a landscape design method

In addition to the selection criterion 'ongoing process', we used other criteria linked to physical characteristics to select the case-study area. We looked for areas with a green-blue network providing important ecological and economic values. On the basis of these criteria we selected four 'National Landscapes'. National Landscape is the status of regions in the Netherlands with special landscape characteristics (nature values, cultural values) (Ministry of VROM, 2004). Green-blue networks are important structural characteristics of National Landscapes. Spatial development of National Landscapes is allowed, but it may not harm the typical characteristics. Provincial governments are responsible for the implementation of the National Landscapes. We explored four National Landscapes: South-West Friesland, Groene Hart, Groene Woud and South-West Zeeland by interviewing the person responsible for the National Landscape policy in the relevant province as well as a representative of the provincial Environmental Federation (an environmental lobby group that has good insight into different stakeholders and the relationship between different interest parties). In the Groene Hart, Groene Woud and South-West Zeeland, there were no suitable processes in landscape development going on in which we could participate. The Friese Merenproject case arose out of discussions with the province of Friesland about the National Landscape South-West Friesland as a potential case. The project partly overlaps with the National Landscape and met the selection criteria: there was an ongoing spatial planning process for improving wetlands and waterways mainly for recreation, with special attention being paid to biodiversity and landscape values. Biodiversity and landscape are recognised as important values that attract (water) tourism in the region. The province of Friesland was co-ordinating the Friese Merenproject.

Despite its co-operation with the Friese Merenproject, our project was not a formal part of the planning process. We operated more or less parallel to it, principally because the method had never been used before, so both the process and the output were uncertain. Therefore we preferred to test it first, without the pressure of suitable output for a concrete planning process. Another reason was that we thought that the stakeholders involved in the project would feel freer to express their preferences about the development of the area if it had no official status in the Friese Merenproject.

4.4.2 Case-study area: Frisian Lakes

The case-study area, the Frisian Lakes, is located in the northern part of the Netherlands (Figure 4.2). The landscape consists of a mosaic of lakes, wetlands and production grassland for dairy farming. The area in which we conducted our pilot study makes up about 30% of a larger area with comparable land use. The pilot area lies between the towns of Joure and Sneek, and some small villages can be found within the area. Dairy farming is an important economic activity, and highly productive grasslands are the dominant land use.

The open and quiet landscape and nature areas are important factors in its attractiveness for recreation, which is one of the most important economic activities in the area. The

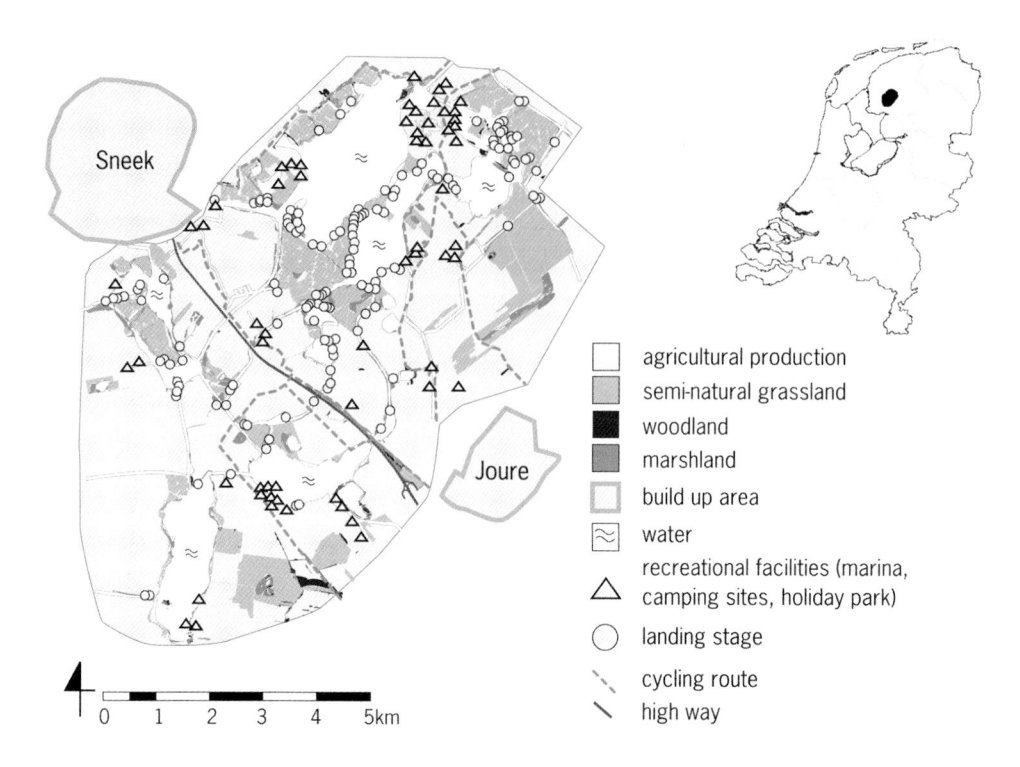

Figure 4.2. Study area with main land-use types and recreation facilities.

area is known for its water-related recreation (such as sailing). Accompanying facilities such as landing stages, marinas and camping sites increase its recreational value. The green-blue network in this area is of major quality because of the wetlands. The wetlands are of international importance for waterfowl. Some of the lakes and wetlands in the area are protected under the Natura 2000 directive, which implies protection by European legislation.

4.4.3 Stakeholders

The various stakeholders had different roles in our project. For clarity we identify them on the basis of their role.
- Advisory group: RITAM is intended for use by the organisation or government responsible for regional planning. In the Netherlands, this is generally the provincial government. Different people from the province of Friesland committed themselves to our project: the leader of the Friese Merenproject, an expert in nature conservation, an expert in rural areas and an expert in spatial development. These experts were also involved in the Friese Merenproject. We call these people 'advisory stakeholders'. They advised us about the

application of RITAM and choices to be made in different steps of the method. At the end of the project, we evaluated the method and the project with them.

The advisory stakeholders recognised the benefits of developing a landscape design method together with the potential users and were willing to function as an advisory board. They expected to benefit from our project, as it could potentially provide them with information about balancing economic and ecological interests in the development of wetlands and watercourses in the area. They helped us with practical aspects of the project when stakeholders had to be contacted (names and addresses, suitable locations for workshops).

- Representatives: other stakeholders were involved in the workshops that we organised and in the choice experiment itself. They represented the most important interest groups and citizens: representatives of the water board (Wetterskip Fryslan), a farmers' organisation (LTO), recreation, nature organisations (Staatsbosbeheer), an environmental organisation (Friese MilieuFederatie) and local government (municipalities of Sneek and Joure). We call these stakeholders 'representatives'. With this group we also discussed the results of the method and we evaluated the method with them. Rather than asking a (random) sample of individuals to participate in the choice experiment, we suggest an approach that is based on the collaboration of representatives of the relevant organisations, agencies and government levels in the area under consideration (e.g. LTO represents farmers, Friese MilieuFederatie represents citizens who are concerned about the environment, local government represents inhabitants of municipalities). There are high costs and a long turnaround time between the design of the choice experiment and the analysis of the results, and this can have a negative effect on the use of a choice experiment as a decision tool for assisting spatial policy makers. A representative approach such as we used has two main advantages, namely (1) the representatives are, in general, quite interested in, and knowledgeable about, the issue, and through their involvement a wealth of local knowledge becomes available, which can be used to develop the relevant scenarios in an efficient and timely manner; and (2) representatives are more concerned with, and actively involved in, the area under consideration than random participants and are therefore assumed to be more willing to participate in the choice experiment.

4.4.4 Application of RITAM in the Frisian Lakes area

We provide a timeline to clarify the different activities involved in the application of RITAM in the Frisian Lakes area (Table 4.1). We divided the different activities into eight steps, which spanned about 10 months altogether. We explain the different steps with an emphasis on the interaction between the stakeholders and the research team to elucidate the different types of input from science and practice.

Willemien Geertsema, Arianne de Blaeij and Martijn van der Heide

Table 4.1. Timeline illustrating the RITAM application activities in eight steps, highlighting the roles of the research team and the stakeholders.

	Research team	Stakeholders
1. Select case-study area	• setting criteria, contacting province of Friesland	advisory group: • decide to participate and indicate boundaries of case-study area when contacted by the research team
2. Identify key stakeholders		advisory group: • identify stakeholder organisations and representatives to participate in RITAM
3. First workshop	• organisation and preparation • introduce the project • suggest spatial characteristics needed for target realisation	representatives: • identify targets for planning area (different for different interests) • identify spatial characteristics needed for target realisation
4. Prepare choice experiment	• design different spatial alternatives based on results of first workshop: spatial characteristics needed for target realisation • decide how to include willingness to pay • design choice experiment	advisory group: • comment on the design of choice experiment
5. Execute choice experiment	• place choice experiment on the internet • contact stakeholders to participate in the choice experiment	representatives: • participate in choice experiment: indicate preferences for spatial alternatives and willingness to pay
6. Analyse choice experiment	• statistical analysis of results of choice experiment	
7. Second workshop	• present results of choice experiment • evaluation of RITAM	representatives: • discuss results of choice experiment • give input for evaluation of RITAM
8. Evaluation	• evaluation of RITAM and process of co-operation research group and advisory group	advisory group: • evaluation of RITAM and process of co-operation research group and advisory group

4. Development and application of a landscape design method

4.4.5 First workshop

Interests in the planning area

The motivation of local stakeholders to change the spatial structure of the landscape in the planning area is at the basis of the design of the green-blue networks. The question is what the arguments behind the motivation are: what are the targets for the planning area? The research team and the advisory group made an inventory of groups or organisations with an interest in the case-study area and were able to set targets for the development of the area. The advisory group knew which people to contact, so that we could approach them personally. The aim was to have stakeholders that represented the 'sustainability triangle' of people-profit-planet, with representatives of government, market and NGOs.

Representatives of local and provincial government, nature and environmental organisations, recreation, agriculture and the water council were invited to participate in the workshop. All interest groups took part: government (4 people), nature/environment (3), recreation (1), agriculture (1), water management (1). Many of the workshop attendees had not met before, despite the fact that they were all involved in the development or management of the area. They appreciated meeting each other. It was recognised by stakeholders from all interest groups that nature and landscape in the area were the reasons for the area's appeal for recreation.

Target setting

The representatives identified their targets for the area at a plenary discussion. The research team had prepared this discussion with information provided by the advisory group about the formal goals of the Friese Merenproject. The first important target was the development of the recreational appeal of the area, to increase the economic strength of this sector. The second important target was to improve and protect the nature quality of the area, basically within the legal obligations for the area – some of the lakes are Natura 2000 areas, thus requiring protection because of EU regulations, and many of the lakes and wetlands fall within the National Ecological Network (Ministry of Agriculture, Nature Conservation and Fisheries, 1990), thus requiring protection because of national law.

Selection of spatial characteristics

In this workshop, we wanted to get input from the stakeholders about which characteristics of the landscape should be varied in the choice experiment. Available scientific knowledge about the relationship between the spatial characteristics of the landscape and the level of ecosystem functions was the starting point. An almost infinite number of spatial characteristics and their levels are possible (e.g. amount of marshland and the spatial configuration of marshland patches, number of landing stages for boats and their position in

Willemien Geertsema, Arianne de Blaeij and Martijn van der Heide

relation to bird breeding areas, etc.). Large numbers of variables are unusable for application in a choice experiment; therefore, we wanted to select spatial characteristics for inclusion in the choice experiment that reflected the priorities of the key stakeholders. The workshop participants were asked to indicate which spatial characteristics of the landscape were of importance for the realisation of their targets in the area. The input of stakeholders was elicited in three ways:

1. They were asked to comment on the list of characteristics proposed by the research team. The participants accepted the list proposed by the research team and added the following characteristics: openness of the landscape and water quality. The different characteristics could be selected or rejected independently of each other.
2. They were asked to indicate how important the characteristics were for the realisation of their targets, using 15 coloured stickers to indicate their preferences. The number of stickers and the spread of the colours made it immediately clear which characteristics were important to which groups of stakeholders. Each interest group had its own colour (see Figure 4.3).
3. They were asked to indicate the level (qualitative or quantitative) of the characteristics. The desired level was related to the current situation. This meant that the current situation was indicated on an axis. The participants could indicate with coloured stickers whether they were satisfied with the current situation or wanted a certain increase or decrease in the level of this characteristic, e.g. the number of landing stages for boats, the area of wetlands, different levels of water quality, etc.

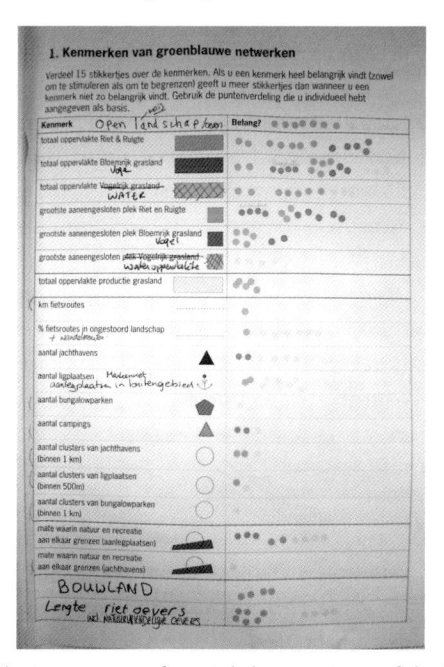

Figure 4.3. Poster showing the importance of spatial characteristics of the landscape for realisation of targets.

4. Development and application of a landscape design method

Development of the choice experiment

The design of spatial alternatives was an important step in the development of the choice experiment. The research team designed the spatial alternatives, but the 'ingredients' were based on the input of the stakeholders in the first workshop. Criteria for the inclusion of a spatial characteristic in the landscape alternatives were either that many interest groups indicated that the characteristic was important or that a strong deviation was present in the declared importance of the characteristic or the desired levels it should take. Table 4.2 shows the characteristics and their levels as used in the development of spatial alternatives in the pilot area.

In addition to the spatial alternatives, we constructed a price tag for the determination of the WTP. Because representatives of interest groups, rather than individual citizens, participated in the choice experiment, the willingness to pay referred to the amount of money that a representative thought the citizens he/she represented would be willing to pay, e.g. through taxes. The price tags used in the choice experiment were: €10, €25 and €80. These amounts were based on experience gained during previous valuation surveys and allow for the derivation of implicit prices for each of the spatial characteristics. The idea, then, is that in order to decide which good or spatial situation they want, people make trade-offs between different combinations of attribute levels at different costs or prices. Of course, it is possible to conduct a choice experiment without the inclusion of a monetary attribute. However, if we want to calculate the welfare measures of a change in the landscape, it is necessary to include a monetary attribute such as price or cost.

Table 4.2. Spatial characteristics of the area and their alternative levels used to construct the spatial alternatives in the choice experiment.

Spatial characteristic	Alternative levels, additional to the current situation
Nature	6 levels (150 ha extra marshland/350 ha extra marshland/150 ha extra marshland and an ecological corridor/300 ha extra natural grassland/200 ha extra natural grassland/100 ha extra marshland)
Water	2 levels (2 alternative extra waterways for boats)
Cycling	2 levels (two alternative extra cycling routes)
Landing stages	2 levels (spatial clustering of current number of landing stages/extra landing stages, dispersed in nature areas)
Yacht basins	2 levels (spatial clustering in part of the area/spatial clustering in total area)
Water quality	2 levels (quality according to the EU Water Framework Directive (European Union 2000)/drinking water quality)

Willemien Geertsema, Arianne de Blaeij and Martijn van der Heide

An animal species functioned as an indicator for the ecological quality of the spatial alternative. The choice of species was based on landscape ecological knowledge about the spatial habitat requirements for viable populations of particular animal species. The relationship between the indicators of ecological value and the spatial characteristics of the landscape were explained in Box 4.1 in the choice experiment. The design of the landscapes (including visualisation) was discussed with the advisory group. No significant changes were needed as a consequence of their comments. An example of a choice set (current situation and two spatial alternatives) is illustrated in Figure 4.4.

Execute choice experiment

Twenty-six spatial alternatives and the current situation in the planning area were visualised for the CE. Each alternative consisted of a unique combination of the spatial characteristics, a price tag and an ecological indicator. The respondents were representatives of interest groups. The experiment was offered through the internet. The advantage of the internet was that respondents were free to choose when to participate. An additional advantage was that respondents participated independently and did not influence each others' answers. A disadvantage was that we could not answer questions that occurred to respondents when engaging in the CE.

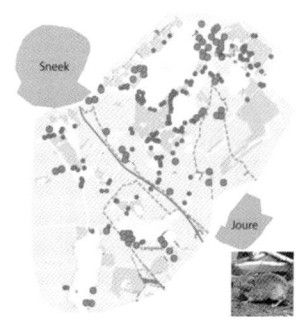

80 euro per household	**25 euro per household**	**10 euro per household**
Current situation	Changes from current situation:	Changes from current situation:
	• extra grassland around Sneekermeer	• extra watercourse via Bokkewiel
	• extra watercourse via Bokkewiel	• extra cycling route southwest of Sneekermeer
	• extra cycling route around Koevordermeer	• water quality: drinking water
	• more landing stages in nature areas	

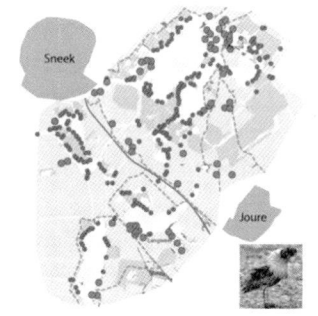

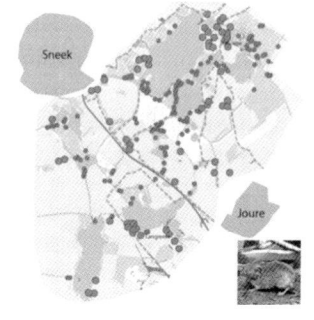

Figure 4.4. Example of a choice set in the choice experiment.

The 26 spatial alternatives and the current situation (status quo) made up 13 choice sets. About 60 representatives of interest groups ('interest stakeholders') were invited to participate through the internet and were asked to forward the invitation to other colleagues. These persons represented a wider range of interests than those that participated in the workshops. We assumed that people in interest groups would be motivated to participate in the CE because their daily work dealt with the area central to the experiment and consequently they would be interested in participating. Half of the invited representatives participated, but in the end only 18 respondents completed the CE. Not everyone was eligible to complete the CE because the explicit requirement was that a respondent should represent the interests of a group of citizens. We of course assumed that they did, but to test that assumption they had to answer one question at the beginning of the CE about their representativeness of citizens. If they answered this question negatively, the internet application of the choice experiment was terminated.

Analysis of choice experiment

Statistical analysis of the CE ascertained the preferences of the interest groups. Because only 18 people completed the CE, the results of the statistical analysis had to be considered with caution. However, the pilot was a test case, and no practical consequences were anticipated, so the results could be used to illustrate the preferences of different interest groups in the Frisian Lakes area. The respondents were divided into two populations. The first group (n=5) consisted of respondents who represented the interests of nature protection groups (nature conservation organisation, water board), whereas the respondents in the second group (n=13) could be broadly classified as representatives of economic interests (especially tourism, recreation and agriculture). No local government representatives took part in the choice experiment. The interests of the local government was expected to reflect the interests of the local inhabitants. Farmers are an important group of inhabitants in the areas, so we expected that the interests of inhabitants would be partly covered by the participation of the farmers' organisation. However, the interests of inhabitants of the towns of Joure and Sneek were expected to differ from the interests of farmers. Nonetheless, there were many similarities between the spatial preferences of the 'nature representatives' and the 'economic representatives'. Both groups of representatives would prefer more nature in the area, but they had different opinions about what type of nature this should be. The 'nature representatives' strongly preferred the establishment of additional marshland vegetations in the southern part of the area, whereas the 'economic representatives' seemed to have a preference for natural grasslands in the north-eastern part of the area. Another difference between the spatial preferences of the two groups related to whether or not an extra bicycle path should be created in the area. The 'economic representatives' preferred such a new bikeway in the southern half of the area – straight across agricultural land – whereas the 'nature representatives' appeared not to be in favour of creating new bicycle trails.

A final, but remarkable, difference between the two distinguished groups was their WTP. We expected that the higher the WTP for a scenario, the less preferable this scenario would be. This negative relationship between preference and WTP was indeed found for the 'economic representatives' but not for the 'nature representatives'. This means that, when completing the survey, 'nature representatives' ignored the price tag for the scenarios. Their preference for a spatial alternative was not influenced by the amount of money to be paid for that scenario.

4.4.6 Second workshop

In the second workshop we discussed the results of the CE with all stakeholders involved and evaluated the method. The group of participants was almost similar to the first workshop. The representatives that had participated in the choice experiment but had not participated in the first workshop were invited but were not present at the second workshop.

Results of the choice experiment

The workshop attendees saw similarities between their own perceptions of the area and the results of the choice experiment. Two things are striking. Firstly, many characteristics of the preferred landscapes were similar to the current situation: the stakeholders seemed to be satisfied with the existing landscape. Secondly, the differences between the two groups were minor. Although we started the project with the idea that there were conflicts between these two interests, this was not reflected in the results of the choice experiment. There was, however, a difference in the preferences for the nature alternatives: the 'nature representatives' preferred development of more marshland, whereas the 'economic representatives' preferred more grassland. Marshland is more related to rare wetland birds, but the openness and visibility of the landscape can decrease, whereas openness of landscape is not decreased by the development of more natural grassland.

Evaluation of the method

We evaluated the RITAM in this workshop by asking the participants to reflect on the credibility, salience and legitimacy of the method. These criteria have been identified by Cash *et al.* (2003) as criteria for knowledge transfer. We formulated questions that make these criteria concrete.
1. Credibility: do the stakeholders think that the science was sound and results trustworthy? The stakeholders judged the scientific quality of the method positively, for example the animal species that were used as an indicator of the ecological quality of the spatial alternative. An important aspect of credibility was the transparency of the method. They were positive about this, for different reasons. First, the use of spatially explicit illustrations of the alternative landscape plans made it clear which landscape changes were planned and where they were planned. Second, the involvement of the

stakeholders in deciding which landscape characteristics to use in the choice experiment was appreciated. However, the step from the list of landscape characteristics identified in the first workshop to the selection of characteristics and their translation into spatially explicit alternatives was not deemed to be transparent.
2. Salience: does the method meet the needs of the stakeholders in the planning process? This question was about the applicability of the method in spatial planning processes. The stakeholders recognised its salience, because the method meets the current focus on stakeholder participation in spatial planning. RITAM enables stakeholders to meet each other and learn from each other. The stakeholders thought that the method was suitable for the early stages of a planning process, for the exploration of conflicts or convergence between the ambitions of different stakeholders. In the pilot, we used only an economic indicator (willingness to pay) and an ecological indicator (indicator species). There was deemed to be a need for indicators for, e.g. recreational quality.

    Salience was somewhat hampered because different interest groups could interpret the written information in the choice experiment on the internet differently. For example, in most of the alternative landscapes, there was an increase in the nature area. For nature interest representatives this meant a 'potential increase in biodiversity', but for agricultural interest representatives this meant implicitly a 'decrease in agricultural area'. Both are true, and the information that we gave with the choice experiment could have been more exclusive, by clearly regarding this trade-off between land-use types.
3. Legitimacy: are the interests of the different stakeholders getting enough attention and is there no bias towards particular interests? According to the stakeholders, legitimacy increased with increasing numbers of interest groups involved. They thought that the important interests were represented by the different stakeholders groups. Another issue relating to legitimacy was the fact that the stakeholders involved in RITAM were not always the people who had the power to make the political decisions about the landscape changes. However, it is expected that a landscape design that is based on the input of different stakeholders can count on more political support than a design developed by scientists alone.

Evaluation with advisory group

With the advisory group we evaluated the project as a whole. This evaluation concerned more than just the choice experiment, which had been evaluated in the second workshop. We discussed whether the results of the choice experiment were going to be used in the Friese Merenproject. The problem was of course that the response rate to the choice experiment was too low to claim that the most preferred landscape that came out of the analysis was indeed the landscape most valued by different interest groups and citizens in the area. Even more relevant, however, was the question of whether the advisory group would use RITAM in the future for landscape design situations. This was answered positively. Although improvements could be made (see also the section on credibility, salience and legitimacy), the advisory group was positive about the potential of RITAM.

Willemien Geertsema, Arianne de Blaeij and Martijn van der Heide

When we started, there were actual questions in the case-study area about changing the spatial structure of the area in order to increase its value for ecology and economy. Simultaneous to our project, within the Friese Merenproject it was decided that the next few years' development of the area (until 2013) would deal mainly with facilities for recreation (e.g. bridge constructions to improve accessibility for boats, or sanitary facilities at landing stages, etc.). This change of focus was the result of the discussions held within the Friese Merenproject, more or less simultaneously with our project. We were not involved in these discussions. The consequence was that the results of our project were not implemented in the Friese Merenproject. The problem behind this is the mismatch in timing between our project and the decisions about the priorities in the Friese Merenproject. Perhaps if we had had the results when the priorities were being defined, they would have been used.

But how representative is this shift in priority from the original goal (i.e. integration of ecology and economy) of a landscape development project to the concrete measures taken (e.g. focus on measures for the support of recreation)? Our impression is that, when it comes to concrete measures, economic arguments are given higher priority than ecological arguments, especially outside nature areas with a legal protection status.

We discussed the different roles of the stakeholders (including the advisory group). Stakeholders were asked both to advise on the development of RITAM and to participate in its application. Although individual stakeholders fulfilled in general just one of these roles, the different roles were experienced as confusing. More clarity about the roles from the outset of our project would have helped to prevent this problem.

We also discussed the role of the advisory group in our project. They appreciated the fact that they were involved in the contacts with the other stakeholders and found it interesting to be a study case. They recognised that our project was not an official part of the Friese Merenproject and that that may have been an important reason for the low response in the choice experiment. A related factor was the uncertainty about how the answers in the choice experiment influenced the planning process. The advisory group concluded that RITAM had potential in planning processes, but that more explanation was needed about the process, the role of the answers in the choice experiment and the way the spatial alternatives in the choice experiment related to the results of the first workshop.

RITAM seemed to be suitable, at the beginning of planning processes, to explore the different preferences of stakeholder groups and to make design and evaluation methods spatially explicit. The advisory group acknowledged that RITAM was a suitable tool for combining ecological and economic values.

4.5 Conclusions and lessons learned

We conclude that RITAM is a promising method for participative landscape planning. The different ways of involving stakeholders through workshops and a choice experiment were appreciated both by the stakeholders and scientists, and by the provincial governance that functioned as the principal and was expected to use the results. RITAM is a suitable method for integrating ecological and economic values.

The RITAM method was applied for the first time in a practical situation, with the support of an advisory group from the study area. It appeared to be possible to go through all the stages of the method. We succeeded in participating with the stakeholders in the different stages. We also succeeded in integrating ecological and economic values in the design of a landscape. This integration took place not only in the design of the landscape (by targeting both economic and ecological ambitions), but also in the interaction between the stakeholders in the workshops. Discussions about the landscape and discovering which different landscape characteristics were appreciated by the different interest groups were valuable for mutual understanding.

The method is suitable for discovering which landscapes represent the preferences of different interest groups; it is also possible to identify one landscape that combines the different preferences of different interest groups. The discovery of preferred landscapes does not always have to stay within the boundaries of, e.g. legal agreements, when the aim is to explore the preferences of different groups, using creativity for the design of future landscapes. In such a situation, borders imposed by legal conditions such as Natura 2000 or official agreements for expansion of built-up areas can be ignored.

Below, we reflect on the project and identify aspects of RITAM that could be improved. The following issues are discussed: the degree of participation, the decision to work with representatives and the role of visualisation of landscapes and their values. We conclude with a reflection on the role of this research in the sustainable development of the Frisian Lakes area, and implications for other areas.

4.5.1 Degree of participation

Unfortunately, we were not able to get a sufficient response to the choice experiment to provide enough data for reliable conclusions about the most preferred spatial development. Despite the low response, the application of RITAM in the Frisian Lakes area can be used to illustrate what kind of output the method produces. In that sense, we realised the aims that we had with this first application of RITAM.

The degree of participation in the choice experiment might have been higher if RITAM had been an official part of the planning process. However, for a pilot and a first try-out, we think that it was the right decision to emphasise the experimental phase of RITAM. In relation to other methods, in order to answer the question of whether the support of stakeholders in the real situation is higher than in the experimental situation, it would be interesting to know whether they were first tested in a practical but experimental situation, or whether they were first implemented in 'real' situations.

For an experimental as well as a 'real' application of RITAM, the challenge for research projects that participate in planning processes is to know the timeline of the spatial development process, in order to find the most suitable time for applying RITAM. Thorough communication with the relevant parties and analysis of critical steps and alternative routes in the timeline of the planning process are ingredients that support successful application and the commitment of participants.

4.5.2 Working with representatives

We chose to work with representatives, rather than individual citizens, on the assumption that the selected representatives would represent all the individuals in the relevant population of citizens. In addition, representatives were assumed to know the spatial preferences of the people they represented, and they were supposed to answer the trade-off questions according to these preferences. Representatives were also expected to know how much the people they represented would be willing to pay for the various spatial characteristics. Thus, we assumed that the person representing the farmers in an area was profoundly aware of the type of landscape ultimately preferred by the majority of the farmers. When participating in the choice experiment, this farmer representative was faced with alternative hypothetical scenarios, and was supposed to choose the scenario that the farmers in the area would prefer the most. Consequently, the farmers' representative needed to separate his or her individual self-interested choices from the choices to be made as a representative of the farming community. The context prompted the representative participants in the choice experiment to act for the good of the community they represented. As mentioned earlier, it would be interesting to find out whether this was really the case. From the answers of participants in the choice experiment, we got the impression that some of the representatives claimed be well aware of the preferences of the people they represented, whereas others were more doubtful about the preferences of those people. A detailed comparison between our representative approach and a 'regular' approach (based on a representative sample of individuals) using quantitative methods would be required to test the assumption of representativeness.

Through the choice experiment on representatives of various interest groups (rather than on a representative sample of individuals), we assessed the importance of various spatial attributes and showed how these attributes determined the preferences of these respondents (and thus for the people they represented) for the structure and character of the landscape in the area. Unfortunately, due to the fact that the representatives of the nature interest groups seemed to be indifferent about the price of a landscape scenario (WTP), our case-study work did not give statistically testable information about the WTP for the spatial changes in landscape patterns. They probably found the different sums of money (including the highest amount of €80) too low for it to influence their preferences. Yet, the amounts are comparable to those used in other choice experiments relating to environmental goods (Alvarez-Farizo and Hanley, 2002: environmental impact of wind farms, Hanley *et al.*, 1998: external benefits of public forests). Another explanation for the indifference to WTP may be that the sums of money did not differ enough to discriminate between different scenarios in the choice experiment. Also, we do not know how the preferences were influenced by the fact that representatives were asked about the WTP of the citizens they represented rather than the respondents' own WTP. There is, therefore, still considerable potential for future work, especially with respect to comparing our representative approach with a 'regular' approach (based on a representative sample of individuals).

4.5.3 Visualisations and indicators of value

An important step in our RITAM was the translation of the spatially implicit information from the first workshop into spatially explicit alternatives for the landscape in the study area. This was done by the research team without input from the stakeholders. Scientific knowledge was used to select the obvious locations of, for example, new nature areas (e.g. adjacent to existing areas) or new cycling routes (e.g. around lakes). In the evaluation, the stakeholders identified this as a weak point; transparency was judged to be low. A solution could be to have stakeholder involvement in this step, in the design of the spatial alternatives. Different methods for the design of spatial alternatives can be examined with a view to their incorporation in RITAM in order to have stakeholder involvement in this step (e.g. Bulens and Ligtenberg, 2006; Opdam *et al.*, 2006; Zetterberg *et al.*, 2010).

We saw that stakeholders preferred landscapes with both ecological and economic values – in this study, value for biodiversity and value for recreation. This value cannot be made concrete without translating complex scientific knowledge about the relationship between landscapes and how they function into applicable knowledge. This relationship can be represented by visualisations of the landscape structure by simple maps, as we did, accompanied by short descriptions, money tags and the picture of an animal as the indicator of the ecological value. In this study, we developed an ecological indicator for the spatial arrangement of the green-blue network. Stakeholders reported that there was a need for indicators for other ecosystem services (or land-use functions) as well.

To develop these indicators, knowledge is required about the relationship between the spatial structure of green-blue networks and the functioning of the ecosystem service. There is also a need for a greater understanding about how to link the demands and needs of society (from national politics to local citizens) to the ecosystem services. And at least as important: the knowledge should be in such a form that it can be applied, understood and trusted by stakeholders in design and valuation situations (Nassauer and Opdam, 2008).

4.5.4 Final remarks

As we saw in this chapter, the stakeholders involved in the development and application of RITAM in the Friese Merenproject were rather positive about the method. They recognised that, with the application of RITAM, the preferences of different interest groups in society could be revealed, a key issue in sustainable landscape development. The solid basis in ecological and economic science was also recognised. Yet, the concrete effect of our project on the measures taken in the case-study area are expected to be minimal, at least in the short term. Reasons include the emphasis on the experimental nature of the project and uncertainty about the results of the choice experiment.

We expect RITAM to be a useful tool for other situations where stakeholders want to develop a landscape for ecology and economics. The suggested improvements to RITAM mentioned in this chapter should first be realised. Clarifying what willingness to pay means and involving stakeholders in the spatial design of the scenarios will help us to apply RITAM in sustainable landscape development.

Acknowledgements

This research was financed by NWO, the Netherlands Organisation for Scientific Research, within the Stimulating Biodiversity Programme. We would like to thank the province of Friesland, especially Mr J. Goos from the Friese Merenproject, for their co-operation and practical support of our work in Friesland.

References

Alvarez-Farizo, B. and N. Hanley, 2002. Using conjoint analysis to quantify public preferences over the environmental impacts of wind farms. An example from Spain. Energy Policy 30: 107-116.
Barkmann, J., K. Glenk, A. Keil, C. Leemhuis, N. Dietrich, G. Gerold and R. Marggraf, 2008. Confronting unfamiliarity with ecosystem functions: the case for an ecosystem service approach to environmental valuation with stated preference methods. Ecological Economics 65: 48-62.
Benayas J.M.R., A.C. Newton, A. Diaz and J.M. Bullock, 2009. Enhancement of biodiversity and ecosystem services by ecological restoration: a meta-analysis. Science 325: 1121-1124.
Bonnieux, F. and P. Le Goffe, 1997. Valuing the benefits of landscape restoration: a case study of the Cotentin in Lower-Normandy, France. Journal of Environmental Management 50: 321-333.
Brosi, B.J., P.R. Armsworth and G.C. Daily, 2008. Optimal design of landscapes for pollination services. Conservation Letters 1: 27-36.

Bulens, J.D. and A. Ligtenberg, 2006. The MapTable, an integrative instrument for spatial planning design processes. In: AGILE, 2006 Shaping the future of geographic information science in Europe. University of West Hungary, College of Geoinformatics, Székesfehérvár, Hungary.

Campbell, D., 2007. Willingness to pay for rural landscape improvements: combining mixed logit and random-effects models. Journal of Agricultural Economics 58 (3): 467-483.

Cash, D.W., W.C. Clark, F. Alcock, N.M. Dickson, N. Eckley, D.H. Guston, J. Jäger and R.B. Mitchell, 2003. Knowledge systems for sustainable development. Proceedings of the National Academy of Sciences of the USA 100: 8086-8091.

Council of Europe, 2000. European Landscape Convention, European Treaty Series - No. 176, Florence, Italy.

De Groot, R.S., M.A. Wilson and R.M.J. Boumans, 2002. A typology for the classification, description and valuation of ecosystem functions, goods and services. Ecological Economics 41: 393-408.

European Union, 2000. Directive 2000/60/EC of the European Parliament and of the Council of 23 October 2000 establishing a framework for Community action in the field of water policy. Official Journal of the European Union L 327: 1-73.

Feld, C.F., P. Martins da Silva, J.P. Sousa, F. de Bello, R. Bugter, U. Grandin, D. Hering, S. Lavorel, O. Mountford, I. Pardo, M. Pärtel, J. Römbke, L. Sandin, K.B. Jones and P. Harrison, 2009. Indicators of biodiversity and ecosystem services: a synthesis across ecosystems and spatial scales. Oikos 118: 1862-1871.

Garrod G. and K.G. Willis, 1999. Economic valuation of the environment; Methods and case studies. Edward Elgar, Cheltenham, UK, 400 pp.

Giordano, L.C. and P.S. Riedel, 2008. Multi-criteria spatial decision analysis for demarcation of greenway: a case study of the city of Rio Claro, São Paulo, Brasil. Landscape and Urban Planning 84: 301-311.

Goldman, R.L., B.H. Thompson and G.C. Daily, 2007. Institutional incentives for managing the landscape: inducing cooperation for the production of ecosystem services. Ecological Economics 64: 333-343.

Hanley, N. and E.B. Barbier, 2009. Pricing nature; Cost-benefit analysis and environmental policy. Edward Elgar, Cheltenham, UK, 353 pp.

Hanley, N., R.E. Wright and V. Adamowicz, 1998. Using choice experiments to value the environment. Environmental and Resource Economics 11 (3-4): 413-428.

Hanski, I., 1985. Single-species dynamics may contribute to the long-term rarity and commonness. Ecology 66: 316-328.

Harrison, P.A., M. Vandewalle, M.T. Sykes, P.M. Berry, R. Bugter, F. de Bello, C.K. Feld, U. Grandin, R. Harrington, J.R. Haslett, R.H.G. Jongman, G.W. Luck, P. Martins da Silva, M. Moora, J. Settele, J.P. Sousa and M. Zobel, 2010. Identifying and prioritising services in European terrestrial and freshwater ecosystems. Biodiversity and Conservation 19: 2791-2821.

Hensher, D.A., J. Rose and W.H. Greene, 2005. The implications on willingness to pay of respondents ignoring specific attributes. Transportation 32: 203-222.

Higgins, A., S. Hajkowicz and E. Bui, 2008. A multi-objective model for environmental investment decision making. Computers & Operations Research 35: 253-266.

Howarth, R.B. and M.A. Wilson, 2006. A theoretical approach to deliberative valuation: aggregation by mutual consent. Land Economics 82 (1): 1-16.

Johnston, R.J., S.K. Swallow and D.M. Bauer, 2002. Spatial factors and stated preference values for public goods: considerations for rural land use. Land Economics 78 (4): 481-500.

Kerkstra, K., 1998. De blik van de architect; stand van zaken II. In: F. Feddes, R. Herngreen, S. Jansen, R. van Leeuwen and D. Sijmons (eds.), Oorden van Onthouding; Nieuwe natuur in verstedelijkend Nederland. Nai Uitgevers, Rotterdam, the Netherlands [in Dutch], pp. 70-71.

Lynam, T., W. de Jong, D. Sheil, T. Kusumanto and K. Evans. 2007. A review of tools for incorporating community knowledge, preferences, and values into decision making in natural resources management. Ecology and Society 12 (1): 5. Available at: http://www.ecologyandsociety.org/vol12/iss1/art5/.

MacMillan, D.C., L. Philip, N. Hanley and B. Alvarez-Farizo, 2002. Valuing the non-market benefits of wild goose conservation: a comparison of interview and group-based approaches. Ecological Economics 43 (1): 49-59.

Millennium Ecosystem Assessment, 2005. Ecosystem and human well-being: biodiversity synthesis. World Resources Institute, Washington, DC, USA.

Ministry of Agriculture, Nature Conservation and Fisheries, 1990. Natuurbeleidsplan. Ministerie van Landbouw, Natuur en Visserij, The Hague, the Netherlands [In Dutch].

Ministry of VROM, 2004. Nota Ruimte. Ministry of Housing, Spatial Planning and the Environment, The Hague, the Netherlands [In Dutch].

Naidoo, R., A. Balmford, R. Costanza, B. Fisher, R.E. Green, B. Lehner, T.R. Malcolm and T.H. Ricketts, 2008. Global mapping of ecosystem services and conservation priorities. Proceedings of the National Academy of Sciences of the USA 105: 9495-9500.

Nassauer, J.I. and P. Opdam, 2008. Design in science: extending the landscape ecology paradigm. Landscape Ecology 23: 633-644.

O'Neill, J., 2007. Markets, deliberation and environment. Routledge, London, UK, 238 pp.

Opdam, P., R. Pouwels, S. van Rooij, E. Steingröver and C.C. Vos, 2008. Setting biodiversity targets in participatory regional planning: introducing ecoprofiles. Ecology and Society 13 (1): 20. Available at: http://www.ecologyandsociety.org/vol13/iss1/art20/.

Opdam, P., E. Steingröver and S. van Rooij, 2006. Ecological networks: a spatial concept for multi-actor planning of sustainable landscapes. Landscape and Urban Planning 75: 322-332.

Paar, P., W. Röhricht and J. Schulere, 2008. Towards a planning support system for environmental management and agri-environmental measures - the Colorfields study. Journal of Environmental Management 89: 234-244.

Perrings, C., 1995. The economic value of biodiversity. In: Heywood, V.H. (ed.), Global biodiversity assessment. University Press, Cambridge, UK, pp. 823-914.

Sayadi, S., M.C. González-Roa and J. Calatrava-Requena, 2009. Public preferences for landscape features: the case of agricultural landscape in mountainous Mediterranean areas. Land Use Policy 26: 334-344.

Steingröver, E.G., W. Geertsema and W.K.R.E. van Wingerden, 2010. Designing agricultural landscapes for natural pest control: a transdisciplinary approach in the Hoeksche Waard (The Netherlands). Landscape Ecology 25: 825-838.

Turner, W.R., K. Brandon, T.M. Brooks, R. Costanza, G.A.B. da Fonseca and R. Portela, 2007. Global conservation of biodiversity and ecosystem services. BioScience 57: 868-873.

Termorshuizen, J.W. and P. Opdam, 2009. Landscape services as a bridge between landscape ecology and sustainable development. Landscape Ecology 24: 1037-1052.

Van der Heide, C.M., J.C.J.M. Van den Bergh and E.C. Van Ierland, 2003. Towards an ecological-economic theory of nature policy. In: S. Dovers, D.I. Stern and M.D. Young (eds.), New dimensions in ecological economics: integrated approaches to people and nature. Edward Elgar, Cheltenham, UK, pp. 121-145.

Van der Heide, C.M., A.T. De Blaeij and W.J.M. Heijman, 2008, Economic aspects in landscape decision-making: A participatory planning tool based on a representative approach. Discussion Paper No. 41, Mansholt Graduate School of Social Sciences, Wageningen, the Netherlands.

Verboom, J., J.A.J. Metz and E. Meelis, 1993. Metapopulation models for impact assessment of fragmentation. In: C. Vos and P. Opdam (eds.), Landscape ecology of a stressed environment. Chapman and Hall, London, UK, pp. 172-191.

Zetterberg, A., U.M. Mörtberg and B. Balfors, 2010. Making graph theory operational for landscape ecological assessments, planning, and design. Landscape and Urban Planning 95: 181-191.

5. Linking training, research and policy advice: capacity building for adaptation to climate change in East Africa

Catharien Terwisscha van Scheltinga and Jouwert van Geene

Abstract

It is increasingly acknowledged that adapting to climate change is important in developing countries, where the majority of people depend on agriculture and natural resources for their livelihoods, and their capacity to adapt to change is low. These people are especially vulnerable to climate change. This vulnerability was addressed together with options to adapt in a context of sustainable development at a two-week training course on climate adaptation. The course was developed and organised by a group of scientists from Wageningen UR with partners in East Africa. In addition to the training course, the team worked on the set-up of a collaborative process with partners from the region and policy advice, all with the support of the Dutch Ministry of Agriculture, Nature and Food Quality. The development of the training course is the focus of this chapter. The course assisted in bringing researchers, policymakers and practitioners together to learn about climate change adaptation in agriculture and natural resources management. The development of a conceptual framework as a joint understanding of climate change adaptation was an important element in the learning process.

5.1 Introduction

In developing countries, due to poverty and limited resource availability, people have a limited capacity to adapt to climate change (Tompkins and Adger, 2004). These may be farmers and other rural people who need to adapt their cropping pattern and livelihood strategies because of changes in temperature and/or precipitation, but they may also be policymakers, practitioners and researchers who need to adjust their day-to-day activities in order to enhance the adaptive capacity of farmers and other rural people. Adapting to climate change at the national level therefore requires external resources and support. To support policymakers, development practitioners and researchers in developing countries, the Netherlands Ministry of Agriculture, Nature and Food Quality (LNV) initiated a bilateral policy support research project in 2008. A group of scientists from Wageningen University and Research Centre (Wageningen UR), together with partners from the region, have engaged in developing and implementing a support programme for climate change adaptation in East Africa (Van Geene and Terwisscha van Scheltinga, 2008).

The three partners were the East African Regional Office of the International Union for the Conservation of Nature (IUCN - EARO), the Regional Universities Forum for Capacity Building in Agriculture (RUFORUM) and the Association for Strengthening Agricultural Research in Eastern and Central Africa (ASARECA), a network of agricultural scientists in

Catharien Terwisscha van Scheltinga and Jouwert van Geene

Southern and Eastern Africa. Later on, the Horn of Africa Regional Environmental Centre (HoA-REC) also joined as partner for training activities in the support programme. The partners from within the Wageningen UR network were Alterra, Wageningen UR centre for Development Innovation[2], Agricultural Economics Research Institute and Plant Research International.

The aim of the LNV policy support programme was to develop the capacities of scientists, policymakers and practitioners in East Africa to address the issue of climate change adaptation and to enhance integration of the issue of climate change adaptation into agricultural and rural development and natural resources policymaking processes, at both the national and the local level. A training course would assist in achieving this, but it was important that the training should not take place in isolation, but rather be a capacity building activity. Following Ritzema *et al.* (2008), capacity building is perceived as engaging people in knowledge creating processes (Nonaka and Takeuchi, 1995) that link applied research with training and policy advice. For our case, it meant linking the training to the professional setting of policymakers, practitioners and researchers in East Africa, i.e. knowledge and policy processes in the agriculture and natural resources management (NRM) sectors. This implied an interactive process in which the training would be developed with partners from the region involved.

There are still a limited number of climate change adaptation activities in the agriculture and NRM sectors, as staff are not (yet) able to translate the (inter)national policies and knowledge on climate change adaptation into programme design and implementable projects. The current way of thinking is along the lines of sustainable development (Brundtland, 1987). In order to be able to translate climate science into practical knowledge in agriculture and natural resources management, it should be linked to the mainstream sustainable development knowledge.

Furthermore, climate science focuses on the biophysical system and is a beta science. Little attention is given to stakeholder participation and change processes, which fit more into the category of gamma science. For effective implementation of climate change adaptation projects in agriculture and NRM, the translation from climate science into sustainable development and change processes thus also needs to take account of the different perspectives of beta and gamma science.

According to the Intergovernmental Panel on Climate Change (IPCC), climate change adaptation also entails addressing uncertainty and complexity. Uncertainty is the degree to which a value is unknown (IPCC, 2007), but it is understood in a wider sense in this chapter, also encompassing the degree to which a situation or a process is unknown. Complexity means that there are at least two or more interconnected elements in the process. From this perspective, climate change in a setting of sustainable development can then be considered

---

[2] Then called Wageningen International.

5. Linking training, research and policy advice

as a complex process in which stakeholders and ecological systems interact at various levels. This view was incorporated at an early stage of the LNV policy support programme.

In addition, the IPCC regards learning as an important element of adaptation (Parry *et al.*, 2007). If new knowledge, skills and attitudes are not acquired, adaptation cannot take place.

To address the issues of enhancing integrated (policy) approaches, uncertainty and complexity and hence a focus on social learning and societal action, a multi-track approach was followed, *combining research, policy, and training activities*. This capacity building approach can be summarised as:
- Linking training for researchers, practitioners and policymakers to knowledge exchange between these researchers and policy support activities at the level of the participating policymakers as well as at the (inter)national level.
- Linking scientific and practical knowledge on climate change and climate change adaptation to scientific and practical knowledge on sustainable development and change processes.
- Exploring the uncertainty and complexity of climate change, and translating this into the day-to-day practice of the participants on the training course as people need not only knowledge, but also skills and the attitude to deal with uncertainty and complexity.
- Using a learning approach, i.e. creating an environment for the participants to acquire new knowledge, bring in their own knowledge, reflect, practice new skills and experience new situations, all of which can contribute to attitude change.

To develop the LNV policy support programme, Wageningen UR and partners jointly organised two scoping workshops, in June and November 2008. In these scoping workshops, policymakers, researchers and other stakeholders (e.g. NGO representatives)[3] from Kenya, Ethiopia, Uganda, Tanzania, Rwanda and Burundi jointly formulated the issues to be addressed in the support programme. As outcomes, the participants indicated that both new knowledge and competencies were needed in order to adapt to climate change, and that more effort was needed to fully integrate climate change adaptation into agriculture and natural resource sector plans and economic development policies and strategies. They noted that capacity building for climate change adaptation was about learning to deal with uncertainties, both in science and in policy development and implementation (Van Geene and Terwisscha van Scheltinga, 2008).

---

[3] The first workshop in June 2008 in Nairobi was attended by 35 participants from Kenya, Ethiopia, Uganda, Tanzania, Rwanda and Burundi, among which 13 policymakers, 13 researchers, 2 education and 3 non-governmental organisations, together with 3 representatives of the FAO and the Netherlands embassies in Kenya and Rwanda (Gordijn *et al.*, 2008). The second scoping workshop in November 2008 in Nairobi was a follow-up to the first scoping workshop, which a few of the first workshop's participants attended. There were 18 participants from Kenya, Ethiopia, Uganda, Tanzania and Burundi (Gordijn and Woodhill, 2008).

For instance, during the first scoping workshop, participants made a rough analysis of different ecological zones in East Africa distinguishing agriculture, mountainous, rivers and wetlands, dry lands and grazing areas. Some of the conclusions from this were:
- 'Climate change is real, it creates uncertainties and opportunities and it is a complex problem. It involves many factors, one thing feeding into the other. For instance, wetlands may increase or decrease, we do not know. Micro changes are unclear but they will have an influence on the larger scale. Because of climate change there is an increased need for sharing, networking and institutional support. We need to involve policymakers, communities, researchers, etc. for interactive policymaking.'
- Some participants reflected that: 'climate change should be understood across sectors, each sectors should know about impacts, and an integrated approach and interdisciplinary work are very important. There is no single approach. Climate change is a set of interactive complements, it includes my friend and my enemy. How can we interact?'

Follow-up activities in the LNV policy support programme as concluded in the scoping workshops were:
1. To prepare a training course for researchers, policymakers and practitioners on climate change adaptation in agriculture and natural resources management.
2. To support high-level national policy processes in the region for adaptation to climate change, enhancing the linkage between the national and the international level as well as the link between national policymaking and local level action.
3. To develop and exchange knowledge, link up and co-ordinate activities between Wageningen UR and other regional and international climate change adaptation initiatives, such as for instance AfricaAdapt (Gordijn *et al.*, 2008; Gordijn and Woodhill, 2008).

As a first step, a two-week training course was developed and implemented in which the above capacity building approach combining research, policy and training was translated into training activities. This was done by staff from Wageningen UR in collaboration with partners at ASARECA, IUCN and RUFORUM. The course was held in Addis Ababa, Ethiopia in June 2009, and was attended by 23 representatives from four countries.

In order to enhance the capacity to develop and organise training on climate change adaptation, a partner in the region, HoA-REC, was identified among the contacts of Wageningen UR, ASARECA, RUFORUM and IUCN. HoA-REC is a recently started network organisation of environmental organisations in the Horn of Africa (www.hoarec.org). Its small secretariat is hosted by the University of Addis Ababa. At HoA-REC, a combination of research, training and policy support activities takes place. Therefore, HoA-REC could provide a good 'home' in East Africa for the training course to be developed, as this also entailed research, training and policy advice. Furthermore, the staff of HoA-REC had a keen interest in participating in the learning process of developing and implementing the course.

5. Linking training, research and policy advice

In this chapter, we present the experiences around the development, implementation and follow-up of this two-week training course. The course turned out to be a boundary process, in which researchers, practitioners and policymakers from different backgrounds learned together about climate change adaptation in agriculture and NRM. The development of a joint conceptual framework for climate change adaptation played an important role.

5.2 Guiding climate change adaptation in agriculture and NRM in East Africa

5.2.1 Training approach: knowledge, skills and attitude change

Capacity development for climate change adaptation is the starting point for the development of the training programme. The approach followed to develop the course derived from the concept that training should not take place in isolation, but should link training with research and policy, and that competencies for adaptation to climate change should be developed. Ritzema *et al*. (2008) describe this competency development as a knowledge-creating process where tacit knowledge is made explicit, in order to learn. It creates the capacity to take up new tasks, in this case adaptation to climate change. In the knowledge-creating process, the supply of knowledge is provided by advisory services, and research is the activity to improve knowledge; these two are linked in a cyclical process with education as a means to disseminate knowledge (Figure 5.1).

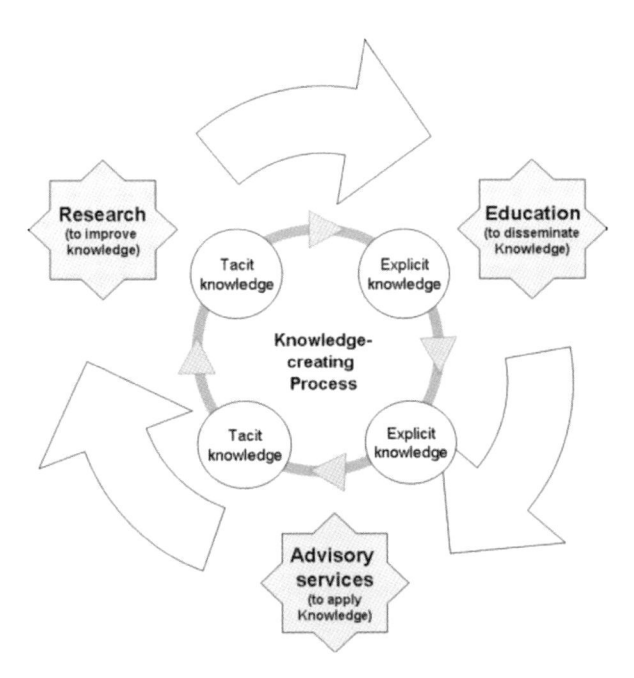

Figure 5.1. Capacity development as a knowledge-creating process. (Ritzema et al., 2008).

Catharien Terwisscha van Scheltinga and Jouwert van Geene

In change processes relating to climate change and sustainable development, addressing uncertainty and creating a good learning environment are important elements. Different societal stakeholders, by learning and reflection, try to find innovative and acceptable solutions that will contribute to a more sustainable world (Wals, 2007). This brings in the link between climate change adaptation, sustainable development and change process, or, as Wals (2007: 500) states: In short 'the key to creating a more sustainable world lies precisely in learning'.

In order to operationalise our concept of capacity development, joint development of a conceptual framework bringing these different elements together and shared by all parties involved was necessary. In the preparatory process therefore, participants with a background in different sectors (science, government, NGOs) were invited to the initial programme scoping workshops and also later to the training course itself.

In the initial scoping workshop, a gap in the research-policy interface was acknowledged and specified by the participants: there was need for a knowledge base, political commitment and interactive policy development. In turn, this made the linkage between research, (policy) advice and training (Ritzema *et al.*, 2008) an important topic for the training course. As explained in the next sub-section where the programme is presented, there were specific sessions in the training course to understand and assist in further developing the different skills and attitudes of scientists and policymakers to address climate change adaptation.

The Dutch agricultural counsellor stated that researchers should be much more policy centred and indicated that this implied that they should try to involve policymakers in their research right from the start. In this way they could create and reinforce research linkages with policymakers and take advantage of any windows of opportunity for research that might arise in the light of policymaking.

In preparatory meetings of the project team, and discussions with climate scientists, policymakers and the training experts involved, it was emphasised that knowledge, skills and attitudes all needed to be addressed. It was felt important that knowledge aspects should be well balanced with skill and attitude aspects, in order to achieve high quality training, i.e. training that assists participants to improve their competencies. For example, a competency to deal with climate change adaptation is assumed to include the ability to acquire and use knowledge of climate change adaptation and to translate this into proposals for implementable projects in the agriculture and NRM sectors. For climate change adaptation, knowledge on the climate system and its change is important, as well as an understanding of the international, national and local issues with regard to adaptation. Furthermore, participants require the skills to link the different levels, and undertake action, e.g. formulate fundable research or implementation projects, or find relevant information on the internet. Attitude elements important to address climate change adaptation are, for

5. Linking training, research and policy advice

instance, the attitude that complexity should not deter one from action, and that different types of knowledge are important and should be combined.

This determined the choice of module topics, the course flow and the session design, as well as the attitude of the training co-ordinators. A programme with building blocks that could be used flexibly depending on the interaction with the participants was prepared, with a multitude of information documents and tools available, also to be used flexibly, depending on the interaction with, and needs of, the participants.

Lecturers, practitioners and policymakers with different professional backgrounds participated in the training in order to bring in different types of knowledge and different points of view. This ensured a strong link between practical examples and academic thinking. Diversity could be experienced by participants, such as: 'I do not know enough, as others know more', and therefore re-assurance and valuing of all participants' contributions were very important elements of the course. Work in small groups was included, where different types of knowledge would be required (on climate change, on sustainable development aspects as well as on change) so all participants could contribute from their own expertise and knowledge.

Therefore, most of the 'knowledge-heavy' sessions were included at the beginning of the course. Because this quickly updated everyone on different aspects of climate change adaptation, a level playing field for all the participants was created.

Kolb's (1984) experiential learning cycle formed the basis to guide the learning process throughout the training (Figure 5.2). Learning, according to Kolb, is a process of experiences, in which people analyse situations, experiment in new situations, act as the situation evolves and reflect afterwards. This learning cycle is not experienced by everyone in the same way, in other words not everyone learns in the same way, and this translates into different entry points in the experiential learning cycle.

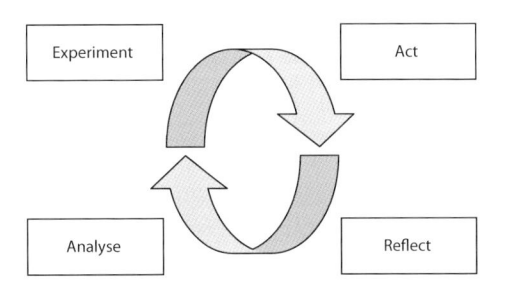

Figure 5.2. Learning cycle. (Kolb, 1984)

Climate change adaptation requires people to learn. There is a need to share knowledge and determine a line of action, given newly available information about an uncertain and complex future. Further, it is only during the intended development process itself that some of its steps may become clear. Thus, learning in this context is inherently complex, making it important to understand how people learn.

The concrete experiences of participants were the foundation of the course. For instance, participants were asked to complete a pre-course assignment in which they explained their work, how it related to climate change; and they prepared a first description of the impact of climate change on a particular hotspot. Every day participants also reflected on their observations during the course in a learning diary, and each participant made a practical action plan at the end of the course.

People tend to change their attitude when they get to know and understand other people's perspective (Argyris and Schön, 1978). This is why the course included many interactive elements such as group work to develop a joint stakeholder analysis and hotspot analysis, the field work and seminar. This forced participants to express their own views and actively listen to others.

5.2.2 Training programme

While the training programme was being developed together with the partners in the region, the following objective was formulated and then translated into the competencies required.

The objective was:

> To enable participants to contribute meaningfully in the debate on climate change adaptation, either in the policy process and or in providing knowledge to the policy process – including enhanced capacity in the implementation of adaptation measures. In order to be able to do achieve this, it is expected that participants need knowledge (climate change adaptation, adaptation options etc), skills (how to deal with uncertainty, vulnerability, how to create adaptive capacity) and attitude (open for change, accepting uncertainty).
>
> <div align="right">(Van Geene <i>et al.</i>, 2010)</div>

More explicitly, this requires the following three competencies:
1. For climate change adaptation, *a knowledge base with shared knowledge on the climate system, climate change and adaptation options* is important, as well as an understanding of the international, national and local issues with regard to adaptation. Adaptation, for instance changing a cropping pattern because of changes in precipitation due to climate change, needs to be locally specific in order to be effective. This requires knowledge of

5. Linking training, research and policy advice

local examples, as well as knowledge of national and international policies to which this local change relates.
2. Adaptation takes place at the local level, whereas the policies are made at the national and international level. Therefore the *competency to link the different scales* for climate change adaptation is required. For instance, policymakers, researchers and practitioners should be able to formulate fundable research or implementable projects where local level adaptation options are effectively linked to (inter)national policy options.
3. In addition to the knowledge on climate change and the competency to link different scales, an *ability to address complexity and uncertainty and to work across disciplines* is required. For adaptation to climate change it is, for instance, important to have the attitude that one will not be deterred from taking action, although there is uncertainty, or the attitude that different types of knowledge are important and should be combined.

The training programme was developed, using a training flow diagram, in which different building blocks together formed the training. This is presented schematically in Figure 5.3. The blocks are:
1. Introduction
2. Problem description
3. Current situation
4. Assessing vulnerability
5. Adaptation framework
6. Application of adaptation framework

Overall course flow (with hotspot approach)

1. Introduction
2. Problem description
3. Current situation and current responses at different scales (national, regional and global)
4. Assessing vulnerability
5. Adaptation framework

Hotspot approach:

Identification	Situation analysis	Adaptation options	Adaptation strategies	Implementation

6. Application of adaptation framework in own context/situation Output: action plan/proposal

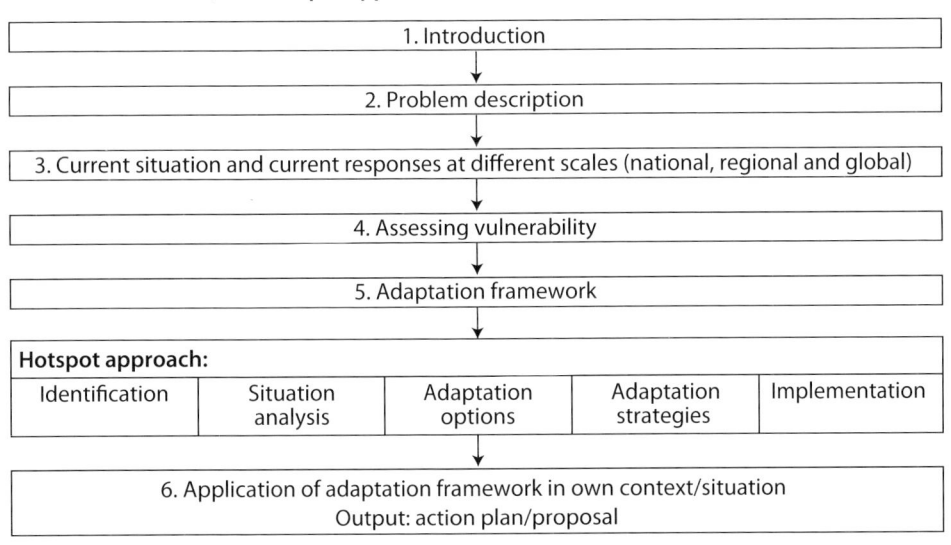

Figure 5.3. Overall flow of the training course. (Van Geene et al., 2010).

Catharien Terwisscha van Scheltinga and Jouwert van Geene

The different building blocks were each worked out in more detail and translated into learning activities during the two-week training course. The blocks are described in more detail below. Based on the experiences during the training, lessons learned were formulated.

Block 1: Introduction

In the introduction, the set-up was presented, first giving an introduction to the course, highlighting the course objectives as mentioned above, and the expectations of the participants and trainers. In light of the expectations expressed, the training programme could be adjusted to include specific interests articulated by participants. In discussion with the participants, the trainers included more information-oriented activities (knowledge) or practical actions (oriented towards competency development).

Block 2: Problem description

In this part, first the climate change problem was elucidated, with some general lectures on climate change. The lectures provided a common knowledge base for everybody and were provided by acknowledged (inter)national or regional experts on climate change.

The link to sustainable development was introduced in an interactive discussion session with the statement 'The best adaptation is sustainable development' as a starting point. Similarities and differences between climate change adaptation and sustainable development led to two equally valid approaches: 1. starting from development priorities and towards integration of climate change, or 2. working from a climate change perspective and defining adaptation strategies. Both have their benefits and lead to no-regret measures for development (Van Geene *et al.*, 2010). In the discussion session, these two approaches were identified, and the discussion led to a shared understanding that both approaches were valid.

Role play was organised as an activity to acknowledge complexity and uncertainty as key aspects of the way climate change adaptation can be analysed and addressed. The goal of the activity was to experience uncertainty and to make the reaction to uncertainty explicit. In the role play, participants were given coloured cards as an asset that they could exchange with other participants, based on an initial instruction about the value of the different cards. During the role play, the instruction was changed from time to time, creating a situation without a clear overview of what would happen next to the value of the cards, although the exchange still continued, thus requiring a strategy to deal with the highly uncertain situation. After the role play, the participants were asked to make their experience of uncertainty explicit, and to share it with the other participants. As most people are deterred from action when they are facing uncertainty, this was a hands-on activity where this reflex to withdraw was experienced, but also the feeling that 'I developed a scenario and continued acting, while adjusting my scenario based on new information'.

5. Linking training, research and policy advice

Block 3: Current situation and current response at different scales (national, regional and global)

To help all participants to increase their knowledge and skills on climate change and climate change adaptation, the current situation was presented by different scientists, preferably also involved in the IPCC, presenting the responses at different scales, e.g. highlighting the role of the National Action Plans on Adaptation (NAPAs) for the different countries in the East African region, and the international discussion on the matter of climate change adaptation.

This training block also addressed the research-policy interface. Policymakers are generally well aware of the necessity to address climate change, but lack the information and competencies to adapt existing and new sectoral policies to climate change (Van Geene *et al.*, 2010). For researchers, the main challenge is to make research results available and applicable to the context of policymakers, even when the research itself is not yet fully completed. Because of climate change, the research-policy interface, as the interaction between policymakers and researchers, needs to be cognizant of these positions of policymakers and researchers. Both may feel uncertain, and this needs to be taken into account.

A half-day seminar was organised as an example to experience the communication between science and policy. It also provided an opportunity to introduce policymakers to climate change adaptation in a short time, without their necessarily having to follow the two-week course. In this half-day seminar on the science-policy interface, the participants presented the results of their analysis of so-called hotspots (explained below). This combined a knowledge, skill and attitude element. Presentations (by participants) and a forum discussion were used as tools. In the forum, invited policymakers made a short statement on a range of subjects previously identified and communicated to them by the organisers.

The knowledge element required the participants to make their newly acquired knowledge explicit in their presentations; this afforded them the opportunity to share it with the policymakers who were also interested in climate change adaptation because it would enhance their learning. The presentation as well as the forum discussion provided the course participants as well as the participating policymakers with the opportunity to hone their presentation skills. The attitude element required the researchers to be interested in what policymakers would like to know, rather than only focusing on the academic results of their research. Both the course participants and the policymakers present had an opportunity to learn to appreciate each other's knowledge and contributions.

During the course, there were specific sessions where video images combining reflection and discussion were used to understand the different paradigms of scientists and policymakers as well as their different approaches to deal with reality. Scientists mostly search for 'the truth', gathering sufficient evidence to make conclusions. Policymakers look for quick answers, often biased from a certain political point of view. To influence policies, researchers need to take advantage of windows of opportunity that emerge in the policy process and use research findings to propose practical policy solutions.

This block also contained various elements focusing on skill development. For instance, participants were asked to look for particular sets of information in IPCC documentation to strengthen their information management skills.

Block 4: Assessing vulnerability

Vulnerability assessment was also introduced. Vulnerability is generally understood as people, livelihoods or an environment at risk. This is a sustainable development perspective. Vulnerability in the climate change discussion is about the hazard of climate events and depends on exposure, sensitivity and adaptive capacity. In this course, the two ways of thinking were combined in the so-called hotspot approach, where the vulnerability of people, their livelihoods and the environment were seen in the context of the longer-term risks due to climate change. On the course, hotspots were identified first as important issues known to the participants as having a noticeable risk of climate impact.

First, hotspots can be identified using climate information to pinpoint areas where climate change is likely to be more severe. Then, vulnerability can be analysed from a sustainable development perspective by identifying the most vulnerable people, livelihoods and environment. The combination of these two analyses provides relevant information on climate change hotspots from a sustainable development perspective. The hotspots formulated in the training were pastoralists in south-eastern Ethiopia, and forest coffee collection in western Ethiopia.

During the analysis in the group work on hotpots in this block, the participants not only acquired knowledge, but also honed their analytical skills.

Block 5: Adaptation framework

The adaptation framework was presented during the course, preferably using local examples. In the adaptation framework, situational analysis was first presented and practiced, then adaptation options were identified, and then adaptation strategies and implementation options were discussed.

In this block, the IPCC definition of adaptation – which does not include a reference to sustainable development – was discussed. In an interactive discussion session, a new definition of climate change adaptation in the framework of sustainable development was developed. The IPCC definition of adaptation was used as the starting point, and the participants reflected on what should be added from the point of view of sustainable development. Then a reformulation was proposed, including all the aspects suggested by the participants. This added to the shared understanding of climate change adaptation.

In order to start using newly acquired knowledge, and to translate it into practical situations and action, a field trip was included in the training programme. During the one-day trip, a particular local climate change hotspot was visited and analysed by the participants, using secondary data (rainfall, temperature) and interviews with local people. Different groups of participants studied the hotspot from different perspectives using the sustainable development framework. In the second week of the training course, the different groups presented the results of their field work for discussion and reflection.

Skills imparted in this block included the ability to prepare the statements for the seminar on the research-policy interface, to strengthen presentation and communication skills by practicing 'elevator pitches' and to be actively involved in the presentations during the seminar.

Block 6: Application of adaptation framework in own context/situation

In order to improve the applicability of lessons learned during the course, the following tools were used and applied; these help to translate ideas into working situations. Firstly, the 'learning journal'; on a daily basis participants were requested to reflect on the learning points, as well as to think and write something about their follow-up for this course. The ideas on future action as individually noted in the learning journal were brought together by the participants in an action plan. This could be a research proposal, an article, a policy or implementation plan, etc. At the end of the course, the action plans were presented, and feedback and suggestions were given by the other participants and the course coordinators.

Secondly, a daily 'recap and reflection' was tasked to a sub-group of participants who had to make a seven-minute presentation with the most important messages of that day's session at the start of the next day's session. The participants were sub-divided into three sub-groups for this purpose, every sub-group taking the Recap and Reflection task every third day throughout the course. The different activities of the course for each block and learning phase are presented in Figure 5.4.

During the training process, we tried to enhance learning by making explicit tacit technical/substantive knowledge about climate change, its impact, adaptation strategies, and the linkage with sustainable development and social change processes. Most of this was done during the design of the module and during the implementation of the training.
- The seminar during the training: participants appreciated the seminar because of its format. The format was an open forum discussion. The participants liked it because it provided an open discussion between researchers and policymakers, where all could share their knowledge.

General Course Programme – June 2009

	Day 1	Day 2	Day 3	Day 4	Day 5	Day 6
Week 1 15-21 June	• Context • Keynote speakers climate change and implications • Getting to know each other and discuss programme • Conceptual framework • Informal gathering	• Concepts theoretical understanding • Climate change adaptation + NAPAs, IPCC • CCA and sustainable development	• Paradigms • **Hotspot approach** • **Identification of hotspots:** People-Planet-Profit • Uncertainty • Financing adaptation • Presentation of posters	• Vulnerability framework impacts and risk management • Environmental impact assessment and competing claims • Prioritisation of hotspots and boundary	• **Situation analysis** • Stakeholder processes • Institutional analysis • Scenarios • Policy process mainstreaming	• Excursion/ field work

	Day 7	Day 8	Day 9	Day 10	Day 11	
Week 2 22-27 June	• **Adaptation options** • Indigenous knowledge and coping strategies • Conflict management and competing claims	• **Adaptation strategies** • Lobby/advocacy, communication • Preparation for seminar	• Implementation: **adaptive management** and M&E • Seminar/presentation: embassy, government, NGOs, media, NL case, Ethiopia case	• Translating hotspot approach to own context • Personal action plans and proposals and funding mechanisms • Negotiation	• Presenting product/ output: proposal/ policy brief, etc. • Ways forward-planning next steps • Evaluation	• Departure

Figure 5.4. Training programme 'Climate change adaptation in agriculture and natural resources management: integrating climate change into policymaking for sustainable development', Addis Ababa, June 2009. (Van Geene et al., 2010).

- The assignments that participants completed during the training course, like the pre-course, individual and group assignments, seminar presentations, and action plans provided an opportunity for participants to make their knowledge explicit. Participants appreciated both the assignments where this was done individually (on paper) as well as group-wise (where knowledge was made explicit and shared verbally).
- After the course, the tacit knowledge elaborated upon in the course was collected and documented in a manual (Van Geene *et al.*, 2010), thus being made explicit and available to share with a wider audience.

5.3 Outcomes and observations

To achieve capacity development, training should be more than just knowledge transfer, and this was clear throughout the course. The participants joined actively in the discussion sessions, assignments, role play, Learning Journal sessions, etc. In this section, we firstly present our main observations on the process of implementation of the course, followed by some specific observations on roles, knowledge and learning.

5.3.1 About the training process

In the early part of the course, information was provided on the basics of climate change and climate change adaptation, such as global circulation and the theoretical background of global warming, as requested by participants. We observed that the participants were very much concerned with, and looking for, explicit knowledge about climate change and climate change adaptation strategies. Therefore we included as much information as possible in the programme, and an extra session with basic climate information was added during the course. One reason why the participants wanted information was that the subject was new to most of them.

It should be noted, however, that a lot of the knowledge presented is currently still under development and being debated internationally in a complex scientific debate, so the demand for 'un-debated' knowledge could not always be met. Mostly unaware of the scientific debate, the participants would easily take any knowledge as established and uncontested. Therefore the course facilitators tried to balance the wish for more knowledge with a focus on explaining the debate.

The wish for un-debated knowledge also revealed different views on knowledge. Whereas in the beta sciences the view that science provides 'facts' that are 'true' is common, in social sciences a more gamma-oriented view prevails, where knowledge is debated and contested. The different paradigms or mindsets were part of the course, and this situation in which different participants had different demands with regard to knowledge on climate change was introduced as an example in the discussion on paradigms.

If participants want new knowledge, it is important to meet this demand (listen to them), otherwise the learning situation may not be optimal, because people will not be open to other activities (listen to others). On the course, we did succeed, however, in creating a safe ground to explore new areas – which meant that, for instance, researchers in agriculture and researchers in meteorology jointly explored adaptation options with livestock development workers, and new ideas emerged, as discussed in e.g. the paradigm shift sessions. The discussion on adaptation and sustainable development, where the participants jointly formulated a new definition, is an example.

A level playing field had emerged, and there was a lot of willingness to participate in more skills- and attitude-oriented activities as well as in subjects not directly related to climate science, but to change related to climate change such as the science–policy interface, or the complexity of the international discussion on adaptation. The assignment on the IPCC documentation was done, despite internet access sometimes being difficult due to limited power supply and internet connectivity. The organisers had foreseen this and provided a lot of information on CD Rom, which was useful.

During the hotspots assignment, the participants resolved cases on pastoralists in south-eastern Ethiopia and on forest coffee in western Ethiopia. Systematically, the steps in the programme were followed, and participants came back to those cases to apply the new knowledge. These cases were presented in the seminar. It is relevant to note that six months after the course, when case-study research was to be identified, these cases formed the basis of the case-study research. In the communication with policymakers, these hotspots identified during the course were also taken as a starting point. The capacity development was in this case certainly wider than only providing training: Wageningen UR and HoA-REC staff involved in the training also became involved in the research and policy support activities of the support programme.

During the discussion on climate change adaptation in relation to sustainable development and change processes, a new definition of climate change adaptation was formulated by the participants:

> Climate Change Adaptation…entails longer-term programmes, activities, policies undertaken to address the negative and positive impacts associated with climate change within the broader setting of sustainable development taking into consideration the social, environmental and economic perspectives; addresses issues of vulnerability, uncertainty and complexity, which are dynamic and appear at different scales; needs capacity to become resilient; and it aims for changes in values and beliefs, understanding, behaviour and practices, institutions and structures using a learning approach.

This contributed to the shared understanding about climate change adaptation.

5. Linking training, research and policy advice

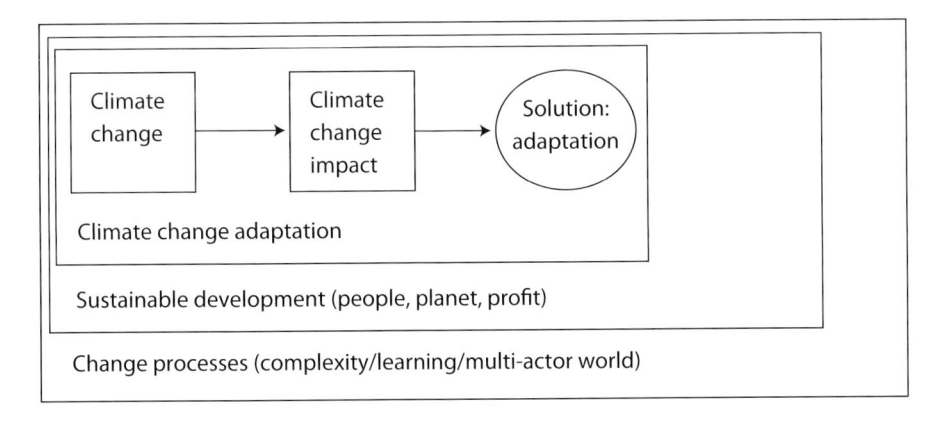

The description of climate change adaptation in the framework of sustainable development firstly focuses on climate change adaptation and its link to sustainable development. It can then be extended further to include the change process towards sustainable development: adaptation to climate change as change processes (Figure 5.5). It can now encompass elements of complexity, learning and multi-stakeholders, changing the science-policy interface and change agents in a multi-actor world, elements that also guided the development of the training course.

The added value of this frame was that participants from different backgrounds could now communicate about climate change adaptation in a language that allowed them to bring in their own expertise and experience. Different perspectives could be explained and understood. With regard to one of the hotspots, the pastoralists in south-eastern Ethiopia, it was understood that there was not a sustainable development situation in the area that would lead to changes in society; this was then aggravated by changes in the climate. This provides the possibility for researchers from different backgrounds to work together on the issue of vulnerability to climate change, to identify possible adaptation strategies and to assess these in the light of sustainable development (Verburg *et al.*, 2010).

5.3.2 About roles, knowledge and learning

Throughout the course, knowledge was made explicit and exchanged, and the policymakers, researchers and others involved developed a shared frame of understanding of climate change adaptation from which they could learn and upon which they could act. Here, we highlight the observations on the roles of the partners and participants, their knowledge base and learning.

Figure 5.5. Climate change adaptation in the framework of sustainable development as a change process.

The aim of the interactively developed capacity building programme was primarily to bring about knowledge development. The role of the training organisers in this exercise was to bring in (technical) knowledge and repackage it for application in a development-oriented setting, as well as to think through and reflect on ways and means of providing, for example, the course participants with the competency to address climate change adaptation.

The lecturers involved through HoA-REC were asked to contribute to the course because of their specific scientific expertise, on the assumption that they would be up to date with the most recent examples of climate change adaptation. However, there were still not many explicit examples in 2009. So the lecturers referred more readily to international knowledge, for instance from the IPCC, rather than highlighting local examples. This resulted in a gap between international policy and knowledge, and local practice.

There also appeared to be two different paradigms among the lecturers as well as the course participants: firstly, the more conventional beta-science paradigm built around the notion of creating models or frameworks about climate change adaptation in East Africa, which could then be tested and experimented with; secondly, a more gamma-oriented action-learning paradigm, which requires fewer theoretical models to start with, but assumes that these will be created and tested along the way. This difference in paradigms was observed between the scientists involved as lecturers as well as among the participants. The difference in attitude based on the difference between the two paradigms sometimes caused uneasiness during the training. Beta scientists indicated a low appreciation for – in their eyes – 'soft' approaches, and compared this to lectures where they got 'real' knowledge. The organisers tried to value all the different types of knowledge and bring the different mindsets to the surface, so that the differences could be made explicit, and be discussed and understood.

5.4 Lessons learned

This chapter has shown that training can be used as a process to bring researchers, practitioners and policymakers together to go beyond professional and other boundaries and to enhance joint learning for collective action in climate change adaptation. The development of a joint conceptual framework was instrumental in this process. Capacity building proceeded from multiple learning activities to which knowledge exchange (presentations from lecturers) and policy support (such as the seminar) were linked. The uncertainty aspects, which are inherent to climate change, were addressed not only at the knowledge level, but also at the skill and attitude level through role play. The more detailed lessons learned are discussed below in more detail.

The framework in which climate change adaptation was conceptualised as a change process within the framework of sustainable development is new, academically as well as to the participants and the organisers of the course. The framework helped the researchers involved in the development of the training course to explain the complex issue of climate change adaptation to the participants. Most of the participants came from a background of sustainable development in which climate change needs to find its place.

The preparation of the training course did not start with a pre-set idea to develop a joint conceptual framework. Rather, it came about during the implementation of the training course itself. Though not very well planned or organised, the discussions around the framework for development were crucial for enhancing mutual understanding among the participants.

The framework provided a link between scientific and practical knowledge on climate change and between climate change adaptation and scientific and practical knowledge on sustainable development and change processes. It also assisted in bringing the different mindsets together, the more beta-science-oriented as well as the more gamma-science-oriented participants.

Acknowledgements

The research activities presented in this chapter were conducted in the framework of climate change adaptation policy support research funded by the Ministry of Agriculture, Nature and Food Quality in the Netherlands. The project was implemented by different partners from Wageningen UR and in East Africa. The authors wish to thank the course participants for their active participation and their openness to learn. Special thanks to the other members of the project team, Jan Verhagen, Eric Arets, René Verburg, Bette Harms and Fulco Ludwig, and further to the other members of the training sub-team, Mekuria Argaw, Fons Jaspers and Femke Gordijn, for the joint learning we achieved together. Also, special thanks to the Ministry of Agriculture, Nature and Food Quality, and in particular Hayo Haanstra and Geert Westenbrink, who as senior policymakers expressed their trust in and support for our approach. Without their commitment to assist developing countries to adapt to climate change, this research would not have been possible.

References

Argyris, C. and D. Schön, 1978. Organizational learning: a theory of action perspective. Addison-Wesley Publishers, Reading, UK.
Bruntdland, G. (ed.), 1987. Our common future: the world commission on environment and development. Oxford University Press, Oxford, UK.
Gordijn, F. and J. Woodhill, 2008. Proceedings follow-up meeting climate change adaptation and policymaking. November 19-20, 2008. Nairobi, Kenya. Available at: http://portals.wi.wur.nl/files/docs/file/climate%20change/Report%20follow-up%20meeting%2019-20%20Nov%2008.pdf.

Gordijn, F., J. Woodhill, C. Terwisscha van Scheltinga and J. Verhagen, 2008. Climate change and policy making in agriculture and natural resource management for policy makers in East Africa. Proceedings scoping workshop climate change adaptation and policymaking. June 12-13, 2008, Nairobi, Kenya. Available at: http://portals.wi.wur.nl/files/docs/File/climate%20change/Proceedings%20scoping%20workshop%20climate%20change%2012-13%20June%202008%20final%20small.pdf.

IPCC, 2007. Glossary, Annex 2 of the summary for policy makers of the fourth assessment report. Available at: http://www.ipcc.ch/pdf/assessment-report/ar4/syr/ar4_syr_appendix.pdf.

Kolb, D.A., 1984. Experiential learning: experience as the source of learning and development. Prentice Hall, Upper Saddle River, NJ, USA.

Nonaka, I. and H. Takeuchi, 1995. The knowledge-creating company. Oxford University Press, New York, NY, USA.

Parry, M.L., O.F. Canziani, J.P. Palutikof and co-authors, 2007. Technical summary. In: M.L. Parry, O.F. Canziani, J.P. Palutikof, P.J. van der Linden and C.E. Hanson (eds.), Climate change 2007: impacts, adaptation and vulnerability. Contribution of working group II to the fourth assessment report of the Intergovernmental Panel on Climate Change. Cambridge University Press, Cambridge, UK, pp. 23-78.

Ritzema, H.P., W. Wolters and C.T.H.M. Terwisscha van Scheltinga, 2008. Lessons learned with an integrated approach for capacity development in agricultural land drainage. Irrigation and Drainage 57: 354-365.

Tompkins, E.L. and W.N. Adger, 2004. Does adaptive management of natural resources enhance resilience to climate change? Ecology and Society 9(2): 10. Available at: http://www.ecologyandsociety.org/vol9/iss2/art10.

Van Geene, J., C.T.H.M. Terwisscha van Scheltinga, F. Gordijn, A.M.J. Jaspers and M. Argaw, 2010. Trainers' manual on climate change adaptation and development: integrating climate change in policy making for sustainable development in agriculture and natural resources management. Alterra Report 1991, Alterra, Wageningen. Available at: http://library.wur.nl/edepot/133717.

Van Geene, J. and C. Terwisscha van Scheltinga, 2008. Supporting capacities for climate change adaptation in Eastern Africa. Policy brief. Available at: http://portals.wi.wur.nl/files/docs/Extended%20Policy%20Brief%20Climate%20Change%20Adaptation%20East%20Africa.pdf.

Verburg, R., E. Arets, J. Verhagen, C. Terwisscha van Scheltinga, F. Ludwig, R. Schils and J. van Geene, 2010. Climate change in East Africa. Towards a methodological framework on adaptation and mitigation strategies of natural resources, Alterra Report 2018, Wageningen University and Research Centre, Wageningen, the Netherlands.

Wals, A.E.J. (ed.), 2007. Social learning, towards a sustainable world. Wageningen Academic Publishers, Wageningen, the Netherlands.

6. Action research in a regional development setting: students as boundary workers in a learning multi-actor network

Jifke Sol, Pieter Jelle Beers, Simon Oosting and Floor Geerling-Eiff

Abstract

The educational experimental project 'Bridge to the Future', which took place between 2002 and 2007, aimed primarily at supporting the regional development process by action-oriented student research. The second aim was to develop students' roles as boundary workers in the co-creation of knowledge in a regional setting. Our basic assumption, like Gaventa and Cornwall (2001), is that collaborative research is empowering and innovative because it links science and society in such a way that it involves peoples' own critical reflection and learning. Actors' roles need to be redefined during this process. This causes uncertainty which needs coaching and facilitation. The 'Bridge to the Future' project started with a kick-off meeting in the area with regional stakeholders, students, supervisors and a project leader. The integrated research question developed there represented the complexity of the regional issues and provided an interdisciplinary starting point for the students who had to conduct their thesis-research in the framework of the collaborative project. As such the research question became a boundary object, which created possibilities for communication, interaction, learning and reflection. During monthly meetings different viewpoints were exchanged and discussed in a multi-stakeholder setting, which slowly developed into a learning community, providing a base and network for regional actors to develop plans collaboratively. As boundary workers the students and their research empowered the people from the area and provided a stronger sense of identity. Important impact of the project in the area is a LEADER network, rural art and rural tourism projects, international exchange visits and the actual development of biomass installations. We conclude that collaborative landscape research can be valuable if actors learn to take on new roles, are supported in creating boundary objects, organise reflection and are able to develop new knowledge, for sustainable development and the management of landscapes.

6.1 Introduction

In this chapter we discuss a higher education experiment in the Westerkwartier region in the province of Groningen, the Netherlands. Students and their supervisors acted in a network of co-operating stakeholders working together for regional development. The experiment, called 'Bridge to the Future'[4], started in 2002 with the aim of bridging gaps between research, college education and regional development. Although the project lasted for five years, we reflect primarily on the first year of the project in this paper.

---

[4] A collaboration between Wageningen University and the agricultural colleges Van Hall and Larenstein in the Netherlands.

Jifke Sol, Pieter Jelle Beers, Simon Oosting and Floor Geerling-Eiff

The region of interest was the Westerkwartier in the province of Groningen, which saw a stagnation of rural development. Farmers expected a decline in their incomes due to world market liberalisation and needed more land to enlarge their farms. Nature organisations perceived slow nature development and anticipated the transformation of more farmland into nature areas. Villages became less attractive places in which to live, because jobs and people migrated to other areas. These issues required an innovative approach towards sustainable development. One farmer, representing a large nature organisation of farmers, faced the dilemma of agricultural development or nature (vs. integrating them both). The local state forestry manager was looking for ways to both improve nature and to work with farmers. These two actors started bridging their regional values and interests, right at the time when Wageningen UR commissioned a project with doctoral students on the subject of rural development. The project team consisted of one project leader and three lecturers from educational institutions within Wageningen UR. The project team approached the regional actors in the Westerkwartier and so the project 'Bridge to the Future' project started. It was aimed primarily at supporting the regional development process and chose an action research approach in order to amplify joint learning and co-creation of new knowledge. The second aim was to let students work and learn in such a way that they could be the bridging actors in the co-creation of knowledge in a regional setting.

At a kick-off meeting in the area, regional stakeholders, students and project team members (the students' supervisors and the project leader) formulated the following shared problem statement and research question:

> How can we simultaneously maintain the landscape as it is, keep farming economically viable and improve the region's vitality?

This integrated research question represented the complexity of the regional issues and acted as a point of reference in which the various stakeholders could recognise their own interests and problem perceptions. Meanwhile it provided an interdisciplinary starting point for the students, inviting them to align their disciplinary backgrounds with the integrated reality of the region. As such the research question became a boundary object, which created possibilities for communication, interaction, learning and reflection on the interrelated issues at stake.

Regional stakeholders were the State Forestry Department, agricultural nature organisations, heritage organisations, three municipalities, the province and rural tourism entrepreneurs. Supervisors came from Rural Innovation Education at Van Hall Larenstein (a Dutch professional higher education institute) and the Animal Science Group at Wageningen University. The project involved students that originated from different disciplinary backgrounds, such as animal sciences, landscape management, social sciences, and rural innovation management sciences.

6.1.1 Role shifts

The project operated in a context of democratic power relations, in which regional stakeholders were challenged to articulate their own wishes. As meaning and knowledge are (re)negotiated in the process of knowledge creation, the actors involved have to reconsider their own position, perspective and role. This might mean that both researchers and social actors have to redefine their roles and develop a set of common values, norms, terminology and procedures (Friedman, 2001). Traditional and formal roles of all the actors involved might shift slightly towards coaching roles. This can create uncertainty, miscommunication and even distrust, all possible causes of friction between the actors concerned. The students, their supervisors and regional stakeholders thus faced uncertainty about both their own and others' roles during the action research process. Indeed, what can people expect from each other when formal roles no longer wholly apply?

In regional development and complex issues within these processes, knowledge cannot just be brought in from outside, it has to be co-created in learning networks together with regional actors. In such a case people create networks or arrangements, called knowledge arrangements (Geerling-Eiff *et al.*, 2007), or multi-actor innovation networks (Beers *et al.*, 2010), in which learning is emphasised and knowledge is actively created and disseminated by all parties in the professional existing network. Why do we speak of 'transdisciplinarity' in the context of this regional development project? Local knowledge is assumed to be an important contribution to the development of novel and more adequate solutions to local problems. The role of local knowledge is key here, because 'transdisciplinary research goes beyond multi- or interdisciplinary research by crossing the borders (if any) between science and society'. Also by performing transdisciplinary research, knowledge from different social and academic actors is integrated (Regeer, 2009).

How does the regional development project contribute to student learning? According to Wenger (1998), students learn as they engage in meaningful practices and are provided access to resources that enhance their participation in those practices. By 'opening their horizons,…they can put themselves on learning trajectories…they can identify with, and [be involved in] actions, discussions, and reflections that make a difference to the communities that they value.' Although that is not the role of the student in traditional education, it is exactly what we, as a project team, aimed for.

In summary, there were exciting challenges ahead, mostly related to new roles in action-oriented research. The challenges were threefold. Firstly, how would regional actors see their roles in the action research process, and how would they act? Secondly, it was the first time the students would work in an action-oriented research manner. The challenges for them were: how to behave in the field, how to cope with uncertainty, how to work with each other's disciplines and characters and how to conduct participative fieldwork, co-create new knowledge and deliver a thesis? Would they – being trained as traditional scientists

– merely behave as observers, or would they really participate? Thirdly, the project was an educational experiment, which meant that the supervisors had to explore their new roles as facilitators, project team members and coaches instead of being the 'traditional' senders of knowledge (Friedman, 2001).

So the basic focus of this paper is on role dynamics and boundary work in the process of action research in the context of the project on integrated regional development.

6.1.2 Bookmark

In Section 2 we address the approach of the research. We detail the theoretical arguments to be chosen for the action research approach in the context of rural development, and describe how we designed the action research process. In Section 3 we discuss process and implementation, answering questions such as: how did the design work out, what did we observe with regard to interaction among the stakeholder groups, region, students and project team/supervisors? What was the role of the scientist vis à vis the stakeholders and what sort of frictions did we encounter? In Section 4 we turn to the lessons learned, in which we also address the meaning of our results for action-oriented research -with students- in a regional context. Conclusions and recommendations are discussed in Section 5.

6.2. Approach

6.2.1 Theoretical justification

The application of scientific knowledge to real-life problems is not always the best solution, for it lacks an orientation towards action. The actual disconnection between knowledge institutes (science) and regional development (society) (Nowotny *et al.*, 2001) is illustrated by the lack of innovative solutions for complex problems such as climate change, poverty and hunger in ecologic, economic and social sustainability issues (Friedman, 2001). The disciplinary approach of traditional scientists leads to partial awareness and lack of integration. Secondly, the traditional way of knowledge creation leads to a lack of commitment for action, for this knowledge is not embedded with stakeholders (Gaventa and Cornwall, 2001). In order to overcome these problems new approaches for the creation of knowledge are needed. We see action research as a possible approach for building new bridges between different stakeholders. In action research, the researcher is one of the stakeholders involved. As a stakeholder, his/her goal is to involve stakeholders, to learn collaboratively, in a transdisciplinary manner, and to co-create innovative and contextualised knowledge (Senge and Scharmer, 2006; Tress *et al.*, 2003).

The role of the researcher here is to create conditions under which practitioners (such as farmers, managers, and social workers) can build and test 'theories of practice' for the purpose of learning (Friedman, 2001). Action research is not a single recipe for a simple

problem, it is more of a 'family of approaches' that share several commonalities (Reason and Bradbury, 2001):
- action research engages people in collaborative relationships, opening new collaborative spaces, in which dialogue and development can flourish;
- it draws on different sources of knowledge; for example both experiential and scientific knowledge;
- it is strongly value-oriented, searching for issues that are significant for specific communities; and
- it is a living, emergent process which cannot be pre-determined.

Action research is recognisable by its approach on 'inquiry in action' (Reason and Bradbury, 2008) and can be a vehicle for building new relationships between academia, development agencies and society at large. It creates a platform for new modes of learning to understand societal needs. 'Action researchers do not only observe and describe the situation; they also take action to improve the situation' (Kibwika, 2006). Action research, according to Kibwika (2006), enables scientists to intervene and participate in development with the community in order to gain experiences that can make research and education more relevant. This also means that knowledge is jointly constructed: 'Truths become products of a process in which people come together to share experiences through a process of action, reflection and collective investigation' (Gaventa and Cornwall, 2001). Indicating that there should be a certain level of equality, 'research can be a partner in a coalition, not a body that is to gain special knowledge, or sit in judgment on the other actors' (Gustavsen, cited in Kibwika 2006).

An action researcher has to take a different role from a traditional scientist. In order to really be a partner in a regional development process, relations between regional actors and scientific actors have to become more equal and democratic. They need time and effort to increase their engagement with each other's lives, perceptions, values and interests. 'The core contribution of research is to create relationships between actors and arenas where they can meet in democratic dialogue' (Gustavsen, cited in Reason and Bradbury, 2006). Democratic dialogue requires first that those who are directly affected by the research problem at hand participate in the research process. Secondly, it requires the recognition that knowledge is socially constructed and embedded. And thirdly, it requires that different forms of knowledge are recognised. Doing so opens up the possibility for new communities with new ideas (Gaventa and Cornwall, 2001).

Action research invites its participants to take action towards the desired change process through reflection and self-analysis by all participants. The specific settings in which this process take place can have a pivotal influence on its success: the exchange of multiple perspectives must be possible, and plurality and multiple pools of knowledge should be accounted for and stimulated. This in turn creates mutual commitments to further contacts and joint efforts between participants (Gustavsen, 2004, cited in Braun, 2006).

Jifke Sol, Pieter Jelle Beers, Simon Oosting and Floor Geerling-Eiff

Our basic assumption, like Gaventa and Cornwall (2001), is that action-oriented research is empowering and innovative because it links science, knowledge and democratic society in such a way that it creates more democratic forms of knowledge, it generates action by relative powerless groups in society and it involves people's own critical reflection and learning. Clearly, action research differs from traditional research, in which members of a system are subjects or objects of the study. In contrast, action research focuses on how all stakeholders, not only the researchers, can engage in the process of inquiry (Coghlan and Brannick, 2010). As Friedman (2001) puts it: 'The goal of action-oriented science is research *in* practice, not research *on* practice.'

Historically, action research projects are underpinned by the concept of collaborative learning and change, making action research a choice methodology to assist learning organisations, learning regions and regional networks in new innovation projects (Braun, 2006). Regional development projects are good examples of the multi-faceted arenas that include complex issues. Scholars increasingly speak of 'learning regions', crucial places in which learning processes, knowledge development and innovation take place (Wiskerke, 2007). In such a region, the various stakeholders involved form a learning system that, if successful, better equips the region for coping with continuous change and uncertainty (Wals, 2009).

The developing process of new collaborative research methods is called boundary work. Action-oriented research makes the connection with society by opening up the boundary between science and society, and by engaging in action, joint formulation of research questions and the definition of possible indicators. At the interface of both worlds regional questions can be translated into research questions and scientific knowledge can be translated into practical and usable knowledge. The interface is not a clear and sharp boundary, but a fuzzy area where science and region overlap (Turnhout *et al.*, 2007). In this fuzzy area science and society engage in joint knowledge production. As different cultures, perspectives and languages of the multi-stakeholder network meet here, some communication problems might arise.

If knowledge, experiences and perspectives are shared across boundaries, this might lead to co-creation, which possibly leads to new knowledge. The process of crossing boundaries is accompanied by uncertainties and often requires new competences. The new methods that prove to be helpful and supportive are called boundary objects (Regeer, 2009). A boundary object is an object with different meanings in different worlds, but a structure sufficiently common to act as a means of translation. Boundary objects facilitate discussion, negotiation, and decision-making. The creation and management of these objects is a key process in developing and maintaining coherence across intersecting social worlds (Turnhout *et al.*, 2007). Crossing boundaries of disciplines or practices is one of the main challenges of transdisciplinary research, especially when cultures clash or differ greatly from each other (Regeer, 2009).

Boundary work operates at the interface of different communities, for example communities of experts and communities of decision-makers. With boundary work the prevalence of different norms and expectations are mediated (Cash *et al.*, 2003). Boundary work needs to be managed by 'boundary organisations' with functions in communication, translation and mediation. These boundary workers need mandates to act as intermediaries between science and society (or policy). Moreover, when investments in these communications are made, then knowledge is more effectively connected to action and the salience, credibility, and legitimacy of the information is higher (Cash *et al.*, 2003). In order to ensure these effects dual accountability is needed, by which boundary managers operate on both sides of the boundaries (of science and society) in order to build effective information flows. This in turn can create a boundary object which facilitates discussion among parties with multiple interests, regarding differences in perspective, values and desired outcomes. Interestingly, Cash *et al.* (2003), note that in many cases single individuals play 'key boundary spanning' roles, independent of their particular organisational affiliations. They operate as the 'lubricant' for overcoming frictions at the boundaries.

6.2.2 Design of the research process

In order to establish bridges between science and society (our primary aim), through which research can contribute to society, sustainability and to the empowerment of local actors, we took a democratic, bottom-up approach (Gustavsen, 2001) in our action research approach, where methods for crossing boundaries (Sarkassian *et al.*, 2010; Regeer, 2009) could be applied. A secondary aim was to create a learning network consisting of regional stakeholders, supervisors and students. As these students are the scientists, policy makers or entrepreneurs of the future, the action research by students should be performed in such a way, that they could be the learning and bridging actors in the co-creation of knowledge in a regional setting.

The fieldwork took place between January and June 2003. The research plan included three ways in which the students could communicate perceptions and questions, experiences, and knowledge from their fieldwork. The first way of interaction was at several meetings, such as a kick-off meeting, monthly meetings and a regional day. The second way concerned student disciplinary interaction as a group working on a transdisciplinary question. The third way was through their personal encounters in their fieldwork doing interviews and try-out workshops with regional stakeholders. Communication events such as the regional day, which were organised for the first time as part of the research, were expected to pique the curiosity of local people, and to involve them in the project. In other words, we wanted these events to cause local people to cross their own boundaries, and participate in the ideas and opinions of other stakeholders.

So what did we decide to do in the Westerkwartier, knowing and assuming that certain boundaries might be there? First, the project's action research approach required us to adopt a learning-by-doing attitude, and not follow a fixed research plan that was prepared without input from local stakeholders. Furthermore, we knew that the students were inexperienced in collaborative research, in working in a trans- and interdisciplinary manner. And soon after the start of the project we knew from different fieldtrips of the students that the region was well known for its 'I do it my own way' attitude. As you can imagine, the project took several interesting turns that allowed us to reflect on and learn about the options for regional development. As the project evolved, it went through the following series of steps:

A. Regional commitment — October - November 2002
B. Students need extra coaching — January - June 2003
C. A kick-off day — February 2003
D. Creating a learning community; by monthly meetings — March 2003 - December 2003
E. Dealing with role expectations — April 2003
F. Who owns the problem? — continuously
G. The first regional day — June 2003

In the following section we provide examples (one for each of the above steps) of boundary work that demonstrate our collaboration with societal stakeholders. In the next section, we reflect on each of the above steps, and, if applicable, we highlight whether or not shifts in roles occurred, and to what extent role expectations and requirements led to friction.

6.3. Process and implementation

6.3.1 Changing roles of supervisors, students and regional stakeholders

In the research plan, we included a student visit of a couple of weeks to the area, to connect, interact and understand the language, perceptions, culture and values of the regional stakeholders. The plan included several opportunities for the students to meet the stakeholders, and we instructed the students, as a group, to plan these few weeks of fieldwork in the area.

A. Regional commitment

Before attracting and enrolling students for the project, the project team (supervisors and project leader[5]) paid a visit to the region and talked with the two of the most engaged stakeholders. One farmer, representing a large nature organisation of farmers, faced the dilemma of agricultural development versus nature (vs. integrating them). The local state forestry manager was looking for ways to both improve nature and work with farmers. These two actors started bridging their regional values and interests, which made them interesting for the research project. Both actors were also quite powerful in the area in the sense that they could attract many others to form a regional network. Furthermore, they were in a rather good negotiating position with their constituencies. Also, these two regional actors

---

[5] One of the supervisors and the project leader are authors of this chapter.

were very willing and committed to start an experiential learning process with students on these issues. They realised that agricultural and landscape issues needed a new and more integrated approach, which meant that a collaborative research approach appealed to them.

B. Students face uncertainty

As the action research was to be conducted by the students, they would be guided by their supervisors on a weekly basis and to a lesser extent (monthly) by the regional actors. However, the role and the tasks of students were very unclear in the first weeks of the project (before the kick-off, see below). What were they expected to do; could they just formulate their own research agenda (as they were used to doing) or not? The students had no experience, training or education with any form of community-based action research, transdisciplinary work or the process of co-creating knowledge. In other words, they were ill-prepared for their role and expressed several uncertainties. Therefore, they needed support in developing a 'learning-by-doing' attitude. As the project team was not experienced in guiding students in collaborative research, they called in help from a professional process coach. This enabled the students to organise workshops and engage with regional actors, or in other words, to work in a transdisciplinary fashion, and cope with complexity and uncertainty.

C. A kick-off day

Early in the project we decided that several regional stakeholders were to be invited for a kick-off day. Together with their coach, the students organised this day in order to gain insight into the complexity of issues on declining agricultural incomes, questions about scale, landscape deterioration or preservation and viability in different aspects in several villages. The aim of the kick-off day was to formulate a shared regional problem statement. Indeed we succeeded in that; the shared problem statement was: *how can we simultaneously maintain the landscape as it is, keep farming economically viable and improve the region's vitality?* The shared problem statement provided a focus for the students' projects, while the regional actors also recognised it as their own issue. Furthermore, the kick-off day resulted in contacts between all actors involved. It increased trust from the regional stakeholders in the regional development project as a whole and acted as a stepping stone for further committed actions.

D. Developing a learning community

Participatory approaches hold that knowledge is socially constructed, and call for methods to stimulate collective awareness and knowledge creation towards a learning community. With this in mind, we established monthly meetings with a selection of the regional stakeholders. The resulting network operated as the steering group for the students' research. In these meetings the students would present their research plans and their ongoing insights and doubts. Furthermore, the students, the project team members and the regional stakeholders (farmer, forestry-manager, administrator, cultural heritage preserver, tourism entrepreneur and others) exchanged views and experiences in relation to the students' research. The discussions which took place were experienced as a rich learning process, from which every actor could learn.

E. Dealing with role expectations

After a while the first results from the students' projects started to come in. The project team wondered what role the different regional stakeholders would take. Would they expect 'bite-sized chunks' of knowledge, in answer to their questions? Or would they prefer to work collaboratively on the creation of new knowledge? At one of the monthly meetings, halfway through the students' fieldwork, the project team discussed possible roles with the regional stakeholders. This yielded an interesting perspective on coaching the students. Attention had shifted towards providing students with a network and contact persons in the field. After that meeting, the regional stakeholders asked several times what they could do to better guide the students. This is illustrative of the responsibility they came to show for the wellbeing of the students and the process of knowledge co-creation. Apparently, the regional stakeholders were prepared for a shift in their role: from being a passive receiver of external knowledge to being an active coach and partner.

F. Who owns the problem?

An important issue in the relationship between scientists and stakeholders was ownership and power. Who was taking ownership of the issues surrounding farming, landscape and vitality (Derkzen, 2009)? Was it the emerging community of learners (the informal new owners so to speak) or should it be the formal owners such as the municipality and the province? Here, the ambivalent attitude of formal representatives from the municipality and the province proved problematic. They showed up many times, but did not take a formal hold on the problem statement, preferring to wait and see. This created a power inequality considering commitment. The grassroots representatives (farmers and state forestry and historic preservation committee) were fully committed but did not have any formal power, whereas the formal representatives, with decisive power over time, money, and other resources, were only moderately committed. They took an ambiguous role, by representing themselves in person, but not as a committed organisation. This created tension within the stakeholder network and made it hard to empower the learning community. It also frustrated the project as a whole, because it limited much of the action-oriented part of the research to be carried out. So, the *informal* stakeholder network, in which the municipality participated, wanted to get going, but *formally*, the municipality did not endorse the new research.

It took the municipality and the province several years to adopt the recommendations of the new regional platform, called 'Regional Initiative Westerkwartier' (WSI) [6]. The

---

[6] WSI is a rural regional platform foundation, consisting of a broad range of regional stakeholders.

municipality and the province never explained their previous ambivalence, but it was clear that it had occurred to them that they could get up to speed with regional policies, and quickly get results within the LAG[7], because the bottom-up process had already taken care of co-creating shared knowledge.

G. The first regional day

The first regional day was intended to inspire the region by 'giving back the stories, experiences and advices' from the fieldwork in a series of interactive and creative workshops. The regional day attracted 60 people from all levels, sectors, and from both formal and informal positions, meaning that the research process was not only connecting science and society, but connected also regional actors themselves. Evaluation showed that the regional day was inspiring, with plenty of networking and talking, through which all kinds of processes in the region became interwoven. The formula of a regional day has since then been repeated year after year, attracting more people, more actors every time. It became a success formula -both for the project, for sharing knowledge from the platform with a wider audience in the region- and for the region, because it became 'the place to be' for artists, farmers, officials, students, teachers, NGOs and other regional organisations.

6.3.2 Concrete results and outcomes of the 'Bridge to the Future' project

After a period of shared experiences, feelings of respect and friendship among stakeholders involved in the project grew and the learning network developed into a learning community. The students learned that they were regarded as relatively neutral agents; they were allowed to make mistakes and ask many 'stupid' questions. They were perceived as unthreatening, curious and interested in local affairs, as demonstrated by the fact that the students stayed in the area for several weeks. The students learned that action research requires an open learning-by-doing attitude and that they were able to act as such, with the support of many others. This provided them with experience, connections and information. As such, the students became more aware of the nature of action-oriented research, its connective power, and the associated uncertainties. Furthermore, they became more confident in their role as boundary workers. This provided them with stepping stones for their careers in rural research, policy and development. One student, for example, was appointed as secretary of the WSI foundation and later became a provincial civil servant. The supervisors experienced the project as a scientific adventure and concluded that it is possible to contribute to societal development when really engaging – as a scientist – and coaching one's students well.

The students' fieldwork stimulated the regional actors to be more aware of, and reflective about, their surroundings and 'their landscape'. What was its beauty? Were there more

---

[7] LAG=Local Action Group, consisting of max 50% formal representation, and at least 50% informal local representation. The LAG formulates policy advice considering rural regional policy and is financed for 50% by EU rural LEADER policy.

possibilities than they ever dreamed of or did they just have to accept the state of the art? During the monthly meetings these questions and issues would also be topics for discussion, through which the regional actors became more aware of their power and identity.

The experiment turned out to be a catalyst for rural development. As a result, the region established a stronger administrative capacity. By the end of the first year of the project the 'Working group regional initiative Westerkwartier' (WSI) was founded, which was a direct effect of the experiment. The WSI represented (and still represents) a wide range of regional actors and their interests. It provided a base and network to share ideas and to develop plans collaboratively. As such it empowered the people from the area and provided a stronger sense of power and identity. Many wishes and ideas were discussed, such as a landscape fund, the appointment of a regional co-ordinator or the promotion of tourism in the area. At that stage it was hard to implement them because of a lack of resources and political commitment Although the first year did not yield very concrete results, it did generate funding from Wageningen University for three more years, which paved the way for the further development of the WSI. Several integrated projects with a natural-cultural-historical-educational character have begun since then. Regional stakeholder collaboration became stronger and more institutionalised both in the WSI and the LAG. The increased awareness of regional identity is apparent from a number of regional initiatives. Examples are:

- Theatre on location about local politics and regional identity.
- The 'Abel Tasman route': a walk through the local museum of the village Lutjegast, its landscape and heritage.
- The 'Baak' (see Figure 6.1): a cultural-educational meeting point, marking the historic landscape and future land use.
- A country house and a country café where local actors can meet and exchange ideas.
- The development of biomass as a way of turning dry and wet 'waste' from hedges and farms into energy, and using it to for example heat the local swimming pool and the local home for the elderly.
- The creation of sustainable co-operation between knowledge institutes and regional initiatives is being shaped by 'a Working Place Westerkwartier' (Werkplaats Westerkwartier) where rural and scientific actors can meet and – very importantly –, where students can learn to play a professional role as boundary workers.

The bottom-up empowerment and the different initiatives and projects that resulted from it slowly impressed and engaged the regional government. This led a few years later, to the establishment of a Local Action Group (LAG group in the context of the European LEADER network) with support from the WSI foundation. The creation of the LAG is an expression of regional development, with a monetary commitment of seven million euros. This LAG in turn gave way to a broad range of projects on biomass, tourism and cultural heritage preservation activities, of which landscape and farming were central aspects.

6. Action research in a regional development setting

Figure 6.1. 'The Baak'.

International exchange followed within the ENLDT network[8], with visits to Ireland and Finland and the organisation of a countryside exchange, with five countries visiting the Westerkwartier for mutual learning and exchange.

In summary, all the above-illustrated initiatives are the practical impact of the original research question, which shows that this transdisciplinary research provides tangible results and concrete sustainable regional development.

6.4. Lessons learned

6.4.1 Further development and concepts for collaborative landscape research

In our project, regional stakeholders were invited and challenged to articulate their own wishes during the collaborative research process. By posing questions and talking with them at the kick-off day, at the monthly meetings and during the interviews carried out by the students, regional actors were reflectively questioned about diverse aspects of their lives. This caused a certain degree of awareness, or consciousness (Cornwall and Gaventa, 2001). They emphasised the importance of a democratic dialogue for the development of new categories of knowledge. This view is useful since power-inequalities can be hidden or invisible in the collaborative process. Stepping stones for the further development of collaborative landscape research can be found in the notion of research as a partner in coalition where partners meet in democratic dialogue (Kibwika, 2006), the creating of new platforms for new modes of

---
[8] ENLDT: European Network for Local Development Teams.

Knowledge in action

learning (Friedman, 2001), where different actors learn to cope with uncertainty in the process of social learning (Wals, 2009), for building new relationships between science and society (Reason and Bradbury, 2008) and where single individuals play key boundary roles (Cash *et al.*, 2003).

6.4.2 Practice, roles and positions of students, their supervisors and stakeholders

The kick-off meeting demanded new roles from all actors involved, but new roles develop over time, as a result of action and reflection. Through multi-actor interaction boundaries between life worlds may become visible or may become fuzzy. Boundary objects can be helpful when traditional roles (e.g. 'mode 1' researcher, university lecturer) do not provide connections for overcoming the boundaries. In our project, the kick-off meeting and the integrated research question provided stepping stones for the creation of new roles. For example, it legitimised the students to participate and plunge into the regional complexity with openness and real interest.

During the communication events and especially during the reflection (in April 2003) with the stakeholders, participants became more aware of their possible roles. Regional actors were not expecting to be 'passive consumers' of new knowledge brought in by scientists, they were willing to become active informants and maybe even change agents. Several regional stakeholders also indicated that they would like to play a role in guiding the students. This led to the appointment of a few regional contact people, to whom students could go for information, networks and daily issues. The roles of supervisors changed in the sense that in university/college they were lecturers, in the collaborative research they became more of a process coach for the students concerning social competences and coping with insecurity. This indicates that in collaboration and learning roles change and that all actors should be made aware of this by reflection on action (Van Mierlo, 2010).

At several workshops and meetings during the project, supervisors also acted as facilitators, in order to guide the learning and searching process of all actors involved. Although students could have behaved as objective, distanced researchers, they instead developed a participatory attitude, by really engaging and listening and actively contributing to the regional development process in interviewing, organising workshops and participating in the monthly meetings. They learned to translate regional complexity into research, which became valuable for the area. They also learned to cope with uncertainty and anticipate unexpected events (Derkzen, 2009). They gained a deeper understanding of regional complexity, power issues and empowerment. By working as a team and connecting with real-life issues in the region students and supervisors became more aware of the possible roles of science, that is, not only the production and dissemination of knowledge, but also being a partner, co-learner and boundary worker in co-creating knowledge and facilitating collaborative processes (Dillon and Wals, 2006). In fact, students had 'key boundary spanning' roles (Cash *et al.*, 2003) in the research and in the area.

The main lesson is that it is necessary to facilitate collaborative action research processes on the spot, for bridging differences in (role) expectations, language, knowledge and beliefs. This is important for regional stakeholders, but even more so for the students involved, since they sometimes felt insecure and anxious with the many goals and uncertainties in the action research process. Furthermore, it appears that training the students' social skills helped them to deal with these uncertainties and shifting roles. The multi-stakeholder evaluation at the end of the first year revealed that the students were very enthusiastic about this way of learning-by-doing; they indicated that they had learned more than ever before, especially new social competences such as being flexible, open and communicative – competences they needed for their new role as boundary workers.

Although the regional stakeholders were positive about the project, they had some mixed feelings after the first year of the project. The farmers, for example, had wanted more 'practical farm-level advice.' However, they too were very satisfied with the regional process results, such as having a regional platform, regional awareness and a stronger negotiating position with higher authorities. The farmers had become aware of the long-term advantages of these regional collaboration and empowerment processes. The role of the governments (municipalities and province) may have been a new role, but its ambivalent character frustrated the further development of, for example, a landscape fund, the appointment of a regional coordinator or the promotion of tourism in the area (Derkzen, 2009).

The lesson for the supervisors was that by engaging students in collaborative research, they spend relatively more time on the process, means and methods than on analysing, reading literature and writing their thesis. This is a point of attention for the future role of higher education in action research. Also in judging the students on their competences as future scientists, the scientific curriculum might provide credits for process competences and boundary work as such.

Another lesson has to do with power inequalities, differences in problem-ownership and commitment. Regional stakeholders from public organisations such as municipality and province saw the collaborative research and its democratic dialogue at first more as a thread to regional plans than as a contribution, for the outcomes of the research could bring new and unexpected knowledge and action. This caused an ambivalence which only ended a few years later, when outcomes turned out to support the regional alignment process between actors and speeded up the regional policy. When such situations arise, it might be better to ask or demand formal problem ownership from all actors involved in some sort of contract or intention in which – if possible – expectations about roles and output are made explicit. In this case boundary objects did not directly empower actors in dealing with their constituencies and department superiors. Therefore boundary objects seem not to negotiate power differences as such, they merely provide the option to make differences more transparent and as a result perhaps negotiable. This gives us the impression that boundary objects are valuable in a multi-actor setting, but maybe to a lesser extent in a governance setting in which powerful actors can 'stay within their boundaries' and are not willing or able to develop new roles.

To summarise, collaborative landscape research can be valuable if actors are able to define and take on new roles, are supported in creating boundary objects, are stimulated to reflect on action and know how to engage constituencies, in order to construct new integrated applicable knowledge, for sustainable development.

6.4.3 Valuable methodologies, methods and tools: the research question as a boundary object

The integrated research question formulated at the kick-off day became a boundary object (Regeer, 2009), which created possibilities for communication, interaction, and reflection on the interrelated issues at stake.

The impact of the research question was threefold. First, it generated an umbrella under which several disciplinary research questions of the students could fit and develop. As such the research question supported the 'crossing of disciplinary boundaries' (Tress *et al.*, 2003). Second, it created a central point of focus for the regional actors involved, and as such provided an aligning effect between the regional actors; they discovered there were several historical, cultural and economic reasons for co-operating and collaborating. The research question turned out to be a sort of 'social glue' in the area. Third, the question generated a new consciousness and unexpected new insights (Tress *et al.*, 2003) for all actors involved; they could no longer defend their own sectoral or disciplinary interests or viewpoints; they were challenged to integrate perceptions and values into some new joint point of stake, into a system analysis. The impact was a broadening concept of landscape as an element of culture and identity which became anchored.

Students with their open and explorative attitude are nearly *boundary objects*; with key boundary spanning roles (Cash *et al.*, 2003). People are more open to students, because they are regarded as more neutral, less powerful and still in a learning position with relatively less influence. Students have no interest except for learning and knowing, they are not in a position of regional decision-making and they hardly ever have hidden agendas. This makes them attractive to talk too. Stakeholders in the area could learn from the questions posed by students because they had to explain their obvious knowledge to relative outsiders. By doing so they became more aware of their own viewpoints and values. During the monthly meetings these viewpoints could be exchanged and discussed in a multi-stakeholder setting, through which perceptions sometimes merged and shifted or got reframed in the process of social learning. As such students have a lubricating role in connecting and exchanging the views and values of various stakeholders in an open and therefore approachable manner.

The monthly meetings and the regional day provided bridges for all actors involved, for exchanging views and experiences. In that sense these 'interactive moments' were effective as platforms on which new modes of learning (Kibwika, 2006; Friedman, 2001) could evolve, as if they were boundary objects in the sense that actors were stimulated to take on new roles (as coaches and participative students). As a boundary object these meetings provided stepping stones for learning to cope with uncertainty (Wals, 2009) and the cautious trying out of new roles in the research process to come. As such boundary objects might support and speed up the development of new roles needed in action-oriented research.

The first year of the project featured relatively little in the way of natural sciences-social sciences interaction, because the students predominantly chose social sciences topics, despite their mixed disciplinary backgrounds (animal sciences and social sciences). However, in the subsequent years other students chose more natural sciences research for their thesis[9], which meant that the transdisciplinary character of the research question provided room for the students to choose their (social sciences or natural sciences) research.

Our conclusion is that boundary objects are valuable and necessary for action research because they lubricate the bridging points, between the diverse values, languages, expectations, interests and viewpoints of the different actors involved. They create opportunities for building new relations between science and society (Reason and Bradbury, 2008) with mutual commitment (Friedman, 2001), for understanding, alignment and collaboration in the multi-actor network. This empowers the actors and their new and shifting roles in the network. Therefore it stimulates the social learning process and the network as a new emerging community of learners with new ideas (Kibwika, 2006).

6.5. Conclusions and recommendations

This chapter describes about one year's worth of action research. In reality the whole project took 5 years. The yield of this ongoing interaction is larger than anyone dared to dream of in the first year. Approximately 50 students conducted their thesis in the whole period on a diverse range of regional issues. The regional platform used the research reports and the regional workshops to acquire a stronger position in relation to the provincial authorities and increased its trust with the regional actors. A special effect of the attention given by all the students to the region was a greater self-awareness about regional culture, identity and qualities. This self-awareness helped to forge bonds between different regional actors. Establishing the LAG was one of the highlights, for it generated various powerful and meaningful projects that helped the community to generate welfare and income. Through these projects, farming, nature and viable villages created sustainable connections for the future of their region. The use of biomass for regional energy needs is only one of the results. We conclude that the action research set-up yielded very important and tangible results for the regional stakeholders, which they perceived as useful, credible, and legitimate.

---

[9] For example, research on the small-scale water storage in the area, and other water management issues.

Of course, this process was a bumpy road with many uncertainties for all actors involved; 'Action research is not what a person already knows and tells that sharpens the countenance of a friend, but what that person and friend together do not know – it is recognising ignorance and programmed knowledge that is the key to action learning' (Kibwika, 2006). The question is how to create the circumstances to make participants comfortable in new and challenging situations, in which 'not-knowing' seems to be the default. When new relations emerge between academics, students and regional actors, when interaction takes different forms, and when struggles are shared, it becomes easier to deal with uncertainty (Bockbank and McGill, 2006). Not by reducing uncertainty, but by giving it a place in the collaborative process.

For action research in a regional multi-actor setting it is important to be clear about expectations on the one hand and to be flexible on the other hand, because the interaction is marked by unpredictable dynamics and shifting roles. The boundaries between actors' perceptions, between formal and informal, between traditional roles and new roles are fuzzy. Therefore the roles of students, teachers and regional stakeholders change over time and expectations about these roles need to be managed. The learning process between the actors involved can be particularly vulnerable when power inequalities between actors are at stake. This happens when people do not feel safe or respected in their (un)defined role. Expectation management and reflection on action might help to sort out different formal and informal roles and expectations about the input for, and the output of, the research process.

The value of action-oriented research for science is threefold. First, it contributes through collaboration, shifting roles and crossing boundaries to more alignment with societal issues through which research impact becomes more valuable, sustainable and legitimate. Second, it gives more insight into reflective learning methods, and the use of them for landscape-oriented science. Third, through its participative and learning nature it offers future scientific boundary workers real and safe learning circumstances to experiment in.

Students have a special position in action-oriented research because they are not perceived merely as instruments for knowledge transfer. Society knows that they are still learning and therefore they are allowed to experiment and make mistakes. Society will expect much higher knowledge input from researchers. This means that students fit the role of action researcher particularly well; as boundary workers they are 'the lubricants' of multi-actor learning networks.

In closing, we give a few recommendations to reconnect universities to the field of regional development and landscape planning through action research, and to contribute to more valued, equitable and sustainable landscape management. The following recommendations are relevant for action researchers in regional contexts:
- Re-examine the meaning of knowledge and learning, allow room for failure and ignorance.

- Put a strong emphasis on reflecting upon the learning process.
- Manage expectations about the project, the process and roles at an early stage.
- Organise the role of an independent facilitator, who takes care of uncertainty, new roles and the creation and use of boundary objects.
- Work together with students in transdisciplinary landscape research, and assess, coach and train them in the competences they need for boundary work.

6.5.1 Future research

It is very interesting to make a closer study of how processes of social learning in multi-actor networks can be organised and facilitated. What is the role of power inequalities, trust and commitment in the ongoing learning process? How do they influence the emerging communities of practice? How can these social learning processes be facilitated from the perspective of action-oriented research? Can reflective learning contribute to this? What is needed from the different actors? When these questions are better addressed and understood then we can better anticipate how action research can contribute to learning and knowledge in regional development for scientists, students and regional stakeholders alike.

Acknowledgements

The research activities were conducted in the context of the educational innovation project called 'Bridge to the Future' in the period 2002-2007. The project was implemented by a project team consisting of lecturers from van Hall-Larenstein, Wageningen University and an external project leader. The project was financed by a one-year innovation fund from Wageningen University. It was then extended for a further three years. The experience, the results and the reflection on the process led to this paper.

References

Beers, P.J., J. Sol and A. Wals, 2010. Social learning in a multi-actor innovation context. Paper presented at the International Farming Systems Association conference, Vienna, Austria (3-7 July).
Brockbank, A. and I. McGill, 2006. Facilitating Reflective Learning Through Mentoring & Coaching. Kogan Page, London, UK.
Braun, P., 2006. Action Research and Network Development: Creating Actionable Knowledge. Centre for Regional Innovation and Competitiveness (CRIC). University of Ballarat, Australia.
Cash, D.W., W.C. Clark, F. Alcock, N.M. Dickson, N. Eckley, D.H. Guston, J. Jager, R.B. Mitchell, 2003. Knowledge Systems for sustainable development. Proceedings of the National Academy of Science of the USA 100: 8086-8091.
Coghlan, D. and T. Branninck, 2010. Doing action research in your own organization. Sage Publications, London, UK.
Dillon, J. and A.E.J. Wals, 2006. On the danger of blurring methods, methodologies and ideologies in environmental education research. Environmental Education Research 12: 549-558.

Derkzen, P., 2009. Geleerd in het Westerkwartier. Een onderwijsproject in een dynamische regio 2003-2008. Wageningen University, Wageningen, the Netherlands [in Dutch].

Friedman, V.J., 2001. Action Science: Creating Communities of Inquiry in Communities of Practice. In: P. Reason and H. Bradbury (eds.), Handbook of Action Research, Sage Publications, Thousand Oaks, CA, USA, pp. 159-170.

Gaventa, J. and A. Cornwall, 2001. Power and knowledge. In: P. Reason and H. Bradbury (eds.), Handbook of Action Research, Sage Publications, Thousand Oaks, CA, USA, pp. 70-80.

Geerling-Eiff, F., H. Kupper, M. De Beuze and A. Wals, 2007. Steen in het water. Een handreiking voor het werken met kennisarrangementen. Wageningen University, Wageningen, the Netherlands [in Dutch].

Gustavsen, B., 2001. Theory and Practice: The Mediating Discourse. In: P. Reason and H. Bradbury (eds.), Handbook of Action Research, Sage Publications, Thousand Oaks, CA, USA, pp. 17-26.

Kibwika, P., 2006. Learning to make change. Developing innovation competence for recreating the African university of the 21st century. Wageningen Academic Publishers, Wageningen, the Netherlands.

Nowotny, H., P. Scott and M. Gibbons, 2001. Re-thinking science; knowledge and the public in the age of uncertainty. Blackwell Publishers, Oxford, UK.

Reason, P. and H. Bradbury (eds.), 2008. Handbook of action research. Sage Publications, Thousand Oaks, CA, USA.

Regeer, B.J., 2009. Making the invisible visible. Analysing the development of strategies and changes in knowledge production to deal with persistent problems in sustainable development. Uitgeverij Boxpress, Amsterdam, the Netherlands.

Sarkassian, W., D. Hurford and C. Wenmann, 2010. Creative Community Planning, Transformative Engagement Methods for Working at the Edge. Earthscan, London, UK.

Senge, P.M. and C.O. Scharmer, 2006. Community Action Research: Learning as a community of Practitioners, Consultants and Researchers. In: P. Reason and H. Bradbury (eds.), Handbook of Action Research, Sage Publications, Thousand Oaks, CA, USA, pp. 238-249.

Tress, B., G. Tress, A. van der Valk and G. Fry, 2003. Interdisciplinary and Transdisciplinary Landscape Studies: Potentials and limitations. Delta series 2. Wageningen University, Wageningen, the Netherlands.

Turnhout, E., M. Hisschemöller and H. Eijsackers, 2007. Ecological Indicators: Between the two fires of science and policy. Elsevier, Amsterdam, the Netherlands.

Van Mierlo, B., B. Regeer, M. Van Amstel, M. Van Arkesteijn, V. Beekman, J. Bunders, T. Cock Buning,. B. de Elzen, A.C Hoes and C. Leeuwis, 2010. Reflexieve Monitoring in actie. Handvatten voor de monitoring van systeeminnovatieprojecten. Wageningen Universiteit en Vrije Universiteit. Uitgeverij Boxpress, Amsterdam, the Netherlands [in Dutch].

Wals, A.E.J. (ed.), 2009. Social learning towards a sustainable world. Wageningen Academic Publishers, Wageningen, the Netherlands.

Wenger, E., 1998. Communities of practice. Learning, meaning and identity. Learning in doing: social, cognitive and computational perspectives. Cambridge University Press, Cambridge, UK.

Wiskerke, J.S.C., 2007. Robust Regions. Dynamics, connectedness, and diversity in the metropolitane landscape. Inaugural Speech, Wageningen University, Wageningen, the Netherlands.

7. The soil-plant-animal system as a boundary object for collaborative knowledge development

Marian Stuiver

Abstract

This article will assess the potential role of boundary objects when farmers and scientists meet and start to work together on collaborative knowledge development. Boundary objects are entities that are shared by actors coming from different communities. The boundary objects create opportunities for alignment between the actors. Thus, they are instrumental in developing a shared discourse, the clustering of knowledge and building a new community of discourse among the farmers and scientists. The case study is the 'VEL and VANLA Nutrient Management Project' in Friesland in the Netherlands that took place between 1999 and 2004. Farmers that were members of the environmental co-operatives VEL and VANLA worked together with a heterogeneous group of scientists to reduce the nitrogen losses at their dairy farms. During this project, the participants adopted a shared perspective: the so-called soil-plant-animal system. This soil-plant-animal system represents nitrogen flows on a dairy farm and introduces the notions of a system approach which means the importance of acknowledging the interdependency of different physical, chemical and biological subsystems. The development of the soil-plant-animal system is analysed as a boundary object. The article will address the learning processes of the participants in developing a shared discourse as well as the conflicts that emerged between the scientists and farmers. The article will conclude with the new role of scientists as boundary workers within this type of collaborative knowledge development.

7.1 Introduction

In the past few decades, a societal demand for agricultural products that produce fewer risks for human health and natural pollutions has been articulated (Beck, 1992; WRR, 2003). New demands enter societal and political discourse; sustainability is one of these demands. Sustainable agriculture aims for agri-businesses being more environmental-friendly, economically viable and also concerned with the social organisation of agriculture (Henkens and Van Keulen, 2001; Van Bavel *et al.*, 2004).

The move towards sustainable agriculture needs to be supported by knowledge and understanding of sustainability. Traditional ways of knowledge production are not sufficient to meet this challenge. There is a general trend to move from scientific endeavour in a traditional research context to knowledge production that is engaged with other communities and useful for multiple audiences (see Bouma *et al.*, 2008; Nowotny *et al.*, 2001). In fact, there are non-traditional ways of knowledge production going on in other communities, outside the universities and research institutes.

Marian Stuiver

This article will assess the potential role of boundary objects when actors from science work together with other communities on collaborative knowledge development. Boundary objects are entities (e.g. maps, soil profiles, software packages, visual representations, see Kent *et al.*, 2007; Ewenstein and Whyte, 2009) that can be shared among both scientists and actors from non-scientific communities and are often interpreted and used differently by each of them. This case study will also assess the new role of scientists within this type of collaborative research.

The case study is the VEL and VANLA Nutrient Management Project in the Northern Frisian Woodlands in the Netherlands that took place between 1999 and 2004. Local farmers founded the environmental co-operatives of VEL and VANLA in 1992: a regional organisation in which the farmers collaborate to integrate environmental values into their production process (Glasbergen, 2000) in co-operation with local, regional and national agencies. Their goal was to experiment with a new approach to dairy farming in a small-scale landscape (Reijs *et al.*, 2007). The co-operatives developed a form of self-organisation (Ostrom, 2005) to meet these challenges. They called into existence a board with elected members (a chairman, a secretary and a treasurer) and they built their own constitution with their own rules and rights.

In the VEL and VANLA Nutrient Management Project farmers of the environmental co-operatives worked together with a heterogeneous group of scientists to reduce the nitrogen losses at their dairy farms. The participants adopted a shared perspective: the so-called soil-plant-animal system. This soil-plant-animal system represents nitrogen flows on a dairy farm and introduces the notions of a system approach which means the importance of acknowledging the interdependency of different physical, chemical and biological subsystems. The development of the soil-plant-animal system was composed of learning processes that involved conflict and alignment between the scientists and farmers.

7.2 Nutrient Management Project of VEL and VANLA

In the 1990s the issue of nitrogen pollution of groundwater and ammonia volatilisation was a growing concern in the Dutch national political debate. To reduce ammonia volatilisation from manure, farmers have been required since 1995 by law to inject their manure into the soil, instead of traditional broadcast surface spreading. The VEL and VANLA farmers assumed the negative side effects of soil injection, like effects on soil fauna and the risk of further soil compaction, due to the heavy equipment.

The farmers of VEL and VANLA claimed that their management systems (including broadcast surface spreading) were at least as effective to reduce ammonia volatilisation. They looked for co-operation with scientists which led to the creation of the VEL and VANLA Nutrient Management Project (see Atsma *et al.*, 2000). In 1994, the Dutch government agreed with a proposal to initiate an experimental research programme, to prove the

7. The soil-plant-animal system as a boundary object

claims being made. Moreover, the farmers participating in the research programme were allowed to apply broadcast surface spreading. In return, the farmers promised to achieve the environmental targets set by the government faster than other farmers. By means of nutrient accounts and scientific reports the farmers had to account for their activities.

7.2.1 Inclusion of scientific disciplines and societal actors

In 1997 a social scientist and an animal scientist from Wageningen University in the Netherlands met a farmer in the Frisian Woodlands and exchanged their ideas and observations. The farmer collected his own farm data. He interpreted the data and wondered why the organic matter content of his manure was decreasing over the years. The animal scientist wanted to test his ideas on the relation between dairy cattle diet and manure quality, in co-operation with a group of farmers. The social scientist was interested in the farmer's knowledge and the potential innovations that were hidden in the farmer's practices of the environmental co-operatives. They met each other, in the hope of starting a nutrient management project with neighbouring colleagues in the Frisian Woodlands. In 1998, the farmers and scientists started to negotiate with various stakeholders, like the Province of Friesland and Wageningen University, to obtain finances for establishing a nutrient management project.

In 1998 they decided to draw up the nitrogen balances of 93 VEL and VANLA farms, based on the period from May 1995 until May 1996 (Verhoeven, 2000). A nitrogen balance is the difference between the amount of nitrogen taken in and the amount of nitrogen excreted or lost. Farm nitrogen efficiency is nitrogen in milk and meat divided by the nitrogen in feed and fodder and fertiliser. Cow nitrogen efficiency is nitrogen in milk and meat divided by the nitrogen in feed and fodder. Soil nitrogen efficiency is nitrogen in own fodder divided by the nitrogen in manure and fertiliser. The animal scientist proposed to look at the nitrogen flows from a systems perspective. The question was: what are the N flows and N efficiencies of the total farming system? What were the losses and what was the nitrogen use efficiency per farm? From these balances, it became evident that there were huge differences in nitrogen flows (and in nitrogen use efficiency) among the 110 farms (with an average ranging between 10 and 28%) (Sonneveld *et al.*, 2007).

After discussing these findings, the scientists decided that they wanted to have a better understanding of the farms that were experiencing lower nitrogen losses. The hypothesis they formulated was that the total loss in nitrogen within the farming system could be effectively reduced. Moreover, nitrogen use efficiency in the plant-soil system varied more among the farms (between 68% and 31%) than nitrogen use efficiency in the animal (between 24 and 8%). This observation suggested that there is more to gain from increasing the nitrogen use efficiency in the plant-soil system than in the animal (Verhoeven, 2000). The leading question now was: how do some of the farmers within the VEL and VANLA co-operatives achieve high nitrogen use efficiency in the total farming system? What can be learned from their experiences?

In 1998 and 1999, the scientists started visiting the farmers of the environmental co-operatives. They visited the chairman of the environmental co-operatives and asked them which farmers would be interested in and suitable to join a possible scientific project. For this purpose they organised a series of study meetings. They explained to the farmers present that they wanted to start a project that focused on management options to increase the nitrogen efficiency of the dairy farm. The farmers reacted with enthusiasm: 'We could not continue farming within the prevailing policies of the government. The ideas of the importance of the nitrogen cycle within the farming system made a lot of sense to us at the time and we decided to work on the soil-plant-animal system together with the researchers.'

In October 1998, the Nutrient Management Project of VEL and VANLA had taken off in the area. The first series of study meetings between these 60 farmers took place. Twelve groups of five farmers were formed and decided to meet on a regular basis. The project involved a wide selection of farmers, with various styles of farming, education levels, milk yields and environmental achievements.

7.2.2 Aims and objectives of the knowledge development process

The goal of the Nutrient Management Project was to find cost-effective solutions for environmental problems, which would meet the government's environmental targets and which would be appropriate to the local community's needs (i.e. the local farming systems and the agro-ecological and social environments). The collaborative research activities therefore focused on nutrient management and in particular on decreasing the use of fertiliser, improving the quality of manure, adapting the application of manure and improving the soil quality. The aim of the Nutrient Management Project of VEL and VANLA was to develop co-operative knowledge activities that could answer the question how to improve the dairy farming systems in such a way that the surplus of nitrogen emitted in nitrate and ammonia could be decreased (Verhoeven *et al.*, 2003).

At the beginning of the project, a research council was established to help design and govern the Nutrient Management Project. The research council meetings were held twice a year and its results were reported back to the scientific and farmers communities. Various scientists participated in the research council, including agronomists from the Research Institute for Animal Husbandry and Plant Research International, as well as social and soil scientists from Wageningen University (Goede *et al.*, 2003, Sonneveld and Bouma, 2003). The chairmen of the farmer communities were members of the research council as they had numerous and various contacts with government authorities, with the right network within the area and with agribusiness and farmers' organisations. They had experience in improving social cohesion within the co-operatives and in mobilising the right farmers to participate in the experiment.

The team of researchers was composed of three different groups. The first group was composed of scientists that were actively promoting and implementing the three main promising innovations (Reijs *et al.*, 2007). The second group was composed of scientists that researched soil science and grassland management. These researchers wanted to develop new lines of research; for example, they studied the interactions between farm labour and physical soil characteristics, developing in different directions (Sonneveld *et al.*, 2007). The third group was composed of researchers affiliated to the Animal Sciences group and researchers from Plant Research International. They were involved in grassland experiments and research into additives (Goede *et al.*, 2003).

7.2.3 Nurturing new modes of knowledge production

Within the Nutrient Management Project VEL and VANLA, new modes of knowledge production were experimented with that aimed to find patterns for developing ways towards sustainability. The following three modes of knowledge production can be distinguished: (1) controlled circumstances; (2) exchange, circulation; and (3) natural history. These modes of knowledge production are derived from Rip (2002: 120).

In this mode of knowledge production, knowledge is the outcome of (experimental) findings under controlled circumstances. Part of the research activities were based on experiments under controlled circumstances, for instance with additives and soil conditions (e.g. Van der Stelt, 2007).

In this mode of knowledge production, knowledge is a by-product of actions of and interactions between local practices. When different actors meet and exchange their knowledge, new knowledge with an added value can be produced. Exchange and circulation were the basis of the innovations formulated among the farmers and the researchers during the research council of the Nutrient Management Project and the study meetings. They discussed their observations and analyses among each other and within their own communities. Furthermore, the research activities – for a large part deliberately – were performed on location, namely in the fields and at the farms of the dairy farmers involved. The interaction between the different actors in the research council and at the study meetings was crucial. During the discussions within the research council, a shared understanding of the promising innovations to be investigated was developed. Study meetings were an important way of enhancing the exchange of information. During these group meetings, the farmers' findings were discussed, compared and contrasted.

Natural history means that knowledge is the outcome of the collection and accumulation of experiences and findings across space and time. The soil plant animal system of the Nutrient

Management Project is an example of creating such a coherent pattern. The actors try to make an overall system more explicit and consequently recognise meaningful patterns within this system. Other examples can be found in the field studies of Bouma *et al.* (2008) and Sonneveld *et al.* (2009). The emphasis is on collecting, systematising and classifying observations in space and time, to find patterns and routines.

7.3 The Nutrient Management Project as boundary work

The activities of the Nutrient Management Project can be framed as boundary work by forming a temporary community of practice where scientists and farmers coming from different epistemological communities (Wenger, 1999) deliberately engage in a process of collective learning over an extended period of time, with the aim of gaining insight and alter the social order in the long run. The participants all want to engage in learning and developing knowledge about this domain. As Wenger argues himself, communities of practice are learning practices: social engagements between actors where learning takes place (Wenger, 1999).

Within communities of practice, two processes are essential for creating mutual understanding: the first process is participation and the second process is reification. These two processes have a dual relationship with each other. Participation implies that the members of the community shape their identities in relation to each other. The relationships can have different forms; they can be based on conflict and harmony and they can be intimate as well as political (Wenger, 1999). Reification means that the bits and pieces of knowledge that are learned are communicated in a reified form (i.e. tools, language or artefacts) within the community of practice and to the outside world. Reification refers to actions within the community of practice like designing, naming, encoding, interpreting and describing (Wenger, 1999).

One example of reification in the Nutrient Management Project is the development of boundary objects (Starr, 1989): objects that serve as an interface between different communities. Boundary objects are entities (e.g. maps, soil profiles, software packages, visual representations, see Ewenstein and Whyte, 2009; Kent *et al.*, 2007) that are shared by several different communities and are often interpreted and used differently by each of them. Boundary objects create opportunities for alignment between different communities. Thus, they are instrumental in developing a shared discourse, the clustering of knowledge and building a new community of discourse among the actors.

Boundary objects can be visible through indicators. Indicators provide simplified representations of complex phenomena. Indicators can be developed in science and advisory schemes, but can also be developed on the basis of experiential knowledge. They show something specific and indicate something more comprehensive or general. Thus, indicators influence observation and experience. Indicators focus observation; the experience of something comprehensive is reduced to something specific. Indicators enable and sharpen observation but also narrow it. Indicators may cause blindness to other phenomena that are not indicated, thus literally becoming blinding insights. A farmer, who is focused solely on the quantity of milk, may – unwittingly – neglect the quality of the milk or the health of his cows. In social learning processes, indicators have an additional function: they provide a shared perspective. By using the same indicators, people focus on a common dimension, which facilitates comparison.

7.3.1 The soil-plant-animal system as a boundary object

From the beginning, a diagram was used as the basic guideline of the Nutrient Management Project. The diagram depicted the soil-plant-animal system interactions, a pattern of linkages within a dairy farm (Verhoeven *et al.*, 2003). The first diagram was drawn in 1998, to assist the other farmers in understanding how they could improve nitrogen efficiency at a farm level. The soil-plant-animal system highlighted the existence of the different, relevant subsystems; cow, manure, soil and plant. All these relevant subsystems needed to be reorganised in such a way that a new equilibrium could be created (Van Bruchem *et al.*, 1999).

In the course of time, the following story about the management of the soil-plant-animal system took shape and was supported by the research done:

> First we try to influence the quality of manure by reducing the amount of mineral Nitrogen in the manure. We do this by altering the feeding strategy. Using the silage of our own farm becomes more important. The cows are fed with limited amounts of concentrates. Instead we use silage from our own farm with a higher fibre and lower protein content. Efficient protein feeding reduces the amount of mineral Nitrogen (Reijs *et al.*, 2007). The advantage of these diets is that the indicator C/N increases in the manure. This reduces ammonia volatilisation and nitrate leaching and it contributes to organic Nitrogen in the soil.

The hypothesis was that a change in the composition of the diet towards less crude protein (RE) and less surplus protein (OEB) would enhance the conversion of nitrogen from feed into nitrogen into milk. An increase in dietary fibre (RC) was promoted to stimulate rumen functioning and hindgut fermentation. Increasing the amount of RC was also supposed to increase the organic nitrogen (Norg) of the manure. These adjustments were expected to lead to changes in manure composition with a higher C/N total ratio, lower mineral N contents (Nmin) and a larger proportion of Norg, less susceptible to losses through volatilisation and leaching (Reijs, 2007).

One important indicator to measure the effects of the use of fibre-rich and protein-poor diets was the carbon-nitrogen ratio (C/N ratio). The C/N ratio in manure depends on the amounts of protein and fibre (which contains C) used in the feed and fodder. Increasing C/N of the slurry implied a change in the cows' diets, reducing the amount of protein and increasing the fibrous content. In addition, straw was added to the slurry and some farmers used additives which were expected to further improve the C/N ratio (Reijs, 2007).

The soil-plant-animal system has been variously named. It has also been called the systems perspective, since it highlighted not just one element (the cow) but all the relationships within the total farming system. The members of the project referred to the systems perspective as the 'VEL and VANLA' method (Figure 7.1). The soil-plant-animal system is the specific version of the systems perspective as it developed within the Nutrient Management Project of VEL and VANLA. Variations of the systems perspective were also present in the research design of the experimental station APM Minderhoudhoeve (Hylkema, 1999) and at the Dutch project *Koeien en Kansen* (Aarts et al., 1988). Within the Nutrient Management Project of VEL and VANLA, the version included the management practices of the farmers who optimised the systems perspective in their own practices.

The systems perspective became the challenge among all the participating farmers to optimise their nitrogen efficiency. Farmers focused on improving the soil, changing feeding patterns towards more fibre and less protein and minimised concentrate use and proteins. Moreover they improved manure application and minimised fertiliser use in combination with broadcast surface spreading.

The systems perspective legitimised and bundled the joint activities of the farmers and the scientists. Together they created an understanding of the background of the data of the

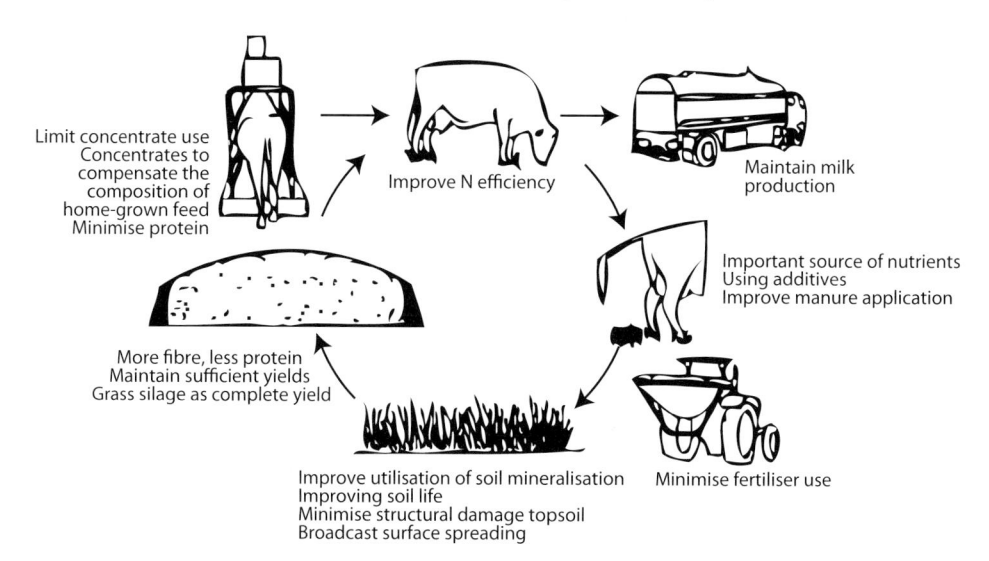

Figure 7.1. The systems perspective and associated farm practices of the VEL and VANLA experiment.

7. The soil-plant-animal system as a boundary object

system and their interrelations. They came to understand the nutrient flows at the farm, and how the farmer managed these flows. The farmers provided hypotheses to understand the system perspective and collected data of their farms, which scientists used to parameterise and calculate the soil-plant-animal system of each farm (Groot *et al.*, 2003).

In the course of time, the systems perspective (and its accompanying management tools and indicators) became visible in publications and presentations to the farming communities (see Verhoeven and Noorduyn, 2003). Several knowledge activities contributed to the soil-plant-animal system: the stories of the farmers about the relation between diets and manure quality, the research on soil life (Goede *et al.*, 2003), manure (Reijs, 2007) and the grassland experiment (Van der Ploeg et *al.*, 2007) as well as the research on the relationship between Nmin and ammonia volatilisation (Huijsmans *et al.*, 2004) New research themes based on the systems perspective were published, e.g. the contents of the soil, soil life and biological processes in the soil, a rehabilitation of specific methods of manure application and the use of additives. New indicators appeared, like the RC, RE and the C/N ratio.

7.4 Conflicts about the soil plant animal system

Within the Nutrient Management Project a debate took place about the validity of different scientific methods and hypotheses. This debate led to the eventual emergence of two groups of actors with differing ideas about the utility and relevance of the systems perspective and the role of scientific and farmers' knowledge.

The first group was composed of narrators of the systems perspective. They aimed to change academics' view of the question 'what is true knowledge?' First of all, this group perspective considered the interdependence between different aspects of farming to be an important part of the analysis. Secondly, with the systems perspective, they integrated farmers' knowledge and innovations (Van der Ploeg *et al.*, 2007) as a crucial element of scientific enquiry.

The second group did not deny the significance of the systems perspective as a hypothesis but still wanted to gain more insight into the crucial factors that resulted in changes in the farming system. They criticised the specific use of the systems perspective as performed by the first group. They claimed that there was no proof based on the systems perspective to support the argument that it would be better to apply manure by traditional (broadcast surface spreading) methods rather than using modern methods of shallow injection. In their opinion, the research that was performed by the first group did not provide enough evidence that the systems perspective would create a radical new set of management options.

Here are two situations in which the two groups became visible. First in 2001, a dispute took place following the publication of the book *Good manure does not smell* (Eshuis *et al.*, 2001). Second, a meeting of the research council in 2003 is analysed where scientists and farmers participated in a discussion about the relationship between science and practice.

Marian Stuiver

In 2001 a dispute took place between the authors of the book (Eshuis *et al.*, 2001) and a researcher from Plant Research International. In the book the soil-plant-animal system is investigated as a valuable option for Dutch dairy farming. It explores the management options it entails. Farmers' experiences with making manure are presented as valuable innovations. A plea is made for using high-fibre and low-protein diets. It is presented as a valuable option for the farmers to optimise nitrogen efficiency and reduce the nitrogen losses. The researcher criticised the scientific validity of the claims made in the publication.

First of all, in his opinion, the specific claims of the farmers and Van Bruchem that a combination of changes in feed, manure and soil would result in a system innovation were no more than a hunch, or a hypothesis, and not a sufficiently validated theory. Secondly, he argued that the Nutrient Management Project of VEL and VANLA could not make an exclusive claim on these findings. Other nutrient management projects in the Netherlands worked with their own variations of the systems perspective. For instance, de Marke, Centre for Dairy Farming and Environment and closely connected with the animal sciences group of Wageningen University, also introduced the systems perspective as a means to overcome the crisis in dairy farming at the end of the eighties. Finally, he stated that the scientific quest would be to discover the crucial factors within the system that are responsible for the changes in N efficiency. In his opinion, looking at a lot of factors (like the diets, additives and straw) at the same time, as it happened within the Nutrient Management Project of VEL and VANLA, did not help the farmers, but only blurred the scientific analysis, since there could also be factors included in the systems perspective that were completely irrelevant. He thought it was the task of the Nutrient Management Project of VEL and VANLA to avoid burdening the farmers with measures that were not effective.

In 2003 during a research council meeting scientists and farmers disputed the value of the systems perspective. One farmer stated:

> Although research until now has maybe not given sufficient scientific evidence for some of our management tools in the systems perspective, for us as farmers scientific evidence is not the most important thing. The mental change is important: a change to more sustainable farming and that is where the systems perspective is useful for.

A scientist responded by asking for more measurable criteria to show that the systems perspective really worked. The farmer replied that for him it started with using less fertiliser and then with changing the feeding strategy. A colleague added that the main topic was to make more use of one's own manure. In other words, the farmers responded by highlighting different adjustments in their management decisions based on the systems perspective. The scientist repeated his question about the measurable indicator. 'What', he said, 'would have happened if a farmer had only used less fertiliser. Would there be a difference with what he has achieved now?' The farmer stated in response that, in his opinion, it was impossible to reduce it to one factor and that 'you have to think in systems.' The farmers stated that it was

7. The soil-plant-animal system as a boundary object

important that, what they considered to be the 'vested knowledge infrastructure', would adopt their perspective. This is shown by the following quote from a farmer called Atsma:

It is up to the scientists that work with us to translate our ways of farming into science and politics. We, as farmers, are convinced it works, because we see evidence in the results of the farm. Now scientists translate it into scientific results, but not in a reductionist way as scientists are often used to.

In short, during the Nutrient Management Project, two views on 'what is valid knowledge' developed among the participants, during processes of conflict and alignment. The first group of actors from the scientific community argued that knowledge development should be based on the analyses and experiments of neutral (or objective) scientists that produce theories on the basis of the analyses and measurements of facts. The second group, consisting of farmers and scientists embraced an epistemology in which farmer's knowledge and new interpretation schemes like the system perspective were considered to be valid sources of knowledge. The latter view on knowledge became the dominant perspective in the debates and publications of the Nutrient Management Project.

7.5 Lessons learned

7.5.1 Boundary objects as instruments for coherence

Boundary objects such as the soil-plant-animal system created coherence between members of two epistemic communities that were previously separated. Over time, with the development of the boundary object, the farmers and (one group of) scientists started to speak a similar language, they started to 'understand' each other. Boundary objects are therefore instruments that enable the farmers to access the outside world of science and politics and vice versa.

The boundary object of the soil-plant-animal system became a carrier of a new body of knowledge within the group of scientists and farmers that experimented with nutrient practices. To make the boundary object more robust, different forms of alignment were necessary. Within the Nutrient Management Project, individual experiences with manure were accepted by one group of actors as proof, for example stories told by farmers about the soil. Others within the Nutrient Management Project needed the boundary object to be more robust. In their opinion, proof cannot simply be based on stories of individual farmers or experiences within farms, but needs to be translated into scientific language, indicators and management options.

An important role was given to indicators (i.e. professional terms used by the farmers and scientists) that enabled the farmers and scientists to speak the same language. Indicators are simplified representations of complex phenomena. When farmers and scientists use the same terms in reference to complex phenomena, they more or less assume that they are all talking about the same meaning and interpretation. The indicators suggest a common understanding of the complex phenomena. This means that farmers and scientists have a shared perspective. For instance, the smell and consistency (thickness) of manure are used as indicators for the complex phenomenon of the quality of manure. For a specific group of actors, thick manure is an indicator for a sustainable way of farming and a trajectory for sustainable agriculture. In other words, the indicators that reflect and confirm the boundary object, also create mutual understanding, internally and externally.

7.5.2 Conflicts as valuable encounters

Within the Nutrient Management Project of VEL and VANLA, both scientists and farmers learned about the soil-plant-animal system. This collaborative knowledge development was accompanied by conflicts and differences in opinion. In this section I will explain why conflicts are valuable encounters in knowledge development and why scientists should engage in these encounters.

First of all, it so happens that there are various categories of knowledge present when different stakeholders gather to produce knowledge. During their interactions, the actors automatically reproduce the various categories of knowledge (e.g. scientific knowledge and farmers' knowledge) discursively and give them a new meaning. This variety of sources of knowledge and their mutual confrontations is not an obstacle but a challenge during collaborative knowledge development. Therefore, it is unwise to present one source of knowledge as superior and debunk other sources of knowledge.

Secondly, parties are more inclined to accept knowledge when they have been involved in the generation of that knowledge. This is especially true when parties come into conflict. A lack of involvement may lead to rejection of one of the other bodies of knowledge (i.e. scientists' or farmers' experiments). Creating a sense of shared ownership of knowledge is conducive to that knowledge being accepted by all the parties concerned. In addition, being involved in a process of 'joint fact-finding' can bring conflicting parties together. One way to build good relationships is through the acceptance of different points of view. In this way a community of practice can arise in which the different participants 'agree to disagree' and consider disagreement as an important source of renewal.

7.5.3 The role of boundary workers

When a scientist experiments with collaborative knowledge production, the boundaries between science and non-science become part of his reflexive research design (Huitema and Turnhout, 2009). The category of scientists as boundary workers was often presented at the meetings of the Nutrient Management Project VEL and VANLA as well. There are competencies that scientists as boundary workers can develop in the processes of examination, communication and conflict and alignment during collaborative knowledge production.

First, there is the (multi-disciplinary) examination and support of various types of knowledge and expertise. Therefore, crucial responsibilities are the identification of (the principles that define) innovative trajectories of research and methods. Boundary workers need to broaden and deepen their understanding of the potential and transformative nature of innovative hypotheses and approaches. This requires considerably creative and analytical skills considering the high levels of embeddedness (Eshuis *et al.*, 2001).

Second, there is the challenge how to transfer locally produced knowledge to different times and places. There is a risk that its robustness is scrutinised within other localities, as we have seen in the controversy about the systems perspective. Although it has been increasingly acknowledged that scientific knowledge does not necessarily represent the objective truth, it is not often expressed by scientists when they communicate with the outside world (Leeuwis *et al.*, 2006). More and more scientists have become aware that scientific knowledge is considered to be robust when it is accepted by one of the several scientific communities of practice. Therefore, scientific knowledge is also contextual knowledge, but in another temporal, spatial and social context than that of farmers' knowledge. However, internal tensions within the scientific community tend to be shielded from the outside world and conflicting views and controversies are not to be brought out into the open (Leeuwis *et al.*, 2006). One challenging aspect for scientific communities is the fact that the 'social' construction of all forms of knowledge is made more transparent to outsiders, and that it becomes clear that scientists are actively engaged in this process even when this is accompanied by struggle and conflicts about competing knowledge claims.

Third, knowledge production (including scientific processes) contains processes of conflict and alignment. Scientists should actively and intentionally discover the sources of knowledge that are present during the interactions. The conflicts that take place can be a good way of discovering these various sources of knowledge and epistemologies. The conflicts sharpen the different standpoints and make the different sources of knowledge and their possible contributions to collaborative knowledge production more explicit.

Acknowledgements

These research activities were conducted within the framework of the Nutrient Management Project and the Innovative Project North Frisian Woodlands from 1999 till 2004. I would like to thank Professor Jan Douwe van der Ploeg, Professor Han Wiskerke from Wageningen University and Professor Arie Rip from Twente University for their intellectual contributions. Furthermore, I would like to thank Transforum Agro and Groen, the province of Fryslân, the Wageningen UR Knowledge Base 1 research programme of the Ministry of Agriculture, Nature and Food, the Association Northern Frisian Woodlands, the Agri- and

Horticulture Organization North and all those directly involved for making this project and my role in it possible. This chapter could not have been written without the data and support provided by this project.

References

Aarts, H.F.M., E.E. Biewinga, G. Bruin, B. Edel and H. Korevaar, 1988. Melkveehouderij en milieu, een aanpak voor het beperken van mineralenverliezen. CABO Verslag nr. 79. CABO-DLO, Wageningen, the Netherlands [in Dutch].

Atsma, G., F. Benedictus, F. Verhoeven and M. Stuiver, 2000. De sporen van twee milieucooperaties. Vereniging Eastermar's Lânsdouwe en Vereniging Agrarisch Natuurbeheer en Landschap Achtkarspelen. NLTO, Drachten, the Netherlands [in Dutch].

Beck, U., 1992. Risk Society: Towards a new Modernity. Sage, London, UK.

Bouma, J., J.A. De Vos, M.P.W. Sonneveld, G.B.M. Heuvelink and J.J. Stoorvogel, 2008. The role of scientists in multiscale land use analysis: lessons learned from Dutch communities of practice, Advances in Agronomy 97: 175-234.

De Goede, R.G.M., L. Brussaard and A.D.L. Akkermans, 2003. On farm impact of cattle slurry manure management on biological soil quality. NJAS Wageningen Journal of Life Sciences 51 (1-2): 103-133.

Eshuis, J., M. Stuiver, F. Verhoeven and J.D. Van der Ploeg, 2001. Goede mest stinkt niet. Wageningen Universiteit, Wageningen, the Netherlands [in Dutch].

Ewenstein, B. and J. Whyte, 2009. Knowledge Practices in Design: The Role of Visual Representations as 'Epistemic Objects'. Organization Studies 30: 7-30.

Glasbergen, P., 2000. The Environmental Cooperative: Self-Governance in Sustainable Rural Development. The Journal of Environment and Development 9(3): 240-259.

Groot, J.C.J., W.A.H. Rossing, E.A. Lantinga and H. Van Keulen, 2003. Exploring the potential for improved internal nutrient cycling in dairy farming systems using an eco-mathematical model. NJAS Wageningen Journal of Life Sciences 51 (1-2): 165-194.

Huijsmans, J.F.M., J.M.G. Mol, M.C.J. Smits, B.R. Verwijs, H.G. Van der Meer, B. Rutgers and F.P.M. Verhoeven, 2004. Ammoniakemissie bij bovengronds breedwerpige mesttoediening. Agrotechnologies and Food Innovations B.V., Wageningen, the Netherlands [in Dutch].

Henkens, P. and H. Van Keulen, 2001. Mineral policy in the Netherlands and nitrate policy within the European Community. Netherlands Journal of Agricultural Science 49: 117-134.

Huitema, D. and E. Turnhout, 2009. Working at the science-policy interface: a discursive analysis of boundary work at the Netherlands Environmental Assessment Agency Environmental Politics 18(4): 576-594.

Hylkema, I., 1999. Eiwitarm en structuurrijk voer kenmerken Minderhoudhoeve. NLTO, Leeuwarden, the Netherlands [in Dutch].

Kent, P., R. Noss, D. Guile, C. Hoyles and A. Bakker, 2007. Characterizing the use of mathematical knowledge in boundary-crossing situations at work. Mind, Culture, and Activity 14: 64-82.

Leeuwis, C., R. Smits, J. Grin, L. Klerkx, B. Van Mierlo and A. Kuipers, 2006. Equivocations on the post privatization dynamics in agricultural innovation systems. The design of an innovation enhancing environment (Working paper 4). TransForum, Zoetermeer, the Netherlands.

Nowotny, H., P. Scott and M. Gibbons, 2001. Re-thinking science. Knowledge and the Public in an age of uncertainty. Polity Press, Cambridge, UK.

Ostrom, E., 2005. Self-governance and forest resources. In: P.J. Shah and V. Maitra (eds.), Terracotta reader: a market approach to the environment. Academic Foundation, New Delhi, India, pp. 131-154.

Reijs, J.W., M.P.W. Sonneveld, P. Sorensen, R.L.M. Schils, J.C.J. Groot and E.A. Lantinga, 2007. Effects of different diets on utilization of nitrogen from cattle slurry applied to grassland on a sandy soil in the Netherlands Agriculture. Ecosystems and Environment 118 (1-4): 65-79.

Rip, A., 2002. Science for the 21st Century. In: P. Tindemans, A. Verrijn-Stuart and R. Visser (eds.), The Future of the Sciences and Humanities: Four Analytical Essays and a Critical Debate on the Future of Scholastic Endeavour. Amsterdam University Press, Amsterdam, the Netherlands, pp. 99-148.

Sonneveld, M.P.W. and J. Bouma, 2003. Effects of different combinations of land use history and nitrogen application on nitrate concentrations in the groundwater. NJAS Wageningen Journal of Life Sciences 51(1-2): 135-146.

Sonneveld, M.P.W., J.J. Schröder, J.A. de Vos, G.J. Monteny, J. Mosquera, J.M.G. Hol, E.A. Lantinga, F.P.M Verhoeven and J. Bouma, 2007. A whole-farm strategy to reduce ammonia losses following slurry application. In: International Conference on Ammonia in Agriculture: Policy, Science, Control and Implementation, Ede, The Netherlands, 19-21 March 2007. Wageningen Academic Publishers, Wageningen, the Netherlands.

Sonneveld, M.P.W., J.A. De Vos, W. De Vries, M. Knotters, J. Kros, J. Roelsma, A. Bleeker, A. Hensen and A. Frumau, 2009. 3MG: Meervoudige Milieu Monitoring voor Gebiedssturing; Een case study voor de Noordelijke Friese Wouden. TransForum Working Papers 9. TransForum, Zoetermeer, the Netherlands [in Dutch].

Starr, S. and J.R. Griesemer, 1989. Institutional Ecology, 'Translations' and Boundary Objects: Amateurs and Professionals in Berkeley's Museum of Vertebrate Zoology, 1907-39. Social Studies of Science 19: 387-420.

Van Bavel, M., J. Frouws and P. Driessen, 2004. Nederland en de Nitraatrichtlijn. struisvogel of strateeg? Wageningen Universiteit, Wageningen, the Netherlands [in Dutch].

Van Bruchem, J., H. Schiere and H. Van Keulen, 1999. Dairy farming in the Netherlands in transition towards more efficient nutrient use. Livestock Production Science 61: 145-153.

Van der Ploeg, J.D., J.C.J. Groot, F.P.M. Verhoeven and E.A. Lantinga, 2007. Interpretation of results from on-farm experiments: manure-nitrogen recovery on grassland as affected by manure quality and application technique. 2. A sociological analysis. NJAS Wageningen Journal of Life Sciences 54 (3): 255-268.

Van der Stelt, B., 2007. Chemical characterization of manure in relation to manure quality as a contribution to a reduced nitrogen emission to the environment. Wageningen University, Wageningen, the Netherlands.

Verhoeven, F.P.M., 2000. Een Nieuw Milieuspoor: Tussenevaluatie Mineralenproject. Wageningen University and Research Centre, Wageningen, the Netherlands [in Dutch].

Verhoeven, F.P.M. and L. Noorduyn, 2003. Natuurlijk in balans, kringloop. Almelo: Lulof Druktechniek

Verhoeven, F.P.M., J. Reijs and J.D. Van der Ploeg, 2003. Re-balancing soil plant-animal interactions: towards reduction of nitrogen losses. NJAS Wageningen Journal of Life Sciences 51 (1-2): 147-164.

Wenger, E., 1999. Communities of practice. learning. meaning and identity. Cambridge University Press, Cambridge, UK.

WRR (Wetenschappelijke Raad voor het Regeringsbeleid), 2003. Naar nieuwe wegen in het milieubeleid. WRR rapporten aan de regering. SDU uitgevers, The Hague, the Netherlands [in Dutch].

8. Learning from learning: the experiences with implementing adaptive collaborative forest management in Zimbabwe

Tendayi Mutimukuru-Maravanyika and Conny Almekinders

Abstract

Convinced that participatory resource management is the way forward in the conservation of natural resources, despite the increasing criticism of participatory approaches, the Centre for International Forestry Research (CIFOR) initiated a multi-country adaptive collaborative management (ACM) research programme. The programme aimed to test the approach and check whether it did indeed result in improvements in both resource conditions and human well-being. Multi-disciplinary teams were set up to spearhead the implementation of the ACM approach in collaboration with local stakeholders in eleven countries (including Zimbabwe) where the research was initiated. Adaptive collaborative management is an approach that is based on action research and learning, and aims to develop people's capacity to adapt to the ever-changing State Forest in Zimbabwe. The chapter shows that doing collaborative research with local stakeholders is easier said than done and several challenges are faced at different levels: within the multi-disciplinary research team itself and between the research team and the local stakeholders. The chapter also shows that, though it is difficult to conduct, collaborative research can indeed result in positive improvements in both the resource status and human well-being. However, these changes will not be sustained if such initiatives fail to explicitly address issues of power and politics as well as put in place clear rules for the management of resources and the means of enforcing them.

8.1 Introduction

Following the failure of centralised top-down approaches to the conservation of natural resources, attention has shifted in the last two decades to participatory approaches. Participatory resource management projects, however, have also produced disappointing results (Alpert, 1996; Barrett and Arcese, 1995; Emerton, 2001; Gibson and Marks, 1995; Kiss, 1990; Oates, 1995; Wells *et al.*, 1992). Conservationists therefore see their argument that the participation of local people increases degradation and biodiversity loss confirmed (Kramer and Van Schaik, 1997; Oates, 1999; Terborgh, 1999). However, proponents of participation consider reverting to top-down conservationist approaches a 'reinvention of the square wheel' (Wilshusen *et al.*, 2002). They call for alternative approaches that combine improvements of both human well-being and the status of natural resources. Researchers from the Center for International Forestry Research (CIFOR) at the head office in Bogor Indonesia were convinced of the urgency to pursue the development of such approaches. Influenced by the work of Terborgh (1999) and Wirkramasinghe (1994) and based on their experiences in two different CIFOR projects (i.e. 'Criteria and Indicators' and 'Devolution and Livelihoods') which showed that both the forest conditions and communities were continuously changing, they concluded that 'adaptation' was crucial. This gave birth to a new programme called 'Local People, Devolution and Adaptive Collaborative Management of Forests'. In this programme adaptive collaborative management (ACM) was conceptualised as an approach that combined research with development and was to address environmental and human problems, while contributing to researchers' understanding of processes involved (Colfer, 2005a, b). The programme was implemented in and around forest sites in 11 countries, (namely, Cameroon, Ghana, Zimbabwe, Malawi, Indonesia, Philippines, Nepal, Kyrgyzstan, Madagascar, Brazil and Bolivia), and had expanded to 30 field work settings by 2002 (Colfer, 2005a). The programme was framed as an action learning programme with learning at different levels. The CIFOR ACM team learnt to implement action research in practice and, through action research, they managed to develop the ACM approach further. They also learnt together with other stakeholders (local communities and the Forestry Commission[10] officers) how to operationalise ACM in specific country contexts. Community members also learnt to better address the challenges they faced using action research.

This chapter describes the experiences of the ACM team in implementing the ACM approach in Mafungautsi forest, Zimbabwe, from 1999 to 2003 as well as the post-project developments. It describes how the ACM team, together with the FC officer and local community members, used action learning to try and find ways to sustainably manage their forest. It later reflects on the experiences of the ACM team and thereafter, by analysing the findings from a follow-up study, and explaining why the ACM approach could not meet its expectations. For understanding the levels of learning it is important to realise that the first author of this chapter was part of the Zimbabwe ACM team. Through her MSc research in Wageningen University in the Netherlands, Tendayi had familiarised herself with interdisciplinary research. When she became part of the CIFOR ACM team, she however did not have practical skills in Action Research. The refection on the implementation of the ACM project in Mafungautsi, the follow-up and overall analysis form part of her PhD research (Mutimukuru-Maravanyika, 2010), and follow an additional level of learning and reflection.

As already mentioned above, in Zimbabwe, the ACM research project was implemented around Mafungautsi State Forest. Like all the other state forests in Zimbabwe, Mafungautsi State Forest was managed by the FC. In 1954 this forest was classified officially as a protected state forest. For the state, the forest is valued as a remnant of the original vegetation type of the Mafungautsi Plateau and also as a water catchment area for important rivers in the country. For local communities the forest represents potential future arable land, especially because of the numerous wetlands found within the forest. For the indigenous people, the

---

[10] The FC is the state body specifically mandated to provide advice on, and control, management and exploitation of forest resources. The FC has regulatory roles as well as extension roles.

forest is also their ancestral home, a place where they used to stay before it was converted into a protected forest.

Despite being a protected forest, local communities from areas surrounding the forest continued to access forest resources illegally, leading to a continued degradation of the forest. In 1994, with funding from the Canadian International Development Agency (CIDA), the FC embarked on a pilot resource sharing project (RSP) and invited communities to participate in the management of the forest as well as benefit from some of the forest resources. The project envisioned ecotourism and wildlife management within the forest boundaries and harvesting of non-timber resources like broom and thatch grass, mushrooms and firewood by people living around the forest. This pilot project went beyond the provisions of the existing Forestry Act which does not allow anyone, except the FC, to extract or harvest resources from state forests. The RSP was, however, not successful and over time the FC officers and local people found themselves entrenched in their perceptions about each others responsibilities and behaviour. Top-down control from the FC continued as well as illegal extraction of the forest resources that were not included under the RSP agreement (Matose, 2002; Mutimukuru-Maravanyika, 2010) until in 1999, when the CIFOR approached the FC for collaboration in developing the Adaptive Collaborative Management approach in Zimbabwe. The FC selected Mafungautsi forest as a pilot site.

8.2 The ACM approach

The ACM approach has its roots in ideas from several disciplines relating to complex system behaviour. These include adaptive management, social learning and other theories about human co-operation and competition; the forest and the people together forming the complex system (see the underlying assumptions, Box 8.1). The conceptualisation and operationalisation of ACM were meant to evolve over time, through reflection on the experiences in the projects. Based on the principles of action learning, the joint monitoring of the implementation process and its outcomes would generate lessons for next steps. Recently, ACM has been defined as a quality-adding approach whereby stakeholders interact, negotiate a vision for their resource, and consciously undergo shared-learning in developing and implementing their plans (Colfer, 2005a, b; Hartanto *et al.*, 2003; Kusumanto *et al.*, 2005; Prabhu *et al.*, 2007; Prabhu and Matose, 2008).

ACM is essentially an action-research and learning approach. ACM is expected to lead to a self-improving system of resource management based on improved flows of information, decision-making following from experimentation, communication and negotiation among stakeholders, and learning among resource users that result in changes in management systems (Prabhu and Matose, 2008). It aims to 'strengthen and enhance the capacity of people to adapt quickly and more appropriately to changes that confront them rather than through ad hoc trial and error' (Prabhu, 2003:12). In order to improve the adaptive capacity of groups in resource management, ACM focuses on three main elements: (1) strengthening

> **Box 8.1. The assumptions underlying the ACM research approach (CIFOR, unpublished data; Colfer, 2005b).**
>
> These included:
> - Forest-dependent people are part of a complex and dynamic forest-human ecosystem that is constantly changing, making predictions impossible and surprises inevitable.
> - Forest-dependent people have the capacity to act, have agency and invaluable knowledge about their systems. It is therefore important for them to participate in the management of their natural resources.
> - Resource management efforts that ignore the issue of equity are doomed to fail as inequity results in conflicts and violence. Most community-based projects are hijacked by the elite, with marginalised people ignored or playing a peripheral role in the project. Efforts therefore need to be put into empowering the marginalised groups so that they also play an active role in resource management. Social capital is an important precursor to collective action, and should therefore be enhanced.

social and human assets of groups; (2) enhancing social learning (i.e. joint learning) and adaptation by stakeholder groups through the creation of opportunities for them to share their knowledge and experiences; (3) broadening the knowledge base upon which decisions can be made by improving collaboration beyond immediate actors to include other key stakeholders and helping to identify who they are (Prabhu, 2003).

The expected societal impacts of the ACM approach include improved policy-making processes, improved local governance, improved capacity of the stakeholders to collaborate, negotiate and act (Box 8.2). These improvements were considered intermediate impacts which would contribute to final impacts: empowerment of local people and combined improved human well-being and sustainable forest management.

National country teams were expected to address the following research questions (CIFOR, unpublished data; Colfer 2005b):
- Can collaboration among stakeholders in forest management, enhanced by processes of conscious and deliberate social learning that results in conscious adaptation of management, lead both to improved human well-being and the maintenance of forest cover and diversity? If so, under what conditions?
- What approaches, centred on social learning and collaborative action among diverse stakeholders, can be used to encourage sustainable use and management of forest resources?
- In what ways do the processes and outcomes of ACM affect social, economic, political and ecological functioning and how does this feedback reinforce or weaken forest management?

> **Box 8.2. Envisioned impacts of the ACM projects.**
>
> Intermediate impacts
> - Improvements in policy-making processes: by strengthening mechanisms and incentives, policy makers would become more responsive to local community strengths and needs as managers; there would be improvements in avenues for information flow from local level to the policy process level.
> - Improvements in local governance: e.g. by improved transparency in how information is collected, communicated and used locally, development would be more flexible, (responsive), representative and resilient in local institutions.
> - Improved collaborative and negotiation capacity: stakeholders can recognise and choose to act on opportunities to increase human well-being and forest conditions via negotiation and collaborative action.
> - Improved adaptive capacity: stakeholders are better able to develop management strategies that take into account both biophysical and social systems, they are better able to anticipate system responses to their management actions, and they are better and more rapidly able to interpret the impacts of their actions and adjust management in response.
>
> Final impacts
> - Empowerment & decision-making: marginalised forest actors have a greater ability to act on their interests; forest stakeholders are enabled to think more critically and longer term regarding forest management.
> - Linking forest and human well-being: better managed forests for both local people's well-being and conservation interests; livelihoods and livelihood strategies improve.

The objectives and outputs were defined in a rather general way at the international programme level, and the CIFOR-ACM teams in the different countries were to test and further develop the ACM approach in their own specific context, based on the learning at the level of the communities and with other collaborators, and at the level of the CIFOR team. The Zimbabwe team came up with its own objectives for the ACM project after reviewing the available literature on earlier experiences in Zimbabwe (Bradley and McNamara, 1993; Nhira *et al.*, 1998; Thomas, 1993) and also the global ACM documents. These included: (1) to facilitate the improvement of current management systems and policies of forest managers at both local and national levels; and (2) to facilitate the development of locally appropriate collaborative monitoring arrangements. The ACM team in Zimbabwe also planned a series of steps for operationalising the ACM project in Mafungautsi. Together these activities formed the ACM process and were to be implemented during the three-year project phase from 1999 to early 2003. The experiences with the implementation of these steps are further described below.

8.3 Implementing the ACM approach in practice

8.3.1 The ACM team, their learning and their collaborating partners

The CIFOR-ACM team was formed by national researchers (the first author of this chapter was part of this team) from different backgrounds, including social and natural scientists. Scientists from various disciplines were represented including sociologists (responsible for facilitating learning processes), economists (tracking the socio-economic impacts of the project) and ecologists (responsible for tracking the ecological impacts of the project). The roles of the researchers in the team were specified in their contracts with CIFOR and their outputs were formulated yearly in the form of performance contracts. Among the outputs were one or more scientific papers and publications related to the ACM research questions (see Section 8.2). These papers were meant for the team to learn about the concepts applied in the ACM approach and to reflect on their experiences. To this end, there were regular team meetings to discuss the concept notes and papers that the team members produced. Among the papers was, for example, one on social learning, developed by the first author of this chapter (Mutimukuru-Maravanyika, 2010). The writing of the paper involved an extensive literature review.

There was no fixed implementation plan for the ACM project. During the project the team had monthly meetings and many informal encounters in their offices in Harare to reflect on experiences, discuss progress and formulate subsequent steps. Various ACM teams in different countries also got opportunities to learn from each other on how the ACM processes were unfolding in different contexts. Such opportunities included global meetings where all team members met and shared their experiences. Global and in-country capacity-building opportunities were also created for ACM team members, including the global scientific writing workshop that was organised towards the end of 2001.

For influencing forestry policies in Zimbabwe, the CIFOR team wrote policy briefs which they presented to policy makers including the FC. They also organised look-and-learn-tours for policy makers to field sites, and created opportunities for them to participate in international conferences to enhance their learning on different forestry policies and their outcomes. The CIFOR researchers also organised policy round table discussions for policy makers on emerging findings from the field, and invited them to participate in ACM training workshops. For the implementation of the ACM project, the CIFOR researchers teamed up with the FC officers in Mafungautsi. The CIFOR team also organised regular update meetings with the FC top management where they briefed them about the ACM activities and findings. It is also important to note that the first CIFOR team leader joined the project on secondment from the FC, to ensure active involvement of the FC in the whole process.

Local community members in Mafungautsi included local traditional leaders (chiefs, headmen and village heads), resource management committees (RMC) formed as part of the resource sharing project and later on community members organised in resource user groups focusing on three key resources namely, broom grass, thatch grass and honey. In each of the three communities where the researchers worked, they were assisted by a community partner who the community had identified. The community partners' main role included facilitating learning processes, conducting research and record-keeping of all meetings and activities organised by local communities when the researchers were away. These community partners received monthly allowances for their work.

8.3.2 Preparing the stage

The CIFOR ACM-team in Zimbabwe began by approaching the FC, the authority responsible for the management of forests in Zimbabwe to get permission for CIFOR to conduct forestry research in Zimbabwe. Upon signing a Memorandum of Understanding (MOU) in Harare, the FC officials selected Mafungautsi State forest as the ACM research site. As mentioned in the introduction of this chapter, the ACM project aimed to improve the situation around the resource sharing project in Mafungautsi which started in 1994 but so far had failed to produce positive outcomes. The CIFOR researchers therefore had to work with the FC field officers in Gokwe District, (where the forest was located and were responsible for managing it), but had to continuously update the FC top managers in Harare on the developments in the field so as to influence the forestry policy formulation process.

Because the FC officers in the field had no clue about the ACM approach, the ACM researchers initially facilitated all the processes in the field. The FC officer responsible for the resource sharing project participated in all the activities to familiarise himself and build up his own capacity for using the ACM approach. The ACM researchers also organised and facilitated special ACM training workshops for the Mafungautsi FC officer in which several field officers from other districts also participated. As the project advanced, the ACM team increasingly involved the FC officer in the facilitation of the joint learning processes with the community members where they identified solutions to their problems, implemented them and reflected on their impacts in order to learn. Eventually they handed over the facilitation to the FC officer while still giving him considerable support (the researchers attended all the activities and meetings that the FC officer organised and assisted him whenever he got stuck). As the officer became more and more confident about working on his own, the CIFOR team support became less important and eventually, towards the end of the project, they were mere observers in the process.

The CIFOR team in collaboration with the FC and other relevant stakeholders in Gokwe District, selected three sites where the ACM project would be implemented. These are Batanai, Gababe and Ndarire. In each of these sites, the CIFOR team identified a community partner to help them conduct research, facilitate learning processes and keep a record of all meetings organised while they were away. To equip these community partners with the necessary skills for carrying out research and record-keeping, the team organised a capacity-building workshop for them. In the workshops they were introduced to the principles of conducting research, record-keeping and facilitation.

8.3.3 Context studies and capacity-building

After agreeing with the FC and the local authorities on the sites for the ACM project, the CIFOR researchers undertook context studies. These studies were an important opportunity for both researchers and communities to share information, and develop their views on current resource issues. The context studies consisted of an ecological part and a socio-economic part. For the ecological surveys, the ecologists made an inventory of the resources (both grasses and trees) and their quantities present in the forest. The survey also assessed the rate of tree cutting in the forest for either timber or harvesting of honey. This information was later presented to the communities, in a report-back meeting organised by the CIFOR researchers. The socio-economic surveys were conducted by the social scientists (including the first author of this chapter) using participatory rural appraisal (PRA) techniques. They identified organisations working in the study sites, the type and location of resource extraction activities and problems faced by communities in collecting and utilising forest resources.

The social-economic context studies confirmed the differing views on the forest. Whereas the FC officer considered the forest as a fragile water catchment area that needed to be protected from human activity, the community members considered the forest as potential land for agriculture and settlement. But the study also showed that communities around the Mafungautsi forest were not homogenous groups of people. The communities were composed of groups who had different backgrounds and had settled in the area at different moments in time. These groups had different interests, perceptions and views concerning the role and use of the forest. Some community members saw the forest as land for cultivation and settlement, whereas others saw the forest as an area from which they could extract resources. Another group, those who had been removed from the forest by the FC in the early '60s and had re-settled on the eastern edge of the forest, still considered the forest as their ancestral home. Apart from the differing views on the forest, the context study showed that local community members were passive about resource management activities, and that they felt poorly represented in the Resource Sharing Project. In the Resource Sharing Project local Resource Management Committees had been formed by the FC, to act on behalf of the communities. These committees were responsible for overseeing the extraction of forest resources that community members were allowed to extract: honey, thatch and broom grass. The committees did so by selling permits for the extraction of limited, defined volumes of the resource and by patrolling the area. Community members claimed, however, that these committees were non-functional, embezzled incomes from the permits and gave themselves the best parts of the forest for harvesting grasses, while overexploitation of the forest, tree cutting and poaching continued. The top-down management approach by the FC, and unfulfilled promises in the RSP, disillusioned many local community members.

The ACM team recognised that these diverging views and interests would need to be addressed before collaboration among the different stakeholders could be expected. The ACM team decided to organise capacity-building interventions to set the stage for participatory action research, a key component of the ACM approach. Training was organised by the CIFOR team for members of the resource management committees and the traditional leadership authority in the form of workshops: a Training-for-Transformation workshop, a conflict resolution workshop and later a leadership training workshop. The workshops involved empowerment training, conflict resolution processes, leadership training. The conflict resolution workshops brought out conflicts that stakeholders had not talked about, such as the top-down organisation by the FC, and the illegal harvesting of resources outside of the Resource Sharing Project agreement by some community members, and the suspicion of embezzlement of money received for permits. By using scenarios and visioning tools to stimulate creative ways of thinking the workshops helped stakeholders break out of established patterns of assessing their situations (Wollenberg *et al.*, 2000). The capacity-building processes as well as the use of visioning for action planning made community members reflect on their situation and their mindset, imagine and describe future situations and define options for addressing their challenges. This resulted in particular community members standing up and speaking out, and stimulated exchange of views and knowledge (see Mutimukuru-Maravanyika, 2010). The training sessions opened up the community members and allowed the CIFOR team to start interesting them in participatory action research.

8.3.4 The formation of resource user groups

From the context studies the CIFOR team had learnt that not all community members were equally interested in all forest resources and issues. The team therefore decided to form groups with people who shared an interest in a particular resource. These groups would later engage in PAR. People were invited to form groups around thatch grass, broom grass and honey; these were the products that community members were allowed to harvest under the resource sharing project agreement. The CIFOR team made it explicit that the membership of the resource user groups was voluntary. Group members discussed the problems they faced, learned from each other about best harvesting practices, and found ways to add value to the harvested products, like in the case of the brooms (Box 8.3). The CIFOR team was responsible, during the early stages, of facilitating the PAR and were supported by the community partners. Many meetings were organised and community members spent a lot of time in resource management meetings and workshops during the 2001-2002 period. Initially, a huge number of people came to the resource user group meetings and participated in the early stages of the PAR process, maybe out of curiosity. Most people, however, dropped out as time went on and only a few people remained and participated in all stages of the research.

Box 8.3. The Machije experiment.

At the inception of the resource sharing project in 1994, in an effort to enhance learning together about sustainable harvesting of broom grass, community members in the Batanai area, on initiative from the Forestry Commission, had decided to conduct an experiment in Machije wetland (the area where Batanai RMC harvests broom grass). The experiment was conducted in two small plots staked out jointly by the broom grass resources users and the FC. In one of the plots, resource users harvested grass by digging. In the other plot they harvested the grass by cutting, using sickles. The stakeholders then monitored to see how the grass would grow in each of the plots. In the seasons that followed no new broom grass germinated in the plot where grass was harvested by digging. Instead, a new grass variety which could not be used for making brooms emerged. Stakeholders concluded that the best method for harvesting their grass was by cutting. For two years after the experiment, no one dug broom grass in Batanai RMC. However, after the two years, people resumed digging despite the fact that they knew about the negative impact. Having heard this, the ACM team decided to organize several meetings to share experiences and identify and plan for possible improvements. During these meetings with broom grass resource users, the team learned that several factors had contributed to the sudden return to the old harvesting methods. One of them was the continued market demand for 'dug brooms', i.e. brooms made from dug/uprooted grass. Customers alleged that uprooted brooms lasted longer than cut brooms because the grass did not loosen so easily. This made many of the Batanai residents return to the practice of digging the broom grass. One woman from the Batanai RMC (who according to the wealth ranking exercise was considered very poor) explained her experiences at one of the meetings:

> One day I went to Gokwe [Gokwe is about 15 km from Batanai] to sell my brooms which were a scotch cart load. When I arrived in Gokwe, all the customers rushed to see the brooms and all they were saying was, "*une magaro here? Une magaro here?*" which means "Are they dug brooms? Are they dug brooms?" Not even a single broom was bought when the people realised that I had cut brooms. I had to go back home all the way from Gokwe with all my brooms untouched. I was really pained from all the time and effort I had wasted.

The woman just ended by shaking her head and saying, '*Ah, zvinorwadza veduwe*' meaning 'Ah, it is very painful, I tell you.' Another woman had a similar experience which she shared with others as well:

> Last year, I also went to Gokwe with a scotch cart full of cut brooms and when I arrived, a group of customers asked me to bring my brooms since they wanted to buy them. I pushed my scotch cart to where the customers were standing and as they were looking at the brooms and putting aside the ones they wanted to purchase, another seller came by and started shouting that she had dug brooms. All the customers who were about to buy my brooms threw them back into the scotch cart and rushed to the newly arrived seller. We actually had a big fight, me and the newly arrived seller ended

8. Learning from learning

> up at Gokwe police station. I presented my case to the police and told them that the other woman was selling illegal brooms, since they were dug and not cut, and this was not allowed in our RMC. The police however dismissed the case and said that there was no such law written down. I finally left the police station angry and disappointed.
>
> After hearing these experiences, the people present decided they would do something about it. Their decisions included the following:
> - Everyone, including those who were not present at this meeting, should tell the RMC members whenever they see someone digging broom grass. The RMC members themselves could not be expected to be solely responsible for controlling: it was a voluntary job and they had to work in their fields as well.
> - Instead of giving resource harvesters permits before harvesting their grass, it was suggested that it would be better if the RMC members would give out permits after resource users had harvested their grass. This would enable the RMC members to inspect and check if the grass was harvested by cutting or digging.
> - In order to deal with the problem of the market preference for 'dug brooms', resource users suggested four options: (1) all broom grass harvesters (within and outside the Batanai RMC) to co-operate and only sell cut brooms. This would force consumers to buy cut brooms since these would be the only ones available on the market; (2) RMCs to negotiate with the Gokwe Rural District Council for a law to prohibit the sale of dug brooms. This would then force all broom grass collectors to cut instead of dig the grass; (3) broom grass harvesters to come up with new bundling methods that could make the cut grass brooms more beautiful and last longer. This would make customers prefer buying the cut brooms; and finally, (4) advertise the brooms so that customers would come to Batanai instead of the Batanai sellers taking the brooms elsewhere. This would give more opportunity for the RMC to inspect and check if all the sold brooms are cut brooms and not dug brooms.
> - Participants also suggested to organise a 'look and learn' workshop in which they would share their experiences with other RMCs around the forest. They could visit the plots in the forest and see for themselves.

Not long after the ACM project ended, the PAR processes that the resource users were engaged in stopped. Initially, the FC officer took over facilitation of the joint leaning processes when the CIFOR project ended in 2003. He had developed the skills and he had gained the trust and respect of community members, but he lacked the resources to operate at the level of the resource user groups. When the ACM project ended, community partners no longer received money and they also stopped facilitating learning processes in the communities. Initially the FC officer managed to facilitate the exchange of experiences at the RMC level for about two years with some financial support from CIFOR. However, these learning processes stopped after the FC officer died in October 2005.

8.3.5 The resource management committees

As mentioned in the introduction of this chapter, the resource management committees that were put in place by the FC under the RSP project to represent the community were not functional when the ACM project started. When the RMCs were formed, they received a constitution that was developed by the FC and was legalised by the Ministry of Youth, Gender and Employment Creation. This constitution (which was in English and not translated into the local language) gave the RMCs limited decision-making power as their decisions were subject to approval by the FC officer. The members of the RMCs were only accountable to the FC and following their constitution, they had no formal obligation to the existing traditional leadership authority and no mechanism of accountability to the rest of the community was included. This lack of downward accountability provided conditions for mistrust. Community members, for instance, were suspicious that the RMC members were embezzling the generated community funds. Meetings called by the RMCs were poorly attended because according to the local traditional leaders, they had no right to call the community to come for meetings.

At the start of the ACM project the CIFOR team concentrated on dealing with the key issues emerging from the context studies and the training workshops. It was not until 2002 that they paid more attention to improving the functioning of the RMCs and make them downwardly accountable. The CIFOR team and FC officer organised multiple meetings for the RMC and community members to discuss the issues of permits, embezzlements of funds, and other elements that had rendered the RMCs non-functional. It is in these meetings that the capacity-building of community members paid off. With the support of the FC officer they resolved conflicts, identified more functional mechanisms of monitoring, compensation for the people involved and permit handling. They also were able to organise regular meetings in which the RMC members gave an account of their work, thereby creating transparency and downward accountability (see Mutimukuru-Maravanyika, 2010). The FC officer continued with his support to the RMCs after the end of the ACM project as these were part of the RSP project. The officer however, died in October 2005.

The new officer had little knowledge of the ACM approach when he took over the office. Since 2003 a political and economic crisis had developed in Zimbabwe and this was also seriously affecting the area around Mafungautsi. Land invasion became politicised and many people continued to move and settle in the forest. They cleared forest areas for settlement and for agricultural fields. The new settlers appropriated resources in the forest areas by staking-out and fencing-off plots, and members from communities around the forest area could no longer access forest resources freely. The new settlers even set fees for the extraction of resources like broom grass from the staked-out fields. There were no sanctioning forces to stop the invasion of the settlers and protect the interests of the communities around the forest. Economic necessity made more and more people move into the forest. There was

8. Learning from learning

increased cutting down of live trees and poaching of wild game. It was therefore not surprising that the new FC officer focused on evicting the illegal settlers instead of facilitating learning.

8.4 Reflection on the experiences of the CIFOR team

The CIFOR team met several challenges in doing collaborative research in Mafungautsi. These are discussed below.

- *Working together as a multi-disciplinary team of researchers was not easy*. Even though both the social and natural scientists belonged to the ACM team, operations on the ground were conducted individually, with each group of scientists teaming up for their activities. This was mainly because individual researchers had their own personal contracts as members of the team and had to produce certain agreed upon outputs or publications. This sometimes made it difficult for the different researchers to see the big picture that their work was trying to achieve as each one struggled to meet his/her own promised outputs. In practice, the social scientists concentrated on facilitating the ACM interventions as well as the learning processes on the ground, whilst the ecologists focused on their own activities like conducting the ecological surveys using completely different methods to those being used by the social scientists. Also, when they went to the field together, because of their different beliefs and methodologies, this sometimes caused conflicts among the researchers. An example of conflicts that came about because of differences in methodology between disciplines is presented in Box 8.4.

  To overcome the challenge of the researchers working independently and losing sight of the big picture, the ACM team leader occasionally organised ACM meetings for the team members to update each other on their progress and findings. These were complimented by the annual writing retreats that were organised for the team members to work on their outputs, give each other feedback and co-author some publications together in which they tried to address the global ACM questions. This was helpful to a limited extent. For example, before her PhD studies, although she had some idea of how some elements of the research complimented each other, the first author of this chapter was still not clear on how all the various elements fitted together in the big picture.

- *Working with local communities sometimes involved going beyond the call of duty*. One example is the case of the community partner for Ndarire, one of the ACM research sites. One day when ACM team members visited him to get an update about what was happening in his area, they discovered that his child who was ill had passed away. When they saw the CIFOR researchers, elders in the community who were attending the funeral then asked them to help carry the corpse from Gokwe Business Centre to their village as they did not have transport to do so. They clearly stated that if the researchers did not assist them, the child would be buried at Gokwe Centre. This was an uncomfortable situation for the researchers and because they were working with the community partner and wanted to continue doing so, they felt obliged to do so. The researchers went back to Gokwe and sent the driver to ferry the corpse back to the village. Their work for that day had to be postponed.

> **Box 8.4. An example of problems encountered when working as a team.**
>
> ACM team members usually started their field trips by visiting the community partners in each of the research sites to get an overview of processes, developments, challenges and key activities taking place. One day during their visit at Batanai, they discovered that the community partner for Batanai, Mr. Lizwe Sibanda, was very ill and suffering from malaria. Mr Sibanda was no longer able to speak and had spent the past few days in bed. As they were seated in Mr Sibanda's hut talking to his wife, the ecologists suddenly asked the social scientists what CIFOR's policy was concerning sick employees. He went on to say that there was no option but for the CIFOR team to take the community partner to hospital so that he could get treatment. The two social scientists were shocked by this proposition and they excused themselves from the hut so as to deliberate on this issue on their own. When outside, one of the social scientists told the ecologist that from their point of view this was not the right way to handle this issue – they argued that it was wrong to impose their decision on the family by telling them what to do. They however agreed that if the wife had asked for the teams' help to take her husband to the hospital, then they were willing to help. The ecologist was angry and accused the social scientists of not being sympathetic to the person who was helping them to do their work. He went on to say that even if there was no policy from CIFOR to pay for a community partner who was ill, he would pay the bills from his own pocket. The social scientists later convinced the ecologist that at least they should ask for the opinion of Mr Sibanda's wife on what she wanted to do about her husband's illness. When they went back into the hut, Mrs Sibanda told the team that her husband was already receiving treatment from a local traditional healer and that if after this treatment, he did not get well, then she would probably ask them to take him to hospital. When the team members came to visit the community partner a few days later to check how he was doing, they found him up and about, and he was back to his normal self.

- *The turnover of staff at the FC made the collaboration process complicated.* The change in personnel from the FC at different levels (from management level to the field level) complicated the collaboration process between the FC and CIFOR. For instance, when top management personnel left, there was need to update the new recruits on what ACM was and what the project was trying to do. At the field level, when the first officer responsible for the project left, there was need for the new officer to be equipped with the ACM approach as well as updated about the project. The officer, however, passed away and the new officer who was appointed to take over had a different focus and he also passed away two years later.
- *How to keep community members interested in the process when tangible benefits are not yet realised.* When helping stakeholders to go through joint learning processes to solve their problems, it takes time for tangible benefits to be realised. Keeping local stakeholders interested in the process was therefore a challenge. In Mafungautsi, some people who came during the early stages of the learning processes dropped out later on, probably

because they did not see the benefit of participating in such processes. The ACM team, however, tried to deal with this challenge by asking resource users to start working on simple problems with simple answers. For instance, when broom grass resource users came up with a new bundling method for their grass, the newly bundled brooms sold at a higher price and this acted as an incentive for them to continue participating in the joint learning processes.
- *Working in a deteriorating socio-economic and political climate in the country made the work complex and difficult.* The ACM team members worked under the watchful eyes of local politicians and this made their work more difficult. Team members had to report to the ruling political party offices to notify them of their presence in Gokwe area each time they went to the field as a means to ensure their security. During training workshops, the team also had to strategically invite other government departments like the Central Intelligence Organisation (CIO) to grace the occasions and prevent suspicions that the researchers were involved in political activities. Failure to do so would have resulted in their workshops being mistaken for political functions, a move that would have endangered their lives. Also, because of the declining climate, more and more people who were key to some of the facilitated processes became mobile in their search for a living. This slowed down progress by the resource user groups. Community partners who used to also assist in facilitating joint learning processes also stopped doing so when they started participating in cross-boarder trading in search of a living.

8.5 Outcomes of the ACM project and follow-up study

The ACM project brought some improvements in the situation around the Mafungautsi forest. First, community members benefited from capacity-building (e.g. the Training for Transformation workshop). Otherwise marginalised community members, especially women, gained confidence and engaged in PAR to deal with some of the problems faced in the resource harvesting. The capacity-building workshops had also been instrumental in normalising the relationship between community members and the FC. Community members discussed and resolved hidden conflicts with the FC officer; they began to work together to try and solve some of their problems. For instance, the FC officers encouraged broom grass resource users to try a new bundling method for the brooms to enable sustainable harvesting methods for the grass (Box 8.3). The community also took its joint responsibility for managing the forest resources more seriously. Before the ACM project, only the resource management committee (RMC) members participated in the management of resources, but later members of resource user groups supported the RMC in this effort and also helped to impose management sanctions. The improved relations and mechanisms put in place allowed the community members to put pressure on their RMCs to be downwardly accountable.

The improved relations had a positive impact on the resource management practices. Community members also exchanged knowledge on the areas, amounts, location, quality of grass resources and harvesting methods (e.g. cutting broom grass instead of digging). Beekeepers began seriously to consider options to prevent the cutting down of hollow trees and reduce forest fires due to honey harvesting. The improved resource management also slightly increased the income of the community members from permits and the commercialisation of honey and broom grass. In Gababe the community even managed to build a house for one of the teachers from the money they had collected by selling permits. These examples of positive changes indicate that capacity-building and participatory action research did generate learning and supported collective action, as was the goal of the ACM approach.

However, a follow-up study over the four years after the project had ended showed that the improvements obtained through the joint learning were not sustained. As previously mentioned the participatory action research of the resource user groups stopped after the ACM project ended because community partners no longer received compensation. The deteriorating economic situation in the country was the reason why many people became mobile and turned to gold panning and cross-border trading to earn a living. Having become more effective in the management and monitoring of the forest resources, the Resource Management Committees went into a downward spiral when the FC commissioner passed away. It became clear that without the FC officer an important pressure, accountability, had disappeared. Thus the situation reverted to the way it was before: the communities became suspicious that RMC members were embezzling funds from selling permits. These issues were left unaddressed as the RMC members stopped reporting to their communities. Furthermore, the increase in the number of new invasions in the forest and its associated further deterioration were an important demotivation for the RMCs to function as the monitoring and sanctioning bodies. The request for support by the RMC members to the FC Forest Protection Unit could not be fulfilled because the FC lacked transport and other essential resources.

8.6 Why the positive outcomes were not sustained

Although a first assessment might lead to the conclusion that the deteriorating socio-economic and political climate in the country put an end to a beautiful initiative in its infancy, a critical analysis shows differently. Increased poverty and land scarcity as a consequence of the crisis in the country can easily be used to explain the invasion and deterioration of the forest and the collapse of what the ACM project had achieved. However, upon closer scrutiny, using a political ecology[11] and new institutionalism[12] perspective, shows the sustainability of the positive outcomes from the ACM project was highly unlikely, even if the subsequent crisis in Zimbabwe had been averted.

First, it is clear that in the conceptualisation phase, both in Bogor, Indonesia, and in Zimbabwe, there was an overestimation of what a research team could achieve in a period of three years. The team invested heavily in setting the stage for PAR with context studies and capacity building. The capacity-building in the form of workshops was necessary to develop positive relationships between the local community members and the FC: without mutual understanding, joint learning through PAR –the crucial backbone of the ACM approach – would not take off. The actual project was therefore far too short and ended when resource users were just beginning to implement their first action plans and before the crucial collaborative monitoring system was implemented. In addition, even after the three-year project period, some of the bigger conflicts still remained unaddressed.

Next to the realisation that realistic time-frames are needed for teams to engage with local people and develop local capacity, it is necessary to consider the complexity of issues of power and politics associated with change. The CIFOR team did little to respond to this issue, apart from engaging in some capacity-building with marginalised groups. People not interested in the forest resources were deliberately left out. The team assumed that building the capacity of interested stakeholders and marginalised groups through empowerment training would break their apparent passiveness and prepare them to step up and 'participate' in resource management activities effectively. The prevailing assumption of ACM team members was that these structural conflicts could be placed in abeyance. They expected that through participatory action research (PAR) process and learning together the tensions between FC and community members and between community members with differing backgrounds would dissolve, and that by gaining capacity and confidence they would succeed in tackling the bigger land issue in the area later. This is to assume (or imply) that 'participation' is such a powerful tool that it can serve as a counter-balance to sovereign power. At the very least, there is no real evidence, anywhere, that it enjoys such potent

---

[11] Political ecology describes empirical research-based explorations to explain linkages in the condition and changes in social and environmental systems with explicit consideration of relations of power. The research is directed at finding causes, rather than describing symptoms of problems. Political ecological research reveals winners, losers, hidden costs and differential power that produce social and environmental outcomes (Robbins, 1994).

[12] The New Institutionalists argue that credible commitment combined with mutual monitoring, under the protection of certain institutional arrangements, can motivate individuals to become more engaged in the realisation of shared goals and visions (Ostrom, 1990). Under this approach, individual decision-making is not only influenced by individual preferences and the optimisation of behaviour (as argued by many economists) but by institutional (i.e. group) preferences as well (Bates, 1995; Ostrom 1990).

properties. Belief in the power of participation to resolve the land issue seems in retrospect to be nothing more than wishful thinking. Several researchers (Chauveau and Richards, 2008; Kaimowitz and Shell, 2007; Logan and Moseley, 2002) have suggested that resource management initiatives will not succeed even in their most limited conservation aims if they shy away from analysis and resolution of fundamental societal conflicts. The assumptions underlying the ACM approach also aspire these thoughts.

All this means that initiatives like the ACM project have to include active lobbying for changes in the Forestry Act, allowing community members to harvest from the forest and legalise local governance mechanisms. At the local level, this would mean engaging the local government authorities, the Rural District Council, in developing legally binding by-laws that can be enforced with the help of law-enforcing agents like the police. Such changes are necessary to ensure that at the local level the community and local authority have the support to enforce regulatory frameworks. In the Mafungautsi forest, the community members had nothing to fall back on when the FC officer passed away and the general socio-economical conditions deteriorated. The CIFOR team in Zimbabwe had been trying to influence policy makers by reporting back to the FC officials in Harare, but a project duration of three years can hardly be expected to yield the necessary legal changes, even in a normally functioning country.

8.7 Concluding remarks

Doing collaborative action research with local community members is easier said than done and requires longer time-frames and huge financial and human resource investments. Learning-based participatory resource management projects must be given sufficiently long time frames, especially when external facilitating agents are involved. Long time-frames will enable facilitators to set up a solid base with more chance of enduring success when they finally pull out. There is also a need for adequate long-term financing (covering both pilot and continuation phases). This should also be coupled with appropriate investments in human resources. The learning-based approach to participation is both labour- and skills-intensive.

It is clear from the Mafungautsi forest experience that research teams engaging with local people to bring about change do need to integrate a range of skills and expertise. They need to include skills and expertise for facilitation of participatory processes as well as the broader understanding of societal change. These have to be complemented with specialist expertise on the natural resources involved, entrepreneurship or other development-oriented activities. From the experiences it can also be concluded that true engagement with local people and the systems in which they live can require researchers to be aware that there is an unequal distribution of power, schemes for participatory management of resources are likely to be captured by local elites, while marginalised groups continue to be sidelined. The experiences in Mafungautsi forest indicate that joint learning through action research may be a powerful strategy for building up the capacity of local people to rearrange the use of natural resources, share them more equally, and arrive at more sustainable management practices. However, learning-based approaches do not replace the need for change in power structures. One could consider that in the communities around the Mafungautsi forest a process of changing power structures was set in motion, which was most clearly evidenced by the improved accountability of the resource management committees. However, effective rules in place and means for enforcing them are indispensible.

Acknowledgements

This research was conducted as part of the Centre for International Forestry Research's (CIFOR) Adaptive collaborative management project in Zimbabwe. It was also part of the first author's PhD studies at Wageningen University in the Netherlands. The research was funded by: Rockefeller Foundation; the Centre for International Forestry Research (CIFOR) and its funding agencies (DFID, EU, and IUFRO).

References

Alpert, P., 1996. Integrated conservation and development projects. Bio-Science 46: 845-855.
Barrett, C.B. and P. Arcese, 1995. Are integrated conservation and development programmes sustainable? On the conservation of large mammals in sub-Saharan Africa? World Development 23: 1073-1085.
Bates, R.H., 1995. Social dilemmas and rational individuals: An assessment of the new institutionalism. In: J. Harriss Hunter and C.M. Lewis (eds.), The new institutional economics and third world development. Routledge, London, UK, pp. 27-48.
Bradley P.N. and K. McNamara (eds.), 1993. Living with trees: Policies for Forestry Management in Zimbabwe. World Bank Technical Paper 210. World Bank, Washington, DC, USA.
Chauveau, J.P. and P. Richards, 2008. West African insurgencies in agrarian perspectives: Cote d'Ivoire and Sierra Leone Compared. Wageningen University and Research Center Publications, Wageningen, the Netherlands.
Colfer, C.J.P. (ed.), 2005a The Equitable forest. Diversity, community and resource management. Resources for the Future, Washington, DC, USA.
Colfer, C.J.P., 2005b. The Complex Forest. Communities, uncertainty and adaptive collaborative management. Resource for the Future, Washington DC, USA.
Emerton, L., 2001. The nature of benefits and the benefits of nature. Why wildlife conservation has not economically benefited communities in Africa. In: D. Hulme and M. Murphree (eds.). African wildlife and livelihoods: the promise and performance of community conservation. James Currey, Oxford, UK, pp. 208-226.
Gibson, C.C. and S.A. Marks, 1995. Transforming rural hunters into conservationists: An assessment of community-based wildlife management programmed in Africa. World Development 23: 941-957.

Hartanto, H., M.C. Lorenzo Valmores, C. Arda-Minas, E.M. Burton and R. Prabhu, 2003. Learning together: Responding to change and complexity to improve community forests in the Philippines. CIFOR, Bogor, Indonesia.

Kaimowitz, D. and D. Shell, 2007. Conserving what and for whom? Why conservation should help meet basic human needs in the tropics. Biotropica 39: 567-574.

Kiss, A., 1990. Living with wildlife: Wildlife Resource Management with local participation in Africa. Technical Paper No. 130. World Bank, Washington, DC, USA.

Kramer, R.A. and C.P. Van Schaik, 1997. Preservation paradigms and tropical rain forests. In: R.A. Kramer, C.P. van Schaik and J. Johnson (eds.), The last stand. Protected areas and the defence of tropical biodiversity. Oxford University Press, New York, NY, USA, pp. 3-14.

Kusumanto, T., L.E. Yuliarni, Y. Macoun and H. Adnan, 2005. Learning to adapt: Managing forests together in Indonesia. Center for International Forestry Research, Bogor, Indonesia.

Logan, B.I. and W.G. Moseley, 2002. The political ecology of poverty alleviation in Zimbabwe's Communal Areas Management Programme for Indigenous Resources (CAMPFIRE). Geoforum 33: 1-14.

Matose, F., 2002. Local people and reserved forests in Zimbabwe. What prospects for community development. PhD Thesis, Sussex University, Brighton.

Mutimukuru-Maravanyika, T., 2010. Can we learn our way to sustainable management? Adaptive Collaborative Management in Mafungautsi State Forest, Zimbabwe. PhD Thesis Wageningen University.

Nhira, C., S. Baker, P. Gondo, J.J. Mangono and C. Marunda, 1998. Contesting Inequality in Access to Forests. Zimbabwe Country study, Policy that works for forests and people series, no. 5. CASS, Forestry Commission, Harare, Zimbabwe and IIED, UK.

Oates, J.F., 1995. The dangers of conservation by rural development. A case study from the forests of Nigeria. Oryx 29: 115-122.

Ostrom, E., 1990. Governing the commons: The evolution of institutions for collective action. Cambridge University Press, Cambridge, UK.

Prabhu, R. and F. Matose, 2008. Adversity and the adaptive possibility of local communities: Setting the scene. In: A. Mandondo, R. Prabhu and F. Matose (eds.). Coping Amidst Chaos. Studies on adaptive collaborative management from Zimbabwe. Resources for the Future (RFF), Washington, DC, USA, pp. 15-64.

Prabhu, R., 2003. Developing Collaborative Monitoring for Adaptive Co-Management of Tropical African Forests Final Technical Report for the Period: January 1, 2000- December 31, 2002.

Prabhu, R., C. McDougall and R. Fisher, 2007. Adaptive collaborative management: a conceptual model. In: R. Fisher, R. Prabhu and C. McDougall (eds.), Adaptive collaborative management of community forests in Asia: experiences from Nepal, Indonesia and the Philippines. Center for International Forestry Research (CIFOR), Bogor, Indonesia, pp. 16-49.

Robbins, P., 1994. Political Ecology. Blackwell publishing, Oxford, UK.

Terborgh, J., 1999. The requiem for nature. Island Press, Washington, DC, USA.

Thomas, S.J., 1993. Indigenous woodlands and CAMPFIRE: Complementarities from collaboration. In: G.D. Piearce and D. Gumbo (eds.), Ecology and the Management of Indigenous Forests: Proceedings of an International Symposium held in Victoria Falls, Zimbabwe, July, 1993. Forestry Commission and SAREC Harare, Zimbabwe.

Wells, M., K. Brandon and L. Hannah, 1992. People and Parks: Linking Protected area management with local communities. World Bank, Washington, DC, USA.

Wickramasinghe, A., 1994. Deforestation, women and forestry: The case of Sri Lanka. International Books, Utrecht, the Netherlands.

Wilshusen, P.R., S.R. Brechin, C.L. Fortwrangler and P.C. West, 2002. Reinventing the square wheel: Critique of a resurgent 'protection paradigm' in international biodiversity conservation. Society and Natural Resources 15: 17-40.

Wollenberg, E., D. Edmunds and J. Anderson, 2000 Anticipating change: Scenarios as a tool for adaptive forest management: A guide. Centre for International Forestry Research, Bogor, Indonesia.

9. Northern Thailand case: gaming and simulation for co-learning and collective action; companion modelling for collaborative landscape management between herders and foresters

Pongchai Dumrongrojwatthana and Guy Trébuil

Abstract

Land-use conflicts between villagers and government agencies are common under the current decentralisation of resource management in Northern Thailand. They are frequently due to deep differences in interests, objectives and perceptions of the landscape resources to be managed and their use. As the complexity of the problems to be tackled increases, there is a need to design and test effective integrated, inclusive and adaptive methods fostering the co-management of the land to improve both ecological viability and social equity. Such methods should facilitate communication and the sharing of knowledge and viewpoints leading to mutual understanding, improved trust, and the design of workable co-management plans. Companion Modelling (ComMod) is a highly interactive gaming and simulation approach relying on multi-agent systems used to better understand a complex system through the co-design and joint use of different kinds of simulation models with the field actors concerned. The co-construction of a shared representation of the issue, followed by its use to simulate and assess future scenarios, facilitates multiple stakeholders' co-ordination and negotiation processes. The presentation of ComMod main theoretical references and key methodological principles is used to characterise the original posture of the practitioner who is seen as a category of stakeholder among others. This leads to a specific type of relationship with the models developed, and the local stakeholders. The operationalisation of ComMod in a process to mitigate a land-use conflict between livestock herders and foresters in a highland village is described. Its results, ranging from fostering mutual understanding to the joint design of concrete collective action, are discussed. Based on the lessons from this case study, an analysis of the strong (trans-disciplinary knowledge integration, empowerment of marginal farmers, flexibility of the approach and its simulation tools) and weak (special skills required, local facilitation and process ownership, use in multi-level processes) points of this collaborative modelling approach is proposed.

9.1 Context and changing role of collaborative landscape research in Northern Thailand

The sustainable management of renewable resources at the landscape level involves not only bio-physical dimensions but also the social, economic, cultural and political aspects. The search for improved landscape management is often complicated by the diversity and heterogeneity of the interconnected ecological and socio-economic systems. The fact that the diversity of stakeholders concerned with the collective management of landscape resources and environmental problems is also increasing is adding to the complexity of this task. The dynamics of interactions among such diverse factors at multiple social levels and spatial scales frequently leads to highly complex, non-linear and divergent processes and the emergence of unpredictable new phenomena (Liu *et al.*, 2007; Van Paassen *et al.*, 2008). As change accelerates and uncertainty increases, there is a need to opt for trans-disciplinary research approaches and methodologies to support truly adaptive, inclusive and integrated management of landscapes (Berkes and Folke, 1998).

The decentralisation of local resource management in Thailand started in the early nineties, particularly with the establishment of local administrative bodies called 'Tambon' (sub-district) administrative organisations (TAO). The remote mountainous areas of the Northern region are mainly populated by historically mobile and diverse non-Thai ethnic minority groups who practised the 'art of not being governed' (Scott, 2009) for many decades. Nowadays, differences in interest, objectives, strategies, practices and perceptions on how the forest-farmland interface should be managed leads to frequent land-use conflicts between these highlanders, administrative managers and technical government agencies, especially in headwater and forest conservation areas. During the last two decades, landscape management research, has used geographic information systems and decision support systems approaches for spatial planning, but the role of the local stakeholders was usually limited to the provision of information and consultative participation. More recently a few participatory resource management projects provided the local stakeholders with opportunities to share their different types of knowledge and points of view on issues of common interest. They improve their mutual understanding, and jointly design workable landscape management plans. But, there is still a need for innovative, integrative, inclusive and adaptive approaches for landscape management. Such processes should contribute to improve the ecological viability and social equity in this fragile highland socio-ecosystem by involving the diversity of concerned stakeholders as partners collaborating on an equal footing.

This chapter describes and discusses the implementation and main findings of a collaborative gaming and simulation process relying on the Companion Modelling (ComMod) approach. Its main goal was to mitigate a conflict over the access to grazing land between local herders and forest conservation agencies in a Hmong village located in an upper watershed of Nan province. This process was guided by an interdisciplinary research team based at the Department of Biology of Chulalongkorn University. It was initiated at the request of officials from the recently established Nanthaburi National Park (NNP) who took part in a similar collaborative modelling experiment conducted on a similar topic one year earlier at a nearby site (Barnaud *et al.*, 2008; Ruankaew *et al.*, 2010). The intended outcome of this collaborative landscape research was better co-ordination among the local farmers, foresters and park rangers for the co-management of the forest-farmland interface.

Following the presentation of the theoretical inspirations of the ComMod approach and the scientific posture of its practitioners, its main methodological principles and key tools are introduced. Then the collaborative landscape modelling process implemented in Doi Tiew village of Tha Wang Pha district, Nan province, is described. The subsequent section discusses the main findings regarding the production of knowledge, the influence of research and scientists on the other stakeholders taking part in the process, and the effects, especially learning ones, and impacts of this collaborative landscape research within the studied context.

9.2 Collaborative companion modelling for landscape management: theoretical perspectives and applied research methodology

In the fast growing family of collaborative modelling approaches, Companion Modelling (ComMod, http://www.commod.org) for renewable resource management is used by researchers and local stakeholders to design and implement highly interactive and inclusive modelling and simulation processes. They are designed to facilitate communication in multi-stakeholders platforms, to co-construct shared representations of given complex issues at stake, and to use them to explore possible solutions through the simulation of future scenarios (ComMod group, 2003). Two complementary general objectives of ComMod processes are (1) to better understand a complex socio-ecological systems (SES) through the collaborative construction and joint use of different types of gaming or/and computer simulation models integrating stakeholders' diversity of knowledge and points of view, and (2) to use these models within platforms for collective learning and to facilitate stakeholders' co-ordination and negotiation mechanisms leading to the definition of collective action plans.

9.2.1 Key theoretical references

The ComMod approach did not emerge in the late nineties from theoretical debates among researchers involved in renewable resource management, but from the fact that they were facing common problems in the implementation of empirical research on complex objects of study. Because the back and forth process between theory and practice, between the laboratory and the field, is a key characteristic of this approach, the dialogue between its practitioners and several relevant schools of thought has been intensified in the past decade and with the implementation of many case studies. Below are descriptions of the main theoretical inspirations and perspective adopted by ComMod practitioners as described in a recent collective publication (Collectif ComMod, 2009).

Drawing on the science of complexity, ComMod considers socio-ecological systems (SES) as complex systems characterised by unpredictable behaviour and that are driven by successive temporary organisations framed by local interactions (Langton, 1992). Of particular interest is the analysis and interpretation of the emergence of properties at the whole system level, which cannot be understood through the observation of its individual components, but that result from interactions. This concept of emergence supports the choice made by the ComMod approach to facilitate the exchange of points of view, the integration of knowledge from various disciplines and sources (empirical, technical, expert, scientific, institutional), and a focus on interactions at the interface between biophysical and social dynamics. Complex SES, such as the spatially heterogeneous and highly variable fragile highland agro-ecosystems of Northern Thailand, are evolving continuously, in an unstable and uncertain environment, and their behaviour cannot be predicted. These characteristics have major implications on the design of ComMod processes operating iteratively, with an evolving focus in each of the successive cycles of collaborative activities depending on the process dynamics crafted step by step by the participants. They also influence the methodological choice of an agent-based modelling approach because of its openness and flexibility. Such characteristics are important for reaching an improved collective understanding of the system and for identifying the key interactions determining its functioning. Later on, the effects of these interactions can be explored in simulations run with the stakeholders to discuss how to drive the system towards a more desired state.

The concepts of resilience and adaptive management also underline the need for a better collective understanding of how the SES works as a way to improve the adaptive capacity of the stakeholders. It is also a necessary step towards the improvement of key properties like self-regulation and self-organisation. Recent definitions of these key concepts insist on the importance of interactive learning (Holling, 2001). Adaptive management of a SES implies flexibility, diversity, and redundancy in regulation and monitoring activities, leading to corrective responses and experiential probing of the ever-changing circumstances. The adaptive capacity of stakeholders is dependent on knowledge, its generation and free interchange, the ability to recognise points of intervention and to construct a bank of options to improve resource management. A ComMod process is a kind of communication and co-ordination platform to stimulate interactions among stakeholders for the generation and interchange of knowledge. This social process improves mutual understanding and creates new kinds of interactions facilitating the co-management of resources. Co-management is defined as a partnership in which local communities, resource users, government agencies, non-government organisations, and other stakeholders share the authority and responsibility over the management of a territory or set of resources. Many ComMod processes aim at setting up such co-management mechanisms (this is the case in the application presented below) and some of them may also lead to the devolution of decision-making power over resource management.

ComMod also relates to theories about collective action and the collective management of common resources and public goods (Ostrom *et al.*, 1994). The link with game theory to create institutional settings favourable to sustainable resource management is of special interest. Sustainable resource management requires agreed-upon but evolving access rules defined and enforced by the users. Trust, social capital, and the relations with institutions at higher levels in the social organisation play important roles in their creation (Ostrom, 2005). This is the reason why ComMod researchers use gaming to explore possible co-ordination and negotiation mechanisms among heterogeneous stakeholders. These games are collective learning processes taking place amongst social networks. Through the games, stakeholders experiment with different management and co-ordination options, so that acceptable solutions can emerge. Previous ComMod processes carried out in the Thai context demonstrated the usefulness of role-playing games used as simulators with the concerned stakeholders to represent the ecological and social dynamics linked to concrete collective problems. In particular, they create a non-threatening atmosphere adapted to the local cultural context (Bousquet *et al.*, 2005a).

The ComMod approach also borrows from the constructivist epistemology when it tries to make explicit and share the different stakeholders' points of view and representations of the system. Reality is multiple, uncertain and subjective as it depends on one's personal experiences, objectives, and interest. Heterogeneous stakeholders perceive a common resource management problem differently; they refer to different kinds of knowledge, values and interests. Stakeholders' actions depend on their perceptions of their (ecological and social) environment, and these different (and partial) contradictory perceptions are frequently at the origin of misunderstandings and conflicts (Röling *et al.*, 1998). To enable stakeholders to modify and align their perceptions, ComMod processes put much emphasis on experiential or discovery learning to facilitate the emergence of a shared collective vision (Röling, 2002).

Post-normal science attaches more importance to the improvement of the collective decision-making process than to the substance of the decision itself (Funtowicz and Ravetz, 1993). The ComMod approach adopts such a posture because of the high level of complexity and uncertainty of biophysical and human behaviour related to resource management. Researchers in the field of post-normal science consider that people construct their own realities through learning during social processes. Hard sciences can show that the landscape management of a given SES is leading to degradation. But the correction for sustainable land use depends on the outcome of human interactions leading to learning, conflict resolution, agreement, and collective action. The role of interdisciplinary teams including biophysical and social scientists is to facilitate, understand and strengthen collective decision-making processes through platforms of interactions. This also explains the importance ComMod practitioners attach to inclusive processes that associate stakeholders with diverse values, perceptions and interest with the aim of a shared representation of the system and the desired management. Specific tools are used to co-construct such a shared representation and the models used in ComMod processes are boundary objects facilitating knowledge integration and exchange to foster mutual understanding, joint learning and the emergence of new ideas among the participants (Carlile, 2002; Vinck, 1999).

From the patrimonial[13] mediation theory of co-management (Ollagnon, 1989), ComMod learned to pay attention to a prospective analysis of the long-term system evolution and the usefulness of scenario explorations for building consensus and agreement about joint goals. A patrimonial representation of the landscape links past, present, and future generations of users and managers; focuses on the owner's obligations rather than his/her rights; and promotes a common vision of landscape sustainability. Mediation is a negotiation approach in which a neutral party facilitates mutual understanding and agreement among different parties in conflict. The view of each party about the issues at stake are made explicit for the others to understand. When people agree on a shared conception of the present situation and how it will evolve, stakeholders are able to define long-term objectives. Then scenarios enabling these objectives to be reached can be collectively identified, simulated and assessed.

9.2.2 Adequacy of ComMod approach and methodology for the specific case

The ComMod approach, and its underlying theory, seemed useful for dealing with several key characteristics of the case in question. There was a need to bridge the gaps, as there was a complete lack of dialogue about the management of the forest – farmland interface: the Hmong farmers cherished their empirical experience of vegetation dynamics and livestock production; the foresters cherished their technical knowledge of forest regeneration, and the university team valued their scientific knowledge about local vegetative biomass dynamics. At the start of the ComMod process, it was important to 'level the playing field', because the herders lacked formal education and there was a language barrier. The herders first needed to know what collaborative modelling was about, to raise their interest and willingness to participate. Furthermore, it was critical to create trust, because there was a deep mutual distrust between the villagers on one side and the foresters and rangers on the other.

Following the recent establishment of agencies in charge of reversing the trend of decreasing forest cover, there was an urgent need for both parties to envision a future agro-ecosystem landscape allowing better relationships between forest conservation and livestock rearing activities.

9.2.3 Key methodological principles and key tools

The scientific posture of the ComMod researcher creates an original relationship between him, the models developed collaboratively, and the field actors and circumstances. Because he/she does not consider him/herself as a neutral outsider but as part of the system under study and to be managed collectively, the ComMod practitioner is involved in an engaged research process. Being an actor in the collaborative modelling process, the ComMod practitioner brings his own knowledge and point of view, while facilitating exchanges

---

[13] Patrimonial is defined by Ollagnon as 'all the material and non-material elements that work together to maintain and develop the identity and autonomy of their holder in time and space through adaptation in a changing environment'.

9. Northern Thailand case

among the participants. The researcher's perception and representation of the system are presented to the participants to be criticised and improved, because the local stakeholders are firmly in the driving seat to stir the process in their preferred direction. Because of this dual role of researcher cum facilitator, ethical issues related to such a posture led the ComMod network of practitioners to define a code of practice (ComMod group, 2003). In particular, this charter recommends the systematic and continuous monitoring of the effects and impacts of ComMod interventions. Full transparency in the use of hypotheses should also be ensured. They should be explicit to other stakeholders and questioned along the collaborative modelling and simulation process.

Figure 9.1 shows a ComMod process usually consisting of several successive and self-reinforcing cycles of analysis (problem analysis), modelling (design and construction of a simulation tool) and field work (specific surveys to fill knowledge gaps, participatory workshops that comprise gaming sessions and/or participatory simulations, plenary debates, individual interviews, definition of the next steps, etc.). This process evolves in an iterative manner.

At the end of each cycle, the conceptual model representing the system under study is revised, as well as the research hypotheses. This succession of collaborative modelling and simulation activities organised in cycles focusing on different key questions, depending on the evolution of the participants' interest, is a fundamental characteristic of a ComMod process (Ruankaew, 2010). The arena of participating stakeholders can evolve from one cycle to the next, depending on the selected focus and on the needs and decisions made by the

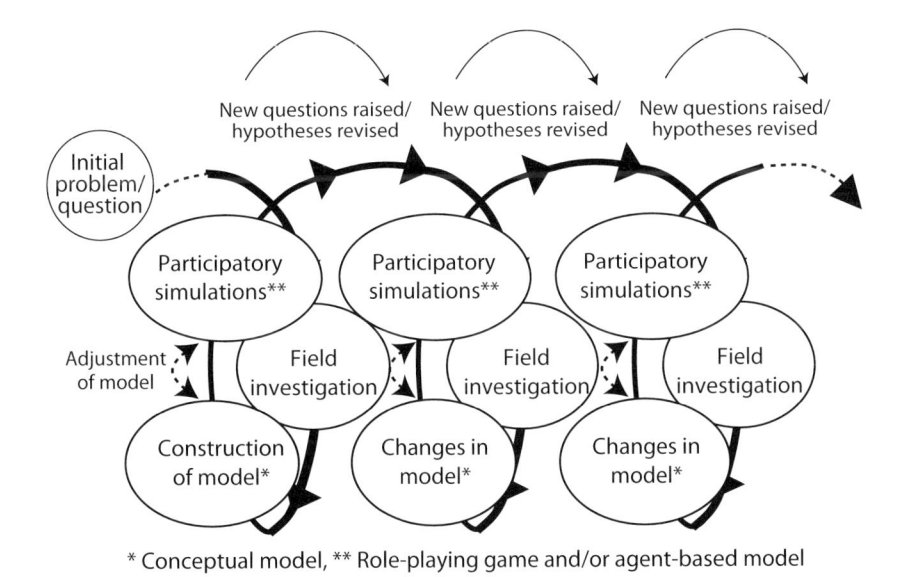

Figure 9.1. The iterative phases of a ComMod process (adapted from Barnaud et al., 2008).

local actors. When the empowerment of 'voiceless' marginal stakeholders is a priority (like in the case study presented below), it takes villagers one or two ComMod cycles before they feel confident enough to invite decision-makers from higher levels in the social hierarchy to join the process.

Multi-agent systems (MAS) is the modelling framework used in ComMod processes because of its suitability in representing SES in a very intuitive way and its capacity to integrate knowledge of a different nature and source in a very open and flexible way (Bousquet *et al.*, 1999, 2005b). In most ComMod processes, the co-design of a conceptual model to synthesise the relevant knowledge on the issue at stake leads to the construction of a role-playing game (RPG). The RPG is used to submit the conceptual model to the local stakeholders and enables scientists to acquire more knowledge from them about the present dynamics and to stimulate exchanges. Several versions of this tool can be used depending on the process dynamics and the evolution of the stakeholders' main interest. Later on, the ultimate version of the RPG validated by the actors is converted into a computer agent-based model (ABM). Having played with the RPG, the participants understand this ABM 'playing the game' that allows far more time and cost-efficient simulations of scenarios selected by the participants, leaving much time to assess their results. This is how ComMod processes make use of the synergy between RPGs and ABMs. Various modes of association of these key tools are found on a case-by-case basis (Bousquet and Trébuil, 2005) and each of these two modelling and simulation tools can help in the construction and improvement of the other.

These simulation tools are used to facilitate individual and collective learning about the present situation, and to run scenario explorations as a way to mediate conflicts and engage people in defining suitable co-ordination mechanisms and negotiating collective action. Therefore, ComMod models are mainly seen as short-term tools. They are mainly built to facilitate communication and sharing of viewpoints and perceptions among stakeholders. Computer enhanced modelling tools are used for interactive learning, but not to predict the state or to pilot the system under study (Bousquet *et al.*, 2007).

9.2.4 Main phases of ComMod methodology and application to the case

The ComMod approach proposes broad methodological principles and flexible tools but does not impose any rigid set of procedures to be strictly followed. This is in agreement with the principle of adaptive management seen as a social process taking into account the specificities of a given set of stakeholder arena and biophysical environment at a given time. Depending on the issue to be examined and the process dynamics, the research team can mobilise the set of tools in the most appropriate and adaptive way. Usually, the following main phases of a ComMod process can be distinguished, even if they do not need to be strictly implemented in succession, especially following the completion of a first cycle.

Initialisation

A ComMod process usually starts from a request made by local stakeholder(s) to a research team to examine a concrete collective resource management problem and to search ways to mitigate it. At this early stage of the mediation approach, it is necessary to make the initial situation explicit to all concerned. The stakeholders need to be clearly informed about the issue at stake and about their interdependence in the search for a solution. A preliminary diagnostic-analysis focuses on the actors involved (their interest, strategy, decision-making and practices), the resource(s) to be managed and it/their own dynamics, and the key human-environment interactions to be represented in the models. Agrarian system diagnosis, stakeholder and institutional analyses, are examples of valuable tools used at this stage. A key challenge in this initial phase is to enable the stakeholders to express their perceptions of the present situation and of its evolution. This leads to the characterisation of the diversity of points of view among the stakeholders at the start of the process, all of them being considered as legitimate and subjective (Barnaud *et al.*, 2008). This diversity of perceptions and viewpoints can be mobilised to let the stakeholders discuss the acceptance of the continuation of the current trends. It is also at this stage that the process facilitator decides, in consultation with the local stakeholders, who will be invited to participate in the first set of gaming and simulation activities. Depending on the choice made, public awareness and sensitising activities may be necessary to level the initial playing field and to deal, for example, with information and power asymmetries. This is because the facilitation of a ComMod process is not a neutral exercise as, for example, a process can be launched and designed to help marginalised and voiceless people to have their say in the decision-making process about resource use.

The Doi Tiew ComMod process was initiated by a request from the rangers from the NNP who, after taking part in a similar process held on a similar issue at a neighbouring site, wanted to examine the problem of cattle roaming in the newly established national park. The initial multi-scale diagnostic study combined an analysis of land-use change in the area based on remote sensed imagery backed by stakeholders' interviews, a characterisation of the different types of farms in the village in relation to livestock rearing, and an ecological survey on how grazing could influence the dynamics of the above-ground plant biomass (Dumrongrojwatthana, 2010). The main social aspects analysed in this preliminary diagnosis were the socio-economic heterogeneity of the herder community and the strategies and practices of the two main forest conservation agencies working in this area: the Nam Khang reforestation unit (NKU) of the Royal Forestry Department (RFD) and the NNP. The findings from the ecological survey were submitted to these herders and foresters as a first game based on a vegetation state transition model proposed by the researchers. Pictograms representing the main types of vegetative cover in the area were proposed and had to be ordered to create different successions of vegetative states depending on what human interference with natural dynamics was involved (cattle grazing, bush fire, tree plantations, etc.). This first version was enriched through the addition of relevant missing vegetation states, and validated with a group of five herders and four NKU foresters. The exercise was used to gather more empirical knowledge from the herders and foresters on the effects of cattle rearing on forest regeneration and to make them aware of gaming and simulation techniques (Dumrongrojwatthana *et al.*, 2009). It ended with an agreement on a list of diverse vegetation states to be taken into account, their dynamics and relationships. This shared understanding of vegetation transitions became the core ecological module in the construction of the gaming and simulation tools. Based on this conceptual model of vegetation dynamics, the spatial representation and gaming rules of the first version of a RPG were crafted.

Following these activities, a selection of different types of herders (based on the role and relative importance of this activity on their farms) and NKU foresters (the unit leader and several of his assistants) were invited to participate in the co-design of models to improve their relevance and, hopefully, their use by simulating scenarios of their choice. The NNP rangers were not invited because their leader maintained very tense relations with the Hmong herders by insisting only on the need to keep the herds outside the park. But several young NNP rangers participated in the second field workshop to play their own role. More flexibility was expressed by the NKU foresters. While they complained about the negative effects of cattle roaming in their tree plantations, they were open to a dialogue with the Hmong herders who considered that cattle grazing had mainly positive effects on tree growth and forest regeneration.

Co-design of models and simulation tools between researchers and local stakeholders

Model conceptualisation precedes the construction and use of a first RPG, to be followed by new versions integrating the modifications requested by the stakeholders, or focusing on different questions depending on the evolution of their interest. Throughout the process, the implementation of computer ABMs similar to the RPGs can be used to run simulations in a time- and cost-efficient way when needed. The model conceptualisation phase is a collaborative trans-disciplinary endeavour carried out through discussions, reviews of existing knowledge from various sources, and specific surveys to fill knowledge gaps. Among other possible knowledge elicitation tools, the use of the diagrammatic unified modelling language (UML) is very useful for encouraging the participants to be precise when exchanging their arguments. It also provides successive concrete outcomes and formal representations of the model taking shape gradually. These diagrammatic outcomes make it easier for the MAS modeller to implement the model under a simulation platform. Later on, these outputs also facilitate the verification of the model to check whether the implemented version is a true representation of the conceptual model. In the construction, simplifications are made, but the hypotheses related to them must be explicit, especially when scenarios are planned to be simulated with this tool at a later stage.

In the Doi Tiew case, the choice was made to build a computer-assisted RPG (cRPG) and to use it as the main simulation tool. The design of the cRPG integrated the updating of vegetation states at the virtual landscape level by the computer depending on the players' actions (selection of plots for tree plantation, delimitation of paddocks, grazing intensity in each paddock, etc.). This choice was made to maintain a gaming atmosphere without long breaks in a session. It was tested with bachelor students to improve its calibration before its use with the local stakeholders. From one ComMod cycle to the next, the cRPG evolved progressively to fit the changing main interest of the stakeholders as shown in Figure 9.2. From one version to the next, more rules were also operated by the computer following their validation in the previous gaming sessions (dynamics of cattle population, cattle losses, etc.). Its gradual development paved the way towards the final production of a fully autonomous ABM allowing time and cost-efficient simulation of land-use scenarios related to different landscape management strategies (Dumrongrojwatthana, 2010).

Implementation and validation of ComMod models

On the basis of the initial conceptual model, the RPGs or/and ABMs are implemented during this phase. Later on, they are used as boundary simulation tools in gaming or/and participatory simulations sessions with the local stakeholders. The use of RPGs precedes the introduction of an ABM replaying the game *in silico*. This is to ensure that the local stakeholders understand the components and rules of these simple models to minimise the well-known 'black box effect'. Stakeholders are invited to take part in gaming sessions in order for them:
- to understand the proposed model and relate it to their actual circumstances;
- to propose modifications or validate them after examining the individual behaviour of agents and the properties of the whole system emerging from their interactions;
- to be able to understand and follow ABM simulations run on the computer, and identify scenarios of interest to be simulated and collectively assessed.

No suitable general theory for the validation of such models exists. Therefore, special attention is paid to their validation by the local experts and end users. The co-design of the baseline conceptual model and the use of RPGs to help validate MAS models are important steps in this process of social validation. In the Doi Tiew case study, the three successive field workshops organised at the site were partly dedicated to the validation by the main types of local stakeholders of the successive versions of the cRPG tool.

Scenario identification, exploration and assessment

During the field workshops, the participants take part in iterative investigations in real and virtual worlds that stimulate their creativity. Along the process, they analyse the results of the simulations and identify, discuss and select scenarios of landscape management to be simulated to explore possible futures. This is where, compared to RPGs, ABMs are powerful

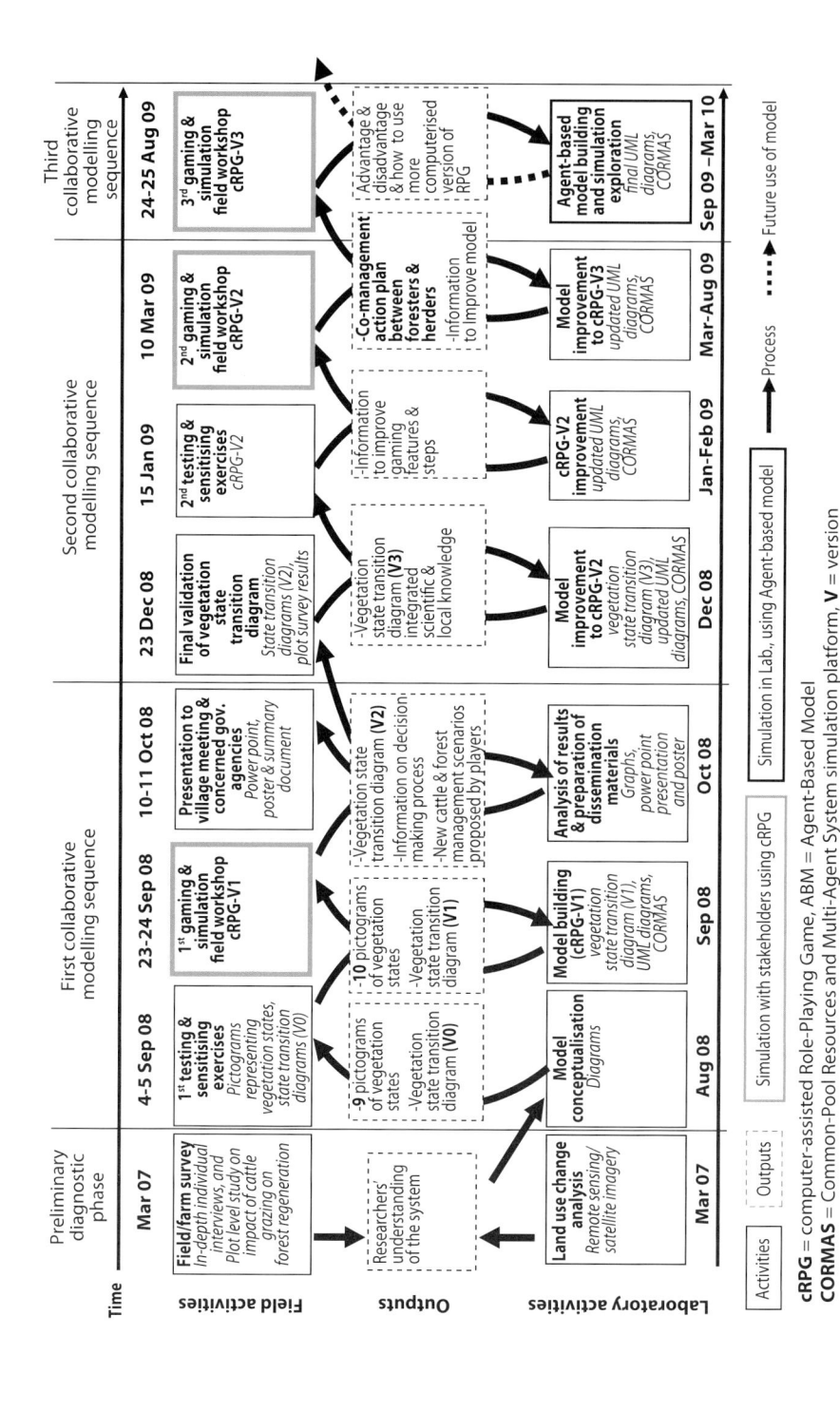

Figure 9.2. Overview of the successive phases of the ComMod process implemented in Doi Tiew village of Nan Province, Northern Thailand, 2007-2009.

for running such simulations rapidly, leaving much time for the discussion of their results. These results are usually presented by using social and ecological indicators previously identified with the stakeholders. In other applications, they can display the different points of view among the stakeholders on the evolution of the system to be managed collectively. Scenario exploration activities are held either in plenary sessions, or within small and more homogenous groups of stakeholders. This depends on what is the best way to promote the most inclusive assessment of the simulation results. Very often, this phase generates new knowledge and questions feeding the preparation of a new ComMod cycle.

In Doi Tiew, the simulations were organised either in plenary sessions or with the herders only. In this second case, at the start of the process, the objective was to familiarise them with the simulation tool and to build up their confidence before playing with the foresters, while in the third cycle the goal was to train more herders in the use of the simulation tool with the help of the former players. By the end of the first field workshop, a scenario of common interest to the herders and NKU foresters was selected. The gaming sessions demonstrated that the establishment of the NNP and the continuation of the current tree plantation and cattle grazing practices were leading to a rapid decrease in grassland areas in the landscape. The herders proposed introducing artificial pastures and the NKU forest unit proposed conducting a joint experiment on a fenced 10 ha plot of their land. The second version of the cRPG simulator integrated this technical innovation and its use showed the herders that a collective management of their herds would allow them to maximise the benefits of cattle grazing in fenced sown pastures. At this stage, district officials were invited to take part in the process and the livestock officer offered to provide *Bracharia ruziziensis* seeds for this experiment. Another administrative officer was also invited by the herders to witness the negotiation of this joint action and its implementation because their trust in the foresters' commitment was still limited.

Monitoring and evaluation of the process effects and impact

There is no suitable monitoring and evaluation methodology for organising a critical and reflexive assessment of such a highly interactive modelling process. But suitable procedures are needed to analyse its different (immediate and longer term, direct and indirect) effects and impacts at individual and collective levels. Recently, a specific reflexive and critical monitoring and evaluation system was published by Jones *et al.* (2009) to be used separately with the designer of the ComMod process and the other participants. This methodology looks at the effects generated by the process in terms of learning about the system, about oneself, the others and the interdependency, the ecological and social dynamics. It also monitors the change in communication (within and between social networks), perceptions, decision-making, behaviour, and finally individual farm practices and collective action. Continuous monitoring is needed to keep track of the process dynamics because much is happening in the field between formal events such as participatory gaming and simulation workshops. A critical assessment of the process is needed at end of each cycle. To organise such activities in a systematic way, a logbook is used to closely monitor the process.

The version used in the Doi Tiew case study comprises three types of documents: (1) an Excel file, providing a chronological account of all the activities related to the implementation of the ComMod process, together with a listing characterising its participants; (2) a set of activity reports, accessible from the master Excel file; and (3) a set of additional documents such as interviews, recorded gaming or simulation sessions, etc. The logbook is filled in every week during the implementation of the ComMod process. The master Excel file provides macro functions allowing automatic statistical treatments of the information. Of particular interest is the analysis of social networks and their evolution along the process. They are used to investigate changes in the relationships between the participants and how they are linked to the implementation of ComMod activities. The logbook data can be processed with the NetDraw software package (available at http://www.analytictech.com) to visualise exchanges among stakeholders and knowledge sharing in each successive phase of the process.

9.3 The companion modelling process in Doi Tiew village

Figure 9.2 provides an overview of the whole collaborative landscape modelling and simulation process implemented in Doi Tiew village over three years to improve the management of the forest-farmland interface at this site. The research team that co-designed and facilitated this process consisted mainly of three researchers. The main process facilitator (and first author of this chapter) was a tropical ecologist and doctorate student specialised in vegetation and animal population dynamics. He was supported by a human geographer cum system agronomist (second author of this chapter), and an ecological modeller with skills in the development of MAS simulation tools (this aspect of the work dealing with tool development is not emphasised in this chapter, for more details see Dumrongrojwatthana, 2010). Throughout the process, this team was assisted by several students who took part in testing sessions to calibrate the simulation tools, and in the facilitation of the successive gaming and simulation workshops. The three sequences of ComMod activities performed are briefly described below to highlight how the process was crafted with the local stakeholders and adapted to changes in the context and the focus of their interest.

9.3.1 First collaborative landscape modelling and simulation sequence

Starting from a situation of mistrust between the two parties, the goal of the first sequence was to facilitate communication between herders and foresters by building a shared representation of forest regeneration at the landscape level in relation to cattle rearing and tree planting activities. The highlight of the sequence was a two-day gaming and simulation field workshop. It was held with 16 herders only in the village on day one to raise their interest in the proposed process and to prepare them to play with the foresters at the district administrative office (seen as a neutral place) the following day. This first version of the cRPG-v1 was used at the village school where a dozen Hmong herders with a low level of formal education were invited to discover, criticise and improve the cRPG-v1 simulation tool. Two groups of herders made decisions on the use of the same virtual landscape in the absence of forest protection activities. One group decided to raise cattle in individual scattered paddocks, while the second group opted for a more collective management of individual herds in a single large paddock. Following the gaming session, the computer displayed, side by side and year by year, the vegetation dynamics resulting from these different choices of cattle management. The herders were able to explain the differences observed in the vegetation dynamics and were introduced to the comparative analysis of scenarios. At the end of the day, half of them agreed to pursue the participatory modelling and simulation activity with NKU foresters at Tha Wang Pha district office the following day.

In the morning session of the second day, the herders explained a replay of the previous day's gaming session to introduce the use of the simulation tool to the NKU foresters. They did it by emphasising the importance of the continuation of cattle rearing for their livelihoods. Then a new gaming session started in which the foresters selected two new plots to be planted with trees at the start of every crop year, before the establishment of the herders' paddocks on the virtual landscape. In the game, the foresters played their actual practice of trying to enlarge patches of tree plantations year after year. But after several years they started discussions with the herders to negotiate their access to the most suitable plots for tree planting. On their side, the herders were interested in negotiating the access to young plantations for cattle grazing when faced with shrinking grassland areas. The dynamics of the gaming session showed them that this would not be enough to make their extensive cattle rearing system sustainable. The afternoon debate showed that there was mutual interest in the introduction of artificial pastures in the landscape. Both parties asked the research team to modify the simulation tool to accommodate this technical innovation. The herders made it clear that they would not take part in a second field workshop if it did not focus on this precise question. Because of their low level of trust in NKU foresters, they also requested the presence of district administrative and technical officials to witness the following part of the process.

The gaming workshop allowed the participation of a few players only, and it was important to communicate about what happened and to disseminate the lessons learned from this event to the wider community of local stakeholders. Several participating herders presented the main results with a slide presentation to the whole village community during a monthly meeting. A document summarising the findings was also distributed. Similar presentations were also made by the research team to the foresters of the neighbouring Sob Khun Royal Project, the District Livestock Development (DLD) Office and at the Nanthaburi National Park (NNP) headquarters. Two large-format posters in the local language showing the process of this first gaming and simulation sequence and its main results were posted in the village and at the NKU office to facilitate further exchanges between players and non-players.

9.3.2 Second collaborative modelling and simulation sequence

At this stage, the local herders and foresters agreed to hold a dialogue about the landscape management issue. But they insisted on focusing the process on their preferred way of mitigating the land-use conflict to allow the continuation of livestock rearing in parallel with forest regeneration. To satisfy this request, the second sequence was designed and implemented to facilitate the design of a co-management action plan. This sequence was composed of four complementary activities as follows: (1) final validation of vegetation state transition diagram following the integration of *Bracharia ruziziensis* artificial pastures as requested by the herders; (2) modification of the cRPG to produce a second version integrating the simulation of the new cattle and land management techniques proposed by stakeholders; (3) test of the cRPG-v2 simulator with NKU and NNP officers (introduction of this tool and its use to the NNP rangers who joined the process at this stage); and (4) implementation of a second gaming and simulation field workshop at the site, with more diverse participants (i.e. NNP and DLD officials) to design a collective action plan. The final validation of the state transition diagram took into account the improved understanding of interactions between cattle rearing, tree plantation activities and forest regeneration achieved at completion of the first sequence.

A similar gaming and simulation session to that in the first sequence was organised in which the national park occupied the highest part of the virtual landscape with NNP rangers playing their role by punishing the owners of cattle trespassing in the park. The same kind of comparison of different cattle-grazing strategies and practices as in the first sequence was implemented. One of them showed that the advantage of introducing artificial pastures would be maximised through the collective management of individual herds (Dumrongrojwatthana, 2010). The subsequent plenary discussion focused on the preparation of a joint experiment to test this technical innovation on a ten hectares plot of land offered by the NKU foresters. The DLD officer offered to obtain the Bracharia grass seeds and several herders volunteered to provide animals for this experiment.

9.3.3 Third collaborative modelling and simulation sequence

At this stage of the collaborative modelling process, some herders were concerned by the limited number of villagers involved in the gaming and simulation activities so far. They asked to be able to use the simulator to 'train' more herders for them to better understand the concrete action plan agreed upon with NKU foresters. By doing this, they also wanted to engage them in its implementation. They also requested further modification of the simulation tool to integrate key cropping activities in the village such as upland production of rice, a local staple food.

To accommodate these requests, the cRPG evolved into a more autonomous third version (cRPG-v3). It was tested with players who participated in the first and/or second workshops, as well as with other herders who had never participated in this ComMod process. The last phase of this third sequence consisted of the implementation of this fully autonomous ABM to be used to simulate, explore and compare the results of various landscape management scenarios with more participants in further participatory simulations. They will be designed to out- and up-scale the ComMod process at this site because other neighbouring communities are facing the same kind of land-use conflict, while the ABM replay of gaming sessions *in silico* could be used to brief local administrators and other decision-makers about the outcomes of this ComMod process.

Figure 9.3 displays the qualitative and quantitative evolution of the stakeholder participation in the three successive cycles of this ComMod process. If field workshops mobilised between 12 and 27 participants during the three cycles, the out-scaling activities were conducted with approximately one hundred villagers. The increased diversity of stakeholders during the second cycle occurred at the request of the herders. While on the contrary, their new focus on engaging more herders in the collective action by training them to use the ABM simulation tool to simulate scenarios led to a far more homogeneous stakeholder arena in the final sequence.

9.4 Research results and outcomes of the collaborative landscape research process

9.4.1 Knowledge exchange and production for sustainable landscape management

The logbook data permits an assessment of the exchange of different kinds (empirical, technical, expert and scientific) of knowledge during the whole ComMod process. Because more activities were carried out with the Hmong herders, 42% of the time was spent sharing their empirical knowledge with other stakeholders. The research team used 24% of the time to share its scientific knowledge. Inputs of technical and institutional knowledge occurred mainly in the second cycle of the process and represented only 5% of the time spent implementing the whole process for each of this two categories. These data show that in such a process, the farmers are able to express their point of view and arguments at length. This is very different from the classic extension or consultation processes in which they act mainly as receivers of information and knowledge provided by other parties.

These knowledge exchanges led to the production of a common vegetation state transition diagram used to represent vegetation dynamics at the landscape level. The use of pictograms associated with each of the main type of vegetative cover was efficient for knowledge elicitation between researchers, herders and foresters (Dumrongrojwatthana, 2009). The initial series of pictograms and transition rules from one state to another (number of years, natural or man-made change) proposed by the plant ecologist were completed by the herders and foresters. This led to two slightly different versions at the beginning of the first cycle and the researcher merged them into a new conceptual model of vegetation dynamics. This

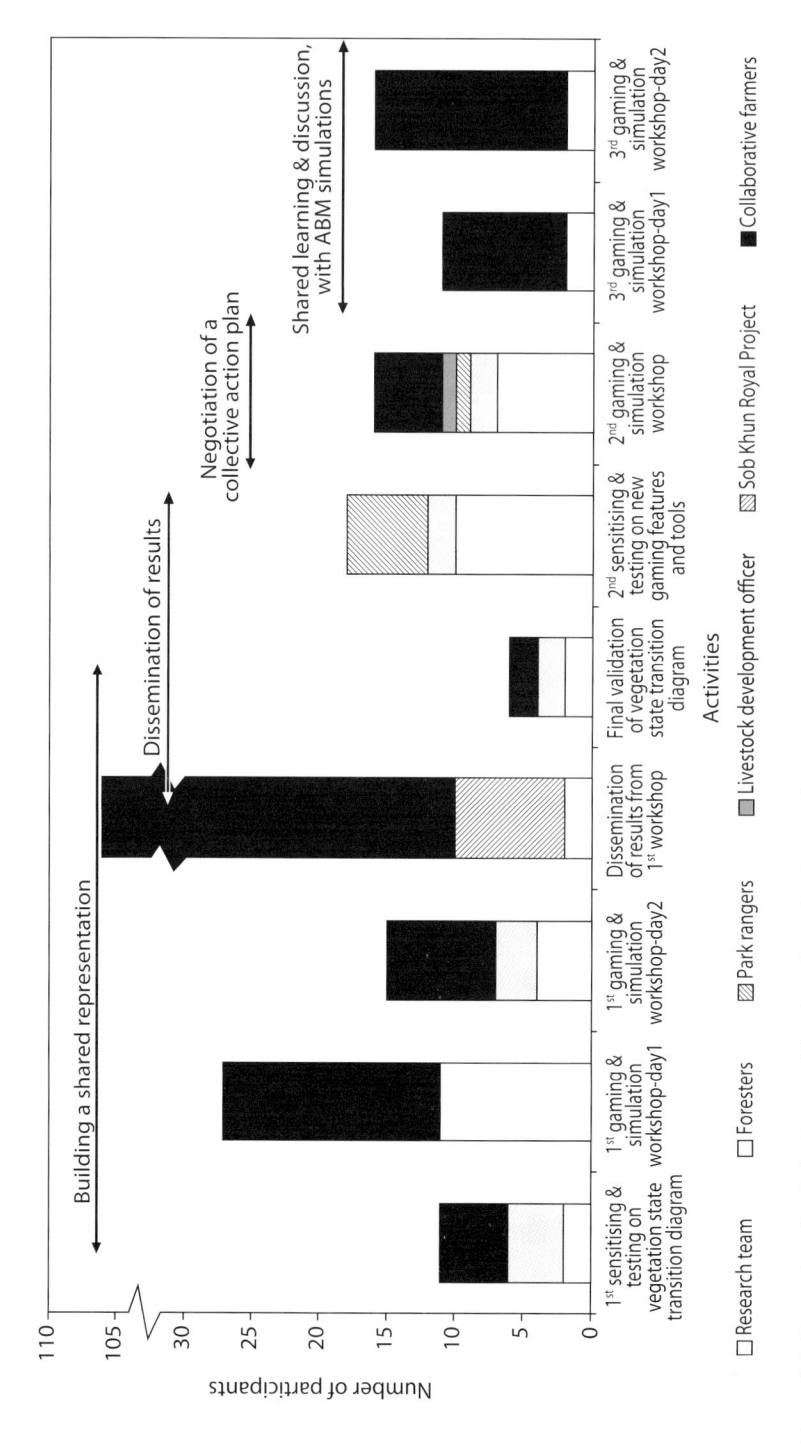

Figure 9.3. Dynamics of stakeholder participation along the ComMod process implemented at Doi Tiew site of Nan province, Northern Thailand, 2007-2009.

9. Northern Thailand case

model was used to regulate vegetation dynamics on the virtual landscape in the gaming and simulation sessions of the first field workshop and was finally accepted by all participants. In the second cycle, the cRPG tool was found to be flexible enough to accommodate the addition of new pictograms (such as *ruzi* pastures, upland rice fields) as requested by the local players.

The virtual landscape shown in Figure 9.4 was based on the 2003 land-use map of the village territory.

A North-South transect comprising a gradient of the main different types of land use and land cover was simplified into a grid where one pixel was equivalent to 3.2 ha. A given pictogram from the conceptual model was assigned to each cell to mimic the main heterogeneities of the actual landscape. The landscape was symmetric to allow two (left and right) groups of 5-6 herders each to play with several foresters to manage one half of the landscape separately by implementing their preferred strategies (for example, individual versus collective management of herds).

At the end of a gaming and simulation session, differences between the two landscape management strategies implemented were displayed, compared and analysed. These debriefings were very interactive and useful to check whether the components and rules of the simulation tool were well understood. Each party provided its explanation of the landscape dynamics displayed and a debate on these arguments facilitated by the research team followed. The rapidity with which the herders assimilated the use of this tool in the first field workshop was rather surprising, as well as their confidence when commenting on the replay of the first gaming session to the foresters the following day. They were clearly taking this simulation tool seriously and used it to enhance communication and mutual understanding with the

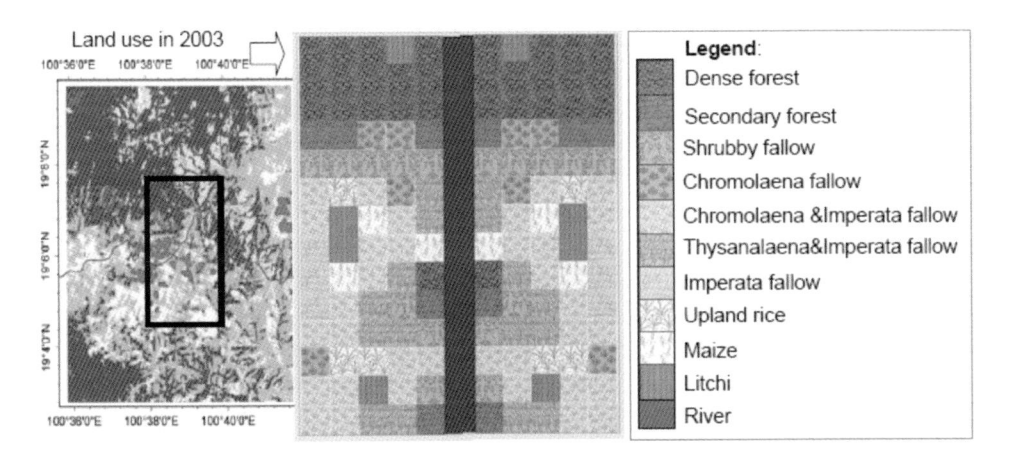

Figure 9.4. Spatial interface of the first version of the computer-assisted role-playing game used in the first ComMod cycle at Doi Tiew site of Nan province, Northern Thailand.

foresters about the importance of livestock rearing to them and the positive effects of this activity on forest regeneration. In the following gaming session, the foresters' strategy for gradually building patches of tree plantations was made explicit and the herders negotiated grazing rights in tree plantations older than five years. But this was not enough to feed the herds as the gradual reforestation of the landscape increased the scarcity of suitable grazing land with herbaceous vegetative cover. This resulted in a decreasing cattle population and poorer quality of cattle carcasses produced under constant grazing pressure. Land use and cattle population dynamics showed clearly that extensive cattle rearing would not be viable in the near future. This prompted several herders to look at how to increase forage production to be able to pursue livestock rearing, while others decided to abandon this activity and focus on crop production. But the transformation of the relationship between herders and foresters generated new ideas during the plenary debate on the results, especially an agreement on the need to test new forage production and cattle management techniques.

Two complementary technical innovations, i.e. the introduction of artificial pastures and rotational grazing, were introduced in the debate by the herders to address the issue of the increasing scarcity of suitable grazing land and for the production of higher quality meat products. They also addressed the foresters' interest in a decrease in the cattle grazing pressure in young tree plantations, as well as the rangers' goal of suppressing roaming animals in the area. This was a bold decision by the herders who have been practising only very low external input, land and labour extensive cattle rearing on natural pastures for several decades. But now they were aware of the fact that such practices would no longer be ecologically or economically viable. The matter became urgent to the herders and their engagement in the process increased. They wanted to sit firmly in the driver's seat and made clear to the research team what should be the focus of the next round of ComMod activities.

The second sequence assessed the proposed technical innovations with the updated version of the simulation tool, with the ultimate goal, depending on the simulation results, of negotiating a concrete co-management action plan. The simulations showed that, while rotational grazing on natural pastures would only be of limited interest, a collective management of herds could maximise the benefits of establishing artificial pastures (Dumrongrojwatthana 2010). This finding influenced the definition of the joint experiment on the introduction of *Bracharia ruziziensis* pastures on ten hectares of land provided by NKU foresters. The idea of launching a joint field experiment on artificial pastures was clearly a step toward a more technical and concrete assessment of this innovation in actual farming circumstances, something that was beyond the role assigned to the cRPG simulation tool.

9.4.2 Influence of research and scientists on the other categories of stakeholders

If the initiation of this collaborative landscape research came from a request made to the research team by the local NNP stakeholder, the scientists played a central role in the design and facilitation of the first cycle of ComMod activities as seen in Figure 9.5a.

9. Northern Thailand case

a. Communication intensity during the first ComMod cycle

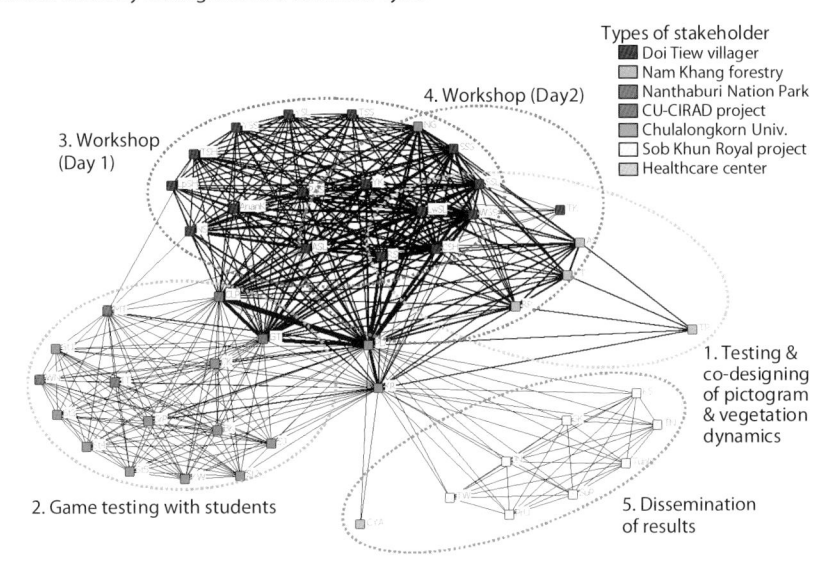

Types of stakeholder
- Doi Tiew villager
- Nam Khang forestry
- Nanthaburi Nation Park
- CU-CIRAD project
- Chulalongkorn Univ.
- Sob Khun Royal project
- Healthcare center

3. Workshop (Day 1)
4. Workshop (Day2)
1. Testing & co-designing of pictogram & vegetation dynamics
2. Game testing with students
5. Dissemination of results

b. Communication intensity during the second ComMod cycle

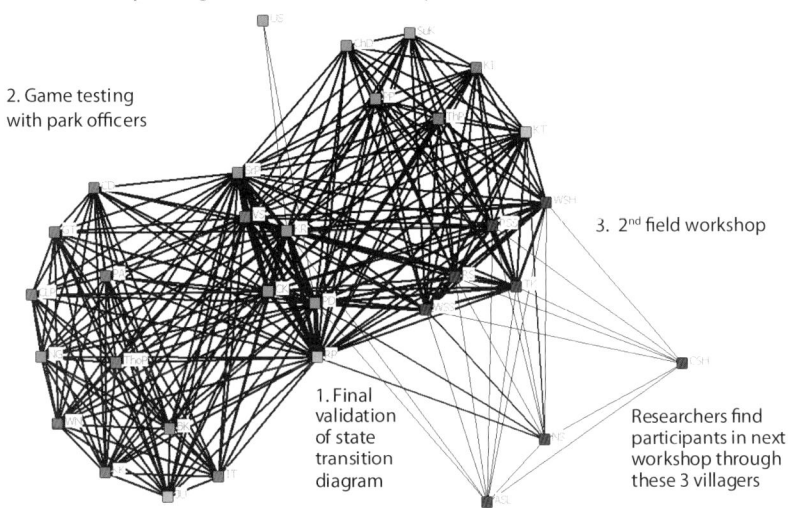

2. Game testing with park officers
3. 2nd field workshop
1. Final validation of state transition diagram
Researchers find participants in next workshop through these 3 villagers

Figure 9.5. Communication intensity among the different categories of participants in the first (a) and second (b) ComMod cycles implemented at Doi Tiew site of Nan province, Northern Thailand (line thickness is proportional to time spent interacting).

The figure displays the intensity of communication among the different categories of participants. The thickness of the lines is proportional to the intensity of communication between two given participants in the process. This was unavoidable because of the initial deep mistrust between the parties in conflict. But by the end of the fist sequence, the interactions between herders and foresters increased. More intensive exchanges between these two categories of key stakeholders are shown in Figure 9.5b displaying communication among the participants in the second cycle on testing innovative cattle rearing techniques and negotiating a collective action plan. Most of the participants being already familiar with the simulation tool, the role of the research team in this second round was mainly to facilitate the simulation exercises and the exchanges among local stakeholders.

By the end of the first cycle, the local stakeholders were driving the process. They were rather surprised to see that the researchers accommodated their wishes and modified their models according to their wishes. Compared to their previous experiences with researchers, there is no doubt that this behaviour contributed to more trustworthy relationships between the process facilitators and the villagers. This was again the case at the end of the second cycle when the herders asked the research team to spend time out-scaling the process with them by training more villagers on using the more autonomous and less time-consuming third version of the cRPG simulation tool. At this stage, the experienced players who took part in the previous field workshops were able to explain what this tool was doing to the newcomers in Hmong language. This was a critical stage for the main process designer and facilitator cum doctorate student who had to keep responding to the requests made by these motivated herders while fulfilling the academic requirements of his degree training in a time-bound framework. It is at this stage that the need for a local facilitator equipped with skills to manipulate the simulation tool with new players became obvious to sustain the positive momentum of the process.

9.4.3 Effects and impacts of the collaborative research process within the studied context

These collaborative landscape modelling and simulation activities established a communication channel between herders, foresters and rangers. The dialogue led to an improved mutual understanding of their respective perceptions of land-use dynamics, objectives and practices. The improvement of trust between the villagers and the forest conservation agencies was also noticeable. Since the negative perception felt during the initial visit of the research team to the village (after which the village authorities checked the institutional attachment of its members on internet through a young migrant working in the tourism industry!), there was a very significant improvement in trust between the villagers and the research team. The ComMod posture of the research team facilitating collective decision-making by local stakeholders and the implementation of a rather longwinded process in their preferred direction clearly helped to achieve that. The villagers clearly said that they understood this team was not in the village simply to make a study and issue recommendations.

Knowledge exchange led to an improved understanding of the on-going dynamics of the forest-grazing land interface for all the participants (including researchers). Most of the herders rapidly understood the features and operation rules of the cRPG simulation tool after a couple of rounds of play (one round simulating one year in a 4-5 year long gaming session). They also made pertinent suggestions (such as the addition of features and options needed for them to make their decisions, the adjustment of technical parameters regarding cattle population dynamics, etc.) to improve its successive versions and to better represent the system they manage. This case study proved the efficiency of combining in a flexible way RPGs and computer simulation tools to bridge the digital gap among users. The process has so far been successful in engaging reluctant villagers who have received no (or only a low level of) formal education in the collective exploration of the future of their surrounding landscape.

But, as expected from the determined Hmong participants, as soon as they made up their mind about ways to practically improve the co-existence between cattle rearing and forest regeneration, the herders requested to move from the virtual world of the agent-based simulation to the negotiation of a field experiment to test the technical innovations found suitable to the parties in conflict. The joint implementation of a rather large-scale experiment on the feasibility to raise pooled herds on *Bracharia ruziziensis* artificial pastures established on foresters land could be seen as a starting point toward the co-management of the forest-farmland interface by local villagers and foresters. During the plenary debate that followed the participatory simulations in the third cycle, the herders expressed their increased awareness of the need for a collective management of their farming activities. They seem ready to move in that direction by testing an acceptable way to allow reforestation of this upper watershed while improving livestock rearing. They proposed a zoning of the village territory between annual crops and animal grazing activities and also suggested inviting the village committee members and the sub-district representatives managing the development funds to join further collaborative landscape simulation activities. Their proposition was backed by the village chief.

9.5 Discussion

9.5.1 Effectiveness of ComMod adaptive methodology and flexible tools for generating knowledge, learning, negotiation, and collective action

Starting from an initial situation characterised by a deep mistrust between the main categories of stakeholders, the ComMod process implemented in Doi Tiew village has now reached the stage of joint implementation of an agreed concrete action plan. The co-design and interactive use of methodological tools facilitating communication, sharing of perceptions, improvement of mutual understanding and trust among the participating stakeholders played a major role in this significant achievement. Compared to earlier ComMod processes implemented in the same region (Bousquet *et al.*, 2005b; Ruankaew, 2010) and their evaluation (Van Paassen *et al.*, 2008) more attention was given in Doi Tiew to preliminary sensitising activities with the disadvantaged marginal Hmong farmers. They were able to better understand the objectives of the process and increased their interest and confidence. They played a crucial role in securing a positive start by engaging the reluctant Hmong herders. Full gaming and simulation sessions with the foresters, and later on with the park rangers, were introduced only when the herders felt ready to confront their opinions and arguments with them.

The simulation tools made extensive use of visualisation techniques (pictograms, virtual landscape, etc.) to avoid face-to-face discussions between the conflict parties and to overcome the severe language barrier (many Hmong herders do not speak Thai). These visuals, that rely on components that farmers could rapidly relate to their actual circumstances (vegetation states, gradient of forest degradation in the landscape, etc.), facilitated the perception and understanding of key phenomena and simulations of landscape dynamics. The choice of a symmetric virtual landscape allowing the visualisation of contrasted management strategies enhanced the assessment of the consequences of decisions made by the players on landscape dynamics. The participants were comfortable with this abstract virtual landscape and never requested a more realistic spatial interface until the agreement on a concrete action plan. While the first cRPG-v1 simulation tool was mainly efficient in stimulating joint learning, the second version was more focused on facilitating the negotiation of a common action plan based on technical innovations introduced by the players. The more autonomous third version was tailored to facilitate communication between already experienced and new participants in the process. These successive versions of the cRPG tool demonstrated how the use of a first prototype creates new users' questions and related needs leading to an evolving process of collective learning and decision-making, up to the beginning of self-organisation in the last phase.

These flexible and rather simple models were designed and modified in a transparent way, and were used as boundary objects (Carlile, 2002; Vinck, 1999) in conflict mediation with the heterogeneous arena of stakeholders. They supported knowledge elicitation (by revealing hidden preferences) and stimulated exchanges of viewpoints and co-learning leading to improved trust. This facilitated joint decisions about the direction of the next steps and the related evolution of these frontier simulation tools. The implementation of this kind of very adaptive collaborative modelling approach places a great demand on ComMod modellers because they have to provide timely responses to stakeholders' changing demands. While being very productive and dedicated to the creation of useful models, this mode of trans-disciplinary collaboration is not easily compatible with the implementation of a research agenda bound by a classic project-based mode of operation.

Time management and the availability of the stakeholders concerned to take part at the right time in time-consuming joint activities, such as a series of gaming and simulation sessions is of paramount importance to create and maintain a productive momentum. This was a limitation in the case study reported here as farmers' priorities determined by the agricultural calendar and academic constraints faced by the main process facilitator cum doctorate student did not allow the implementation of key field activities at the most suitable time. Coding the successive versions of the cRPG tool under the computer simulation platform required special skills to be learned. This was also an obstacle to the timely delivery of the simulation tool meeting the stakeholders' successive shift of interest as field workshops needed to be postponed by a few months.

9.5.2 Organisation of stakeholder involvement and engagement

Legitimacy of the intervention

The status of Chulalongkorn University at the national level and the backing of provincial authorities provided legitimacy to the research team when implementing an action research process in the area. The NNP agency made the initial request to the research team but its local leader at that time still refused to compromise with the herders regarding the co-ordination of cattle grazing and park management rules during the second cycle of the process. Consequently, the negotiation of a co-management plan took place between the Hmong herders and the NKU foresters, with district administrators and technicians acting mainly as observers. From a methodological point of view, plenary debates after simulation sessions were systematically associated with individual interviews with all the participants the following day. This promoted a rather equitable expression of all the participants' viewpoints. The interviews were also used to reinforce the relationship between the modelling process and actual circumstances in the field. The legitimacy of the process could be further improved if, as now proposed by the herders, village committee members and representatives of the well-funded and influential sub-district administration could also participate actively in the process. But for this to happen and to build on promising preliminary results, there is an urgent need to identify and train a local facilitator to replace the process designer and lecturer-researcher in this role.

Evolution of the stakeholders' arena

The heterogeneity of the stakeholders' arena taking part in the ComMod activities was mainly driven by the herders' willingness to play with NKU foresters in the first cycle and their subsequent request to involve land administrators and the DLD technician to monitor and ensure the foresters' accountability and to facilitate the introduction of a technical innovation. Following a third cycle focusing on strengthening the herders' participation, they seem ready to up-scale the process and are advocating the invitation of local administrators up to the sub-district level to take part in collaborative landscape management as well. This proposition is timely as a local facilitator should take over the key role of 'human interface' to increase the local ownership of the process, maintain its momentum and monitor it now that there is less need for new collaborative modelling and simulation inputs.

The cRPG tool used in the first sequences did not allow for the participation of many villagers in gaming and simulation sessions. But the autonomous ABM tool produced at the end of the third sequence allows the involvement of more interested people in a time- and cost-efficient way. The computer simulations of scenarios run with it are also going to be used to disseminate the results to more indirect stakeholders, like projects and other villages facing similar land use conflicts in the neighbourhood. The presentation of such simulations in Hmong language by engaged Doi Tiew herders who took part in the simulation workshops are particularly efficient and convincing.

Figure 9.5 shows the pertinence of using a logbook for qualitative and quantitative analyses of social dynamics and to critically reflect on the process implementation. More detailed visualisations of the intensity of interactions among the categories of participants, e.g. on a cycle-by-cycle basis, are useful, as well as the observation of the evolving centrality of the most active participants (Dumrongrojwatthana, 2010). Filling the logbook on a weekly basis is a somewhat tedious task, but powerful computer tools facilitate the construction of social network graphs and the analysis of their evolution over time. The logbook data can also be used to monitor coalition and power relation dynamics in collective landscape management processes.

Engagement and collaboration of social and biophysical scientists

It is presently widely accepted that improved dialogue and integration of bio-technical and social science perspectives needs to be achieved in the context of sustainable landscape development. The case study reported here showed the usefulness of MAS models (either conceptual models, low tech RPGs or high tech ABMs) to integrate agro-ecological (vegetation dynamics in this case) and social (stakeholders' diversity and their interactions) knowledge. This modelling approach facilitates communication, mutual understanding and decision-making among researchers from different disciplines involved in the representation of a complex system to be examined with local stakeholders. The evolution of the conceptual model and its related simulation tools accompanies the gradually improved researchers' understanding of the land management system and feeds more exchanges across disciplines. Of particular interest are the phases during which hard choices have to be made to keep the model simple and focused on local stakeholders' interest. Each version of the model is associated with selected indicators used to assess simulation results. Usually one deals with the ecological dynamics, the evolution of the area under forest cover in this case study, while the other one looks at the agro-economic performance of the system (change in the size of the cattle population and the quality of the carcasses). Each member of the family of models built over time constitutes a milestone testifying this evolution of the shared representation of the system under study as influenced by the shift of interest and focus of their end users.

9.6 Conclusion

In a ComMod process, local stakeholders are in the driving seat and the course of action is uncertain. The engaged posture of the ComMod researcher could be uncomfortable in a classic project-based research context. This could be further complicated by the multiple roles played by a ComMod process designer and facilitator. As soon as it becomes feasible, it is preferable to let a local stakeholder manage the facilitation activities with the added advantage of increasing the local ownership of the process. But time is needed to identify the legitimate person with the right skills and to transfer the methodology and tools to her. Such a transfer is needed to achieve the objective of an acceptable balance between scientific and societal pursuits of collaborative landscape planning without jeopardising the ComMod researcher situation in academia. Another dilemma deals with the dissemination of this approach in a cost-efficient way. Relying on already trained stakeholders equipped with adapted simulation tools to train new participants can help address this challenge. But further methodological developments are still needed to use such an approach in multilevel processes encompassing larger areas.

Acknowledgements

The authors are grateful to Dr. Christophe Le Page for his very dedicated assistance in the implementation of the simulation tools. They also thank the Challenge Program on Water and Food (CPWF) of the CGIAR, the Ecole Commod Project, Asia IT&C Programme of the European Union, the Science for Local Project under Chulalongkorn University Academic Development Plan, the Office of the Higher Education Commission of the Royal Thai Government, and the French embassy in Thailand for supporting this research.

References

Barnaud, C., G. Trébuil, P. Dumrongrojwatthana and J. Marie, 2008. Area study prior to companion modelling to integrate multiple interests in upper watershed management of Northern Thailand. Southeast Asian Studies 45(4): 559-585.

Berkes, F. and C. Folke (eds.), 1998. Linking ecological and social systems: Management practices and social mechanisms for building resilience. Cambridge University Press, Cambridge; UK.

Bousquet, F. and G. Trébuil, 2005. Synergies between multi-agent systems and role-playing games in companion modeling for integrated natural resource management in Southeast Asia. In: Proceedings of the International Conference on Simulation and Modeling 2005 (SimMod 2005), 17-19 January 2005, Rose Garden Aprime Resort, Bangkok, Thailand, pp. 461-469.

Bousquet, F., O. Barreteau, C. Le Page, C. Mullon and J. Weber, 1999. An environmental modelling approach. The use of multi-agent simulations. In: F. Blasco, A. Weill and F. Paris (eds.), Advances in environmental and ecological modelling. Elsevier, Paris, France, pp. 113-122.

Bousquet, F., G. Trébuil and B. Hardy (eds.), 2005a. Companion Modeling and Multi-Agent Systems for Integrated Natural Resource Management in Asia. Cirad & International Rice Research Institute, Los Baños, Laguna, Philippines, 360 pp.

Bousquet, F., G. Trébuil, S. Boissau, C. Baron, P. d'Aquino and J.C. Castella, 2005b. Knowledge integration for participatory land management: The use of multi-agent simulations and a companion modelling approach. In: A. Neef (ed.), Participatory approaches for sustainable land use in Southeast Asia. White Lotus, Bangkok, Thailand, pp. 291-310.

Bousquet, F., J.C. Castella, G. Trébuil, C. Barnaud, S. Boissau, S.P. Kam, 2007. Using multi-agent systems in a companion modelling approach for agro-ecosystem management in South-east Asia. Outlook on Agriculture 36(1): 57-62.

Carlile, P., 2002. A pragmatic view of knowledge and boundaries: Boundary objects in new product development. Organization Science 13: 442-455.

Collectif ComMod, 2009. La posture d'accompagnement des processus de prise de decision: les references et les questions transdisciplinaires. In: D. Hervé and F. Laloë (eds.), Modélisation de l'environnement: entre natures et sociétés. Éditions Quae, France, pp. 71-89.

ComMod group, 2003. Our Companion Modelling approach. Journal of Artificial Societies and Simulation 6 (1). Available at: http://jasss.soc.surrey.ac.uk/6/2/1.html.

Dumrongrojwatthana, P., 2010. Interactions between cattle raising and reforestation in the highland socio-ecosystem of Nan province, northern Thailand: A companion modelling process to improve landscape management. Unpublished doctorate thesis, Paris Ouest Nanterre La Défense University, Paris, France, 345 pp.

Dumrongrojwatthana, P., C. Le Page, N. Gajaseni and G. Trébuil, 2009. Co-constructing an agent-based model to mediate land use conflict between herders and foresters in northern Thailand. Proceedings of the 24th Annual Landscape Ecology Symposium, Landscape Patterns and Ecosystem Processes. April 12-16, 2009. The Cliff Lodge, Snowbird, UT, USA. p 55.

Funtowicz, S.O. and J.R. Ravetz, 1993. Science for the post-normal age. Futures 25: 739-755.

Holling, C.S., 2001. Understanding the complexity of economic, ecological and social systems. Ecosystems 4(5): 390-405.

Jones, N.A., P. Perez, T.G. Measham, G.J. Kelly, P. d'Aquino, K. Daniell, A. Dray and N. Ferrand, 2009. Evaluating participatory modeling: Developing a framework for cross-case analysis. Environmental Management 44: 1180-1195.

Langton, C.G., 1992. Life at the edge of chaos. In: C.G. Langton, C. Taylor, J.D. Farmer and S. Rasmussen (eds.), Artificial life II, Addison-Wesley, Reading, MA, USA, pp. 41-91.

Liu, J., T. Dietz, S.R. Carpenter, M. Alberti, C. Folke, E. Moran, A.N. Pell, P. Deadman, T. Kratz and J. Lubchenco, 2007. Complexity of coupled human and natural systems. Science 317: 1513-1516.

Ollagnon, H., 1989. Une approche patrimoniale de la qualité du milieu naturel. In: N. Matthieu and M. Jollivet (eds.), Du rural à l'environnement: la question de la nature aujourd'hui. L'Harmattan, Paris, France, pp. 258-268.

Ostrom, E., 2005. Understanding institutional diversity. Princeton University Press, Princeton, NJ, USA. 376 pp.

Ostrom, E., R. Gardner and J. Walker, 1994. Rules, games and common-pool resources. University of Michigan Press, Ann Arbor, MI, USA.

Röling, N.G., 2002. Beyond the aggregation of individual preferences: Moving from multiple to distributed cognition in resource dilemmas. In: C.S. Leeuwis and R. Pyburn (eds.), Wheelbarrows full of frogs: Social learning in rural resource management. Royal Van Gorcum, Asen, the Netherlands, pp. 25-47.

Röling, N.G. and M.A. Wagemakers, 1998. A new practice: Facilitating sustainable agriculture. In: N.G. Röling and M.A. Wagemakers (eds.), Facilitating sustainable agriculture: Participatory learning and adaptive management in times of environmental uncertainty. Cambridge University Press, Cambridge, UK, pp. 3-22.

Ruankaew, N., C. Le Page, P. Dumrongrojwatthana, C. Barnaud, N. Gajaseni, A. Van Paassen and G. Trébuil, 2010. Companion modeling for integrated renewable resource management: a new collaborative approach to create common values for sustainable development. International Journal of Sustainable Development and World Ecology 17(1): 15-23.

Scott, J.C., 2009. The art of not being governed: An anarchist history of upland Southeast Asia. Yale Agrarian Studies Series, Yale University Press, New Haven, CT, USA. 442 pp.

Van Paassen, A., C. Barnaud and I. Patamadit, 2008. Rethinking participatory research in renewable resource management. Proceedings of the World Congress of the International Association for Media and Communication Research (IAMCR), Stockholm, Sweden.

Vinck, D., 1999. Les objets intermédiaires dans les réseaux de coopération scientifique. Contribution à la prise en compte des objets dans les dynamiques sociales. Revue Française de Sociologie XL(2): 385-414.

10. Reflexivity in action research: two spatial planning cases

Marcel Pleijte, Marc Schut and Roel During

Abstract

The purpose of this chapter is to discuss reflexivity in action research, because a lot of action researchers do not pay attention to reflexivity and we find it crucial not only for understanding the position of an action researcher, but also for understanding the process and results of action research. Reflexivity refers to the capability of a researcher to detach from the scientific disciplinary paradigm of his/her discipline and take a different perspective. We start by describing two concepts necessary to understand reflexivity: performativity and self-referentiality. Performativity refers to the way that actors redirect and reconstruct their activities to fit a theoretical model. Self-reference can be defined as the process of reasoning, in which new information in communication is reframed by means of predefined concepts. Two studied cases, Noordwaard and Wieringerrandmeer, demonstrate how citizens mobilise research and researchers to strengthen their negotiating position, because they were marginalised. The action researchers primarily provided action-oriented knowledge, but from their perspective raised very interesting scientific questions about democracy and science. Concerning democracy the issue was raised as to whether planning procedures contradict the inclusiveness that is required to respect the intentions and knowledge that ground alternative plans. At a more scientific principal level the question can be posed if action research can be free of normative positions towards the issue of developments that are preferred or considered inappropriate. The danger of an action researcher who limits his focus to the performance of his knowledge contribution and therefore contributes to self-referentiality can be opposed by reflexivity. We consider it a mission impossible if both positions are equally balanced by one researcher. A first level of reflexivity can be organised by a second action researcher if he/she at least includes a similar theoretical framework. Reflexivity based on a competing theoretical framework should be organised in a secondary analysis.

10.1. Introduction

Action research puts researchers in a compromising position. It is generally expected that their research should play an important role in dealing with increasingly complex problems. It is supposed to provide powerful instruments for analysing problems, exploring possible solutions, and monitoring and evaluating the impacts of actions taken. Action- and impact-oriented research approaches have been proposed as a strategy that allows researches to become embedded and subsequently better understand the context in which research can effectively contribute to exploring sustainable solutions (cf. Schut *et al.*, 2010). In collaboration with stakeholders, research questions are jointly elaborated, as well as the methods, and expected outputs; making research more accessible and robust for stakeholders in the process. However, this kind of 'self-referentiality' may compromise the objectivity of the research process, which has increasingly been studied by social scientists exploring the sociology of science practices (Fuller, 2009; Trigg, 2004). Self-referentiality occurs in research when a researcher refers to him- or herself. Self-reference is related to self-reflexivity and apperception (Foucault, 1966, 1969). Luhmann (1990) defines self-referentiality as a process of reasoning, in which new information in communication is reframed by means of predefined concepts.

The issue of self-referentiality has serious implications for trust relations between science and society. The reliability of scientific research is an important factor in the societal acceptance of problems and proposed solutions. Increasingly, problems that are loaded with scientific evidence are denied by critical groups in society. They are called deniers, and they cannot be convinced by facts or figures. Deniers are driven by mistrust in governments, ideology or religious belief, where the commitment of belief takes precedence over scientific evidence. Disbelievers that have a strong impact on society can be found in debates on climate, evolution, holocaust, vaccine and tobacco (Schermer, 2010). Deniers search for any inconsistency in scientific results and aggravate them as scientific prejudice or false assumptions. On the other hand, scientists who are not open to criticism stereotype their opponents as deniers. There is a particular danger here for the action researcher, who may end up being accused of scientific fraud as a result of the self-referentiality described above.

According to Foucault (1977), the problem of self-referentiality is inherent in scientific research. In his view, a scientific discipline can only function on the basis of concealed presumptions and power inventions that precede the accumulation of knowledge. He clarified the relations of power and knowledge as follows:

Knowledge linked to power, not only assumes the authority of 'the truth' but has the power to make itself true. Knowledge, once used to regulate the conduct of others, entails constraint, regulation and the disciplining of practice. Thus, there is no power relation without the correlative constitution of a field of knowledge, nor any knowledge that does not presuppose and constitute at the same time, power relations. (Foucault, 1977: 27)

This quotation indicates the difficulties action researchers are likely to encounter if they try to avoid getting locked in the stakeholders' or practitioners' self-referential problem definitions. Detaching from them requires the ability to take a different perspective on the problem or use knowledge that has been qualified as controversial. This ability to diverge can be conceptualised as reflexivity; something the action researcher has to combine with useful and effective knowledge that helps to solve the complex issues at stake (cf. Guillemin and Gillam, 2004). In other words, reflexivity refers to the capability of a researcher to detach from his/her scientific disciplinary paradigm and take a different perspective (Kuhn, 1962; Trigg, 2004).

10. Reflexivity in action research: two spatial planning cases

The usefulness of research can be designated as 'performativity': the way actors redirect and reconstruct their activities to fit in a theoretical model. Performativity is an interdisciplinary concept often used to name the capacity of speech and language in particular, but other forms of expressive but non-verbal action as well, to intervene in the course of human events (Austin, 1962; Butler, 1997; Derrida, 1988; Schechner, 2006). What compromises the position of action researchers is the fact that they are expected and required to continuously seek a balance between performativity and reflexivity in their scientific work.

This chapter describes the dilemmas of a simultaneous quest for performance and reflexivity in action research. Before exploring performativity and reflexivity in action research, we will outline the theory and practice of action research. Subsequently, we identify several dilemmas posed by reflexivity as a scientific attitude and the various constraints it puts on performativity in action research. In the light of these constraints and the factors underlying them, we evaluate two action research case studies the authors have been involved in. This evaluation forms the basis for concluding suggestions for the optimisation of the dialectic relationship between reflexivity and performativity in action research.

After the introduction of the key concepts in this section we outline the theory and practice of action research as a scientific practice (Section 10.2). We identify the dilemmas posed by reflexivity as a scientific attitude and the various constraints it puts on action research. Subsequently, we define what can be understood by reflexivity (Section 10.3), and performativity (Section 10.4) in action research. We continue with an evaluation of two action research case studies in which two of the authors have been involved: Noordwaard (Section 10.5) and Wieringerrandmeer (Section 10.6) in the Netherlands. This evaluation will form the basis for an analysis and subsequent conclusions (Section 10.7) about how to optimise the dialectic relationship between reflexivity and performativity in action research.

10.2 Action research as a scientific practice

In this section we briefly discuss the concept of action research, and show how it emerged in a collaborative planning tradition, inspired by the German philosopher Habermas. This collaborative planning tradition focuses on co-operation models and consensus-seeking, in which communicative approaches are assumed to provide adequate answers to problem-solving and planning in an increasingly complex society (Healey, 1997; Allmendinger, 2002). The objective of collaborative planning is to address complexity through a sense-making and sense-seeking process, instead of using traditional blueprint planning approaches. Many have described the need to facilitate harmonious communication between stakeholders so that they can develop new – at least partly shared – problem definitions and cognitions on the basis of creative, participatory social learning processes (Cloke and Park, 1985; Habermas, 1981; Röling, 1994). These theories have inspired spatial planners to invite stakeholders to the planning process and co-create plans so that the complexity of the planning context is reflected in the complexity of the planning process itself. However, in practice these participatory decision-making processes often result in 'arenas of struggle', with stakeholders acting strategically, rather than communicatively (Leeuwis, 2000). Increasingly, action researchers are perceived as a panacea for these paralysing struggles as their knowledge and facilitation skills can bring stakeholders together and bridge different perceptions and objectives. For example, landscape architects have acquired central positions in planning in the Netherlands, because they manage to direct stakeholders towards consensus around their design products (Hajer *et al.*, 2006). In this context landscape architects operate like action researchers.

This quest for consensus is supposed to be favoured by jointly developing so-called integrated or robust knowledge, in which action researchers may play different roles. They are supposed to supply strategic knowledge on 'what works and how to influence i.e. decision-making and implementation processes'. Some researchers refer to this practice as interdisciplinary research (Tress *et al.*, 2003), because it is supposed to combine knowledge from the humanities, the natural and the social sciences. The potential for self-efficacy of the stakeholder group should be enhanced, as a result of this interdisciplinary knowledge. This implies that pragmatics become more important than truth-finding. The stakeholder community might not be interested in truth, but in a reality reflecting their particular view on truth. Then the knowledge in use may be framed into *a priori* assumptions on (their) reality and other fields of knowledge may be excluded. The quest for consensus and a preference for action-oriented knowledge demands that the researcher take on a more active and authoritative role (cf. Hajer *et al.*, 2006) in the planning process.

In this section we now focus on three matters: (1) the communicative approach of Habermas; (2) co-creation of knowledge; and (3) social construction of knowledge in relation to reality. All these concepts are concerned with action research in a communicative approach. Action research can also mean that a researcher is attempting to deliberately create conflict, especially if the planning or negotiation process will benefit from it.

In our opinion action research goes on. Lewin (1946) introduces action research as a concept and has described action research as a comparative study of the conditions and effects of forms of social action and research leading to social action, shaped in a spiral consisting of plans of action, act and reflect on the effects of that action. Central to action research are so-called acting, reflecting, learning and change in a cyclical process. The concepts of performativity (effects of action) and reflexivity can be understood and placed in this cyclical process. Acting may be interpreted as insertion (or withholding) of knowledge, but also in the trend of processing or making choices when it comes to supporting specific (weak) stakeholders.

10.3 On reflexivity in action research

Planning processes that are organised and facilitated towards achieving consensus amongst stakeholders can easily exclude divergent opinions and solutions. This divergence, however, might be important for developing the innovative ideas a group is chasing. A focus on innovation while striving for consensus makes the role of the researcher ambivalent. On the one hand, the researcher may provide a scientific backbone that supports consensus building amongst stakeholders, in a process often designated as *social learning* (Röling, 1994). On the other hand, the researcher may provide knowledge that does not fit the 'groupthink', but does open up new horizons and solution space. Both ways should be negotiated with the stakeholders, which implies that the action researcher has to compromise between the truth value and usefulness of research findings in the process. Within such an approach, research can support certain stakeholder perspectives or facilitate negotiations, but is also itself subject to negotiation (cf. Giller *et al.*, 2008; Leeuwis, 2000).

Reflexivity is both necessary and dangerous for the group's motivations to take decisions and lobby for their interests. If stakeholders are persuaded to accept that other perspectives on a planning subject are just as valid as theirs, they may become dismayed. Reflexivity is also dangerous for the researcher, because it undermines the ontological assumption of one truth, generalisation and therefore the very basis for the fundamental role of science in society. If a researcher just sticks to reflexivity, the planning process will always be judged as situational, creating particularised truth values (Trigg, 2004). As a consequence, every practice is unique and there is no basis left for comparison or generalisation. It is necessary to compare practices, however, in order to select theories and information that may be useful. To put it more generally, the action researcher plays a prominent role in the selection of information that is considered to be of use and, as a consequence, in the rejection of information that is considered inappropriate. This inclusion and exclusion of knowledge requires reflexivity to overcome possible groupthink.

10.4 On performativity in action research

Performativity refers to the way that actors redirect and reconstruct their activities to fit a theoretical model (Austin, 1962; Butler, 1997; Derrida, 1977; Schechner, 2006). For instance, most planning theories include a strong role for governments, which is often implicitly adopted by planning practitioners. When applied to action research, the concept of performativity can be elaborated in a way that corresponds to the discussion on reflexivity given above. In addition to the theoretical meaning of the concept, its practical implication relates to the position of the action researcher in the group. The researcher's theories would be far more effective when having a central and leading position in the group, whereas a peripheral position would entail constant negotiation about the information the researcher is supplying. A striking example can be found in the 'community of practice' theory, which is grounded in the Habermas view on collaborative planning discussed earlier. This view implies a social learning attitude in a planning group and this imperative is normally accepted without debate: no one has questions about this 'community of practice', they were participating automatically and it was also informal, without liability (Tress *et al.*, 2003). If this concept is introduced and implemented by a scientist in a group of planning practitioners, it may strengthen the group's self-referentiality and the focus on sharing information in the group and excluding information from the outer world.

Having discussed the dialectical relationship between performativity and reflexivity as well as the importance of reflexivity in planning practice, we will now discuss two case studies of action research. The cases differ in the position of the researchers involved, illustrating problems of reflexivity in different contexts.

10.5. Case 1. The Dutch Flood Mitigation project: Noordwaard

Flood mitigation policies are currently being deployed by the Dutch government to counter the effects of climate change. Mitigation can be achieved by creating more space for the rivers, increasing river discharge capacities, allowing for natural inundation processes. Since 2003, the Dutch Ministry of Transport, Public Works and Water Management has been working on the sustainable development of floodplains along the rivers Rhine and Meuse, resulting in a government endorsed River Flood Mitigation Plan (Ministerie van Verkeer en Waterstaat, 2006). A wide variety of measures have been planned and implemented to improve water retention and discharge capacity, including the relocation of dikes, the construction of water retention polders and side channels, and the redevelopment of floodplains by changing land use. The plans for changing land use affected a group of farmers and residents of the 'Noordwaard' (Figure 10.1), a polder area in the Biesbosch tidal system, in the south-west of the Netherlands in the province of North-Brabant (Figure 10.2a, b).

Figure 10.1. Picture of the area of Noordwaard. (Rooy, 2009)

10. Reflexivity in action research: two spatial planning cases

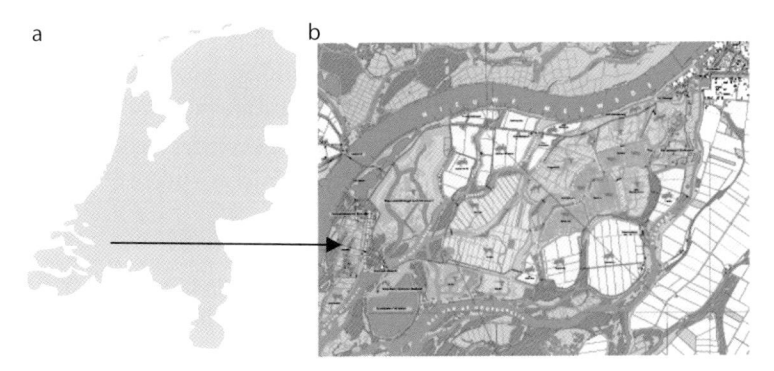

Figure 10.2. Geographical location of the Noordwaard in the Netherlands (a) and a map of the area of the Noordwaard in the future (b). (Ministry of Transport, Public Works and Water Management 2007).

The group organised the *Platform Behoud Noordwaard* (Platform Save the Noordwaard) and objected to the plans of the Ministry of Transport, Public Works and Water Management and its Project Bureau in charge, advised by the Faculty of Hydraulic Engineering of Delft University (Figure 10.3). They got assistance from a hydraulic engineering emeritus professor who was critical of governmental water policies in an earlier phase (Roth *et al.*, 2006; Roth and Warner, 2007). Based on his expert knowledge and the platform's local knowledge of the polder and river area, they developed an alternative to the government's preferred plan. When neither the Project Bureau nor Delft University showed any signs of taking

Figure 10.3. Farmers in the Noordwaard block the way when the Secretary of State for Transport, Public Works and Water Management visits the area. Dutch text: 'Keep your hands off the Noordwaard'. (Photo by Jos Waltheer)

their alternative into account, they called in desperation for help from the Wageningen University Science Shop. The problem was that to take the alternative seriously would entail running a hydraulic model, based on the plans for increasing the river discharge and water storage capacity. The Project Bureau considered these plans contrary to EU policies (Habitat Directive), whereas the university saw such use of the model as a token of disloyalty to their official client (the Ministry).

At this point, two of the authors of this chapter came into the picture, as they were assigned this Science Shop project. The description of the process given below was written from their point of view. A partial account is given in their Science Shop report (Pleijte *et al.*, 2005) and in other articles (Pleijte and During, 2006; Schut *et al.*, 2010). A full account could not be published in an official Science Shop report, for the reasons given below. A discussion on their ability to combine reflexivity with their action research will evaluate the degree of bias in their approach.

10.5.1 Threefold strategy for action research

At first the researchers tried to relate to the official planning process, hoping that their university affiliation would help them to overcome any possible drawbacks in taking the Platform's alternative into account. This attempt was in vain. To put it more bluntly, the only access to the democratic process of decision making went through the hydraulic model put forward by the Project Bureau. Denying access to this model meant no visibility in the political discussion. Alternative models did not exist, because of the huge amount of investment that had been made in this 'official' one. Given this state of affairs, a threefold strategy was deployed by the researchers and the platform:
- underpinning the platform's alternative with a qualitative landscape ecological system analysis;
- critically reviewing the official model and its basic assumptions;
- criticising the democratic process and finding ways to penetrate political agendas.

This resulted in action research that went beyond the original question of theoretical underpinning for the platform's alternative. More emphasis was put on action than on research. Although they were unaware of the discussion on reflexivity and performativity, the positions of the two researchers were split. One of them became the right-hand of the leader of the Platform and was primarily interested in the process and its fallacies. The other took an outside position and gave instructions on how to improve the quality and status of the alternative and how to address politicians. They self-organised this division of labour, which reflected their specific interests and expertise. Below a concise and self-critical account of their activities is given, which follows their threefold strategy.

10.5.2 Action research approach

To improve the status of the platform's alternative, a group of independent scientists (landscape ecologists, physical geographers, river experts from the universities of Delft, Wageningen and Utrecht) were invited to critically review and improve the proposed plan. The experts agreed on the use of a qualitative landscape-ecological system analysis that integrated the local knowledge of the farmer group. This resulted in a higher level of knowledge about the river system and its manageability with which both their alternative could be improved and the official government plan could be criticised. The most important conclusion of this expert meeting concerned the quality of the alternative: there was room for improvement but it was a serious enough proposal to compete with the official plan. The qualitative landscape ecological analysis was flanked by a policy analysis. Again a synthesis was made between the available formal knowledge on the official planning procedure and the local knowledge and narrative-oriented knowledge of the platform.

Placing the government endorsed plan in doubt started with posing critical scientific questions to the Project Bureau and then using the answers to highlight the shortcomings of the model. The questions were derived from scientific literature and the landscape ecological analysis. One of the questions focused on the norm stating the maximum river discharge that was used for the river policy and its theoretical underpinning. Posing such questions revealed that there was no such scientific basis and moreover that the norm did not correspond to the body of knowledge on climate change and the IPCC scenarios[14]. Another question involved confronting the government plan with the disastrous floods of 1993 and 1995. The official plan would cause water from the river Rhine to flow into the river Meuse because of a 90 cm water level disparity. The experts of the Ministry of Transport, Public Works and Water Management claimed that the questions posed were highly inappropriate, because their models could not run such a hypothetical scenario (in fact there was no model available that encompassed both the River Rhine and the Meuse). Finally, the issue of the model structure was questioned, because it turned out that the official model could only calculate water management effects downstream and not upstream. This is out of line with geographic morphological knowledge on changes in natural river behaviour invoked by rising or dropping sea levels (Buijse *et al.*, 2005a, b; Middelkoop *et al.*, 2005; Wolfert, 2001). Moreover, the effect of rising sea level was not included in the official model.

The interaction in which all these questions were posed and answered or not answered, mainly in public hearings and debates, exposed the self-referentiality of the governmental planning group. Criticising the governmental plans was clearly considered 'not done' and as a consequence, positions hardened between the platform and the Project Bureau. This

---

[14] This became one of the key issues in the political debate in the First Chamber of the State General. The Minister could not answer this question and the debate was postponed until the State Secretary returned from a few months' leave. The State Secretary convinced the senators that the norm corresponded to the mid-IPPC scenario: a statement that could not be checked by the politicians and was finally taken for granted.

was reflected in the tone with which the platform was addressed. At first, repeated pleas to be co-operative were made by the Project Bureau, who promised to give clarity soon about expropriation of their lands and houses (Figure 10.4). Due to the resistance the platform organised, the approach changed to one of individualised stalking. Officials of the Project Bureau visited farmers during their work several times per week, unannounced. They were told they were a problem for their neighbours, who were willing to co-operate and their full compliance with the planning process was urgently requested. This approach was certainly effective as the unity in the platform was torn apart and some of the members wanted to give up resistance. This schism occurred in a period in which the parliament had to decide on the national project. Politicians were aware of the resistance from the Noordwaard, but still unaware of the alternative produced by the platform. The researchers of the Science Shop project were invited to participate in an expert meeting organised by the parliament. They accepted the invitation in their capacity as experts and not as platform representatives. In addition to this expert meeting, there was a bilateral discussion with a member of Parliament who chaired the official Parliamentary Committee on Water Management. Although he was from a political party supporting the governmental plan, this member of Parliament expressed his concern about this policy development in general and about the way the officials dealt with the platform's alternative. He convinced his Committee to give a formal assignment to the Investigation and Verification Office of the Senate, to shed light on the accountability of the procedure of the National Flood Mitigation project. The Investigation and Verification Office reported in line with the conclusions of the researchers of the Science Shop, by stating that the Directorate General of Public Works and Water Management failed

Figure 10.4. Protest sign in Dutch: 'Spatial planning for flood mitigation!!!– Where does that leave us??'. (Du Borck, 2007)

10. Reflexivity in action research: two spatial planning cases

to take various well-prepared alternative plans into account (Investigation and Verification Office, 2006). However, this outcome did not affect the decision-making process in the Parliament in any way. During this relatively short period of democratic decision-making the situation worsened in the Noordwaard. It became clear that the pressure on individuals had risen to such an extent that casualties were likely. Receiving this signal from the platform, the researchers decided to stop their activities instantly. They decided not to report a second time to avoid a deepening of the schism in the local community. The platform more or less surrendered during the democratic process.

10.5.3 Analysis and reflection

Any reflection on the role of the action researchers should take the enormous power inequality into account. Within the platform a reflexive position was taken in advance right from the beginning. They were aware that they would have to move their homes for the safety of the country. But they wanted to be convinced that there was no other way, and this was the reason for developing an alternative. A basic and transparent comparison between their alternative and the official plans would have been enough to change their attitudes from resistance to co-operation. Instead, the platform was invited on various occasions to explain their position and their views in public hearings. The members felt very uncomfortable, because they had not being educated for such debates and could not master the computer enough to make convincing PowerPoint presentations. So these invitations deepened their sense of inferiority vis-à-vis the government planning officials. This power play[15] by the governmental agencies caused an increasing lack of trust.

Assistance from the researchers was welcomed, because of their river system knowledge and their strategic insight into the democratic procedure. The researchers considered empowerment as a key issue on the way to taking the alternative into account. The qualitative landscape-ecological system analysis however, although combined with the policy analysis and intertwined with local knowledge, was insufficient to break the self-referentiality of the official government discourse. Nevertheless, the effect of the Science Shop project on the governmental planning process was rather significant: the officials of the Project Bureau felt attacked. The researchers in the Science Shop project inadvertently hardened the relationship between the platform and the Project Bureau. This became more apparent as the researchers organised their level of reflexivity in the political process, acknowledging it as the encompassing level of truth. The adoption of a central position by one of the researchers and a peripheral position by the other proved successful. It turned out to be the right formula for bringing the issue of the disregarded alternative into the political arena. As a consequence, a strategic combination of scientific arguments arose. Due to a lack

---

[15] In the official Science Shop report there are several examples of power play and misleading information. One example may illustrate this: one of the Provincial Deputies stated in a newspaper that being co-operative would result in a more forward position in expropriation with regard to the total of the National Flood Mitigation Project and therefore in higher prices for the expropriated lands.

of communication about contents with those in charge of the official planning process, self-referentiality became apparent in the platform too. It was believed that the platform's alternative was better equipped to answer the combined challenge of countering rising sea levels and increased river discharge.

This self-referentiality affected the attitude of the researchers, because it became unclear whether the lower-lying parts of the Netherlands would indeed become a safer place to live when the governmental plans were put into practice. The issue in the Biesbosch changed, because an increase in river discharge in a tidal zone would imply greater access for tidal water during spring tides. This question, addressing the combined effects of increased river water discharge and sea level rise, could not be answered with the existing body of scientific knowledge. This unanswered question plus the lack of scientific underpinning of the norms gave rise to doubts about the whole project. This doubt was not expressed in public debate, but was kept in mind as a dilemma during the Science Shop project, providing the kind of reflexive awareness that inhibits rash actions.

10.6. Case 2. The demonstration project of area development: Wieringerrandmeer

The National Spatial Strategy of the Ministry of Housing, Spatial Planning and the Environment (2006) (VROM in Dutch) forms the basis for development planning or spatial development. The National Spatial Strategy has shifted the emphasis in the policy from 'imposing restrictions' by governments, to 'promoting developments' for decentralised governments, market parties, societal organisations and citizens. The ability to develop is the central consideration, and is promoted through less detailed regulation by central government, fewer barriers and a greater span of action for (1) other levels of government by decentralisation to provincial authorities and municipalities and (2) market parties. One of the main objectives of the National Spatial Strategy is to link spatial policy to the demands of society, and to allow for faster implementation of policy. Some examples are the reduction of regulations, and the modernisation of legislation (embedded in the new Spatial Planning Act and the Interim Urban and Environmental Procedures Act). Central government will make proposals for better use of public private partnerships (PPPs) in spatially defined projects and for recovery and settlement of costs regionally. This will give the public, companies, government authorities and non-governmental organisations new and improved opportunities for putting their ideas into practice. The Ministry actively assists the exchange and dissemination of knowledge in these fields. Development planning or spatial development is a method that makes the implementation of spatial plans, visions and projects the central consideration.

The Ministry, provincial governments and other public and private stakeholders have been jointly setting up 14 demonstration projects for development planning, which had to be ready for implementation by 2005. One of these 14 demonstration projects of spatial

10. Reflexivity in action research: two spatial planning cases

development is Wieringerrandmeer, in the north of the Province North-Holland in the Netherlands (Figure 10.5).

10.6.1 Wieringerrandmeer

Wieringen (Figure 10.5) is a polder located in the province North-Holland that has been part of the mainland since 1924 (Figure 10.6a, b). Its main land-use functions are agriculture and housing. In the mid-nineties the initiative arose to make Wieringen an island again, by developing a lake between Wieringen and Wieringermeerpolder. The proposal was supported by both the municipality of Wieringen and their neighbouring municipality

Figure 10.5. Picture of the present area of Wieringerrandmeer. (Volkskrant, 2008).

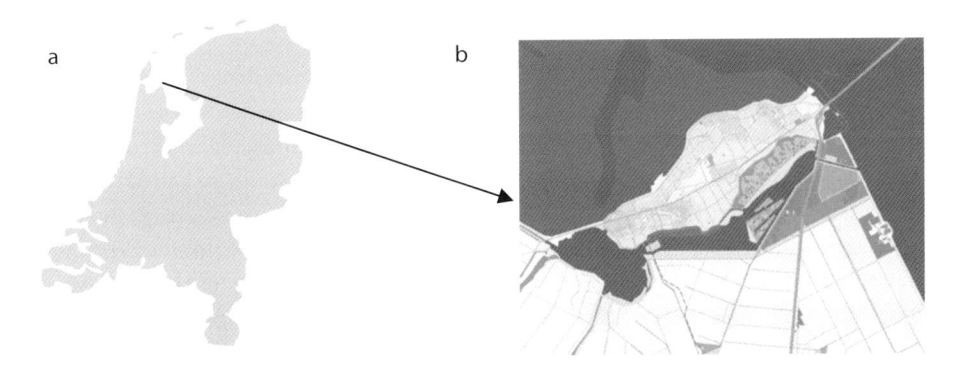

Figure 10.6. Geographical location of Wieringerrandmeer in the Netherlands (a) and a map of the Wieringerrandmeer in the future (b) (SP Noord Holland, 2005).

Wieringermeer. Bearing in mind the objective of this chapter, we will - at this point - make some relatively large jumps in time in the below three sections.

In 1999, the municipalities of Wieringermeer and Wieringen, the local tourist organisation and Waterboard Hollands Noorderkwartier came together in a steering committee and Project Bureau that launched the plan to create a Wieringerrandmeer. The Project Bureau adopted a public private partnership (PPP) construction that would allow for the early integration and collaboration of market players in developing and implementing the Wieringerrandmeer project. A Development Competition for proposals was initiated, in which several large construction companies, engineering firms, design and dredging specialists enrolled.

In February 2004, an independent jury declared one of the proposals as the winner of the Development Competition. The winning proposal would cover a total area of 2,200 ha including a 9 km long canal, a new border lake of 800 ha, water storage locations of 100 ha, a nature area of 200 acres, 50 acres of beaches, 1,300 dwellings in the new area and 1,300 dwellings in the nuclei of Wieringen and Wieringermeer.

In the spring of 2007, a meeting was organised by several residents of Wieringen, who had serious concerns about the plans for the Wieringerrandmeer that would – according to the residents – lead to massive and unjustified interference with the landscape. At that time, 30 farms were located in the area, which were most likely to be resettled to create space for the project. The municipalities and the province argued that the future of agriculture in the region was uncertain and offered no 'long-term perspective', although the farmers doubted this. However, an eminent consequence of the project was the suggested change in water level in the region which would have negative impacts on the agricultural land.

During this meeting it became clear that other stakeholder groups also shared the concerns about the planning of the Wieringerrandmeer. The stakeholders established themselves formally under the name 'Wierings Beraad', by then composed of residents from the municipality of Wieringen, the Environmental Federation of North Holland, Landscape North Holland, and the Foundation for Landscape Wieringen. Wierings Beraad specifically worked with LTO, a farmers' organisation. One of the first activities was sending a letter to four ministers ((1) Transport, Public Affairs and Water Management, (2) Agriculture, Nature and Food Quality, (3) Housing, Spatial Planning and Environment and (4) Economic Affairs), urging them to take a good look at the plans. According to Wierings Beraad, the design of the Wieringerrandmeer did not adequately respect the qualities of the current landscape, did not sufficiently take into account the adverse effects on the environment, provided insufficient socio-economic benefits, and could lead to major financial risks and risks for the water system and infrastructure. Wierings Beraad expressed their deep concerns about the current plan for the border lake that should be paid from a housing development plan that initially would include the construction of around 2,600 dwellings (Figure 10.7).

10. Reflexivity in action research: two spatial planning cases

Figure 10.7. Poster which articulates that a lot of houses are built in the area to realise nature and water retention. Dutch text: 'Wieringen awake! Wieringen + a border lake = a sea of houses. So much red for a little green. Do not do it!!!'. (Landschapszorg Wieringen, 2006).

Moreover, they stressed that the number of dwellings was growing because of problems with the exploitation of the whole plan.

10.6.2 Action research approach: research towards an alternative spatial plan

In April 2008, Wierings Beraad initiated the development of an alternative plan in collaboration with Alterra[16], Oosterhuis Architects and Mapsup[17] (Wierings Beraad *et al.*, 2008). Alterra was approached by the spokesperson of Wierings Beraad who knew one of the researchers that had experience with integral, sustainable planning and process management. This researcher subsequently involved the landscape architect and Mapsup.

Knowledge of landscape architecture and a digital map-table, used to integrate different kinds of maps, were used to design an alternative plan. Additional knowledge and expertise were provided by Alterra, the Environmental Federation of North Holland, Landscape North Holland, LTO and the Foundation for Landscape Wieringen. Hydraulic data was provided by the Waterboard.

---

[16] Alterra is part of Wageningen University & Research Centre focusing on the green living environment.
[17] Mapsup supports spatial planning processes by offering GIS tools to non-GIS users to improve communication and decision-making.

Two researchers at Alterra played a facilitating role in the process. One of the authors of this chapter was involved. During the development of the alternative proposal, the Alterra researchers fulfilled different roles. One of the researchers was involved as action researcher in the planning process and became the right-hand of the spokesman for Wierings Beraad. He played an active role in the process by participating in various meetings, acting as a knowledge broker. He contributed to: (1) formulating the alternative plan; (2) advising the Wierings Beraad on the appropriateness and accuracy of the environmental impact assessment (EIA) procedure; and (3) the spatial planning procedure. The other researcher was positioned in the periphery of the project and gave advice about these three topics in a more reflexive manner. This split was not organised on their own account but has grown, in this case directed not by the researchers themselves, but by the spokesman for Wierings Beraad.

Simultaneously, the researchers also conducted more policy-oriented research for the Ministry of Agriculture, Nature and Food Security (LNV). To avoid discussions about participation in action research within the organisation Wageningen University Research Centre, the involvement of the researchers was not formalised in a project. This provided the researchers with a degree of flexibility, and avoided conflicts of interest within the organisation. The Ministries of the central government has decentralised the spatial planning process to the provincial authority and the municipalities involved. The provincial authority could have experienced the involvement of Wageningen University and Research Centre as controlling or as a critical attack on the decentralised process commissioned by the Ministry of Agriculture, Nature and Food Quality.

The research started by exploring why Wierings Beraad had failed to successfully mobilise an alternative spatial plan in the formal spatial planning procedure. Several attempts had been made to discuss the planning for Wieringerrandmeer, without the desired result. Different perspectives and assumptions about the usefulness and necessity of developing the Wieringerrandmeer project did not provide sufficient space for successfully presenting alternatives. Alternatives were continuously perceived as threats rather than opportunities, whereas having multiple scenarios could offer increased flexibility through time, taking into account changing assumptions and contextual factors. Another conclusion was that citizens and civil society had been insufficiently involved during the early stages of the project, when the PPP-construction was developed. Citizens had been informed through the media and clear participation and communication structures were absent.

With regard to the appropriateness and accuracy of the EIA, the researcher advised Wierings Beraad to criticise the EIA and to ask them to examine the content of their alternative. When reviewing the EIA, the researchers advised Wierings Beraad to specifically emphasise the quality of the landscape, and to present the Alternative Wieringerrandmeer Proposal as the 'most environmentally friendly alternative' to the Steering Committee.

We believe that in a spatial development project of this size two major questions should be asked: (1) what is the usefulness of a spatial development plan and (2) what is the necessity of a spatial development plan? Wierings Beraad found the necessity of creating a Wieringerrandmeer to have been unconvincingly demonstrated. The need to construct houses was mainly legitimised by poorly informed and outdated socio-economic data. This data was moreover used to justify the compensation of adverse environmental impacts. Moreover, serious environmental consequences, such as stagnant mobility and increasing salinity were not studied. The implementation of the proposed plan required a comprehensive housing programme, which would disturb the existing rural character of the area and not contribute value to spatial quality in general; an unacceptable sacrifice according to the Wierings Beraad.

Due to the premature development competition and elaborated PPP construction, limited time and space was provided for citizen participation, not to mention for the elaboration of citizens' alternatives. Lastly it was concluded that civil society organisations and citizens had hardly been involved in discussions about the usefulness and necessity of the proposed plan, and in thinking about alternatives. The proposed spatial plan came from governments and builders, not from citizens and other societal stakeholders. Supporting Wierings Beraad's criticism of the spatial planning procedure, the researchers provided some points for consideration:

- The Elverding Committee (2008) recently found that in many large projects the exploration phase is missing or of limited quality. There is (also) little evidence of participation by civil society organisations and citizens when it comes to discussions about usefulness (value) and necessity in large projects, which leads to problems for governments and the private sector later in the process.
- The conditions under which the project was initiated had changed, but proposals that respected and incorporated these changed conditions were not given the opportunity to be submitted and equally studied in the spatial planning procedure.

10.6.3 The Alternative Wieringerrandmeer Proposal

On the 27th of June 2008, Wierings Beraad presented their Alternative Wieringerrandmeer Proposal. In this plan less land would be depoldered, fewer houses constructed, the houses could be located closer to the lake, and fewer farmers would have to be resettled.

The alternative plan suggested a number of advantages vis-à-vis the existing plan for the area:
- focus on strengthening existing spatial qualities in the area: quiet, open land, green recreation, cultural history of the area;
- smaller scale, thus more flexibility in the future, and better control of (financial) risks;
- preservation of good agricultural land, no large-scale expropriation or displacement of farmers (Figure 10.8);
- improvement of water quality, and fresh water for agriculture;

Figure 10.8. Farmers from the Wieringerrandmeer ask governments and project developers to keep their hands off agricultural land. The Dutch signs say 'Province, do not let your farmers drown' and 'Use your mind, do not waste fertile land'. (Agrarisch Dagblad, 2008)

- strengthening of economic activities (green recreation), stimulate the local marina promoting the economy of regional farming produce;
- strong contribution to the National Ecological Network (EHS);
- space for the construction of up to 750 houses, in line with the original objective of the border lake, in line with local and regional housing needs;
- broad public support, including residents, farmers and environmental conservation organisations.

The Alternative Wieringerrandmeer Proposal was submitted to the Steering Committee Wieringerrandmeer, suggested to be adopted as the 'most environmentally friendly alternative' within the EIA. Surprisingly, the Steering Committee brought in their own most environmentally friendly alternative. In their official response to the Alternative Wieringerrandmeer Proposal, the Steering Committee mainly based their conclusions on a number of presentations, not seriously respecting the perspectives and considerations underlying the alternative. Incorrect assumptions and findings were analysed, and the real vision and outline behind the 'Alternative Wieringerrandmeer Proposal' were not evaluated nor discussed. The Steering Committee concluded that the Alternative Wieringerrandmeer Proposal was lacking financial foundation, and therefore not considered feasible. The report was written without the co-operation or consultation of Wierings Beraad, who were also not provided with the opportunity to prepare written remarks.

10. Reflexivity in action research: two spatial planning cases

Simultaneously with the development and assessment of the Alternative Wieringerrandmeer Proposal, Wierings Beraad had periodic contact with the Ministry of Housing (VROM), the Wieringerrandmeer Project, Steering Committee Wieringerrandmeer, and parliament's Housing Commission. Independently of the Steering Committee, they were asked to consider the alternative proposal, and allow it access to the formal spatial planning procedure and EIA procedure. Again, the Wierings Beraad was told that the alternative lacked a clear financial plan and underpinning, which made it unrealistic.

The Steering Committee's socio-economic and financial evaluation of the Alternative Proposal was submitted for review by Wierings Beraad to reputable independent experts. As part of this strategy, a financial consultation organisation was asked to underpin the alternative financially, and make a comparison with the preferred alternative by the government. The consultation included an analysis of how the diversification of risks were allocated between public and private parties. Furthermore, the analysis showed that calculations for the preferred alternative had been made on the basis of underestimated true costs, especially costs related to acquiring agricultural land. A war of reports started.

As part of a lobby for national political support, members of two large political parties in the parliament were invited to visit the Wieringerrandmeer. One of the authors joined an excursion by the parliament members to the area and participated in the debate that arose between the Wierings Beraad and some members of the Second Chamber.

10.6.4 Analysis and reflection

In the planning process for Wieringerrandmeer there was little room for jointly exploring a plan for the region. The Steering Committee was not open to collaborating in a constructive way, which led to tensions and conflict between them and Wierings Beraad.

The Steering Committee would unconditionally hold on to their own principles and plan, so that they were no longer open to innovative and improved understanding of the changing circumstances. They continuously referred to democratic decisions (approval by the province and municipalities), ignoring the lack of public support for the plans.

The case of Wieringerrandmeer can provide lessons for action research and the role of action researchers, because: (1) researchers interacted with societal organisations and citizens to develop an alternative plan; (2) researchers mobilised formal explicit knowledge of different disciplines that led to a more integral and sustainable alternative; (3) the researchers brought in tacit knowledge about other demonstration projects of spatial development which can be advantageous, i.e. knowledge about usefulness and necessity; (4) the researchers mobilised knowledge about legal procedures to improve the communication and relations between politicians and other stakeholders and to make optimal use of existing procedures and citizens' rights in the spatial planning procedure.

One of the researchers (researcher A) had a particular role as a knowledge broker, using his explicit formal knowledge for integrated, sustainable planning and for process management. He worked in a Habermas-like manner; focusing on the self-referentiality of the stakeholders, by paying a lot of attention to the communication and consensus-seeking through negotiation. The other researcher (researcher B) worked much more in a Foucault-like way, by focusing on the inequalities in the negotiation process and conflicts. He advised in a strategic manner to influence the planning process.

The performative researcher (researcher A) had a more central position in the process, the role of reflexivity was much more restricted to reflection on the activities of Wierings Beraad. The involvement and embedding of researcher A in developing an alternative plan influenced the performativity of research, whereas the involvement of researcher B influenced the reflexivity. Because the action researchers worked independently, reflexivity and performativity did not specifically reinforce each other. Reflexivity and performativity met in the person of the spokesman of Wierings Beraad, who combined the knowledge of both action researchers. However, it was not a joint interactive job between the action researchers and the spokesman, which makes it necessary to criticise the self-referentiality of researchers in an action-research approach. Of course, this applies equally to the PPP construction and Wierings Beraad.

When reflecting on the role of the two action researchers, some observations and preliminary conclusions can be drawn. Both researchers operated from a different perspective on spatial planning. One saw his role as becoming part of the collaborative planning process, and connecting stakeholders and networks. The other researcher focussed more on the inequality of power relations. As a consequence they gave contradictory information and advice. Whereas the knowledge broker insisted on keeping the relations with the PPP positive and attempted to negotiate a marginal influence, the reflexive researcher raised more fundamental issues of legitimacy and democratic openness of the official planning process. Both recommendations were strategic towards the planning process, but in a different way. These differences did not cause great problems, because the spokesman for Wierings Beraad could handle them. He used them as options to be discussed in his group. These two approaches could probably have been used more efficiently if both researchers had taken a more interactive and reflexive stand towards the process of negotiation and its underlying principles. Contrary to the previous case this subdivision of reflexivity and performativity between two researchers seems to have been suboptimal here.

10.7 Discussion and conclusions

The objective of this chapter is to describe the dilemmas of a simultaneous quest for truth and performance in action research, and to discuss the possibilities and limitations of reflexivity as a scientific attitude and the various constraints it puts on performativity in action research approaches. By systematically analysing the key concepts, and providing

10. Reflexivity in action research: two spatial planning cases

examples from the two case studies we have tried to highlight what appear to be the key drivers that influence this.

In both cases the spatial planning process between government and citizens was the central topic. Both Noordwaard and Wieringerrandmeer demonstrated how citizens mobilised research and researchers to strengthen their negotiating position. Nonetheless, we have also seen that eventually government or dominant parties took insufficient account of alternative plans that emerged from community resistance. Both cases differ in relation to the mechanisms that caused this lack of inclusiveness. In the Noordwaard case the government felt responsible for the common interests of safety for the lower parts of the country in the long term and believed that a group of citizens and farmers was not qualified to interfere with the hydraulic complexity of river management. Self-referentiality emerged around the hydraulic model for river management. In the second case of Wieringerrandmeer, the interests of private investors in the PPP caused self-referentiality. The forecasted financial revenues and profits led to a lack of flexibility in accounting for community-based concern around Wieringen.

Another similarity between the cases is that preferred solutions for the two studied areas were designed, discussed and approved at a very early stage in the spatial planning procedure. (Democratic) decisions, taken during this phase, were used as a backstop to ensure that decisions did not have to be discussed again, regardless of whether or not the conditions under which these decisions were taken (i.e. public support, new research on discharge peaks, changes in the price of agricultural land) had changed or not. The Government's procedures appear to be too static to deal with this changing context. Moreover, essential procedures or models in decision making, like the EIA (Wieringerrandmeer) and hydraulic model (Noordwaard), were not accessible to serve the interests of citizens or social movements. In this way the government used them as instruments of power to control access to formal procedures. In both cases there was a combination of knowledge regarding the content of the problem (e.g. discharge capacity), knowledge concerning the process, and political lobbying. And there was a good reason for this. The reflective capacity of the researchers formed the basis for this approach of multilevel networking, coalition-building and conflict management.

In both cases there was a potential conflict of interest between researchers and their clients (Platform Save the Noordwaard and Wierings Beraad), and their main institute and principal (LNV). This may consciously or unconsciously have influenced performativity. In other words, power politic will affect the (unconscious) choice between performativity and reflexivity.

It was the combination of knowledge about the content, process/procedures and political lobbying in both cases that created possibilities for bargaining. Hidden in this is a 'right' configuration of performativity and reflexivity: knowing what to do to create an opening in the process (reflexivity), then mobilising substantive insights and alternatives that can give the process a new direction (performativity).

Performativity is stakeholder-dependent. As we indicate in the introduction, research is not only mobilised in negotiations by stakeholders, it is also subject to negotiotiation itself. In other words, the value of research is negotiable. This focus on the 'performativity' of research, clearly stakeholder-related, means that research is used as a 'weapon' in negotiation processes (Foucault). From a 'reflexivity' point of view this perspective would be completely different; since one could say it is unjust to deliver stakeholder A arguments, but not stakeholder B. From this perspective it creates legitimacy for research to support the goals of stakeholder A, while excluding the goals of stakeholder B.

In both cases action researchers were involved at the request of marginalised groups. Reacting to marginalisation, the action researchers primarily provided action-oriented knowledge. Although it can be argued that this orientation towards an emancipating approach may inhibit the researchers' vision on truth in these cases, their perspective raises very interesting scientific questions about democracy and science.

Concerning democracy the issue was raised if planning procedures contradict the inclusiveness that is required to respect the intentions and knowledge that ground alternative plans. It seems that procedures are too organised around the contents and procedures of a formal planning process, focusing only on individual citizen participation or community resistance. The fact that resistance can lead to interesting alternative plans does not fit into the procedure.

At a more scientific principal level the question can be posed whether action research can be free of normative positions towards the issue of developments that are preferred or considered inappropriate. The action researcher has to take a clear position, but by taking a reflexive stand he can escape the group think that is discussed in the first half of this chapter. This normative position can be problematic later, but the solution seems quite obvious. A combination of action research and a subsequent scientific analysis can be used to take advantage of the action-oriented perspective on planning, while using the findings for scientific progress in the understanding of spatial planning practices. The case study of the Noordwaard indicates that it can be advantageous to combine action research with reflective re-analysis, when reflection is organised in a participative way close to the actual planning events. The case study of Wieringerrandmeer showed that a reflexive analysis sometimes cannot coincide with action research, because of incomparable planning beliefs underlying performativity of knowledge and reflexivity of observations.

The danger of an action researcher who limits his focus to the performance of his knowledge contribution and therefore contributes to self-referentiality can be opposed by reflexivity. We consider it a mission impossible if both positions are to be equally balanced by one researcher. A first level of reflexivity can be organised by a second action researcher who at least includes a similar theoretical framework. Reflexivity based on a competing theoretical framework should be organised in a secondary analysis.

Acknowledgements

These research activities were conducted in the processes of area development. The knowledge was developed for and with citizens of two areas: Noordwaard and Wieringerrandmeer, both in the Netherlands. Scientific support for the research activities was provided by Alterra, Wageningen University and Research Centre, the Netherlands. The action research projects were financed by the Science Shop of Wageningen UR (Noordwaard) and by Knowledge Basis 7: Transitions, institutions, government and policy of Wageningen UR (Wieringerrandmeer). This chapter could not have been written without the data and support provided by these two projects.

References

Agrarisch Dagblad, 2008. Boerenprotest tegen Wieringerrandmeer. Available at: http://www.agd.nl/upload/1864769_661_1205832974002-VRP_3kol.jpg. 18-03-2008.

Allmendinger, P., 2002. Planning Theory. Palgrave, New York, NY, USA.

Austin, J.L., 1962. How to do things with words, the William James Lectures delivered at Harvard University in 1955 (Londen 1962, revised edition 1967). Clarendon Press, Oxford, UK.

Butler, J., 1997. Excitable speech, a politics of the performative. New York, NY, USA.

Buijse, A.D., F. Klijn, R.S.E.W. Leuven, H. Middelkoop, F. Schiemer, J.H. Thorp and H.P. Wolfert (eds.), 2005a. Rehabilitating large regulated rivers. Archiv für Hydrobiologie Supplement 155, Large Rivers 15. 738 pp.

Buijse, A.D., F. Klijn, R.S.E.W. Leuven, H. Middelkoop, F. Schiemer, J.H. Thorp and H.P. Wolfert, 2005b. Rehabilitation of large rivers: references, achievements and integration into river management. In: Buijse, A.D., F. Klijn, R.S.E.W. Leuven, H. Middelkoop, F. Schiemer, J.H. Thorp and H.P. Wolfert (eds.), Archiv für Hydrobiologie Supplement 155, Large Rivers 15, pp. 715-738.

Cloke, P.J. and C.C. Park, 1985. Rural Resource Management: A Geographical Perspective. Croom Helm Ltd., Sydney, Australia.

Derrida, J., 1988. Signature event context. In: J. Derrida (ed.), Limited Ins. Northwestern University Press, Elvanston, IL, USA, pp. 1-23.

Du Borck, B., 2007. Blogspot. Available at: http://duburck.blogspot.com/2008/03/cordinator-voor-bewoners-noordwaard.html.

Elverding Committee (Advies Commissie Versnelling Besluitvorming Infrastructurele Projecten), 2008. Advies Sneller en Beter. 28 pp.

Foucault, M., 1966. Les Mots et les choices. [the Order of Things]. Gallimard, Paris, France.

Foucault, M., 1969. L'archéologie du Savoir [The Archaelogy of Knowledges]. Editions Gallimard, Paris, France.

Foucault, M., 1977. Discipline and Punishment. Tavistock, London, UK.

Fuller, S., 2009. The sociology of intellectual life. The career of the mind in and around academia. Sage, London, UK.

Giller, K.E., C. Leeuwis, J.A. Andersson, W. Andriesse, A. Brouwer, P. Frost, P. Hebinck, I. Heitkönig, M.K. van Ittersum, N. Koning, M.T. van Wijk and P. Windmeijer, 2008. Competing Claims on Natural Resources: What role for Science? Ecology and Society 13: 18.

Guillemin, M. and L. Gillam, 2004. Ethics, Reflexivity and "Ethically Important Moments" in Research. Qualitative Inquiry 10: 261-280.

Habermas, J., 1981. Theorie Des Kommunikativen Handelns. Band 1: Handlungstrationalität und gesellschaftliche rationalisierung. Band 2: Zur kritik der funktionalistischen vernunft, Suhrkamp Verslag, Frankfurt am Main, Germany.

Hajer, M., D. Sijmons and F. Feddes (eds.), 2006. Een plan dat werkt. Ontwerp en politiek in de regionale planvorming. Nai Uitgevers, The Hague, the Netherlands [in Dutch].

Healey, P., 1997. Collaborative Planning, shaping places in fragmented societies. UBC Press, Vancouver, Canada.

Investigation and Verification Office, 2006. Verificatie PKB Ruimte voor de Rivier. Tweede Kamer, The Hague, the Netherlands [in Dutch], p. 33.

Kuhn, T.S., 1962. The structure of scientific revolutions. University of Chicago Press, Chicago, IL, USA.

Landschapszorg Wieringen, 2006. Available at: http://www.landschapszorg.nl/dl%5C060202posterhuizenzee.jpg and http://www.landschapszorg.nl/inhoud.asp?id=2.

Leeuwis, C., 2000. Reconceptualizing participation for sustainable rural development: Towards a negotiation approach. Development and Change 31: 931-959.

Lewin, K., 1946. Action research and minority problems. Journal of Social Issues 2: 34-46.

Luhmann, N., 1990. Essays on Self-Reference. Columbia University Press, New York, NY, USA.

Middelkoop, H., M.M. Schoor, H.P. Wolfert, G.J. Maas and E. Stouthamer, 2005. Targets for ecological rehabilitation of the lower Rhine and Meuse based on a historic-geomorphologic reference. Archiv für Hydrobiologie Supplement 155, Large Rivers 15: 63-88.

Ministerie van Verkeer en Waterstaat, 2006. PKB Ruimte voor de rivier. Investeren in veiligheid en vitaliteit van het rivierengebied. SDU, the Hague, the Netherlands [in Dutch].

Ministry of Transport, Public Works and Water, 2007. Management Ruimte voor de rivier. Ontpoldering Noordwaard. Available at: http://rvdr.flow01.redmax.nl/Noordwaard/menu/Het%20project/Project.

Pleijte, M. and R. During, 2006. Ruimte voor alternatieven? Ruimte voor de rivier in de Noordwaard. Landschap 23: 187-191.

Pleijte, M., R. During, A. Gerritsen en L. Stuyt, 2005. Noordwaard: over stromingen in het denken over hoogwater en natuur. Ruimte voor meer stromen om de Noordwaard. Report 215. Wetenschapswinkel Wageningen UR, Wageningen, the Netherlands [in Dutch].

Röling, N., 1994. Facilitating sustainable agriculture: turning policy models upside down. In: I. Scoones and J. Thompson (eds.), Beyond Farmers First. Intermediate Technology Publications Ltd., London, UK, pp. 245-248.

Roth, D and J. Warner, 2007. Flood risk, uncertainty and changing river protection policy in the Netherlands: the case of 'calamity polders. Tijdschrift voor Economische en Sociale Geografie 98(4): 519-525.

Roth, D., J. Warner and M. Winnubst, 2006. Een noodverband tegen hoog water. Waterkennis, beleid en politiek rond noodoverloopgebieden. Wageningen Universiteit en Researchcentrum, Wageningen, the Netherlands.

Schechner, R., 2006. Performance Studies, an Introduction. Routledge, Abingdon, UK.

Schermer, M., 2010. I am a sceptic, but I'm not a denier. New Scientist, 15 May 2010: 36-37.

Schut, M., C. Leeuwis and A. van Paassen, 2010. Room for the River – Room for Research? The case of depoldering De Noordwaard, the Netherlands. Science and Public Policy 37(8): 611-627.

SP Noord Holland, 2005. Wieringerrandmeer: weer een stap verder richting financieel debâcle. Available at: http://noordholland.sp.nl/bericht/1187/050531-wieringerrandmeer_weer_een_stap_verder_richting_financieel_debcle.html.

Tress, B., G. Tress, A. van der Valk and G. Fry (eds.), 2003. Interdisciplinary and transdisciplinary in landscape studies: Potentials and limitations. Delta Program, Alterra Green World Research, Landscape Centre, Wageningen, the Netherlands.

Trigg, R., 2004. Understanding Social Science. Blackwell Publishing, Oxford, UK.

Van Rooy, P., 2009. Nederland boven water. Programma Gebiedsontwikkeling 2007-2009. Curnet, Gouda, the Netherlands, Available at: http://www.nederlandbovenwater.nl.

Volkskrant, 2008. Aanleg Wieringerrandmeer gaat door. 17 maart 2008. Available at: http://www.volkskrant.nl/multimedia/archive/00105/Wieringerrandmeer_105990a.jpg.

Wierings Beraad in samenwerking met Alterra, OK Architecten en Mapsup, 2008. Het Andere Wieringerrandmeer. Haalbaar, schaalbaar en betaalbaar. Available at: http://www.landschapszorg.nl/lsz.asp?id=5#anderwieringerrandmeer.

Wolfert, H.P., 2001. Geomorphological Change and River Rehabilitation: Case Studies on Lowland Fluvial Systems in the Netherlands. PhD Thesis, Scientific Publications 6, Alterra Green World Research, Wageningen, the Netherlands.

11. Limpopo case: the role of research in conflict over natural resources; informing resettlement negotiations in Limpopo National Park, Mozambique

Jessica Milgroom, Cees Leeuwis and Janice Jiggins

Abstract

Working in a tense political climate with a village to be resettled from a national park in Mozambique, this research looked for a way to be relevant to the complex situation at hand. The objective of the research at the outset was to improve post-resettlement food security. While intending to carry out a formal cycle of action research focused on agricultural practices, the research found its niche in contributing to negotiations of post-resettlement conditions between park staff and village residents. Working interactively with multiple actors, the researcher inquired about and presented information that could increase leverage in negotiations for the village residents while maintaining a balanced perspective about the challenges and limitations encountered by other actors in the process. Although the tangible influence of the research on the outcome of negotiations was subtle, we believe that untraceable consequences may have been more profound. Lessons learned include firstly, an understanding that the process of research can potentially contribute more to problem-solving than polished research results. This potential contribution is dependent on investing in relationships with key actors and being present to witness, document, inquire about and support the process as opportunities arise. Secondly, our experience suggests that research is more likely to bring about change if it is explicitly socially-engaged, interdisciplinary, well-grounded with actors on multiple levels and coupled with information intermediation. Finally, in the type of conflictive context common in landscape development, we suggest that the role of the researcher differs from that in a non-conflictive setting. In the context of conflict, the potential for the researcher to contribute to social change hinges on managing a balancing act between actors in conflict and the researcher, tailoring the research to the people, culture and specificities of each situation, and exploring creative modes of interaction.

11.1 Introduction

This chapter reports on a research process that took place in and around the Limpopo National Park in Mozambique. The Limpopo National Park (LNP) was established as a stepping stone to the creation of the larger Great Limpopo Transfrontier Conservation Area (GLTFCA) that also includes Kruger National Park in South Africa and Gonarezhou National Park in Zimbabwe as well as two other national parks in Mozambique. The creation of this new park led to plans to resettle villages located along the Shingwedzi river that runs through the centre of the park to areas outside or in the buffer zone of the park (Figure 11.1a, b). Although most residents slated for resettlement did not want to leave their homes, the

Jessica Milgroom, Cees Leeuwis and Janice Jiggins

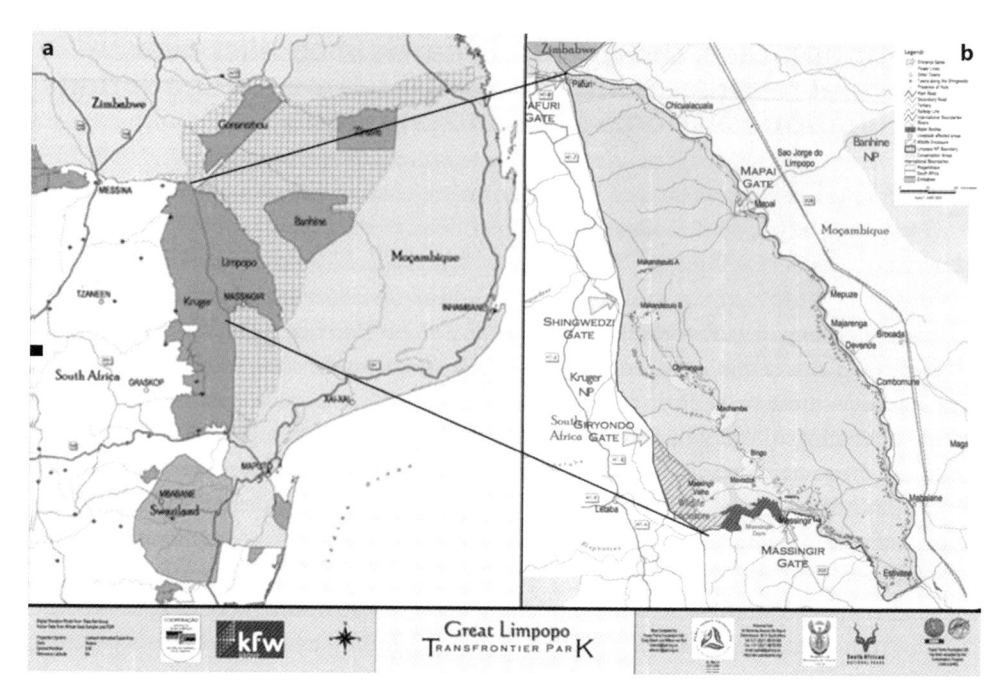

Figure 11.1. The GLTFCA in the regional context (a) and the LNP (b) showing the villages to be resettled highlighted (map by Peace Parks Foundation).

villages have been faced with intensified exposure to wildlife resulting from the translocation of game and the removal of the fence that separated the area from Kruger National Park. Threatened mainly by the increasing number of elephants, some residents gradually became willing to negotiate 'voluntary' resettlement (see Milgroom and Spierenburg, 2008). The resettlement initiative led to a lengthy negotiation process that first focused on land-use of the area inside the park while convincing residents to accept resettlement, and then on land-use and access to resources in the post-resettlement location while determining conditions for resettlement. These conditions included compensation provided to the resettled residents as well as the benefits provided to the host villages. The research reported on in this chapter documented the process from December 2006 to June 2010 and the short-term outcome of the resettlement of the first village, one of the two villages that formed part of the pilot project for resettlement in the LNP. The study was part of a larger interdisciplinary research programme 'Competing Claims on Natural Resources' of Wageningen University and Research Centre, that included twelve PhD projects in total. In line with the philosophy of this larger programme, the research had a natural and social science component and aimed to inform societal negotiation and contribute to problem-solving in this conflictive setting. The researcher was actively involved in the process being studied. In this chapter, we first outline the ideas underlying the larger research programme (see also Giller *et al.*, 2008) and provide some further contextual information. Then we describe some key episodes in the research process in order to describe the different roles played by the researcher and to assess the potential influence of the research on the process and outcome of resettlement. In the discussion section, we reflect on how the roles played by the researcher and the impacts obtained were lined up with the larger programme philosophy.

11.2 The Competing Claims perspective on the role of science in societal negotiation

Conflicts centering on the use of land and water can be regarded as a 'complex' problem setting (Gunderson and Holling, 2002; Hisschemöller and Hoppe, 1996). Many stakeholders try to exert their influence in decision-making and pursue different societal values and interests. At the same time, actors involved face considerable uncertainty regarding the likely constraints, opportunities, consequences and trade-offs associated with different modes of using land and water. In such complex settings, outcomes emerge eventually from multiple interactions across time and space. Such outcomes cannot be pre-planned, and can in many ways be seen as the unintended outcome of many intentional as well as unintentional (inter)actions and inter-dependent activities (Long, 2001; Loorbach, 2007). This series of interactions can be conceptualised as a process of societal negotiation that takes place in multiple networks and social settings, with different degrees of formality and intentionality (Giller *et al.*, 2008). When we speak of 'societal negotiation' we do not imply that formal, organised or planned negotiations are of prime importance. We do, however, suggest that 'outcomes are negotiated' under circumstances where different interests and power dynamics play a role. It is important to recognise that the quality of both formal and informal societal negotiations is often far from optimal in terms of equity, bargaining power, procedural and legal transparency, representation of interests and negotiation skills. Moreover, the availability of and/or access to knowledge and validated information about biophysical and socio-economic dynamics, options, opportunities and constraints is often lacking (Cash *et al.*, 2006) or unequally distributed.

One strategy for improving the quality of societal negotiation is to collaboratively develop relevant insights, or collect, systematise and analyse knowledge and information. Although other forms of intervention could in theory and practice be more forceful in creating 'a level playing field', these are outside the direct mandate and sphere of influence of science as a system of inquiry. Science as an organised human activity can play a useful role in negotiations in complex problem settings, especially if scientists can adapt their conventional mode of operating to practical problem-solving (Funtowicz and Ravetz, 1993; Gibbons *et al.*, 1994; Hisschemöller and Hoppe, 1996; Hoppe, 2005). In situations where both uncertainty and decision stakes are high, Funtowicz and Ravetz (1993) argue that scientists need to engage in *post-normal science*, i.e. become intensely involved in societal interactions and collaborative forms of research and learning in order to contribute to the development of shared views and value commitments, and thus become part of an 'extended peer community', reaching beyond the normal boundaries of professional relationships. The idea of post-normal science has close affinity to 'mode 2' science (Gibbons *et al.*, 1994) (Table 11.1). An implicit assumption in 'post normal' and 'mode 2' science is that scientists have something unique to offer that may improve the quality of societal negotiations.

11.2.1 A sceptical view of the contribution of science

Scientists are faced with a series of challenges that they must overcome in order to play a positive role in societal negotiations. In conflict situations, knowledge and information are strategic resources. Stakeholders select and deploy the data and insights that help them to defend their own specific interests. They tend to ignore or actively seek to undermine the credibility of contrary evidence, or oppose researching certain issues if they feel that the outcomes may be threatening. They also might try to prevent the spread of knowledge and information that they expect to negatively affect their interests. A proposal to carry out research may be welcomed as a delaying tactic or diverted towards innocuous themes or topics that support the cause of the already powerful. Stakeholders also may engage in forming opposing 'knowledge coalitions' (Long and Long, 1992; Van Buuren and Edelenbos, 2004). Research-based solutions and options are often ignored as stakeholders use opportune policy windows (e.g. a time of crisis) in order to push solutions that were designed earlier but languished for lack of support (Warner, 2008).

Moreover, the capacity of science to come up with results and options that are feasible in the context is easily overestimated. The chief reasons are that scientists often fail to take into account contextual conditions and locally specific knowledge when setting priorities, defining the nature of the problem, or designing solutions. Scientists' willingness and capacity to integrate insights from different disciplines and/or about different time and scale dimensions is organisationally constrained. The capacity of science to arrive at firm causal conclusions or predictions about the future that are sufficiently secure for decision-making in messy societal negotiations, also remains limited. Temporal mismatches also come into play – decision-makers often want quick results, while quality, in-depth research often takes more

Table 11.1. Key differences between 'mode 1' and 'mode 2' science (Gibbons et al., 1994).

'Mode 1' science	'Mode 2' science
Academic context	Application-oriented
Disciplinary	Trans-disciplinary
Homogeneous	Heterogeneous
Hierarchic and stable	Heterarchic and variable
Academic quality control	Quality measured on a wider set of criteria
Accountable to science	Accountable to science *and* society

time. Associated with this mismatch is the potential for researchers, with the best intentions of contributing to negotiations, even in 'mode 2' science, to mis-represent important issues due to the lack of a thorough understanding of the nuances of the situation. On the other hand, bringing out information that has never before been defined in black and white terms, like drawing physical boundaries on a map that has traditionally been loosely interpreted, can create more conflict and reduce the space for negotiated compromise. Furthermore, reward structures in science continue to discourage scientists from engaging with societal stakeholders in the first place (see Leeuwis, 2004; McIntyre *et al.*, 2009).

11.2.2 An optimistic view of the contribution of science

Despite the challenges described above, there are several reasons to be cautiously optimistic about the potential of scientists to make a difference to the outcomes of societal negotiations. The fact that knowledge and information can be used as a strategic resource (i.e. as a 'weapon') in a situation of conflict does mean that stakeholders are aware how to access and use that knowledge and information. In line with this, it has been shown that research activity may well serve to initiate the mobilisation of stakeholders in negotiation processes (see also Blackmore, Ison and Jiggins, 2007; Van Buuren *et al.*, 2004). When research is carried out in close collaboration with stakeholders, it has the potential to contribute to the development of common understanding and identify starting points for action. It might also help to improve the quality of the relationships among stakeholders as they begin to engage in 'doing something together'. By exploring or by just documenting previously ignored or misunderstood phenomena, researchers can help to widen the space in which options for action are sought. By introducing different qualitative and quantitative techniques such as modelling (Van Ittersum *et al.*, 1998) and scenario development (Weisbord and Janoff, 1995) research can help stakeholders discover shared values and visions about the longer term. In addition, research can serve to ameliorate uncertainty with respect to some straightforward aspects of disputed issues, even if it is difficult to capture the full complexity of the context. Collecting, analysing, and organising information designed to contribute to the negotiation process, such as, for example, quantifying resources or things not normally expressed in that way can have non-trivial consequences for the way that stakeholders look at things and interact with each other (Collins *et al.*, 2007; Steyaert *et al.*, 2007). And finally, studies in conflict management too have suggested that forms of research and investigation have considerable potential for improving the creativity and quality of negotiation trajectories (Aarts, 1998; Pruitt and Carnevale, 1993).

The methodological approach developed by the larger Competing Claims programme organises collaborative research in multiple cycles that 'start' by making descriptions of the situation from different disciplinary and stakeholder perspectives, and then proceed to gain an understanding of interrelations that have explanatory value. Subsequently, a critical activity is exploration in the widest possible sense, which supposedly leads to the discovery of new options for action that can be integrated in the design of social and technical solutions. Placed at the centre of the cycle is 'negotiation', recognising on the one hand the importance of the role of science as a vehicle for informing societal negotiation processes, and, on the other, that in order to generate knowledge that is legitimate and relevant to the societal problem at hand, ongoing negotiation with stakeholders about research activities is necessary. Figure 11.2 presents the methodological framework for the programme. How the processes of interaction sketched in the figure actually played out in the case considered here is outlined further in the following sections.

The Competing Claims methodological framework resembles the action research cycle of observe, reflect, plan and act. While there are many branches of action research, diverging both in theory and practice, all engage in this type of iterative research and action cycle. What we call the 'design' phase of the research can entail collaborative implementation of an action, but it recognises that the role of the researcher can also be to inform and facilitate the planning of action through improved negotiations. One of the assumptions of the programme is that a positive contribution to societal negotiation may occur when scientists address questions and uncertainties experienced by marginalised parties especially, with the intention of strengthening their position in negotiation processes. Drawing on the action research approach, the programme proposes that research that makes the choice

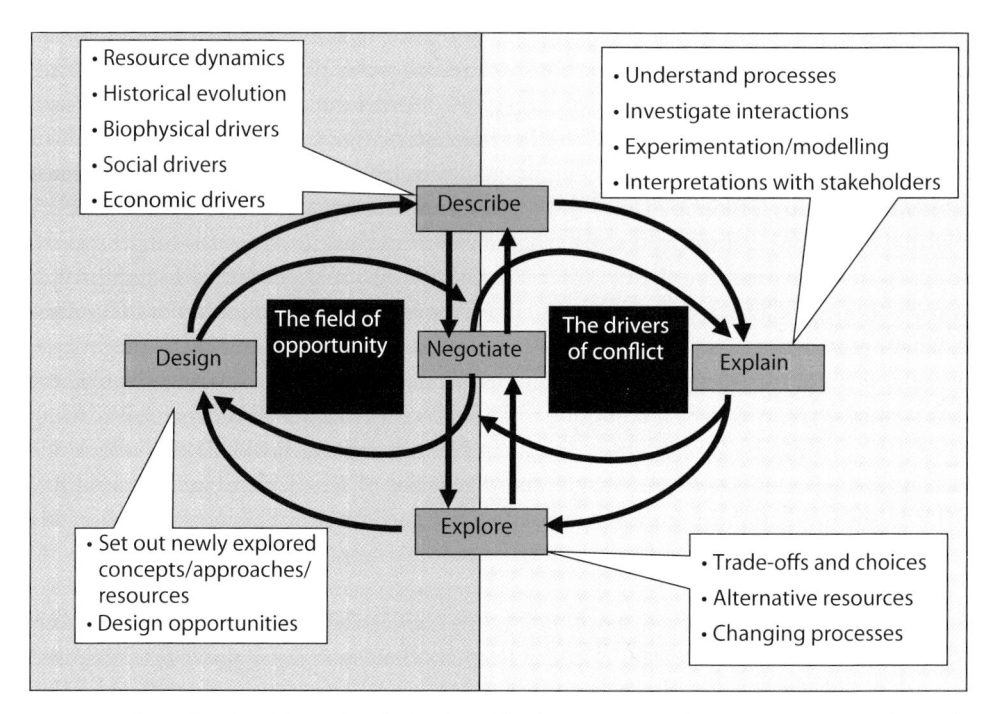

Figure 11.2. Overall methodological cycle developed for the Competing Claims programme, outlining the kinds of activities that guide the interaction between researchers and the stakeholders confronted with competing claims. (Giller et al., 2008).

to be socially-engaged and explicitly political is more likely to contribute to social change (Brydon-Miller *et al.*, 2003). While the programme finds it important to adhere to principles of scientific rigour, and strives to generate answers and conclusions that are as objective and balanced as possible, it thus recognises that science – regardless of whether it is social or natural science – can never be politically neutral since the *research questions* that scientists address tend to be posed by certain parties rather than others, and inherently build on specific societal problem definitions, values and aspirations (Alrøe and Kristensen 2002; Leeuwis 2004). Differing from some approaches to action research, however, we believe that it is necessary to engage with actors from many different perspectives across levels and scales to gain an in-depth understanding of the conflict at hand. This orientation shapes the role of the researcher as someone who can situate the local context in the larger picture, providing information from different sources, as opposed to a participatory action research orientation that is geared more towards collaborative knowledge generation at the local level. Scientists cannot avoid taking value-laden decisions about which and whose questions should have priority, but we believe that they can assist in answering those questions while being explicit about their assumptions, using methodologies that are rigorous and acceptable to conventional science. We believe that data collection should be interdisciplinary, multi-scaled, and can be both qualitative and quantitative. Engaging with actors across levels allows us to understand the structural context of the situation as well as enhancing our potential to make an impact. Similarly, embracing the 'scientific' character of our work was also a strategy to remain a legitimate player in this volatile and conflictive research context. The case study described below illustrates how this approach was applied in practice, the challenges faced and lessons learned about how to contribute to negotiations in a conflictive and tense setting.

11.3 The research context: competition for resources and resettlement in Limpopo National Park

The establishment of the Limpopo National Park (LNP) brought with it a series of challenges both for conservation and for development. The park is home to 27,000 people who depend primarily on natural resources for their livelihoods. Increased numbers of wild animals and efforts to develop tourism in the park has necessitated the resettlement of eight villages situated along the Shingwedzi river to a site outside the park along the Elefantes river. Given traditional land tenure and the lack of land without an 'owner', resettled villages are slated to be situated with host villages that agree to share resources with them.

Resettlement commonly brings a set of risks for resettled residents, from impoverishment to social marginalisation (Cernea, 1997) and new social conflict for both resettled and host villages (Brockington, 2002). In the case of conservation-induced resettlement where original lands are still intact, the risk of residents returning to inhabit original sites or file land claims is significant if the livelihoods of resettled residents are not rehabilitated (De Wet, 2006). The risk that economically and physically displaced residents utilise resources inside the conservation area, or sabotage conservation projects is also considerable if sustainable livelihood alternatives are not available (Chatty and Colchester, 2002). Conservation-induced displacement has also been shown to cause environmental degradation outside and around conservation areas due to an increase in population density and concentration of resource use along the borders (Rangarajan and Shahabuddin, 2006). However, the development of viable and alternative livelihoods is likely to reduce unsustainable use of natural resources. In order for the GLTFCA to be a sustainable land-use option in the long run, local livelihoods of residents directly affected by the establishment of the conservation area must be secured as a first step towards the dual objective of bringing development and conservation through transfrontier conservation initiatives.

Given the difficult agro-ecological climate of the region characterised by low (less than 400 mm) and sporadic rainfall, an ability to cope with vulnerability and adaptation to adverse conditions, such as drought, is crucial for local livelihoods. Resettlement is likely to cause residents to alter their coping strategies. Livelihoods in villages both in and outside the park are based primarily on agriculture, livestock and charcoal production (only outside of the park). While both inside and outside the park agriculture is mostly rainfed, outside the park there are agricultural associations and opportunities to access irrigation. Despite these opportunities and other opportunities for wage labour and market integration, access to natural resources is fundamental for adaptation and mitigation of risk in the natural environment. However, official state-driven modernisation discourse considers salary-based, money-based livelihoods to be better than having livestock and being dependent on agriculture. Government and agents of development consider the area to be too dry and rainfall patterns too erratic to be suitable for depending on agriculture and they believe that small-scale agriculture or livestock rearing does not constitute a modern lifestyle (Milgroom and Spierenburg, 2008). As we will see below, these views and conditions play a role in the negotiation process about resettlement.

11.4 The research process as it unfolded, from the field researcher's perspective

In this section we will describe some key episodes in the research process. The experiences are written from the perspective of the first author (the PhD student who carried out the fieldwork).

11.4.1 Juggling university requirements and research ideals

I began my PhD with a fair dose of scepticism about the role of science and research in solving real problems. I had been involved in large and small research projects before my doctoral research that had left me feeling unsatisfied and uneasy with the balance of resources spent on science and its subsequent relative irrelevance to society. I wanted to explore other ways of engaging in research through my PhD. The questions I had in mind when I began were: how can science contribute to gaining space and leverage for small-scale farmers in negotiations over resources? How can science actively shed light on a local problem? I wanted to carry out interdisciplinary research and be part of a larger project within which other students were also working. I was introduced to the Competing Claims programme and began my research within that framework. As a PhD student I was required to produce a proposal for the Graduate School. My proposal was written after a brief trip to the country (for which I already had relevant language skills) and study site. Given my interests, background and the preliminary experience I had gained interviewing people and visiting the area on my scoping trip, I identified the general research focus as: how can my research contribute to improving post resettlement food security? I had seen that there was a planned resettlement initiative and that food security in the new location could potentially be a problem. Beyond that focus, however, I thought that the process of identifying a more specific research question from the ground was of the utmost importance for carrying out research that is relevant to a local problem. I wanted to keep the research agenda open to be able to identify the specific questions after I had a better grounding in the local environment. However, when I returned from the initial exploratory trip and presented my proposal to the university, various comments were made to the effect that my proposal looked more like development work and not research. Many people asked, but what is the specific research question? Despite being supported by supervisors to tailor my research to a local problem to be defined along the way, eventually I had to specify research questions to meet the academic requirements. Nevertheless, I began fieldwork without any strong theoretical underpinning or specific research questions in mind, forgetting for the time being those I had defined for my proposal. I wanted to have a thorough understanding of the context in which I was working and the problem that I wanted to try to contribute to resolving before narrowing my focus. In order to do this I allowed myself the time to try out topics, bounce ideas off different people and probe the extent to which any results that I might find were likely to be applied or actually contribute to change. While my original intentions of experimenting with how research could be more relevant to society remained present, I did not want to do this from an abstract point of view, or turn it into a research question for my PhD but wanted to take a learning-by-doing approach.

11.4.2 Finding a niche for my research

Using anthropological methods, the first year of my research was based on participant observation, and unstructured and in-depth interviews about livelihoods with a focus on agriculture. I was aware that the context within which I was working, specifically the people involved and my relationships with them, would determine how and whether or not my research could evolve into an action research process. I was aware of the possibility that I may not feel legitimate to 'intervene', and that I could not force the situation or make any decisions under time pressure. I established myself in Nanguene, the first village to be resettled, and began to document the residents' lives and learn the local language. I simultaneously built relationships with the park employees, visiting them each time I came in and out of the park.

I was interested at the outset in contributing to food security and livelihood rehabilitation in post-resettlement. I witnessed the effort invested in agriculture under poor rainfall conditions during the first rainy season and I became focused on working towards improving the agricultural system by trying out social or technical alternatives, as the 'design' phase of my research. I wanted to experiment with and implement alternative agricultural practices together with farmers, driven by their ideas, needs and desires. During this first year I looked for entry points, taking my time to observe and ask questions before beginning anything. Several options were considered and discussed based on residents' expression of the major limitations to production. One idea was to study elephant damage to agricultural production and develop a monitoring system for this that could be used to quantify losses and claim compensation. This idea was abandoned later since it was assumed that such a system would not be of much use after resettlement, and because of lack of consistent support from the park staff. Another entry point considered (and actually implemented much later) was to work on seed systems. In view of an observed low quality of maize seed (little distinction between grain and seed), high demand for new varieties, and market for locally-adapted seed for planting, we thought that improving the seed system could contribute to increased food security in the area by boosting production and also by providing a source of income for those farmers who could invest in seed production. This was not a participatory or collaborative decision, but one that I considered based on interviews and discussions and in light of my own interests and need to write a PhD.

11.4.3 Changing roles: becoming an information intermediary

The idea of finding entry points in agriculture was complicated considerably by the fact that there was no rain during the first two rainy seasons. In the meantime, however, opportunities emerged for following the process of resettlement issue more closely. When I arrived in December of 2006, the village was expected to be resettled by early 2007, but was not actually resettled until two years later, in November of 2008, due primarily to political complications. In mid 2007 I began to recognise an opportunity to become more actively involved in the negotiations.

The Mozambican government (Ministry of Tourism) wanted the resettlement process to occur quickly to be able to focus on developing the national park as a tourist attraction. The donors, however, wanted the process to be participatory, fair and transparent. The first park director lost his job due to this conflict and a second was sent to resolve the resettlement problem. A survey had been carried out in early 2005 in Nanguene to determine who was entitled to what compensation, but the results were not shared with the residents. Models for the houses were built and in an attempt to create a space for participation, residents were invited to see and express their opinions about the houses. Village leaders then began to take a step back, refusing to accept resettlement if the houses were not larger. The park staff changed their strategy at this point and decided to work with the villages that had already agreed to be resettled and that formed part of the pilot project instead of working with all of the village leaders (Milgroom, unpublished data). Higher government officials and World Bank staff were present in meetings shortly after to 'convince' these two villages to sign documents that said they agreed with the model houses, including the size. At this point details about the compensation package had to be decided and a series of meetings ensued. These negotiations about compensation between the park authorities and residents of Nanguene provided the 'arena of conflict' that I followed closely, together with a research assistant from a nearby village. Since I was a resident in the village, or camped at a the park headquarters during much of this time I was in a good position to follow the process. I was invited to meetings between the park and the village and soon became by default a means of communication between the two parties. Cell phone coverage was not reliable so I was asked, as someone with a vehicle, to inform the village leader about a meeting, and to bring him and other village residents with me to meetings. The village residents began to ask me about what was going on with the resettlement process, and the park staff began to ask about what was going on in the village. As the negotiation process for resettlement progressed, and concerns were expressed to me from both sides, I began to take a more active role in information exchange. This role for my research emerged organically, and in the beginning I was not thinking about it as a purposeful action, but more an additional obligation as a researcher, and an opportunity to access different sources of information.

When I perceived the need for information for decision-making about resettlement on multiple levels, and that I could play a role in facilitating that information, I began to see that perhaps the utility of my research was more as a participant in the resettlement process and less as an action researcher of the agricultural system. Originally I had envisaged the collaborative research in which I was to engage as a semi-formal arrangement for the involvement of stakeholders working together in a concerted action research project on a technical issue, such as resolving a piece of the food security puzzle. I did not abandon that idea, but in light of the role as an information intermediary that I was beginning to play, I decided to be more structured and purposeful in the way I collected and shared information.

I think that I was able to find a role as an information courier because both the park staff and the villagers recognised their disadvantages in accessing information that I could gather from both sides. The park staff did not have access to local information because they did not want to or did not have the time nor the contacts. The village residents knew that information was being withheld from them by the park staff and feared that they would be or were being manipulated. Outside observers attempting to make sense of what was going on in the park, such as donors and consultants, were also in need of insight about the resettlement process. One donor representative regularly met with me to discuss what was going on in the field because he felt that his contacts (the park and higher-level government staff) were sharing information selectively. This was specifically the case with respect to conflicts and complications that were arising between village leaders and the park staff, misunderstandings within the village, and pressures exerted by the Mozambican government to override the donors' wishes, those the representative was there to protect. There were no other researchers carrying out fieldwork on the topic of resettlement at the time.

11.4.4 Walking the tightrope: maintaining trustworthiness and managing impressions

In a societal negotiation process information can be highly sensitive. When questions were directed at issues that I felt confident answering, I had to be careful about the provision of information so as not to threaten my relationships with either the park or the villagers, despite the lingering sensation that it was my chance to make a difference, to influence the course of events and gain some ground for the villagers who were to be resettled. Mostly I held my tongue, recognising that what I thought was helpful might actually cause the villagers to lose ground. Thus, when either side asked me clear questions about the other, I would tell them that I would ask and get back to them with the answer the next time. Moreover, I often had to be very clear about the limitations of what I knew. Authorities or interested bystanders would typically ask me to give voice to all villages destined for resettlement with questions such as, 'do people want to be resettled?' etc., and I had to be careful to say that I only felt qualified to talk about the small village in which I was working, and that there was no one single answer for the whole village. Other times they would ask for an opinion about issues at hand and how they should be handled; this was the most difficult for me because I feared influencing things in the 'wrong' way.

With both parties, I spent my time asking questions about perceptions, ideas, preferences, problems and worries. I stated my opinions very rarely to villagers and only when expressly asked to do so. When the villagers expressed doubts about what the park was doing, I would tell them, 'I really don't know, but I had heard that…' and carefully state information which validity I felt very confident about. I wanted to provide clarification without risking misunderstandings because I was unsure of how what I said would be interpreted. I did not want to raise false expectations, or spread incorrect information because I could not be sure that the information that I was getting from the park was the whole story and because I knew that the story was constantly changing. Related to that, I was concerned with being used as a puppet in discussions between the park and the village – I did not want to risk the villagers saying, 'but Jessica said…'. I was worried about this for two reasons: (1) I thought it would change my relationship with the villagers if they thought they could 'use' me, and not just the information that I could provide; and (2) I needed the park to support my research and I wanted to maintain integrity and transparency about my activities. This decision about how and how much information to share was one limitation inherent to the conflictive context. I was unwilling to risk losing access to the research site, or losing the trust of the park staff by explicitly 'taking sides' or by providing information that may, or may not, have been empowering to the village residents. I felt that playing a role as an information intermediary had more potential for positive effects in the tense political environment that a more frontal approach.

However, when I had a chance to converse with park staff, I was more open about my opinions. I felt that there was less at stake, less risk of misunderstanding because I was not working through a translator and because I understood their culture better than that of the rural village. I began to note what types of approaches and timing were more effective, who was receptive to clear transmission of information, and who was receptive to indirect comments, etc. Although I found that staff was most receptive to questions, carefully respecting hierarchy as a foreign woman student (it was clear that they didn't want to feel that I was criticising them or telling them what to do), I tried to suggest constructive ways to deal with conflicts such as calling attention to a need for clarification on specific issues and proposing small, inexpensive improvements for post-resettlement conditions. Some examples of these proposals (that came from conversations with residents) were to provide seedlings of local tree species instead of just domesticated introduced fruit trees such as mangos and papayas, provide seed of new varieties instead of the most common introduced variety that is known to be adopted only partially, to erect a plaque in the original village location after resettlement to mark the social history of the park, and to carry out a history project to document the history of the village.

Over time I began to express my concerns about issues that I thought to be of the utmost importance. For example, I made it clear to all parties that I thought it was necessary to invest first in securing land rights, then in building the houses and to secure enough land to facilitate the growth of the village over time, and to provide land based on family size, not just the same amount of land for each family unit. Park staff felt that the village residents could negotiate their own access to the land that they needed but I was observing growing apprehension on the part of the resettled village, resistance on the part of host village and blatant conflict between the leaders of the surrounding villages about who would cede more agricultural land to the resettled village. Much of the conflict that was arising was the result of actions taken or not taken by the park itself, such as promises made to the host village that were not fulfilled and that therefore led to a diminishing willingness to accommodate resettled residents and their need for access to resources.

With both of the main parties in the study context I had a lot of 'impression management' work to do. Even when I had been working in the village for 18 months, the villagers still asked me every so often what I was really doing and if I was working for the park. This is because villagers would see me at park headquarters and see me interacting with park staff. The concept of being a student for so long and carrying out research activities was also unfamiliar to them and therefore difficult to understand. Among the park staff it was my experience that social researchers were not appreciated in general because of what the staff called 'biased work'. They accused researchers of talking to residents and not to park staff, publishing their one-sided opinions, and of being used by residents to publish lies by writing about things that they did not understand. The LNP had had experiences with researchers criticising their work and with journalists publishing negative statements about the park and its treatment of residents. This was considered especially harmful for a project of its size and fame, because the authorities depended on a positive press for the success of the greater conservation area (including in South Africa and Zimbabwe) in attracting funding and tourists, and in order to promote the development-via-conservation initiative elsewhere in the country. One park staff member said to me, 'There have been a few articles written criticizing the park and resettlement, but really there are two types of judgment: value judgment and fact judgment. Value judgment is difficult because it is based on opinion, personal values of better or worse, but you will be measuring FACT of what there is in one place and the other, what people do in one place and in the other.' [18] This comment was made because of the amount of time that I had spent observing the process, getting to know both sides of the conflicts, and my proposal to quantify differences between pre- and post-resettlement locations with respect to resource endowment.

I was able to overcome distrust partially, especially with the community but with only some of the park staff. The extended period of time during which I was conducting research in the area helped to build my credibility, reinforced by my attempt to ask questions and construct positive alternatives instead of criticising, and by my focus on agriculture (which, although it became secondary, was always present throughout the research process). However, as in the village, I experienced relapses at certain times, when the staff doubted my 'loyalty' to their 'side', especially when they saw me living in the villages and interacting in a friendly way with residents, and even more so during tense political times. For example, when donors or consultants came to visit the project to decide about whether to provide a 'no objection' or permission to go ahead with an important issue, sometimes park staff would facilitate my meeting with them and other times they would make it difficult for me to meet with them if things were not going well, for fear of what I might say.

Some issues that were crucial to this 'walking the tightrope' were the timing of information sharing and maintaining a low profile. Sometimes I would wait months to share a certain piece of information or ask a certain question. For example, when I knew that park staff were busy with political visits or being pressured to perform, I chose to wait to ask about a technical issue until technical decisions were being made again. I felt that otherwise my input would be discarded as irrelevant at that moment. I found it useful to always be flexible and opportunistic about time and plans. Whenever possible I also waited until my information was solicited instead of trying to offer information.

11.4.5 Some examples of research(er) influence

It is impossible to know precisely how my presence, questions and suggestions influenced the events that took place. However, I documented all of the conversations that I had and

---

[18] Interview, LNP staff, Massingir, June 19, 2007.

noticed that sometimes issues that I had raised were taken up again in meetings, debates and informal discussions. On many occasions, issues that I thought were important were not acted upon. A few examples are given below of when they were and were not attached to policy changes and actions.

Influencing resettlement planning

A consultant hired to draw up the resettlement action plans was keen to bounce his ideas off me – knowing that I was in close contact with the village whose future he was planning. As an independent consultant he was not under pressure from the government and he was interested in drafting a fair and equitable resettlement plan as close as possible to the World Bank guidelines for resettlement. He consulted me on issues concerning the local agriculture system, land tenure, and off-farm access to food and money. I would take his questions back into the field and discuss them with the villagers. One example of a topic that we debated and discussed was the access to agricultural land in post-resettlement. He made calculations based on the number of hectares per person a family would need to be able to produce enough food to sustain itself. This was to be the amount of land that each family would receive in post-resettlement. He was under the impression that labour was a limiting factor and that the tendency to have large amounts of land per family was because of soil fertility management practices in shifting agriculture. My research had found that in fact labour was not as limiting as rainfall and that all the hectares available to a family would be used in the case of a good rainfall event. The harvest would then be kept to tide families over until the next harvest – which might not be for several years – and therefore having access to large amounts of land to 'capture the rainfall' when it came, was important for food security. He was also unaware of the opportunistic practices in agriculture that farmers use to respond to spatial variability in rainfall. Their fields within the park were spread across the landscape and farmers planted in one or another depending on the rainfall patterns of that particular year. Because of the ecological consequences of opening up large tracts of land and the economic cost of doing so, he changed the Resettlement Action Plan proposal to include access to more agricultural land that families could open as they needed to, in addition to the fields that would be opened for them in the resettlement location. I also brought up this issue with one of the donor representatives, and the park administrator at the time.

However, the Resettlement Action Plan was adhered to only partially. Instead of providing land on the basis of the size of the family, each family was given a fixed allocation of one hectare and no land was set aside for future agricultural expansion. Therefore the impact of my work on the temporal and spatial variability of semi-arid farming was eventually minimal for Nanguene. Two years after resettlement it is clear that access to land for cropping is a problem, especially for more marginalised residents who are not well connected into the social networks of the host village. It is not just a problem for the villagers, but one that the park is still dealing with, and based on this it has been planned that the next village to be resettled will receive more land.

Correcting the number of houses

The original survey of the families in Nanguene concluded that there were 16 nuclear families. My work in the village concluded that there were 19, according to the definition of family developed and used by the park. I discovered that this discrepancy came about because some people had moved back to the village since the survey that the park was using had been conducted, and some had moved away. The survey had originally been carried out in early 2005 with the intention of moving people that year; however, I began my research in late 2006 and the figures I generated were already different because of these movements. Meanwhile the plans for resettlement were still being made. The leader of the village reported these changes in the composition of the village to the park, but regardless of that, they were not recorded officially in the plans for resettlement. Apparently only 16 families were to be resettled, leaving four families without resettlement opportunity; furthermore, the plans made provision for one family that no longer lived in the original village. I brought up the issue with park staff, consultants, and donors. Eventually someone was sent to the village in 2008 to confirm the survey data discrepancies. It was decided finally that 18 houses would be built in the resettlement area, leaving one woman with four children without a house, as decided by the village itself because she had left her husband's household. Park staff argued that they could not provide her with a house against the wishes of the village (the decision did not reflect the villagers' wishes, but the opinion of one important elder) and never mentioned the case to the donors.

Marking local history

In my discussions with village residents, the issue of the importance of their ancestral land came up. An anthropologist working in the park in 2006-2007, Rebecca Witter, had suggested the idea of a marker, a plaque to document the cultural history of the area. When discussing this idea with the residents I found that they heartily agreed. I brought up the idea with park staff, consultants and donors and they agreed to implement it. In order to decide what to write on the plaque, I brought two historians to the two villages that were included in the pilot phase of resettlement, to record the villagers' oral histories. These histories were to be documented for future generations in case resettlement disrupted the history of the village. The recorded histories were meant to be kept with the park in a place accessible to interested researchers or tourists. However, the park did not follow up on this, nor have histories been shared with the villagers. Without any further consultation with me, the plaque was built and put in place the week after resettlement, so the resettled residents never saw it finished. The plaque erected where Nanguene used to be simply said that 'a village used to exist in this location', but a year after being erected it is broken and no longer legible (Figure 11.3). Residents were pleased that the plaque was to be erected, but were upset that they were never consulted about what would be finally written on the stone, or the design of the plaque. They never knew that I had suggested it to the park staff, but may

Figure 11.3. A picture of the broken plaque, 16 months after resettlement.

have guessed it. I did nothing to follow up on the issue because at that time I no longer had an open channel of communication with the park staff.

Setting agendas for further action

Through my research, another issue emerged that was worrying the residents to be resettled – especially the women. I had carried out a pairwise ranking exercise to explore men's and women's priorities in post-resettlement and it became clear that above and beyond anything else was their concern that they wouldn't be treated well by the host village. How they would be received would determine their eventual access to resources, but also their experience in public places such as getting water and their children's experience in school. I discussed these findings with park staff and the following week a meeting was called with the leaders of the host villages and the leaders of the villages to be resettled to specifically discuss 'how the host village will receive the resettled village'.

The meeting that ensued was long and complicated, and the conclusions not hopeful for Nanguene. There was a conflict about the agricultural land and access to fields. Neither the host village nor the neighbouring village would agree to budge on allowing Nanguene residents' access to their resources. It was agreed that there would be a party to welcome the village, but neither side wanted to contribute to it. At that point residents were in no position to protest because they had already agreed to be resettled, had already received their compensation money and had no leverage to change the situation. I was also in no position to do anything but observe because of tensions that were mounting, as described below.

Compensation for fields

The first step in the actual physical resettlement was the transportation of posts for building their kraals (livestock pens). There had been discussion between park staff and the village leader about when this was to happen, but no concrete date was set. Suddenly the leader was informed that the truck would come the next day, but they had still not received the compensation money for their fields and houses. The leader called the park and said that they would not allow the posts to be transported until they had the money in their hands. Payment was arranged and the transportation was scheduled for another day. However, the payment was based on the survey that had been carried out in 2005. At that time their fields were also measured, but three years later their fields had expanded, other fields had been opened and those families who were not surveyed in 2005 never had their fields measured. The compensation process for cultivated land was not transparent and it was not clear until the very last moment who was going to be compensated for what and how much, especially for those families who were not surveyed in 2005. After the compensation had been paid in cash, it was clear that some families had not been fully compensated. While the people concerned knew that they were not fully compensated, they did not know how much they were still owed. I measured fields in 2008 as part of my research and I happened to be present on the day this discussion was taking place in the leader's house. I offered to compare the number of hectares compensated with the number measured for the families that had doubts.

The leader of the village at that point did something that he had never done before. He used my presence directly to leverage his interests. He said on the telephone to park staff: 'We still have problems here that need to be resolved. I have told Jessica that there are things that need to be cleared up.' He said again that he would not allow the posts to be transported until all of the compensation was fully paid. The park staff member replied that there was nothing missing from the compensation and that the posts would be transported the next day. At this point the leader again (without me knowing it until later) utilised very subtly my presence to make his message heard. He asked my assistant to write a message (sms) from his phone to the park staff in Portuguese. The content of the message is not as significant as the fact that he is very capable of writing his own messages in the local language, but chose to ask my assistant to write it for him in Portuguese, as if to insinuate that I was supporting him, or telling him what to write, or even perhaps writing it myself. At the moment itself I did not realise that she was writing it in Portuguese and assumed that it was in the local language.

Soon after the message was sent, a representative from the resettlement team appeared in the village to smooth over the problem. They promised that all compensation would be paid, that the fields would be measured, but that they had to allow the posts to be transported the next day. The leader gave in to this pressure but unfortunately the fields were never measured and the full compensation was never paid (although a symbolic amount was paid to a few people).

Untraceable consequences?

The events described in the previous section were potentially influenced by my work, although I can never be sure. Howerver, I think that the intangible influences may have been more profound. Some of these have to do with identity and status. Some villagers had the impression that by my presence in the village, and by my studying the resettlement process, they gained leverage with the park.

In May 2007, I was discussing with the leader of the village about the purpose of my research and why I attend the park meetings with them. He said:

> No, the park does not want you to be there. They tell us things that we write down but then we show them later what we wrote and they say, no, we didn't say that. But if you write it down they can't say that they didn't say it. …They don't like you because you are white and they are black and we are black. They don't want you at the meetings, but you should go to them. (Informal conversation, Nanguene, May, 2007)

At this point he was more aware than I was about the park staffs' feelings about my presence in the meetings, that were to surface later.

A year and 4 months later, after an interview in one of the households in September 2008, right before resettlement, I asked the head of the household (whom I was interviewing) if he had any questions for me, as I always do before finishing any interview. He responded: 'No, I would if it was the first time I am seeing you, but I know now what you are doing so I don't have any questions. Those guys at the park are afraid of you. They respect you. Because you are here they know that if they don't do what they should they will go to jail' (interview Nanguene, Sept, 2008).

Despite never having said anything before about me, my role with the park, or my research over the two previous years, he suddenly made this comment out of the blue. While it is unlikely anyone would go to jail, his perception of the influence of my presence in the village was surprising, even for me.

Another less traceable influence of my research was that it may have raised the level of preparedness of community members when interacting with others. When I was finishing my fieldwork, various local residents made comments about the questions that I had asked them over the years. One said clearly, 'All the questions you have asked us prepared us for when other people come to ask us things. We wouldn't have known what to say' (interview new Nanguene, June, 2010). As the first village to be resettled, Nanguene received many visits from donors, WB, NGOs, government officials and interested parties, all asking the same questions: are you happy here? Are you satisfied with resettlement? The work that I had done with them in asking these questions since 2006 about their expectations, and their priorities in resettlement, about the process and the negotiations, and then about the results and their level of satisfaction, requesting them to be specific about justifying their answers apparently helped them to know what to say to others who were intimidating, less specific, etc. The disposable cameras that I had provided them with to document their lives pre- and post-resettlement were also apparently very helpful for them. One resident said, 'Those pictures have really done their job. Every time someone asks me about what my life was like before resettlement, I show them the album. They see the trees that used to feed us, the grass that our animals used to eat, our fields, our river…' (informal conversation, new Nanguene, April, 2010).

11.4.6 Becoming controversial: losing access to the park

In the third year of research, the park director was replaced yet again. This changed the dynamics of my researching process and the role I could have for the park in the resettlement process. The new park director was a forceful presence sent there to make changes to the process of 'getting the park up and running'. Many people became scared of losing their jobs, leading to back-stabbing and political manipulation to gain favour with the new director. Resettlement was the hot political issue of the day and it was well known that it had been the motive for removing the previous two park directors. The development of the park as a game reserve was dependent, in the eyes of the park administration, on removing people from the inside of the park area as quickly as possible. Any real or perceived obstacles to quick and efficient resettlement were problematic from the new director's perspective.

In October 2008 I was told that I was *persona non-grata* in the park (by one of the park's staff with whom I had worked most closely). He told me that he had been told by various sources that I was organising meetings in both the resettling and host village and convincing people not to be resettled or to accept the resettled village. I had been working with him since the very beginning of my research and was very surprised by his change in attitude, since he had always been supportive and facilitative of my research. He knew better than anyone else about my position: my philosophical outlook on the research, my desire for a positive outcome from the resettlement process and my goal to contribute to that positive outcome through my research. Although he never told me so directly, I interpreted his warning as a sign that my relationship with him had suddenly become a threat to his own interests, and his job security. I had become identified by the political authorities as a threat to the success of a quick resettlement process because I was perceived as representing the rights of the first village to be re-settled, and the assertion of these rights was seen to delay the process of resettling other, and larger villages. However, the official reason given for not wanting me to continue research in the park was that my permit was no longer valid, and that I was doing things that were not included in my written permit.

The fact that the park felt threatened by my research reinforced the villagers' impression that my presence was beneficial for them. It also showed the tenuousness of the delicate role that I was playing, and how the potential for acting as an information courier in a process of negotiation and mutual learning depends on a series of conditions that need to be in place to favour that work.

Despite the fact that I was not welcome inside the park, I continued my research in the resettled area. I felt that without access to the opinions and perspective of the park staff, my story suddenly became somewhat one-sided. I did what I could to talk to the people I still had contact with from the park, but had no choice but to focus my work more on the perspective of the residents.

One evening, sitting with the resettled village leader he asked my assistant if she could help him write a letter to the district administrator about some issues important to their situation in the new village. Nervous about creating misunderstandings with the district government, I asked him not to mention that she had helped him write the letter because of her relationship with me. Neither the residents of Nanguene nor I ever talked explicitly about the conflicts that had arisen between myself and the park administration, so I explained. He responded as follows:

> That sounds like the park. It is the same with ORAM[19]. In meetings they say they have an NGO to help communities, but out of the meetings they tell ORAM they don't need anyone to get involved with the communities' issues. They tell them they can't even go into the park and have meetings. The problem is that Mozambique is still in colonialism. Even in the bible there is only a small section written for Negros because they don't want us to know more, they want to keep us in the dark. It is like the Mozambican state, they don't want us to know anything. The park too wants to keep information from us. …But don't worry, even in meetings we say what we want and they understand us. They shouldn't think you are causing any problems because the ideas come from us. (Informal conversation, January, 2009)

While not surprised about the park's reaction to my work, he was also assuring me that the ideas, demands and actions that have proven to be problematic for quick resettlement in fact come from them and not from me. Again this reinforces the idea that any influence that I might have had in the process was not necessarily manifested in tangible terms; the consequences of my work were much more subtle. None the less, it was enough to find myself outside the park gates looking in.

Soon after being barred from the park, one member of the resettlement staff was fired and four more resigned from the park because of the same political changes that excluded me, mainly in response to the leadership style of the new park director. This left only one person

---

[19] An NGO that works with raising awareness about communities' rights (Rural Organization for Mutual Support).

in the resettlement team, that person being someone relatively new to the park staff, and wiped out most of the institutional memory of the resettlement process.

11.4.7 Beyond information intermediation: supporting integration in post-resettlement

In pursuing my ideas about improving agricultural production in post-resettlement, I secured funds for a small project to test new varieties and work on maintaining quality seed through multiplication and conservation. This project was carried out with the host village on the lands of the agricultural associations that have access to irrigation. The intention of the project was to work primarily with Nanguene, but with the lack of irrigation resources where the new fields had been opened, and no rainfall, it proved very difficult to work with them on this project. We therefore carried out the variety trials on the associations' fields, and attempted to include the resettled villagers in the activities. Before the project was implemented I had asked many people in the host area if they thought Nanguene would be welcomed into the associations. Everyone replied 'yes, of course', but when it came to actual implementation, they did not feel comfortable participating.

Leaving aside any potential contributions to food security, this project served as a vehicle to explore the dynamics of integration between the two villages. In this case I was more boldly vocal in pointing out that the very fact that the project existed, and was needed, was as a consequence of the resettlement and used this as an argument to bring the two communities together in a project. I chose not to request anything from the host village for Nanguene, or speak for Nanguene's needs, but continued to invite them to participate as if they had always belonged there. I also asked key hypothetical questions informally about access to resources (mainly rainfed fields) for the newly resettled village, about for example, what might happen in the future when there is more need for land for Nanguene residents' children, and possibilities for entrance into the agricultural association. By doing so, my role changed from being merely an information intermediary to a more activist role where I used technical research activities not only to help solve technical problems but also as a strategy to enhance relationships between the host village and the former Nanguene villagers.

11.4.8 Re-gaining access to the park

When the project activities had finished and I was wrapping up my fieldwork, I requested time from the park to present the results from my research and from the project activities. Around the same time I was contacted by someone involved in monitoring a World Bank project that funds transfrontier conservation areas and also periodically visits the Limpopo National Park on those missions. That person asked me to prepare a presentation to send to the coordinator of the mission to request a slot for me to present to the group involved in the mission. My request to make a presentation at the park was not addressed or responded to until the presentation that I prepared for the WB mission was circulated to the Ministry of Tourism, at which point I received a personal phone call from the same park director who denied the continuation of my permit to work in the park, inviting me to make a presentation to the park staff. He did not attend the presentation, but it was openly received by the other staff members present. Many of the issues were debated and few points of disagreement were raised about my findings, opening the doors again, at least officially, to work in the park and to provide feedback on the resettlement process. Given that I observed and documented closely a process that the team currently working on resettlement had not been witness to (since the park staff present at that time had left) I presented some issues that were unfamiliar to those attending the meeting. I expect that any lingering negative feelings towards my work were simply not expressed and that some park staff members were glad that I had finished my fieldwork for the time being. However, the official 'green light' and access to the park provided me with the opportunity to ask questions and document the perspective of the park staff once again, even if my feedback was not well received. I knew that my research was unable to capture nuances of particular issues and events by speaking only to the village residents and onlookers, and in the last months of my research I was able to fill in important gaps in my data and discuss my findings with some park staff.

I contacted the district government to request time to make a presentation for them and they invited me to their governmental session, but when, supported by park staff, I requested that the presentation be attended by community members, NGOs and other stakeholders, they refused saying that it would be too conflictive and that they were not interested in that sort of meeting.

11.5 Discussion and reflections

In this section we – the PhD student and two members of her supervisory team – reflect on these research experiences against the background of our conceptual assumptions and ideas about the role of science in societal negotiation. Several issues come to mind.

11.5.1 It is not eventual research outcomes that matter

Our involvement in the resettlement process in Limpopo National Park taught us that it was not the research results that influenced the societal negotiations. Only part of the data on resources in and outside the park were analysed, and very few of the findings were written down in a formal report or scientific article in the period described in this chapter. Nevertheless, we can point to clear moments in the process where it is likely that the research as a directed and purposeful activity had an influence on ongoing societal negotiations. The initial 'simple' inventory of people and their resources, for example, did change the views of park authorities on the importance and intensity of agricultural activity in the area, and led them to think more seriously about post-resettlement scenarios. It is also clear that the community used relevant information from the research in their negotiations with authorities. Moreover, there are indications that they felt empowered, or at least supported by the presence of an outsider who recorded their resources and monitored the process.

We suggest it was the process and activity of doing research, especially in terms of three parameters – presence, information and dialogue – that may have contributed to any improvement in the quality of societal negotiation. Our examples indicate that 'presence' is multi-faceted, involving (at a minimum) role, identity, and status; and that it is always in flux in a dynamic of power and an unfolding story that is to a varying degree outside the researcher's control. Research-derived information, provided as basic, descriptive, and aggregated data, clearly played a role in some instances in improving the quality of the information available to the negotiating parties. The dialogue at times was enriched by the simple figures, tables or maps and other graphical representations provided, as in the results of the pairwise ranking exercise about priorities for post-resettlement (see also Schut *et al.*, 2010). In terms of the overall Competing Claims research cycle (see Figure 11.1) this implies that, in order to have influence in societal negotiations, it is not always necessary for the researcher to 'go full circle' – the 'describe' activity alone can already have an impact if communicated to the right actors at a time and in a format that they are receptive to. Inquiry and preliminary results from the process of describing and explaining can spark exploration and design by stakeholders in practice. Systematised, polished, thoroughly analysed and conceptualised research results played no part in the case presented in this chapter. Despite this fact, the researcher was engaged in a constant process of data analysis, and of checking assumptions in a cycle of reflection and action, vigilant about the integrity, ethics and rigour of her research and aware of potential unintended impacts resulting from the research activities. The idea of what kind of 'scientific work' is expected to influence societal negotiation clearly needs reconceptualising.

11.5.2 Combining research with information intermediation

Our experience indicates that performing research activities and producing scientifically credible outcomes may need to be combined with playing the role of an information intermediary. Phrased differently, a researcher can play a useful role in communicating insights and concerns from one stakeholder to another, thus enhancing the transparency in the negotiation process. Without such exchange activities the influence on the societal negotiation process would probably have been less. The intermediary activity involves not simply providing and diffusing information, but rather engages the researcher in a delicate process of 'walking the tightrope' (see Section 11.4.4) in which active maintenance of trust and relationships is of critical importance. Combining these roles proved challenging and required a considerable investment of time and energy. On the other hand, the effort proved informative, contributed greatly to the richness of the research and was key to informing negotiations.

It is relevant to note that information intermediation is clearly not the only role a researcher may usefully play. The fact that this role became so prominent seems clearly related to the specific context in which the research took place – a still ongoing negotiation process in which compensation about existing resources played an important role, where many basic data were lacking and where communication between stakeholders was complicated by a range of practical conditions. Later on, when resettlement had actually happened, the context of the research changed markedly, and so did the role of the action researcher. In terms of the overall Competing Claims research cycle the later roles played by the researcher seem to be more associated with the 'explore' and 'design' activity. An interactive action research cycle of observe, reflect, plan and act was engaged in at earlier stages, informing the researcher's actions about how best to communicate with different actors. Thus, our experience seems to suggest that the role a researcher plays (or can legitimately play) may be contingent on the specific time and space context of societal negotiation. This implies that Figure 11.1 may too simplistically suggest that one can become embedded in a context and go through the full proposed methodological framework.

11.5.3 The importance of independence and informality

It is relevant to point out that the intermediary role played by the researcher was informal. There was no previous agreement between the various parties that such a role would be played. Although the research activity itself had a greater degree of formality in the sense that it was based on a peer-reviewed proposal, and all the required permits were obtained before starting the work in the study area, it remained a relatively independent and low profile PhD project, with no formal connections to the resettlement process. These conditions were probably conducive to making a constructive contribution to the societal negotiations. On the other hand, these conditions do raise questions about sustainability and ethics. The informal arrangements that were forged in the interactions among the various interests depended entirely on the researcher's physical presence in the area. The direct effects of the research did not go beyond the impacts of changes made during the time of fieldwork. Perhaps some indirect effects will prove more lasting, such as facilitated learning and awareness about political processes, but the majority are unknowable, embedded in the lived and felt experience of others in their interaction with the researcher.

One could question the ethics of intervening as an intermediary without explicit agreement on the 'rules of engagement'. Although in this case the researcher acted according to her personal ethics (asking permission to share information, etc.), there was a sense of betrayal among the park staff when they saw her written work for the first time. When asked for feedback on the first article to be published from the research, one of the park staff (electronically in writing) made a few edits and comments about the assumptions made in the paper. Later in person he said 'I was surprised and disappointed that you wrote that paper. I thought you were only interested in agriculture.' Then in reflection said, 'It is necessary that someone document this process and I am glad that it is someone who knows us and understands the issues we deal with' (informal discussion, Maputo, June 2008). Although it had been explained that the research was exploring the process of resettlement from the perspective of multiple disciplines, the response from the park staff can be explained by various motives: it is very different to see your actions and words written down than to live them or say them, and interdisciplinary research is not common. Since he also saw the researcher carrying out more technical research, it is possible that he did not fully understand that the social aspects would also be considered results of the research. He may also have expected the paper to favour the park more than it did because of our friendly relationship that gave way to many hours of discussion and understanding of the problems that they were facing. His response sparked a reflection on whether or not the researcher had explained her research clearly enough to all parties involved.

Overall the question remains of how researchers can manoeuvre themselves into a position to legitimately conduct research and perform intermediary roles in a conflictive setting. No clear institutional arrangements, mandates and finances are available for this in most contexts, and even in many university settings it is not very common to do this kind of work.

11.5.4 The feasibility of doing collaborative research in conflict situations

In our initial ideas about the research in a competing claims setting, particular reference was made to the idea that the research needed to be 'collaborative'. Commonly this notion suggests that the research is deliberately designed and implemented in close collaboration with stakeholders. When looking back at our research, we must conclude that the research was more 'interactive' than 'collaborative'. The interaction between researcher and researched has enormously influenced the direction of the research – the topics deemed relevant shifted all the time based on the input from stakeholders. The stakeholders interacted with the research in different forms, as respondents, key informants and as actors that actively questioned the researcher in an information brokerage role. However, it remains the case that it was the researcher who eventually decided lines of inquiry and the methods to be employed. In hindsight, this way of operating resulted from two circumstances. First of all, the fact that the research was part of a PhD experience, operating on a limited budget, meant that academically-determined factors (such as academic requirements, supervisor preferences and timelines) originating from interests external to the context, had to be taken into account. Major obstacles to a more collaborative research process included the tense political atmosphere, unequal playing field, researcher's fear of being used, blamed, etc., of losing access to the research site, or worsening the conflict. In hindsight, other forms of interaction may have been more powerful, impactful or effective, but in the specific context and timeframe encountered, the researcher consciously and purposefully chose interactive research as the best possible strategy.

In other respects, the conflictive setting – created by a rather disruptive pressure originating from higher and more powerful levels to establish a transboundary park – proved a conducive context in which to do research (as was anticipated in the wider Competing Claims programme). The park staff, the village leaders, government and donors were all on a steep learning curve because this was the first resettlement project to be carried out from a national park with the intention of fair compensation (i.e. by using the World Bank resettlement framework). When the researcher arrived, it was a somewhat vulnerable time for all stakeholders. The process and contours of resettlement had not yet fully crystallised, and the park staff felt caught between the demands from government and donors, and the village residents. It was also an uncertain situation for the villagers because they were negotiating their future in an as yet unknown context, were unused to negotiating with 'superiors', and they knew that they lacked information. This mutual vulnerability might be considered a pre-condition for their information-seeking behaviour and their willingness to invest in learning processes (see Leeuwis, 2000; 2004). In this sense the timing of the research happened to be right. As shown by Schut *et al.* (2010), policy processes tend also to have phases where new information and insights are no longer welcome; such a moment arose when the new park director arrived with a mandate to speed up the process.

11.5.5 Scientific criteria and political engagement

As explained in Section 11.2, an important assumption in the Competing Claims programme philosophy is that science can be combined with engagement with marginalised parties in a negotiation process – in this case, the communities that were to be resettled. Our experiences in this research indicate that this is indeed possible but it requires considerable investment in relationships, and simultaneous effort to ensure that the stronger parties also benefit.

An important implication is that 'engagement' is always and necessarily 'situated' and not necessarily-repeatable. The forging of relationships was important to accessing the information in the first place, to controlling its quality, and for determining how its role in dialogue was shaped. By embedding information in relationships and context, one tends to gain accuracy and precision and lose generalisation and replicability. However, this does not take away from the scientific rigour of the research.

Furthermore, the information provided by the researcher in her intermediary role proved to be relevant not only to the village residents. In fact, one could argue that when residents had access to certain information (e.g. the amount of resources they were using) this information became simultaneously relevant to the park staff as well, if only because it created the need to be able to respond to the claims made by the former. Hence, authorities too valued the information provided through the research. However, when key relationships in the park were replaced, this virtuous dynamic collapsed and the presence of the researcher immediately resulted in conflict that could only be resolved partially (and after considerable time) by renewed effort and investment in building relationships of trust and mutual benefit.

Jessica Milgroom, Cees Leeuwis and Janice Jiggins

11.6 Conclusion

We have seen in this chapter that enhancing the quality of societal negotiations through scientific research is not a matter of identifying the most pressing questions and uncertainties, then returning to scientific 'business as usual', and reporting the findings when all the material has been analysed. It is crucial to be involved in the ongoing negotiation process, and work to enhance transparency about emerging issues on the basis of still rather crude and preliminary data and findings. In essence this means that scientists must adapt both their view about what constitutes 'a useful result' and about when such a result should be delivered. In an ongoing process of societal negotiation, one cannot predict in great detail when what kind of information will be relevant and make a difference. This means that 'being around' and being willing and prepared to give input when an opportunity arises are important requirements for scientists who wish to contribute to understanding and resolving complex problems. Scientists must not only do research, but can also become information brokers, a difficult but important role to play, especially in a conflictive situation. Regarding the 'politics' of science, engagement with marginalised parties by posing non-neutral research questions, and then otherwise refraining from explicit and open political support to specific parties in the conflict, proved workable and meaningful. As anticipated, it led to the generation and exchange of information that could be used strategically by marginalised parties, and hence became relevant to others as well. The choice to leave the real politics, advocacy and strategic information use to the stakeholders, made it possible for the researcher to remain credible and relevant in the long run, albeit with the necessary hick-ups. Working in this manner required a lot of investment in, and maintenance of social relationships with different stakeholders. In the current academic climate, it is not self-evident that researchers have the time, space and competencies to engage with conflict situations in this manner.

Acknowledgements

The first author would like to acknowledge funding from the National Science Foundation (USA) Graduate Research Fellowship Program. Any opinions, findings, and conclusions or recommendations expressed in this material are those of the author(s) and do not necessarily reflect the views of the National Science Foundation. The research was carried out under the umbrella of the INREF funded research programme 'Competing Claims on Natural Resources: Overcoming mismatches in resource use through a multi-scale perspective', Wageningen University, the Netherlands. The final stages of the research were made possible by a seed grant from the Animal Health Environment and Development group.

References

Aarts, M.N.C., 1998. Een kwestie van natuur; een studie naar de aard en het verloop van communicatie over natuur en natuurbeleid. PhD thesis. Wageningen Agricultural University, Wageningen, the Netherlands.

Alrøe, H. and E.S. Kristensen, 2002. Towards a systemic research methodology in agriculture: Rethinking the role of values in science. Agriculture and Human Values 19: 3-23.

Blackmore, C., R. Ison and J. Jiggins (eds.), 2007. Social learning: an alternative policy instrument for managing in the context of Europe's water. Special Issue. Environmental Science and Policy 10(6): 493-586.

Brockington, D., 2002. Fortress conservation: The preservation of the Mkomazi Game Reserve, Tanzania. Indiana University Press, Bloomington, IN, USA.

Brydon-Miller, M., D. Greenwood and P. Maguire, 2003. Why Action Research? Action Research 1(1): 9-28.

Cash, D.W., W.N. Adger, F. Berkes, P. Garden, L. Lebel, P. Olsson, L. Pritchard and O. Young, 2006. Scale and Cross-Scale Dynamics: Governance and Information in a Multilevel World. Ecology and Society 11 (2): 8. Available at: http://www.ecologyandsociety.org/vol11/iss2/art8/.

Cernea, M.M., 1997. The Risks and Reconstruction Model for Resettling Displaced Populations. World Development 25(10): 1569-1587.

Chatty, D. and M. Colchester, 2002. Conservation and mobile indigenous peoples: displacement, forced settlement and sustainable development. Berghahn, New York, NY, USA.

Collins, K., C. Blackmore, D. Morris and D. Watson, 2007. A systemic approach to managing multiple perspectives and stakeholding in water catchments: some findings from three UK case studies. Environmental Science and Policy 10(6): 564-574.

De Wet, C. (ed.), 2006. Development-induced displacement: problems, policies, and people. Berghahn Books, New York, NY, USA.

Funtowicz, S.O. and J.R. Ravetz, 1993. Science for the Post-Normal Age. Futures 25: 739-755.

Gibbons M., C. Limoges, H. Nowotny, S. Schwartzman, P. Scott and M. Trow, 1994. The New Production of Knowledge: The Dynamics of Science and Research in Contemporary Societies. Sage Publications, Thousand Oaks, CA, USA.

Giller, K.E., C. Leeuwis, J.A. Andersson, W. Andriesse, A. Brouwer, P. Frost, P. Hebinck, I. Heitkönig, M.K. Van Ittersum, N. Koning, R. Ruben, M. Slingerland, H. Udo, T. Veldkamp, C. Van de Vijver, M.T. Van Wijk and P. Windmeijer, 2008. Competing claims on natural resources: what role for science? Ecology and Society 13(2): 34. Available at: http://www.ecologyandsociety.org/vol13/iss2/art34.

Gunderson, L.H. and C.S. Holling, 2002. Understanding transformations in human and natural systems. Island Press, Washington, DC, USA.

Hisschemöller, M. and R. Hoppe, 1996. Coping with intractable controversies: the case for problem structuring in policy design and analysis. Knowledge and Policy 8 (4): 40-60.

Hoppe, R., 2005. Rethinking the science-policy nexus: From knowledge utilization and science technology studies to types of boundary arrangements. Poiesis and Praxis 3: 199-215.

Leeuwis, C., 2000. Re-conceptualizing participation for sustainable rural development. Towards a negotiation approach. Development and Change 31: 931-959.

Leeuwis, C. (with contributions by A. Van den Ban), 2004. Communication for rural innovation. Rethinking agricultural extension. Blackwell Science, Oxford, UK.

Long, N., 2001. Development Sociology: Actor Perspectives. Routledge, London, UK.

Long, N. and A. Long (eds.), 1992. Battlefields of knowledge: The interlocking of social theory and practice in research and development. Routledge, London, UK.

Loorbach, D., 2007. Transition Management: new mode of governance for sustainable development. PhD thesis, Erasmus University, Rotterdam, the Netherlands.

McIntyre. B, B.D. McIntyre, H. Herren, J. Wakhungu and R. Watson (eds.), 2009. Agriculture at a Crossroads. Global Report. International Assessment of Agricultural Knowledge, Science and Technology for Development (IAASTD). The Island Press, Washington, DC, USA.

Milgroom, J.M. and M. Spierenburg, 2008. Induced volition: Resettlement from the Limpopo National Park, Mozambique. Journal of Contemporary African Studies 26 (4): 435-448.

Pruitt, D.G. and P.J. Carnevale, 1993. Negotiation in social conflict. Open University Press, Buckingham, UK.

Rangarajan, M. and G. Shahabuddin, 2006 Displacement and Relocation from Protected Areas: Towards a Biological and Historical Synthesis. Conservation and Society 4(3): 359-378.

Schut, M.L.W., M.A. Slingerland and A. Locke, 2010. Biofuel developments in Mozambique. Update and analysis of policy, potential and reality. Energy Policy 38: 5151-5165.

Steyaert, P., M. Barzman, J. Billaud, H. Brives, B. Hubert, G. Ollivier and B. Roche, 2007. The role of knowledge and research in facilitating social learning among stakeholders in natural resources management in the French Atlantic coastal wetlands. Environmental Science and Policy 10(6): 575-574.

Van Ittersum M.K., R. Rabbinge and H.C. Van Latesteijn, 1998. Exploratory land use studies and their role in strategic policy making. Agricultural Systems 58: 309-330.

Van Buuren, M.W. and J. Edelenbos, 2004. Conflicting knowledge. Why is joint knowledge-production such a problem? Science and Public Policy 31 (4): 289-299.

Van Buuren, M.W., J. Edelenbos and E.H. Klijn, 2004. Managing knowledge in policy networks. Organising joint fact-finding in the Scheldt Estuary. Paper presented at the International Conference on Democratic Network Governance, Copenhagen, Denmark, 21-22. October.

Warner, J.F., 2008. The politics of flood insecurity: framing contested river management projects. PhD thesis. Wageningen University. Wageningen, the Netherlands.

Weisbord, M.R. and S. Janoff, 1995. Future search. An action guide to finding common ground in organizations and communities. Berrett-Koehler Publishers Inc, San Francisco, CA, USA.

12. Conclusion: from knowledge for action to knowledge in action

Annemarie van Paassen, Renate Werkdam, Bas Pedroli, Jolanda van den Berg, Eveliene Steingröver and Cees Leeuwis

Abstract

Sustainable landscape development means researchers have to engage in collaborative research to find an informed, ethical and locally-valued balance between ecological resilience and societal pursuits, and build the capacity for co-ordinated adaptive management of the involved stakeholders and governance institutions. In this last chapter we analyse the collaborative research processes, or so-called boundary-spanning-processes, of the case chapters. The timing and the type of boundary objects and methods used more or less define the level of participation of social stakeholders and the role and function of the researcher in the ongoing societal learning, negotiation and innovation process. The cases show the variety of functions and knowledge broker strategies pursued. From the chapters it is not clear whether all research efforts led to concrete impacts; several authors highlighted dilemma's and bottlenecks that they found hard to deal with. We note that each type of problem and context setting requires a specific type of inquiry (theoretical system perspective), researcher role and boundary process, and to be effective the latter should evolve in line with the iterative societal learning, negotiation and innovation process. To be effective, collaborative researchers cannot limit themselves to 'knowledge production for action', but need to engage in 'knowledge production in action'. They have to analyse the situation and embed their research in the ongoing change process; to opt for a multiple-dimensional, flexible research approach, and to wisely combine various types of system thinking and the respective paradigmatic assumptions. With enough background knowledge on various system approaches, continuous monitoring and reflection, collaborative researchers may become competent performers, but at the end of the day collaborative research is an art. Experts have a holistic perspective, 'a feel' for nuances and apply creative thinking in action.

12.1 Introduction

In the first chapters of the book we introduced the topic of sustainable landscape development and the challenge this poses for governance and science. Sustainable landscape development means that within social systems we should find an informed, ethical and locally-valued balance between ecological resilience and societal pursuits. This means we have to build the capacity for co-ordinated adaptive development of the involved stakeholders, multilayered polycentric organisations and institutions. Researchers are called to engage in trans-disciplinary research: problem-driven, action-oriented collaborative research with and between the societal stakeholders. Since the 1980s landscape researchers have been executing trans-disciplinary research, but for about a decade they have questioned whether this research has insufficient impact on societal awareness and decision-making (Opdam, 2010). Dominant research and development frameworks such as Integrated Landscape Planning and Integrated Natural Resource Management are not very precise about the process of knowledge integration and learning required to attain the desired integrated development. Adaptive Management proponents advocate learning, but do not include the influence of the cultural and political context on the learning and innovation process (Leach *et al.*, 2007; Medema *et al.*, 2008; Huitema *et al.*, 2009). Research practitioners operationalise theoretical frameworks differently, which leads to highly different outcomes (*ibid.*). In this book we explore the actual reasoning and role of collaborative landscape research in practice: the applied theoretical frameworks and methodologies and the actual contribution of collaborative research to sustainable landscape development.

In this last chapter we review, analyse and compare the cases presented in the previous chapters to get more insight into the actual research processes, the different roles of researchers, the theories and methodologies applied, results attained and lessons learned. With respect to the lessons learned we focus on the two challenges as elaborated in Chapter 2: the collaborative practices and researcher roles employed, and adequacy of the applied theory and methodology in tackling the issue-at-stake in the specific context. This enables us to reflect on the future perspective of landscape research; to contemplate on what is needed to be more effective in real-life landscape development and governance.

12.2 The cases revisited

As explained in the introductory chapters, sustainable landscape development concerns multiple stakeholders and institutions at different spatial and temporal scales and in various domains, and each of them has their specific perspective and interest. The only way to get agreement on the direction of the development is to bridge the gap between the different life worlds and start a boundary-spanning process (Van Kerkhof and Lebel, 2006; Mollinga, 2008). There are various types of boundary-spanning processes, depending on the phase and focus of the researcher-stakeholder collaboration, the type of boundary objects and methods used, and the level of participation of social stakeholders. Stakeholders can participate in the problem formulation, the situation analysis and exploration of options and risks, the research goal setting, the experiential learning about concrete solutions, and formulation of action strategies (Kloprogge and Van der Sluijs, 2006). Participatory methods focus on different research phases: for instance, discursive risk assessments focus on problem and risk identification; future search and scenario analyses focus on situation exploration and goal setting, while consensus conference and citizen juries try to influence proposed goals and action plans (Van Asselt and Rijkens-Klomp, 2002; Kloprogge and Van der Sluijs, 2006). In the following we briefly characterise the cases according to the type of boundary-spanning processes pursued, the associated type of collaboration with stakeholders and the results attained.

12. Conclusion: from knowledge for action to knowledge in action

12.2.1 Integrating knowledge to find a local-fit solution

In the Red River Delta and the Frisian Lakes Cases, the initiators strived for concrete improvements in the irrigation management and the landscape planning procedures respectively. The proponents in both cases started from their technical knowledge (hard system thinking) and invited stakeholders to inform them about their contextual issues, concerns and priorities to be considered in the design. In the Red River case, researchers involved local stakeholders in the detailed, technical monitoring of the present functioning of the irrigation scheme, which helped researchers and stakeholders to learn about the technical problems caused by local customs and 'to speak the same language'. In both cases, the researchers developed a boundary object (a computer model in the Red River delta case and visualisations of possible landscape structures in the Frisian lake case) based on their scientific knowledge and assumptions, asking local stakeholders to add knowledge, provide their opinion and jointly determine what solutions were feasible and valued, or at least acceptable. The researchers were in the driver seat; they defined the issue-at-stake and consulted local stakeholders to get local-fit solutions. The Red River Case tackled a problem that local stakeholders lived with day-by-day and because Vietnam has quite a hierarchic culture where leaders and their followers value science-based recommendations, the elaborated technical solutions were welcomed and implemented. This was not the case for the Frisian Lake case. Here the researchers experimented with a new planning method parallel to the ongoing planning process, with NGO members representing the local inhabitants. In the end they found out that the focus of the process was not in line with the actual preoccupation of the planning officers. They developed a method to orient landscape development which may have been useful, but was not opportune for the 'issue-at-stake', which was a concrete choice between some small infrastructural elements. In summary, in these two cases researchers assumed the problem was clear (a well-structured problem) and used a boundary object that expressed this problem definition, to consult stakeholders to add contextual knowledge and valuation so as to find a local-fit solution.

12.2.2 Sharing perspectives to jointly define the problem and type of solutions needed

The policy level

In this book the East Africa case is 'one of a kind', but it represents a quite common phenomenon, i.e. high-level policy makers and planning institutes inviting researchers to start a collaborative research process around a new complex issue that requires action (in this case climate change adaptation). Such collaborative research enables them to enhance social learning and awareness about the issue-at-stake, while simultaneously developing tools, methods and routines for learning and the formulation of policy solutions that stakeholders and citizens would support. The East Africa case was inspired by soft system thinking: the sharing of knowledge between all stakeholders to create a shared vision of what is needed, and the notion that stakeholders need methods to help them to make their tacit knowledge and opinions explicit. Though the main participants were national researchers, the initiating Dutch researchers did not engage in collegiate, but rather in collaborative research. The Dutch researchers acknowledge this situation and attribute it to time pressure and long distances. The training itself served as a boundary-spanning method: there were lectures to inform the participants about the available scientific knowledge on the matter, alternated by discussions and joint field studies to encourage participants to study the issue in the field, share and enrich their (tacit) knowledge and opinions on the issue-at-stake and solution orientations. The short-term aim of the workshop and training was to enhance awareness among national researchers and policy makers of climate change adaptation, encouraging researchers to include this topic in special and ongoing research in the country. In this way, they would feed the policy making.

The local level

In the Mafungautsi case, the Westerkwartier case and the Northern Thailand case, researchers explicitly opted for a local learning process. Inspired by soft system thinking, the researchers encouraged local stakeholders to observe their landscape environment; to share knowledge and opinions about the landscape, their interests and their behaviour; to become engaged in and committed to advocacy vis-à-vis higher level decision-makers. Communication with these higher level decision-makers was organised by the researchers in the form of joint workshops, stakeholder attendance to commission meetings, and the formulation of recommendations to policy makers. In the Mafungautsi case as well as the Northern Thailand case, the researchers were inspired by the theory of adaptive management, which focuses on social and experiential learning. In the Northern Thailand case, the researchers used participatory modelling as a boundary method, but in contrast to the Red River case the role-playing game and computer model were quite simple, focusing on actual ecological and human behaviour, and only served to get enhanced sharing of knowledge and discussion about the exact problem formulation and the type of solution to look for. The Mafungautsi as well as the Westerkwartier case used field work, analysis using different perspectives, meetings and discussions, simple scenario envisioning as tools for social learning and creative thinking to break through ordinary thought and decision-making patterns. The boundary process was as open as possible, geared towards social learning and capacity-building. We could characterise the researcher-stakeholder relations as collaborative: researchers facilitated and guided the process of social learning. In the Westerkwartier case, stakeholders organised themselves in a regional platform and their recommendations were adopted by the municipality and province. In the Mafungautsi case (Zimbabwe) and the Northern Thailand case, most government officials still adhered to a top-down planning culture. Some officers, closely involved in the process, saw the advantages of the social learning approach but it was hard to convince the others to take an open attitude and share as equals. In Thailand the simulations convinced Hmong herder that it was impossible to combine traditional cattle-rearing activities with the National Park's tree planting, so they insisted on the exploration of artificial pastures.

12. Conclusion: from knowledge for action to knowledge in action

Foresters agreed to provide the herder with an experimental plot while the district livestock officers provided the seeds needed. After this agreement, efforts were made to inform other herders as well as decision-makers about the issue-at-stake and possible solutions. In this way researchers hoped to build up the adaptive management capacity of the stakeholder for the future. In the Mafungautsi case, much effort was done to involve Zimbabwe policy makers as much as possible in the conferences, round table discussions and workshops to prevent them from perceiving the initiate as 'political' and 'subversive'. Relationships were forged and the local stakeholders plus the forester were trained in facilitation, conflict management and leadership. However, after the project the local and network activities did not last long and the authorities resumed their top-down approach.

In summary, these four cases describe researchers' efforts to include stakeholders in the problem definition. Through basic boundary objects (concepts, theoretical frameworks or simple models) and in-depth inquiry methods they stimulated stakeholders to express their perspective, underlying reasoning, interests and values, in order to create mutual understanding, and a joint vision about the type of development needed. In this way they may have prevented conflict. Through social learning they also worked on capacity-building: they intended to build up trust, engagement and relationships for the concrete search for and development of solutions and action.

12.2.3 Sharing of knowledge for more equitable development

In the Dutch Spatially Planning cases as well as the Limpopo case, the researchers tried to influence the ongoing landscape planning and implementation of the government, in favour of marginalised local stakeholders. They combined reflection on power dynamics and ethics (as promoted by crtical system proponent Ulrich) with strategic knowledge generation and information provision to give voice to/empower the marginalised and to stimulate more inclusive solutions (as promoted by the critical system proponent Jackson). In the Dutch Spatially Planning cases, researchers joined formal coalitions of local inhabitants and helped them to understand legal planning procedures, to formulate a science-based critique of the formal plan and its underlying reasoning, and/or elaborate an alternative solution. The researchers were not formally involved or contracted by the stakeholder coalition, which avoided conflicts of interests in the research institute and ensured a more collegiate relationship with local stakeholders. Nevertheless, researchers played a dominant role as spokesmen in the strategic negotiation process and litigation. As decisions had been taken, government officers felt threatened and esteemed citizens and farmer coalitions were not regarded as qualified to interfere in complex issues. Though the points put forward were scientifically credible, salient and more fair to local interests, in neither of the cases did they lead to a positive change in the landscape decision. In the Limpopo case, the researcher was a foreigner interested in the process of resettlement of local communities outside the Peace Park area in Mozambique. To gain legitimacy, she focused her PhD research on a concrete technical issue (how to improve plant and seed management to safeguard

A. van Paassen, R. Werkdam, B. Pedroli, J. van den Berg, E. Steingröver and C. Leeuwis

local livelihoods inside and outside the park), and networked with local stakeholders as well as the park authorities to gain trust, gather information and slowly start low-profile mediation. Despite the delicate balancing of actions, the political situation was such that the higher level authorities sensed her as a threat and easy scapegoat for the delays in the resettlement process. In the Dutch Spatial Planning cases one action researcher took a more reflexive stance while the other engaged in a collegiate partnership aimed at advocacy and empowerment of local stakeholders. Being knowledgeable about scientific reasoning as well as the planning and litigation procedures, they at times took over the leading role and acted beyond their formal responsibility as researchers. In the Limpopo case, the researcher had to manoeuvre delicately and opted for a strategic consultative-cum-informative approach, based on continuous reflection about the negotiation process, power dynamics and her position in these. In the Dutch Spatial Planning cases elaborated reports and maps were used as detailed boundary objects for negotiation and litigation, but in the Limpopo case all communication was informal, oral and behind the scenes due to the political sensitivity. The dialogue at times was enriched by the simple figures, tables or maps and other graphical representations provided. It would have been too threatening for the local communities and the Park officials to openly share thoughts about the argumentation, negotiation, power dynamics and the consequences for the resettlement communities. Hence, in this latter case the research aim was understanding and influencing the societal negotiation concerning landscape development, rather than capacity-building for empowerment and more interactive learning & decision-making routines.

In these cases, the researchers got involved in negotiation (proving arguments for or against a certain problem frame or type of solution proposed) and/or mediation (providing information about the actual or possible future situation, concerns, underlying beliefs, norms and values of certain stakeholders, to create more understanding and better relationships). Through the provision of bits and pieces of knowledge, researchers tried to influence the ongoing problem framing and negotiation of solutions in favour of the marginalised. Whether they were successful of not, depended on whether the power holders felt independent and powerful enough to impose their perspective or whether they felt responsible and/or interdependent vis-à-vis the marginalised groups.

12.2.4 Sharing of perspectives for capacity-building and institutional change

The Northern Frisian Woodland (NFW) case is a case in which the farmers invited researchers to join their innovation project, as this allowed them to understand the status of 'governance experiment'. This status created some room for manoeuvre vis-à-vis the detailed governmental rules and regulations about obligatory farm practices reducing nitrogen losses at dairy farms. NFW is a farmers' association for nature- and landscape management in the north of the Netherlands. Local farmers initiated the association in 1992 by founding two environmental co-operatives, VEL and VANLA (Eshuis and Stuiver, 2005). They wanted to develop their own approach for reducing nitrogen losses in their dairy farms and improving

12. Conclusion: from knowledge for action to knowledge in action

soil and water quality. The farmers established a board and developed their own rules and rights and a form of self-organisation to meet these goals. Aided by some researchers, as was formally required, the farmers continued their activities from the status of an 'experimental research programme'. This provided space, means and the time to further develop and validate their approach. The story of NFW outlines the collegiate collaboration for joint learning in the Nutrient Management project, which consisted of three working groups, focusing on research for and implementation of soil- and grassland management innovations, fodder production innovations and feed regimes innovations. The story demonstrates the equal relationship between farmers and researchers and the conflict that emerged with respect to the scientific credibility of the boundary object, i.e. the soil-plant-animal system framework. The farmers and some researchers used to share this boundary object and integrate farmer knowledge to get a holistic perspective on the issue and ideas about promising nitrogen management practices. New nitrogen management practices emerged and were accounted for in an experimental research programme, a certification system, nutrient accounts, reports, newsletters and websites.

From other sources, we learned that the farmer co-operatives were also working on additional projects, among which an initiative to develop a local and collaborative approach for the maintenance of the small-scale landscape of hedges and rows of alder trees (Werkman *et al.*, 2010). The co-operatives, which had by then expanded with four other co-operatives, together established the 'NFW Association' which incorporated all the different projects they were working on together and they sought co-operation with the province of Friesland and a regional farmers' organisation. The intention was to pool expertise in order to effectively submit grant applications to the governmental landscape management programme '*Programma Beheer*'. In 2004, the initiative expanded to include the Ministry of Agriculture, Nature and Food Quality and the Ministry of Public Housing, Spatial Planning and Environmental Conservation, the regional water board, and the regional environmental federation. Together, they entered into a covenant that incorporated the mutual agreements, a programme of action and a working structure consisting of a steering group, workgroups and projects. In 2007, the project was incorporated in TransForum, a temporary innovation programme that aims to offer the Dutch agricultural sector a more sustainable and profitable perspective (TransForum, 2007). In close collaboration with the TransForum project team, a group of social scientists conducted interviews with the partners and facilitated a joint interpretation of the results with the association's bureau and the project team. They became members of the steering committee and of various working groups to obtain information, introduce their insights and create commitment and possibilities for stakeholders to start initiatives or projects. They helped organise the initiative, its structure and its activities by helping create more transparency and streamline all ad-hoc initiatives into co-ordinated action; they co-ordinated the participation of other researchers; and they helped to get the initiative on the national agenda.

A. van Paassen, R. Werkdam, B. Pedroli, J. van den Berg, E. Steingröver and C. Leeuwis

However, the NFW association grew more and more frustrated by the detailed governmental rules and regulations that they had to comply with. The association wanted more freedom for self-governance. A meeting organised for policy makers from the Ministry of Agriculture evoked enthusiasm, but not the freedom the association wanted. The association concluded this issue could not be solved at the national level so it was important to know how, where and by whom decisions were made at the European level. The researchers proposed starting an inquiry into the national and European network of decision-making and lobbying, and helping the association to develop networking and advocacy strategies and lines of argumentation. Here, the researchers play the role of advisor and 'think along', but the decisions are made by the association. This initiative is still ongoing.

This case is therefore an example of a research project with an innovation system thinking perspective, that tackles technical as well as organisational problems at various system levels. This means researchers conduct research and present their findings for discussion, or they develop a basic boundary object to jointly explore power, organisational and institutional dynamics, constraints and opportunities. In this way they build the capacity of the stakeholders and create new institutional routines for co-ordinated adapted governance.

The choice of a prime research goal (envisaged societal contribution of the research) more or less determines the kind of boundary-spanning process pursued: the selection of boundary tools and methods of inquiry and negotiation. In fact, it means researchers opt for a certain research or so-called knowledge brokerage role and prime brokerage strategy (see Table 12.1). And these brokerage strategies are intimately related to the type of collaboration with the stakeholders, i.e. the type of collaborative research as defined by Probst *et al.* (2003) (see Chapter 2).

12.3 The role of collaborative research

In the previous section we revisited the different case stories, highlighting the type of boundary-spanning processes pursued, the associated type of collaboration with stakeholders and the results attained. In the next sections, we focus on the two challenges elaborated in Section 2.4: the research practices and the research role employed, and the perceived adequacy of the theory and methodology to tackle the issues-at-stake in the respective contexts. Furthermore, we reflect on the tensions between 'the ways of knowing' (epistemology) of traditional scientists and societal actors, that the researcher had to deal with.

12.3.1 The variety of enacted knowledge broker roles and prime strategies

In the book chapters the authors expressed their reasoning, underlying theories and assumptions. These are the so-called 'espoused theories' (Argyris and Schön, 1996). But what is more important in practice, are the 'theories-in-use': the partly tacit theories and assumptions that guide the actual implementation of the research. In Section 12.2 we provided a short summary of the implementation of the 9 cases. Most research processes focussed on more than one issue (issue-at-stake, creating mutual understanding, institutional embedding and change etc.), but when we look at the overall, most dominant, research focus we can distinguish the prime broker strategies of the researchers as presented in Table 12.1. The most dominant type of boundary-spanning process and type of stakeholder participation pursued, seems logically connected to the envisaged societal contribution of the research. Researchers aim for a certain societal contribution and therewith define their role and prime broker strategy in an ongoing societal negotiations and innovation processes. The various collaborative research approaches served different purposes.

12.3.2 Who determines the overall research goal?

In the previous section, we demonstrated that the different cases aimed at different research goals. They aimed at specific societal contributions. This is in line with the definition of trans-disciplinary research. Trans-disciplinary research involves the integration of scientific and stakeholder knowledge, is problem-driven and action-oriented (Fry, 2001; Tress and Tress, 2001; Tress *et al.*, 2003; 2004; 2005; Wu, 2006; Wu, 2008). Gibbons *et al.* (1994) and Nowotny *et al.* (2001) note that the problem-driven, action-oriented character of the research can only be attained when researchers become more accountable to society. The inclusion of societal actors in the research initiation and formulation ensures that 'the researchers provide answers for the questions posed'. In Section 2.4 we discussed the issue of boundary work: the negotiation between scientists and societal actors about the role and legitimate responsibilities of the researcher and other societal actors in the research and innovation process. Considering the importance of the concepts of trans-disciplinarity and boundary work, the questions arises: who actually initiated the research and defined the overall research goal?

In six of the nine cases the research was initiated by a research institute. In the Red River Delta case (Chapter 3) and the Frisian Lakes case (Chapter 4), national research institutes wanted to generate practical solutions for a technical problem and a planning problem respectively. In the Westerkwartier case (Chapter 6), the Northern Thailand case (Chapter 9), the Mafungautsi case (Chapter 8), and the Limpopo case (Chapter 11), research institutes wanted to support the learning, negotiation and action of local stakeholders in their respective landscape, and try new, more inclusive and 'local-fit' learning and governance approaches. In the East Africa case (Chapter 5), the Ministry of Agriculture in the Netherlands incited Dutch researchers to start a capacity-building programme in Africa to prepare national researchers, policy makers and development practitioners for the effects of climate change, and integrate the issue of climate change adaptation into agricultural, rural development and natural resources policy-making processes. In two cases, the Flood Mitigation case (Chapter 10) and the Frisian Woodlands case (Chapter 7), local stakeholders invited the research to join their coalition so as to enhance their learning and to become stronger in societal negotiations.

A. van Paassen, R. Werkdam, B. Pedroli, J. van den Berg, E. Steingröver and C. Leeuwis

Table 12.1. Comparison of implementation characteristics of the various collaborative research cases presented in the book.

Prime broker strategy researcher	Envisaged societal contribution	Type of boundary-spanning process
A. To integrate knowledge and inform	Generation detailed technical-economical viable, socially acceptable practices/solutions that policy makers perceive as credible, salient and legitimate	Knowledge integration; research to develop comprehensive science-based boundary object, which considers policy concerns and includes local knowledge and/or values.
B. To guide sharing of perspectives	Social learning to create joint vision for collective action, to prevent conflict	Joint further development of basic boundary object (concept, theoretical framework or model) and boundary process, primary aimed at sharing of knowledge, opinions, underlying values and interests related to issue-at-stake
C. To negotiate, to mediate	Inclusion of marginalised interest in ongoing societal learning and negotiation processes, leading to more equitable development and governance	Strategic provision of knowledge; research of issue-at-stake, diversity perspectives, position marginalised, and power dynamics to create boundary objects that put marginalised interests on the political agenda.
D. To empower	Capacity-building for more inclusive learning and negotiation routines Institutional change to enhance innovation for sustainable, equitable development	Joint discussion around piece of information or frame (boundary object), aimed at sharing of knowledge, opinions, underlying values and interests related to issue- at-stake and power, organisational and/or institutional issues

This means that a majority (6 out of 9) of the collaborative research projects for landscape development are primarily initiated and determined by researchers. And the researchers seem to be primarily inspired by the idea of knowledge integration and soft system thinking (5 out of the 6 cases). In the East Africa case, the researchers initiated the research together with policy makers, and they also opted for the social learning strategy. In two cases, researchers initiated their research on invitation of local stakeholders, and they opted for an advocacy and empowerment approach. Hence we can conclude that most collaborative research efforts are still primarily defined by the researchers themselves. They, as well as policy-makers seem to favour research approaches that highlight the joint learning: they want to invite

12. Conclusion: from knowledge for action to knowledge in action

Type of collaborative research	Role of researcher (knowledge broker)	Cases concerned
Consultative	Problem-solving of structured problem	Frisian Lake Red River delta
Collaborative (Collegiate)	Accommodation/facilitation to attain consensus/compromise about development orientation (Implicit) capacity-building for joint learning and decision-making	East Africa Westerkwartier Mafungautsi Northern Thailand the Frisian Woodland
Consultative Collaborative	Advocacy and mediation for more balanced negotiation and equitable development solutions	Limpopo Flood Mitigation
Collaborative Collegiate	Capacity-building more inclusive learning and negotiation routines Institutional change to enhance innovation for sustainable, equitable landscape development	the Frisian Woodland Northern Thailand

stakeholders to join the knowledge integration or learning process. When engaging with marginalised stakeholders, or collaborating with a stakeholder coalition, the researchers tend to opt for advocacy or empowerment approach, and are inspired by theories related to critical system thinking and innovation system theories.

The observation that 7 out of 9 collaborative programmes have been initiated by players who were relative outsiders to the direct societal context in which the researchers were operating is perhaps not totally surprising in light of the dominant modes of research funding, but it is still worth noting. Experience teaches us that it is not easy for locally active stakeholders to have or develop ownership of outsider initiated processes. It would be worthwhile to study how the history of initiation and funding affects collaborative processes, and try alternative funding arangements (e.g. channelling research funds through the stakeholders, rather than through the research institutes) (see e.g. Klerkx & Leeuwis, 2008).

12.3.3 The fit between the espoused theories and actual theories-in-use

In the previous section, we concluded the overall research goal was predominantly determined by the researchers. Now we are interested to see whether the goal and theoretical framework as announced at the start of the exercise (the espoused theory) was the same as the actual implemented goal and theory (theories-in-use). People often say one thing and do another, because there are emotional, sensitive issues or tacit assumptions they do not express, but which do influence their actual behaviour. When we compare the 'theories-in-use' with the initial 'espoused theories' for action that were used to categorise the research cases in Chapter 2, we can show that: the prime researchers' broker strategies A, B, C and D (see Table 12.1), respectively fit well with hard system thinking, with soft system thinking, with critical system thinking, and with innovation system thinking. This means that in the cases, the 'theories-in-use' when enacting the research were not very different from the espoused theories for action. Note that we categorised the Red River Delta case as a research process in which the type A broker strategy was applied, aimed at knowledge integration despite their complementary focus on learning. The reason for this is that they were primarily focused on substantive learning, rather than making in-depth inquiries about each actor's interests, concerns and underlying norms and values to create more mutual understanding and build relationships amongst the actors.

Given that it is quite common to find that 'theories-in-use' deviate from 'espoused theories', it is quite remarkable that we find quite a good fit in this book. It is not entirely clear how we should interpret this. Does theory indeed drive practice? Or did the authors retrospectively fit their theory to the practice as part of an effort to construct a logical story? In Section 12.3.5 below we show that several cases described in the book have adapted both their practice and theory over time. This suggests that achieving a fit may be the result of an iterative learning process in which theory and practice mutually inform each other.

12.3.4 The fit of the theoretical framework and research role with the problem type and setting

Michaels (2009) notes that it is important to better understand the tasks that knowledge brokers undertake within different contexts. In line with the framework about environmental problem types and policy settings of Hisschemoller *et al.* (2001), we elaborate the following ideas (see Table 12.2): in complex situations related to landscape development there is a lot of uncertainty and ambiguity, so it seems wise to opt for an open-learning (Hoppe, 2005) and capacity-building approach (Mollinga, 2008). Innovation system thinking might be useful in guiding the researcher's action. This approach enables researchers and stakeholders to identify and enact vis-à-vis emerging problems. As soon as an emerging problem is identified, different stakeholders will have different perspectives and concerns about the issue-at-stake: there is no consensus about how to approach the issues; what concerns and values prevail in determining the type of action needed. To prevent conflicts, policy makers and researchers may opt for a social learning approach, inspired by soft system thinking, to define a shared vision, consensus, win-win situation or compromise. However, even when there is a kind of consensus about the type of solutions needed, the exact choice of one or another measure may have high consequences for the stakeholders. When this leads to conflicts, researchers are often invited to join stakeholder coalitions or mediate in order to provide the arguments to settle the conflict (Bocking, 2006; Turnhout *et al.*, 2008). In such a situation, researchers need to be aware of the power dynamics surrounding the decision-making, use critical system thinking and opt for an advocacy or mediating role. When stakeholder negotiations or policy makers have led to a clear framing of the problem and the type of solution needed (structure problem), it is the task of the researcher to resolve this problem through knowledge integration.

A question which arises from the table above is: did the perception of the problem type and setting of the research designers, in our cases mostly the researchers, fit the initial and evolving situation as perceived and enacted by the stakeholders? Did the researchers have the feeling they were able to tackle the emerging situations and attain the envisioned research goal and assumed societal impact? In Section 12.2, we noticed the researchers did not always attain the societal impact they hoped for. Several authors mention they encountered problems, mostly related to conflicts, power differences and turbulent political strife that interfered with and impeded the collaborative research and innovation process. This suggests that their initial diagnosis regarding the nature of the problem setting (Table 12.2) may have been limited. In one case (the Frisian Lakes) the authors wonder whether it is worthwhile hooking a design experiment on a real ongoing planning process, or whether it is better to opt for a traditional experiment with a representative sample of individuals. Some authors ask themselves how to go about these issues of conflict and power imbalances (Red River Delta; Westerkwartier case).

Several research teams tried to address this issue of power differences and institutional constraints, and made efforts to overcome them, e.g. by regular contact and early involvement of the authorities. The efforts led to varying outcomes. In the Northern Thailand case this seems successful, because only small favours were asked from the authorities and local actors seemed capable of tackling the main problem via new livestock practices. In the Frisian Woodland case inclusion of the authorities is relatively successful, but the most restrictive rules seemed to come from national and European politics, which is quite high-level. In the Mafungautsi case, the researchers found themselves in a turbulent political environment and they saw their first positive impacts ruined by ongoing political turmoil. In this regard, the lessons learned are that collaborative research is time- and skills-intensive; and research

Table 12.2. The fit between the problem type and setting with the researcher roles.

	Unstructured	Badly structured	Moderately structured	Well structured
Perspective on problem definition and solutions	No consensus	Uncertainty, lack of consensus	Some consensus, but choice of specific solutions has high consequences for stakeholders	Situation of clarity and consensus
Brokering role of researcher	Learning and engagement for innovation; build adaptive capacity	Process role: stimulate social learning, create shared concepts and a joint vision to enhance collaboration Accommodation	Strategically provide arguments and advocate a more equitable solution	Science arbiter, provide credible, salient, legitimate knowledge to support and elaborate solutions
Theoretical perspective	Innovation system thinking	Soft system thinking	Critical system thinking	Hard system thinking

12. Conclusion: from knowledge for action to knowledge in action

teams need skills and expertise for facilitating social learning and negotiation processes as well as the broader understanding about power dynamics and societal change.

For the researchers of the Dutch Spatial Planning cases as well as the Limpopo case, the importance of the divergence of perspectives, power balances and institutional constraints were clear from the start, but they approached them in a different manner with clearly different results. In the Dutch Spatial Planning cases the researchers opted to join coalitions for advocacy and empowerment, while in the Limpopo case the researcher opted for a relatively independent, low-profile and flexible strategy of advocacy and mediation. In the Flood Mitigation case the efforts seemed counterproductive. As the reports and argumentation against the prevailing problem frame came after the closure of the problem formulation phase of the selection of the respective solution, the officials felt attacked and relations hardened. The focus on the contents of plans, the ongoing critique and arguments for alternatives caused both parties to bombard each other with more contents (reports). The processes led to a stalemate and those with most power 'won' this particular case. However, in the long term the issue was put on the political agenda.

In the Limpopo case, the researcher opted for a more mediatory role, which implies a delicate process of 'walking the tightrope' in which active maintenance of trust and relationships is of critical importance. The role a researcher plays is multi-faceted, involving role and identity; and is contingent in the specific time and space context of societal negotiation. In some instances, bits of research-derived information, provided as basic, descriptive, and aggregated data, played a role and improved the quality of the information available to the negotiating parties. Such an independent low-profile approach can make a difference, even though such conditions raise questions of ethics. Furthermore, the researcher faces obstacles such as a tense political atmosphere, unlevel playing field, researcher's fear of being used or blamed, or losing access. In short, critical system thinking and innovation thinking may help to identify the constraints for equitable, sustainable landscape development and governance, but tackling them requires considerable engagement and investment in multilevel relationships.

It is perhaps interesting to note that both 'critical systems' projects (Limpopo and Flood Mitigation) are characterised by a somewhat unorthodox way of funding. The first was mainly funded through an individual research scholarship (complemented with some core university funding), which gave the researcher a great deal of independence and discretion regarding what to study and for whom. The second was funded by a Dutch 'science shop', a facility through which less-endowed groups can gain access to a limited amount of research funding. Here the researchers were actually called in to strengthen the position of a marginal group, in line with the overall 'science shop' objective. One could hypothesise that it is perhaps easier more and acceptable to conduct politically engaged research through such 'non-mainstream' ways of funding research capacity.

12.3.5 The need for a multi-dimensional and flexible research approach

In Chapter 2 we presented a typology of contemporary collaborative landscape research (see Table 2.1):
- research primarily aimed at problem-solving, which tends to embrace hard system thinking but tried to include local knowledge and values;
- research primarily aimed at social and experiential learning, which uses soft system thinking;
- research for balanced negotiations, inspired by critical system thinking;
- research for institutional change, inspired by innovation system thinking.

We can conclude that – although the typology helps in evaluating the differences between the cases – most cases do not strictly follow a general typology like this one.

Collaborative research needs to tackle various issues before being able to create change. Four cases (the Northern Thailand case, the Flood Mitigation case, the Limpopo case and the Frisian Woodland case) did explicitly address a variety of issues, and used various types of system thinking. They explicitly incorporated issues of power differences and/or institutional constraints in their theoretical thinking and research methodology. In these cases, we see that the research simultaneously or iteratively tackles various dimensions of a change process such as the substantive learning and problem-solving; the need for mutual understanding and relationships; tackling power imbalances, etc. Proponents of critical system thinking Flood and Romm (1995) advocate a flexible research approach, iterating between different system perspectives most appropriate to deal with the emerging new problem or issue-at-stake.

Various cases in the book tried to tackle these varying issues, and changed their research focus along the process, amongst others the Mafungautsi case, the Frisian Woodland case and the Northern Thailand case. Table 12.3 shows how in the Northern Thailand case the research focus changed over time.

Table 12.3 illustrates that it is too simplistic to think about programmes as having a single, static and/or clearly identifiable theoretical approach. This simultaneously implies that analysing whether or not there is 'a fit' between espoused theories and theories-in-use, respectively between research roles and the type of problem setting, is something that may need to be done continuously rather than at a single moment in time.

12.3.6 The tension between 'ways of knowing'

Many of the authors of the cases described epistemological dilemmas that consciously or unconsciously influence the choices they make, sometimes without explicitly addressing them. Positivism assumes the existence of a 'true', context-free reality that can be measured,

12. Conclusion: from knowledge for action to knowledge in action

Table 12.3. Evolution of context and research focus in the Northern Thailand case.

Evolution context and issue at stake	Adopted research aim	Related theoretical framework
Park rangers want solution for cattle roaming in the park. Heterogeneous herder community, whose livelihood depends on cattle rearing. Situation of distrust	Workshop for uneducated herders first, to create awareness and prepare them for confrontation with more powerful foresters of NNP	Critical system thinking
Hmong herder are prepared to have workshop together with NNP rangers	Workshop to facilitate communication and trust between herders and foresters by building a shared representation of link forest and cattle rearing	Social system thinking to create trust, mutual understanding and define problem
Foresters and herder realise impossibility of combining tree planting with traditional herding techniques. Herder accepts dialogue	New workshop with inclusion of artificial pastures as option to explore	Hard system thinking
Workshop participants agree on joint experimentation, but herder communities need to be informed and mobilised	Semi-autonomous simulations to inform other herders in villagers and neighbouring communities with similar land-use conflict	Innovation system thinking
Need to brief and get consent of local administrators and other decision-makers about the outcomes of this ComMod process	Development ABM replaying gaming sessions *in silico* to brief wider public	Innovation system thinking

mapped in cause-effect laws, proven and generalised to other contexts. Methodologically, researchers have to comply with the paradigm's scientific standards of validity, reliability and replicability. The constructivist epistemology recognises that all knowledge, including scientific knowledge, is socially constructed (Knorr-Cetina, 1981; Latour, 1987). Through interaction, people create meaning; they construct their reality about the issue-at-stake, their relationships and the ongoing learning and negotiation process, which guide their action. Researchers study how people create meaning, and they search methods that help to change reality perceptions in order to create more favourable outcomes.

In the Frisian Lakes case as well as in the Red River Delta case, the researchers started with their biophysical knowledge, acquired with positivist research methods. In the Frisian Lake case, the researchers invited representatives to add issues and criteria that they esteemed important, but the subsequent choice experiment was meant to attach a financial weight to a 'value judgement'. The method aimed to enhance social learning and exchange, but then concluded with a quantification of values so as to depoliticise the issue and transform it into an economic cost-benefit optimisation. In the Red River Delta case the researchers involved local stakeholders in the monitoring and data collection to compensate for a 'lack of reliable data', 'enhance stakeholder's knowledge and understanding of a system and its dynamics under various conditions'. However, they also invited stakeholders to give their interpretation of the problems and finally asked them to discuss and prioritise the various solutions. By adding some 'qualitative flesh to the quantitative bones' they combined two epistemologies, without compromising the underlying assumptions. The researchers in the Northern Thailand case explicitly opted for constructivism and started with interviews and the sharing of knowledge 'to get a rich picture with all legitimate perspective on the issue at hand'. For them the modelling was meant to trigger debate and jointly create a new reality and meaning about the problem and type of solutions desired.

In the East Africa case, the Mafungautsi case, the Westerkwartier case and the Frisian Woodlands case, researchers feel the tension and consciously balance the ontological and epistemological assumptions that belong to their interactive learning approach on the one hand and positivist assumptions that may characterise their education, institutions and research partners on the other hand. Lessons learned relate to the importance of bringing to light different paradigms among researchers. The Westerkwartier authors conclude it is possible to engage in both worlds at the same time, however their suggestion is to use objective science to understand subjective interpretations and processes, a conclusion which deserves further discussion about how this relates to constructivist basic assumptions. In the Frisian Woodlands case, two groups of scientists and farmers engage in a conflict about the meaning of a systemic model. For the natural scientists, the model means something that should be tested to objectively prove its scientific validity, while for the farmers the model was valuable because it integrated practical knowledge they esteemed relevant and useful for the design of innovations. Lessons learned include that conflicts and discussions about differences in perspectives such as these may be valuable and a source of renewal.

12. Conclusion: from knowledge for action to knowledge in action

In the Limpopo case, the researcher feels her presence as foreigner can only be legitimised by adherring to strict scientific rigour and she strives to generate answers and conclusions that are as objective and balanced as possible. She also recognises that science can never be politically neutral. The researcher assumes that scientists can assist in answering value-laden questions 'while being explicit about their assumptions, using methodologies that are rigorous and acceptable to conventional science'. Highly motivated to develop an approach that actually contributes to local problem-solving, her research proposal is classified by her research institution as 'development work' rather than research. The researcher then defines research questions for her proposal in line with institutional requirements, but starts her fieldwork without specific research questions or theories so as to be open to the existing context, which implies that she ignored the requirements of her institution. Although the researcher eventually did engage in a constant process of rigorous data gathering and analysis, she learned that it was not the research results that influenced the societal negotiations, but rather the process of being there, interacting, gathering information and engaging in dialogue. In the Dutch Spatial Planning cases, something similar happened when the authors described how they chose to avoid discussions about engaging in action research within their own institution in order to increase their scope of action. This provided them with more flexibility in their approach.

To summarise, many of our case chapters, consciously or unconsciously, address some form of tension between positivist, hard system thinking and constructivist, soft system thinking. They describe frictions between 'old' and 'new' researcher roles; between the need for 'hard' knowledge as opposed to learning approaches. They pose questions about what 'valid' knowledge is; and address questions concerning how 'scientific' their collaborative approaches really are, also in the eyes of participants. In some chapters, we notice an assumption that 'hard knowledge is not done', and at the same time, 'hard' knowledge assumptions such as independent, objective, replicable, etc., resonate in their language. In our view hard system thinking is valid and useful for specific issues. However, it is important that researchers are aware of the diversity of focus and paradigmatic assumptions, and subsequently opt for an overall system approach wisely combining different kinds of research methods to tackle different types of problems. Positivist, natural sciences remain of vital importance, to monitor and analyse the dynamics of 'nature' and the biophysical consequences of human activity to inform normative frameworks for sustained land use. Social sciences must play their role among landscape sciences to analyse human activity as the result of intentionality and greed, economic systems, human learning and agreement (Röling, 1997). The mission of collaborative landscape research is to help society learn to live valued livelihoods within the realms of the ecological opportunities.

12.4 Practical recommendations for the future

After the analysis of the cases, and the lessons learned we come to the following recommendations for those who want to engage in collaborative research for sustainable landscape development and governance.

12.4.1 Link up with existing institutions to embed the research in their innovation process

Six out of nine cases in the book were initiated and formulated by research institutes. The best way to ensure the fit between the research approach and needs of the societal stakeholders is to already engage with them during the initiation of the research project and the formulation of the issue-at-stake. The results of collaborative landscape research will not fully contribute to sustainable landscape development if researchers do not link up with government officers, NGOs and other key actors in the decision-making process. Though we as researchers are still largely unused to engaging beyond the border of science, our commitment to existing networks of societal partners is crucial for a thorough alignment and matching of responsibilities for research and action (Klerkx *et al.*, 2009). Hence, it may be wise to embed future collaborative landscape research better in current processes of knowledge-in-action and in multiple networks of societal partners and governmental institutions. This may simultaneously require new funding arrangements that make it easier for stakeholders to exert ownership.

12.4.2 Look at the problem and context to determine the role of the research

Collaborative researchers will always experience a dilemma between their commitment to their professional career for which they need high-rating scientific publications, and their commitment to societal impact (McNie, 2007). The actual role that a researcher will take in the research and innovation process will depend on his or her personal characteristics, funding agency and employer, but is also determined by the problem setting. Researchers as well as societal stakeholders from different cultural-institutional backgrounds have different beliefs about what stakeholder participation and research collaboration is about and what it should accomplish (Webler, 2001; 2002; Probst *et al.*, 2003; Rault and Jeffrey, 2008). As we have seen in the different chapters, collaborative research is diverse and has many functions. The initial and evolving problem type and the context setting (willingness to co-operate, legitimate role and preferred procedures of the societal actors) more or less influence the role that researchers can usefully play to create impact (Hisschemöller *et al.*, 2001; Hoppe, 2005; Chevalier and Buckles, 2008; Opdam, 2010).

12.4.3 Study the various theoretical frameworks and use them flexibly

In Section 12.3.5 we showed the importance of keeping in constant touch with the research context and switching to different strategies to match new situations. In order to deal with diverse, complex and changing research contexts, researchers need a toolbox of different theoretical perspectives, roles and 'stories' that help them to focus on different aspects. For the research process, this means that researchers cannot do without a preliminary problem- and stakeholder analysis, an identification of barriers but also opportunities for change, an appropriate and flexible positioning of the research. Acquaintance with the various theoretical frameworks enables researchers (in deliberation with the stakeholders) to flexibly select the framework and innovation-cum-research methodology most fit for the evolving issue-at-stake and the surrounding socio-political context.

12.4.4 Select the most appropriate type of boundary–spanning process

Landscape development concerns a large variety of stakeholders; hence it is important to develop appropriate boundary-spanning processes: use the right type of boundary object, level of participation, and learning or negotiation method. As Carlile (2002) noted, people from different life-worlds need boundary objects that enable them to exchange information about the issue-at-stake and what it means to them. Simple concepts, frameworks and models are useful as they allow stakeholders to exchange perspectives and to develop them in a way that makes sense to them. It enables them to create a rich picture of a landscape and/or a governance issue; explore a gamut of solutions; negotiate; and finally agree upon some useful ones. At the same time, this joint work engages people and builds relationships for action (Klerkx *et al.*, 2010). Consultation of stakeholders for the integration of knowledge in comprehensive predefined models is only useful for structured well-defined problems. In situations of distrust and conflict about problem formulation and/or proposed solutions, other types of boundary processes and -objects are needed, clearly visualising the issue-at-stake, and the argument to put forward in the negotiation. This may be a model or elaborate report, but in the right circumstances a small piece of information or quote may have considerable impact.

12.4.5 Opt for a reflexive approach and if possible include stakeholders in this exercise

Researchers who familiarise themselves with different theories and methods are more flexible and better able to adapt their strategy to the problem type and setting (Huitema *et al.*, 2009). Landscape development issues concern multiple levels and domains and a variety of perspectives and institutional routines; hence, to advance, researchers need to consider and tackle various emerging problems and constraints in a multi-dimensional or iterative manner. They need to opt for a reflexive approach: continuously monitoring and reflecting upon their action and the evolving context (Leach *et al.*, 2007). It might even be a good idea to involve stakeholders in a reflexive monitoring process to obtain more contextual knowledge and awareness about the socio-political and institutional issues; to better gear research and innovation processes towards the most constraining factors; and to create commitment for effective action that surpasses the local level. There are methods and boundary objects in development for this purpose (Guijt, 2008; Van Mierlo *et al.*, 2010).

12.4.6 Express contrasting paradigms and deal with them

In the previous section we described how researchers may choose and apply different approaches and methodologies depending on the nature of the problem, i.e. researchers use more than one paradigm or worldview to try and understand and act on reality. However, in collaborative research, researchers are also confronted with other researchers and participants who have their own convictions about preferred approaches. The challenge for collaborative researchers here is to find ways for hard and soft system perspectives to meaningfully co-exist. They may even try to integrate them in a new approach, in which stakeholders define the focus of the research, which (partly) needs to be solved by hard system knowledge. From a meta-paradigmatic perspective, it helps if researchers reflect on and understand the different worldviews represented in the collaborative research process and how these affect each other (Feltmann, 1984; Van Dongen *et al.*, 1996). This may enable researchers and participants to create new definitions, starting points and approaches for collaboration.

12.4.7 Remain cautious and modest in a context of diversity and conflict

Landscape research deals with a variety in interests, perspectives and power differences. It is a challenge to develop solutions that are supported or at least accepted by all stakeholders and institutions concerned. By involving stakeholders in the problem analysis and the development of the solutions, researcher enhance social learning to create mutual understanding, and build the trust and relationships needed for agreement and co-ordinated action. However, researchers often work in contexts of political turmoil, economic crisis and competing claims, characterised by uncertainty, conflict, weak social relationships and deep distrust (Bresnen *et al.*, 2003; McEvily, 2003; Van Bueren, 2003; Dietz and Den Hartog, 2006). This induces stakeholders to actively pursue strategic negotiations that are characterised by unequal bargaining power, knowledge access, representation and incompatibility of argumentation skills (Giller, 2005; Huitema *et al.*, 2009). In such a context there is no sense of interdependence and there is a big risk that scientific information will be used as 'ammunition' in the political or economic struggle (Leeuwis, 2000; Hoppe, 2005). Critical system thinking may help the researcher to strategically position him or herself. Depending on the situation and the characteristics of the key actors it may be useful to involve those who might otherwise block the process, and prevent conflicts by the timely introduction of a compromise, creating package deals that combine different interests (cf. Klijn *et al.*, 1995; Edelenbos and Klijn 2005, 2006; Klijn and Koppenjan 2006), or alternatively go on the offensive and put a critical issue on the political agenda that would otherwise be ignored.

12. Conclusion: from knowledge for action to knowledge in action

The actual impact of these efforts depends on contingencies and is often beyond the control of the researchers; hence we need to remain cautious and modest in our expectations.

12.5 Epilogue: collaborative research: belief, science or art?

Being confronted with the limitation of growth, society called upon scientists to engage in trans-disciplinary, problem-driven, action-oriented research. At first, landscape researchers interpreted trans-disciplinary research as an intensified form of inter-disciplinary research for action. However, when research results did not provide the answers required, researchers abandoned the standard approaches of traditional positivist methodology and engaged in collaborative research (Fry, 2001; Wu, 2006, 2008). Scientists are also people, observing the results of their actions, and sometimes being frustrated that the results of their research are not effectively used in landscape development and governance. In many cases this has led to research processes where researchers have taken the initiative to design and control the entire collaborative research process. One could consider this as a belief, a belief that commitment mobilises others and leads to better results in landscape development and governance processes. In recent years, however, a body of evidence has emerged showing that this commitment can be described, analysed and improved in a scientific way. This book contributes to the scientific debate in this realm. But more than a belief or a science-based skill, at the end of the day collaborative research appears to be an art. Problem types and settings diverge and evolve, and it is difficult to foresee all constraints and opportunities at the start of a research process. Books about collaborative research may give you the first rules for deliberation and action. With science-based rules, continuous monitoring and reflection you may become a competent performer. But real experts have a wealth of experience and creativity which allows them 'to feel' nuances in the problem and context setting, exhibit rapid, intuitive, holistic and visual thinking rather than rational positioning (Flyvberg, 2001). Without a holistic, intuitive and creative attitude towards knowledge-in-action, collaborative research risks being ineffective window-dressing legitimising traditional science-based landscape development approaches. Based on thorough commitment, creativity and self-reflection, collaborative research can develop from a scientific activity to provide information enhancing effective negotiations in landscape development processes, into a legitimate involvement in these processes. In short: *from knowledge-for-action* to *knowledge-in-action*!

If this book succeeds in inspiring researchers from different backgrounds to develop initiatives for creative approaches and to engage in ongoing knowledge-in-action, we have at least partly achieved our objectives.

References

Argyris, C. and D.A. Schön, 1996. Organisational Learning II. Theory, method and practice. Addison-Wesley Publishing, Reading, MA, USA.

Bocking, S., 2006. Nature's Experts: Science, Politics, and the Environment. Rutgers University Press, New Brunswick, NJ, USA.

Bresnen, M., L. Edelman, S. Newell, H. Scarbrough and J. Swan, 2003. Social practices and the management of knowledge in project environments. International Journal of Project Management 21: 157-166.

Carlile, P.R., 2002. Transferring, translating and transforming: an integrative framework for managing knowledge across boundaries. Massachusetts Institute of Technology, Cambridge, MA, USA.

Chevalier, J.M. and D.J. Buckles, 2008. SAS2, A guide to collaborative Inquiry and social engagement. Sage, Ottawa, Canada.

Dietz, G. and D.N. Den Hartog, 2006. Measuring trust inside organisations. Personnel Review 35(5): 557-588.

Edelenbos, J. and E.H. Klijn, 2006. Managing stakeholder involvement in decision making: a comparative analysis of six interactive processes in the Netherlands. Journal of Public Administration Research and Theory 16 (3): 417-446.

Eshuis, J. and M. Stuiver, 2005. Learning in context through conflict and alignment: farmers and scientists in search of sustainable agriculture. Agriculture and Human Values 22 (2): 137-184.

Feltmann, C.E., 1984. Adviseren bij organiseren. De Perscombinatie, Amsterdam, the Netherlands [in Dutch].

Flood, R.L. and N.R.A. Romm, 1995. Enhancing the process of methodology choice in Total Systems Intervention (TSA) and improving chances for tackling coercion. Systems Practice 8 (4): 377-408.

Flyvberg, B., 2001. Making social science matter; why social inquiry fails and how it can succeed again. Cambridge University Press, Cambridge, UK.

Fry, G., 2001. Multifunctional landscapes; towards transdisicplinary research. Landscape and Urban Planning 57: 159-168.

Gibbons, M., C. Limoges, H. Nowotny, S. Schwartzman, P. Scott and M. Trow, 1994. The New Production of Knowledge: The Dynamics of Science and Research in Contemporary Societies. SAGE Publications, London, UK.

Giller, K., 2005. Competing claims on natural resources: Overcoming mismatches in resource use through a multi-scale perspective. An interdisciplinary research proposal to the International Research and Education Fund (INREF) of the Wageningen University.

Guijt, I., 2008. Seeking surprise: Rethinking monitoring for collective learning in rural resource management. PhD thesis. Wageningen University and Research centre, Wageningen, the Netherlands.

Hisschemöller, M., R. Hoppe, P. Groenewegen and C.J.H. Midden, 2001. Knowledge use and political choice in Dutch environmental policy: a problem structuring perspective on real life experiments in extended peer review. In: M. Hisschemöller, W.N. Dunn, R. Hoppe and J. Ravetz (eds.), Knowledge, Power and Participation in Environmental Policy Analysis. Policy Studies Review Annual Volume 12: 437-470.

12. Conclusion: from knowledge for action to knowledge in action

Hoppe, R., 2005. Rethinking the science-policy nexus: from knowledge utilization and science technology studies to types of boundary arrangements. Poiesis and Praxis 3: 199-215.

Huitema, D., E. Mostert, W. Egas, S. Moellenkamp, C. Pahl-Wostl and R. Yalcin, 2009. Adaptive water governance: Assessing the institutional prescriptions of adaptive (co-) management from a governance perspective and defining a research agenda. Ecology and Society 14 (1): 26. Available at: http://www.ecologyandsociety.org/vol14/iss1/art26/.

Klerkx, L. and C. Leeuwis, 2008. Delegation of authority in research funding to networks: Experiences with a multiple goal boundary organization. Science and Public Policy 35(3): 183-196.

Klerkx, L., N. Aarts and C. Leeuwis, 2010. Adaptive management in agricultural innovation systems: the interactions between innovation networks and their environment. Agricultural Systems 102: 390-400.

Klerkx, L., A. Hall and C. Leeuwis, 2009. Strengthening agricultural innovation capacity: are innovation brokers the answer? International Journal of Agricultural Resources Governance and Ecology 8 (5/6): 409-438.

Klijn, E.H., J.F.M. Koppenjan and C.J.A.M. Termeer, 1995. Managing Networks in the Public Sector: A Theoretical Study of Management Strategies in Policy Networks. Public Administration 73(3): 437-454.

Klijn, E. and J.F.M. Koppenjan, 2006. Institutional design in networks: elaborating and analyzing strategies for institutional design. Paper for the Eight International Research Symposium on Public Management (IRSPM VIII) 31 March-2 April, University of Economics and Public Administration, Budapest, Hungary.

Kloprogge, P. and J. van der Sluijs, 2006. The inclusion of stakeholder knowledge and perspectives in integrated assessment of climate change. Climate Change 75: 359-389.

Knorr-Cetina, K., 1981. The manufacture of knowledge: An essay on the constructivist and contextual nature of science. Pergamon, Oxford, UK.

Latour, B., 1987. Science in Action. Harvard University Press, Cambridge, MA, USA.

Leach, M., G. Bloom, A. Ely, P. Nightingale, I. Scoones, E. Shah and A. Smith, 2007. Understanding Governance: pathways to sustainability, STEPS Working Paper 2, STEPS Centre, Brighton, UK.

Leeuwis, C., 2000. Reconceptualizing Participation for Sustainable Rural Development: Towards a Negotiation Approach. Development and Change 31: 31-59.

McEvily, B., V. Perrone and A. Zaheer, 2003. Trust as an organizing principle. Organization Science 14 (1): 91-103.

McNie, E.C., 2007. Reconciling the supply of scientific information with user demands: An analysis of the problem and review of the literature. Environ Science and Policy 10(1): 17-38.

Medema, W., B.S. McIntosh and P.J. Jeffrey, 2008. From premise to practice: a critical assessment of Integrated Resources Management and Adaptive Management Approaches in the water sector. Ecology and Society 13 (20: 29. Available at www.ecologyandsociety.org/vol13/iss2/aer29/.

Michaels, S., 2009. Matching knowledge brokering strategies to environmental policy problems and setting. Environmental Science and Policy 12: 994-1011.

Mollinga, P.P., 2008. The rational organization of dissent; boundary concepts, boundary objects and boundary settings in the interdisciplinaryity study of natural resources management. ZEF (Center for Development Research), Bonn, Germany.

Nowotny, H., P. Scott and M. Gibbons, 2001. Re-thinking science; knowledge and the public in the age of uncertainty. Blackwell Publishers, Oxford, UK.

Opdam, P., 2010. Learning science from practice. Landscape Ecology 25: 821-823.

Probst, K. and J. Hagmann, with contributions from M. Fernandez and J.A. Ashby, 2003. Understanding Participatory Research in the Context of Natural Resource Management: Paradigms, Approaches and Typologies. ODI-AGREN Network Paper No. 130. Available at: http://www.odi.org.uk/agren/.

Raul, P.K. and P. Jeffrey, 2008. On the appropriateness of public participation in Integrated Water Resource Management: some grounded insights from the Levant. The Integrated Assessment Journal 8 (2): 69-106.

Röling, N., 1997. The soft side of land: socio-economic sustainability of land use systems. ITC journal 1997 (3/4): 248-262.

Transforum, 2007. Innovatief praktijkproject Noordelijke Friese Wouden, working paper 6. Transforum, Zoetermeer, the Netherlands.

Tress B. and G. Tress, 2001. Capitalising on multiplicity: a transdisciplinary systems approach to landscape research. Landscape and Urban Planning 57: 143-157.

Tress, B., G. Tress, A. Van der Valk and G. Fry, 2003. Interdisicplinary and transdisciplinary landscape studies: Potential and limitations. Delta Series 2, Wageningen. Integrative studies on rural landscapes: policy expectations and research practice. Landscape and Urban Planning 70: 177-191.

Tress, B., G. Tress and G. Fry, 2005. Integrative studies on rural landscapes: policy expectations and research practice. Landscape and Urban Planning 70: 177-191.

Tress, G., B. Tress and G. Fry 2004. Clarifying integrative research concepts in landscape ecology. Landscape Ecology 20: 479-491.

Turnhout, E., M. Hisschemöller and H. Eijsackers, 2007. Ecological indicators: between the two fires of science and policy. Ecological Indicators 7: 215-228.

Van Asselt, M.B.A. and N. Rijkens-Klomp, 2002. A look in the mirror: reflection on participation in Integrated Assessment from a methodological perspective. Global Environmental Change 12: 167-184.

Van Bueren, E.M., E.H. Klijn and J.F.M. Koppenjan, 2003. Dealing with wicked problems in networks: analyzing an environmental debate from a network perspective. Journal of Public Administration Research and Theory 13 (2): 193-212.

Van Dongen, H.J., W.A.M. De Laat and A.J.J.A. Maas, 1996. Een kwestie van verschil: conflicthantering en onderhandeling in een configuratieve integratietheorie. Eburon, Delft, the Netherlands.

Van Kerkhoff, L. and L. Lebel, 2006. Linking knowledge with action for sustainable development. Annual Review of Environment and Resources 31: 1-33.

Van Mierlo, B., B. Regeer, M. Van Amstel, M. Arkensteijn, V. Beekman, J. Bunders, T. De Cock Buning, B. Elzen, A.C. Hoes and C. Leeuwis, 2010. Reflexieve monitoring in actie; Handvatten voor de monitoring van systeeeminnovatieprojecten. Box press, Oisterwijk, the Netherlands.

Webler, T., 2001. Public participation in watershed management planning: views on process from people in the field. Human Ecology Review 8 (2): 29-39.

Webler, T., 2002. Unlocking the puzzle of public participation. Bulletin of Science, Technology and Society 22 (3): 179-189.

12. Conclusion: from knowledge for action to knowledge in action

Werkman, R., C. Termeer, A. Gerritsen and M. Stuiver, 2010. 'We can do it better' Barriers to the integration of selfgovernance principles in existing governing practices in a Dutch initiative for community rural development. Paper for the 23rd Annual Meeting of the Public Administration Theory Network. Ohama, NE, USA.

Wu, J.J., 2006. Landscape ecology, cross-disciplinarity and sustainability science. Landscape Ecology 21: 1-4.

Wu, J.J., 2008. Making the case for landscape ecology; an effective approach to urban sustainability. Landscape Journal 27: 41-50.

About the authors

Conny Almekinders is a staff member of the Technology and Agrarian Development group in the Social Science department of Wageningen University. Her experiences and interest are focused on participatory approaches of technology development, the researcher-farmer interaction in their context. This focus lately brought her to explore action research as a way of generating scientific knowledge.
Affiliation: Technology & Agrarian Development chairgroup, Social Sciences, Wageningen University, the Netherlands.
E-mail: conny.almekinders@wur.nl

PJ (Pieter Jelle) Beers studied Environmental Health Sciences at Maastricht University. He obtained a PhD at the Open University of the Netherlands for his thesis *Negotiating Common Ground: Tools for multidisciplinary Teams*. As a post-doc, he worked at TU Delft on a project called 'Harnessing Multi-actor System Complexity'. PJ is now employed at Wageningen University, on the topic of knowledge and system innovation, and at TransForum, where he is Scientific Theme Coordinator for research on 'Images of sustainable development in agriculture and green space.' PJ's main research interests concern the role of knowledge and learning in the context of complex societal problems and sustainable development.
Affiliation: Animal Production Systems Group, Wageningen University, the Netherlands.
E-mail: pj.beers@wur.nl

Arianne de Blaeij graduated in Environmental Economics at Wageningen University in 1998. She defended her PhD entitled *The value of a statistical life in road safety* at the Vrije Universiteit Amsterdam in 2003. Since 2006, she has been employed as a researcher at the Research Unit Regional Economy and Land Use of LEI-WUR. Her main focus is on valuation of, and payment mechanisms for, ecosystem services and natural resources.
Affiliataion: Regional Economy & Land Use Group, LEI (Agricultural Economics Research Institute), Wageningen UR, the Netherlands.
E-mail: arianne.deblaeij@wur.nl

Pongchai Dumrongrojwatthana is a tropical ecologist and lecturer-researcher in the Department of Biology of the Faculty of Science at Chulalongkorn University in Bangkok, Thailand. He obtained his joint doctorate degree from Paris Ouest Nanterre La Défense and Chulalongkorn Universities in April 2010. The title of his PhD dissertation is *Interactions between cattle raising and reforestation in the highland socio-ecosystem of Nan province, Northern Thailand: A companion modelling process to improve landscape management*.
Affiliation: Department of Biology, Faculty of Science, Chulalongkorn University, Thailand.
E-mail: pongchai@hotmail.com

About the authors

Roel During is senior researcher in Cultural Heritage and Spatial Planning. His PhD research and analysis was made out of pluralist and universalist ideological claims on cultural heritage in Europeanisation. He was assigned several research tasks by the First and Second Chamber of the State General, which gave him a good view of politics-polity interactions. In 2005 he submitted the initiative CULTPLAN, intending to study the intercultural dimension in spatial and landscape planning. In the three-year project that followed he became acquainted with the diversity of regional cultures in Europe and their influences on spatial planning practices. Recently his focus shifted to self-organising communities, their knowledge resources and their political repercussions.
Affiliation: Alterra, Wageningen UR, the Netherlands.
E-mail: roel.during@wur.nl

Floor Geerling has an MA in Communication Sciences from the University of Amsterdam, the Netherlands. She has built up experience in research on knowledge management and communication and innovation studies in the life sciences since 2000. Her research experience and interest is focused on the concept of knowledge arrangements in which research, education, entrepreneurs, citizens and governments work together on the adoption, circulation and co-creation of knowledge. She currently works as programme leader for the policy supporting research programme Knowledge (BO-09).
Affiliation: LEI (Agricultural Economics Research Institute), Wageningen UR, the Netherlands.
E-mail: floor.geerling-eiff@wur.nl

Willemien Geertsema graduated in Biology at Wageningen University in 1994. At Wageningen University in co-operation with Alterra, Wageningen UR she wrote her PhD thesis entitled *Plant survival in dynamic habitat networks in agricultural landscapes* (2002). From 2002-2008 she worked at Alterra and Wageningen University on different applied research projects, studying green-blue networks for biodiversity and ecosystem services and multifunctional landscapes. Since 2008, her work at Alterra has focused on climate adaptation strategies for nature and on the application of scientific knowledge in sustainable landscape development.
Affiliation: Alterra Landscape Centre and Land Use Planning Group, Wageningen UR, the Netherlands.
E-mail: willemien.geertsema@wur.nl

Bette Harms has an MSc in communication science and a BSc in forest and nature conservation from Wageningen University, the Netherlands. She specialises in participatory research methods in natural resource management. She has experience in Africa on connecting local farmer innovativeness in natural resource management and climate adaptation to other stakeholders – public or private, local or global – to contribute to enhance local resilience and sustainable development.

Affiliation: Environment, Nature and Landscape group, LEI (Agricultural Economics Research Institute), Wageningen UR, the Netherlands.
E-mail: bette.harms@wur.nl

Janice Jiggins is a social scientist, former Professor of Human Ecology, at the Swedish University of Agricultural Sciences, Uppsala (Sweden). For more than thirty years she has worked and published widely on small farm development in the tropics, extension systems, farming systems research, participatory plant breeding, natural resource management, integrated pest management, gender issues and, within Europe, on the sustainable management of water in the agrarian sector.
Affiliation: Guest researcher at Communication and Innovation Studies chairgroup, Social Sciences Group, Wageningen University, the Netherlands and Visiting Fellow at IIED, London, United Kingdom.
E-mail: janice.jiggins@inter.nl.net

Bui Thi Kim holds a diploma degree in economics from Technical University Dresden, Germany. She has broad experience in community development issues in Vietnam since 2000. Her interest is in promoting participation and democracy at grassroots levels, women rights and child rights. She specialises in participatory project management; gender mainstreaming in development projects by rural and urban people in Vietnam; trainer on facilitation skills, gender and women rights, child rights, participatory learning and action; facilitator in improving the quality of life for poor people, manager in development projects.
Affiliation: Center for Promoting Development for Women and Children (DWC), Vietnam.
E-mail: kimbt@hn.vnn.vn

Cees Leeuwis is professor of Communication and Innovation Studies at Wageningen University. His research focuses on cross-disciplinary approaches to creating technical and institutional space for change, social learning and conflict management in networks, and the functioning of innovation systems.
Affiliation: Communication and Innovation Studies Group, Wageningen University, the Netherlands.
E-mail: cees.leeuwis@wur.nl

Jessica Milgroom is an interdisciplinary PhD student in the Competing Claims on Natural Resources programme (INREF-funded) at Wageningen University. Her research focuses on population resettlement, mechanisms of participation and negotiation in policy, and adaptive agricultural practices in semi-arid environments.
Affiliation: Communication and Innovation Studies chairgroup (Social Sciences Group) and Plant Production Systems chairgroup (Plant Sciences Group), Wageningen University, the Netherlands.
E-mail: jessica.milgroom@gmail.com

About the authors

Tendayi Mutimukuru-Maravanyika has a PhD in natural resource management from Wageningen University and Research Centre. She also has an MSc in Management of Agriculture Knowledge Systems (MAKS) from the same university, and a BSc Honours in Agriculture (with a specialisation in agriculture economics) from the University of Zimbabwe. Tendayi has vast experience in using the participatory action research methodology as well as other participatory methodologies in solving natural resource management problems. Her research interests include community-based natural resource management, adaptive management, participatory action research and climate change and adaption.
Affiliation: Technology & Agrarian Development chairgroup, Social Sciences, Wageningen University, the Netherlands.
E-mail: tendayim07@yahoo.co.uk

Simon Oosting has a PhD in Animal Sciences. At the Animal Production Systems Group he teaches and supervises research about roles and functions of animals and systems with animals in the Netherlands and in the tropics. Action research in the frame of regional development is one of the instruments used for teaching and learning about the roles and functions of animal systems for societies.
Affiliation: Animal Production Systems Group, Wageningen University, the Netherlands.
E-mail: simon.oosting@wur.nl

Paul Opdam is professor in Landscape in Spatial Planning. Educated as an ecologist, he became involved in the planning and design of conservation networks. Later his research shifted in focus towards planning of multifunctional landscapes. He has been (2003-2010) the co-ordinator of the €8 m/year strategic research programme 'Sustainable spatial development of ecosystems, landscapes, seas and regions' which is funded by the Dutch Ministry of Agriculture, Nature Conservation and Food Quality. His expertise includes planning and design methods for ecosystem networks at various levels of spatial scale, adaptation strategies for landscapes to climate change and the role of green infrastructure and biodiversity in governance processes to develop landscape services. These topics were addressed in some of his recent projects. Paul Opdam combines a leading role in science with advisory roles in the science-practice interface.
Affiliation: Landscape Center and Land Use Planning Group, Alterra, Wageningen UR, the Netherlands.
E-mail: paul.opdam@wur.nl

Bas Pedroli is a senior landscape researcher with an academic background at the University of Amsterdam in physical geography and landscape ecology. He specialised in landscape studies both in consulting assignments and contract research. He is engaged enthusiastically in the future of Europe's living landscapes, developing methodology for landscape and nature conservation planning from a sustainable development perspective, and developing methodology to integrate natural sciences, complex land-use requirements and landscape

perception and appreciation in the management. He has a keen interest in involving civil society in the process of decision support for these purposes. He co-ordinates several EU projects related to landscape and is active in various scientific networks.
Affiliation: Alterra Landscape Centre, Wageningen UR, the Netherlands.
E-mail: bas.pedroli@wur.nl

Marcel Pleijte is a senior researcher in Public Administration and a PhD researcher at Alterra, a knowledge institute for the rural area, and part of Wageningen University and Research Centre (Wageningen UR), the Netherlands. His projects at Alterra focus on policy evaluation, especially the evaluation of area development. His PHD research focuses on public-private partnership in area development and a discourse analysis is made of the discussions about area development between different domains of state, market and civil society. He was involved twice in action-oriented research: in the Noordwaard and in Wieringerrandmeer.
Affiliation: Alterra, Wageningen UR, the Netherlands.
E-mail: marcel.pleijte@wur.nl

Le Quang Anh holds a Bachelor degree in Water Management for Agricultural Development from Prague University, Czech Republic. He is a researcher and senior consultant with over 20 year's experience in Vietnam and Southeast Asia in institutional aspects, especially in Participatory Irrigation Management (PIM) and Impact Evaluation. He has extensive experience in irrigation projects. Mr. Anh has worked in participatory planning, monitoring, and evaluation projects for water resources policies in Vietnam for a variety of clients including the Ministries of Agriculture and Rural Development, Alterra-ILRI, Wageningen University and Research Centre (the Netherlands), World Bank, ADB and some NGOs. His research and interest focuses on participatory methods, impact evaluation, socio-economic aspects, institution and community development.
Affiliation: Center for Training and International Cooperation, Vietnam Academy for Water Resources, Vietnam.
E-mail: aba_anh@yahoo.com

Henk Ritzema obtained a MSc in Civil Engineering at Delft University in 1980 and a PhD at Wageningen University and UNESCO-IHE Delft in 2009. He has thirty years of experience in water management and hydrology for food and ecosystems management in North Africa, the Middle East and in South and Southeast Asia. His experience and interest lie in capacity-building through joint research and education projects in the field of natural resources management.
Affiliation: Irrigation and Water Engineering Group, Wageningen University, Wageningen UR, the Netherlands.
E-mail: henk.ritzema@wur.nl

About the authors

Marc Schut is a PhD researcher at the Communication and Innovation Studies Group of Wageningen University and Research Centre (Wageningen UR), the Netherlands. His PhD research focuses on the role of research in societal negotiations and policy processes. He is currently involved as a policy advisor in Mozambique, conducting research to support the development of a framework for sustainable biofuel production there. Through his case studies and action-oriented research, he hopes to gather insights into the dynamics that influence the effective contribution of research towards sustainable solutions to complex environmental problems.
Affiliation: Communication and Innovation Studies Group, Wageningen University, the Netherlands.
E-mail: marc.schut@wur.nl

Jifke Sol has an MSc in Rural Sociology, Wageningen University, the Netherlands. She has built up experience in Dutch rural development projects in different regions since 1993, working for consultancy desks and universities. She currently runs her own business, aiming at the improvement of co-operation between different stakeholders by supporting the process of social learning. For Wageningen University she works on the topic of knowledge and system innovation. Jifke is specialising in research on and facilitation of reflective learning in multi-actor alliances in regional contexts.
Affiliation: Education and Competence Studies, Wageningen University, the Netherlands.
E-mail: jifke.sol@wur.nl

Eveliene Steingröver has a PhD in plant physiology. Since 2000, she has been working for the Landscape Department of Alterra Green World Research, specialising in landscape ecology. Her interest lies in bridging the gap between science and practice. Her main interest is the application of ecological knowledge in environmental policy and in planning processes that involve stakeholders from different land-use functions. She is involved in developing interactive tools for stakeholders to improve the usage of ecological knowledge in spatial planning.
Affiliation: Alterra Landscape Centre, Wageningen UR, the Netherlands.
E-mail: eveliene.steingrover@wur.nl

Marian Stuiver holds a PhD in Rural Sociology. She performs action research on sustainable entrepreneurship and effective governance, and organises interactive processes. She leads a WUR research programme on sustainable development of areas. Before joining WUR she was a social science researcher at the University of Amsterdam and project developer at TransForum Agro en Groen.
Affiliation: Alterra Landscape Centre, Wageningen UR, the Netherlands.
E-mail: marian.stuiver@wur.nl

About the authors

Catharien Terwisscha van Scheltinga is a researcher and lecturer on climate change adaptation and international water management at Alterra, part of Wageningen University and Research Centre. She has an MSc in International Land and Water Management from Wageningen University, the Netherlands. She has a wide range of experience in water management and rural development in Africa and Asia. Since 1993, she has been involved in different assignments for (inter)national organisations on training, applied research and advisory services. Her research experience and interest is in capacity development for climate change adaptation, and in particular the relationship between climate change adaptation, sustainable development and changing livelihoods of vulnerable groups. Until recently, she was a steering committee member of the Gender and Water Alliance.
Affiliation: Earth System Science-Climate Change group, Alterra, Wageningen UR, the Netherlands.
E-mail: catharien.terwisscha@wur.nl

Guy Trébuil is an agronomist cum human geographer in the Management of Renewable Resources and Environment rescarch unit (GREEN) of the Centre de coopération internationale en recherche agronomique pour le développement (Cirad) based in Montpellier, France. Since 1981, he has been doing research on the transformations of agricultural systems in different Southeast Asian countries. For the past eight years, he was involved in projects using Companion Modelling (ComMod), a participatory approach relying on Multi-Agent Systems, to support decentralised, integrated and inclusive management of renewable resource in Thailand and Bhutan.
Affiliation: CIRAD, UPR47 GREEN, Department Environments and Societies, France.
E-mail: guy.trebuil@cirad.fr

Jolanda van den Berg has an MA in development administration from Leiden University, the Netherlands. She has built up extensive experience in development research in Africa and Southeast Asia since 1993. Her research experience and interest lie in participatory research methodologies, socio-institutional aspects of research and development, particularly in the fields of natural resource management and sustainable livelihoods. She specialises in participatory innovation by rural people, development practitioners and scientists to increase local capacities to adapt to changing conditions.
Affiliation: LEI (Agricultural Economics Research Institute), Wageningen UR, the Netherlands.
E-mail: jolanda.vandenberg@wur.nl

About the authors

Martijn van der Heide obtained his degree in Agricultural Economics from Wageningen University in March 1997. His PhD thesis examined the economic analysis of nature policy (2005). Since 2004, he has been employed as a research scholar at the Research Unit on Natural Resources, with ample expertise in ecological and environmental economics, and with research interests in the field of agriculture, ecology and economics, in particular in monetary valuation of natural resources. In June 2010, Martijn was appointed as lecturer in 'Integrated Nature and Landscape Management' at Van Hall Larenstein, University of Applied Sciences.
Affiliation: Environment & Nature Group, LEI (Agricultural Economics Research Institute), Wageningen UR, the Netherland; Van Hall Larenstein, University of Applied Sciences, Wageningen UR, the Netherlands.
E-mail: martijn.vanderheide@wur.nl

Jouwert van Geene is a social scientist and development practitioner with an MSc in Management Studies from Radboud University Nijmegen, the Netherlands, with a special interest in Development Studies and Public Administration and Development. Jouwert has worked on the international capacity development of NGOs and government since 1995, focusing on participatory methods for community engagement and multi-stakeholder processes. He works mainly in the domains of sustainable livelihoods, food security and natural resource management. Until recently, he was attached to the Wageningen UR, Centre for Development Innovation; he is currently affiliated to The Hunger Project Netherlands.
Affiliation: Centre for Development Innovation, Wageningen UR, the Netherlands.
E-mail: jouwert.vangeene@gmail.com/jouwert@thehungerproject.nl

Annemarie van Paassen is assistant professor in Communication and Innovation Studies. After 11 years of practical experience in development work, notably the training and guidance of facilitators in the domain of community development, agricultural development and natural resource management in Africa, she joined Wageningen University. Her present research focuses on social learning, negotiation and conflict management in multilevel innovation processes; the use of boundary-spanning tools such as simulation models for innovation; the execution of inter- and trans-disciplinary research; science communication; the role of (collaborative) research in innovation processes; and critical/reflexive monitoring & evaluation of collaborative research.
Affiliation: Social Sciences, Wageningen University, the Netherlands.
E-mail: annemarie.vanpaassen@wur.nl

Renate Werkman has a PhD in Social Science from the University of Amsterdam, department of Political Sciences, the Netherlands. Her main interest is in transition and change in organisations and networks and the role of counterproductive interaction patterns in transition processes. Methodologically, she is inspired by action research methods and naturalistic inquiry. She currently runs her own research and consultancy business.
Affiliation: Social Sciences, Wageningen University, the Netherlands.
E-mail: renate.werkman@onderzoekenadvies.org

Keyword index

A
ABM – *See:* agent-based model
ACM – *See:* adaptive collaborative management
action learning 170
action-oriented research 21, 150
action planning approach 68
action research 137, 143, 149, 170, 171, 177, 221, 223, 224, 228, 252, 271
adaptation framework 121, 124
adaptive
 – capacity 173
 – collaborative management (ACM) 170, 171, 172
 – governance 23
 – management 27, 194
advisory group
 – role 94, 104
advocacy 291
aesthetic value 89
Africa 52
agent-based model (ABM) 194, 198, 207
agriculture 75, 234
applicability 103, 106
arena of conflict 257

B
balanced negotiations
 – research 48, 292
belief 299
biodiversity 169
biophysical systems 22
bottom-up governance approach 90
boundary
 – concepts 49, 50
 – objects 49, 50, 134, 138, 146, 147, 149, 154, 158, 163, 195, 214, 279, 281
 – processes 49, 117
 – roles 146
 – simulation tools 201
 – work 33, 44, 138, 158
 – workers 164
boundary spanning process 278
 – appropriate 297
 – type 286
brokerage 268, 270
 – first level 44
 – second level 44
 – systemic 44
broker knowledge 43, 44, 236, 240
Brundtland commission 20

C
capacity building 61, 76, 78, 114, 127, 128, 130, 174, 177, 183, 185, 281
 – approach 116
change
 – attitude 117
 – focus 104
 – process 129
choice experiment 89, 90, 101
climate change 113
 – adaptation 114, 117, 118, 120, 129
co-creation 138
 – of knowledge 134
co-design 200
coherence 163
collaboration type 278
collaborative
 – learning 138
 – modelling 62, 193, 204
 – participation 45
 – planning 240
 – relationships 137
collaborative research 17, 79, 138, 181, 257, 272
 – advantages 50
 – approaches 42

Index

- key dimensions 43
- landscape 145
- types 42, 47, 286

collective
- action 194
- action plan 206
- learning 158
- management 203

collegiate participation 45, 286
co-management 194
combining research methods 295
communication
- intensity 211

communicative approach 224
community
- drainage committee 71
- of practice 158, 225
- participation 61

community-based institutions 19, 63, 64
compensation 264
competing claims 126
complexity 115, 119, 192
complex system 21
computer simulations 216
conceptual framework 113, 197, 200
- evolution 216
- new 207

concerted action 24
confidence 203
conflict 298
- context 258, 298
- functions and values 24
- management 251

consensus 224
constructivist 26, 195, 294
consultative participation 45, 75
contingent valuation method (CVM) 89
contractual participation 45
cost-efficient 216
credibility 31, 102, 139, 149, 260

critical
- monitoring 203
- system thinking 28, 43, 281

CVM – *See:* contingent valuation method

D

decentralisation 192, 232
deliberative valuation 91
democratic
- deliberation 20
- dialogue 137, 145
- process 228

diagnostic study 199
digital gap 213
discourse 33, 158, 231
distrust 20, 196, 260, 297
diverse perceptions 195, 199
drainage system 58, 66, 69, 73, 74
DUFLOW 73

E

East Africa 53, 113
ecological
- services 22
- values 85, 100

ecologists 18
economic
- interests 101
- values 85

ecosystem services 86
ecotourism 171
effect 108, 212
EIA – *See:* environmental impact assessment

embedded 26, 136, 165, 221, 240, 271, 277, 296
emergence 193
empowerment 142, 144, 172, 173, 177, 185, 231, 291
engagement 217, 273
entrepreneurship 186

environmental
- impact assessment (EIA) 236
- values 154
epistemic communities 163
epistemology 163, 195, 294
- dilemma 292
- pluralism 20
equitable 22, 137, 261
- expression 215
- landscape development 17
espoused theories 288
ethics 271
Ethiopia 128
evaluation 102, 203
experiential learning 27, 280
exploration phase 237
expropriation 230
extended peer community 249

F
facilitating 257
- debate on arguments 209
- the design 206
facilitators 136, 146
farmers' organisation 63, 64, 76, 156, 234
field experiment 210, 213
flexible research approach 198, 292
Flood Mitigation 226
food security 255
foresters 199
forest-farmland interface 204
forest management 172

G
gaming workshop 205
geographical focus 52
goal 192
governance 172, 186
- multilayered polycentric 23
- robust 23
- science-based 18, 20

green-blue networks 87
grid 209
Groningen 133

H
habitat networks 88
hard sciences 195
hard system thinking 25, 43, 279
herders 199
heterogeneity 215
human resource investment 186

I
impression management 259
increased awareness 213
independence 271
indicators 100, 203
Indonesia 185
inequalities 240
informality 271
information-oriented activities 122
inhabitants 101
initialisation 199
innovation system thinking 29, 43, 284
institutional
- change research 48
- constraints 67, 70
- development 61, 76
- theory 29, 43
institutions 29
intangible 265
integrating
- perspectives 216
- values 105
integrity 258
intended outcome 192
interaction 157
interactive 92
interdependent 21
interdisciplinary 134
- teams 195

Index

interest   97
– groups   101
intermediary role   259
internet   100
interviews   255
irrigation and drainage management committees   64
iterative investigations   201

J

joint fact-finding   164
joint learning   130, 134, 175, 182
joint stakeholder analysis   120

K

knowledge   119, 123
– action-oriented   242
– arrangements   135
– categories   164
– co-creation   142, 164, 224, 253
– contextual   136, 165
– development   130, 156
– elicitation   200
– exchange   116, 123, 157, 207, 213
– experiential   131, 137, 158, 161
– explicit   78
– formal   229
– indigenous   126
– innovative   136
– integration   86, 115, 224
– interdisciplinary   224
– local-specific   59, 81
– modes of production   153, 157
– narrative-oriented   229
– robust   165, 224
– scientific   131, 137
– socially robust   26
– tacit   68, 78, 81, 127, 280
– translation   86, 107
– true   161

L

landscape   18, 22, 85, 234
– design method   86, 92
– development   21, 232
– ecology   26
– functions   22
– management strategies   209
– science   24, 51
– services valuation   26
land-use   72
– analysis   25
– development   18
– map   209
– scenarios   201
leadership   180
learning   210
– approach   115, 171
– by doing   141, 143
– community   141, 143
– cycle   119
– phase   125
legitimate
– knowledge   32, 103, 139, 149, 252
– process   240
– role researcher   215, 217, 253, 255, 296
level the playing field   196
livelihood   19
lobbying   241
logbook   207, 216
long-term system evolution   196
loyalty   260

M

marginalisation   242
mediation   196, 282, 291
metapopulation theory   88
monetary valuation   89
Mozambique   53, 247, 267
multi-dimensional approach   292, 297
multi-disciplinary   181

Index

mutual
- interest 205
- trust 212
- understanding 105, 164, 194, 212

N
natural resources 169, 253
nature conservation 25, 101
negotiation 173, 205, 210, 221, 225, 240, 248, 252
nested systems 21
Netherlands 52, 53, 223
new institutionalism 185
nutrient management 156

O
objectives 193
objectivity 90
open-access resource 19
options
- generate 210
- prioritise 66
out-scaling 207
ownership 164, 215, 217, 288

P
PAR – *See:* participatory action research
paradigm 127, 298
participant 125
- observation 255
participate 136
participation 158, 185, 237
- active 60
- degree 105
participatory
- action research (PAR) 57, 177, 184, 185
- approach 70, 169
- diagnostic survey 66, 68
- modelling 59, 78, 81
- monitoring 67, 77, 173
- research approach 59, 63
- rural appraisal (PRA) 176
People, Planet and Profit 20, 97
performativity 221, 223, 225, 240, 242
pertinent suggestions 213
Phan Dong area 65, 72
pictograms 207
planning
- blueprint 223
- collaborative 223
- with communities 60
policy implementation 232
political
- activities 183
- ecology 28, 185
positivist 25, 43
post-normal science 195, 249
power 142, 185, 186, 187, 222, 241, 249, 270
- asymmetries 199
- inequality 147, 150, 231
- relations 135
PRA – *See:* participatory rural appraisal
practitioners 136
pragmatic problem 49
preferences 98
preliminary sensitising activities 214
price
- indifference 107
- tag 99
priority 104
problem
- setting 289, 296
- type 289
problem-oriented research 21, 46
problem structure 30, 279, 290, 297
process
- cycles 197
- design 194
public
- distrust 20
- private partnership 232, 234
- support 238

Index

R
raising interest 204
Red River Delta 58, 65, 77
reflexive 221, 223, 225, 240, 241, 297
– monitoring 203
regional development 133, 135, 137
reification 158
reliability 222
representatives 101, 106
requests 212
research
– collaborative 280
– collegiate 282, 283
– consultative 279, 282
– methodology 80, 198
– role 33, 286, 288
researcher's
– perception 197
– role 44, 80, 96, 210, 286, 288
– tasks 44
research-policy interface 118, 123
resettlement 248, 253
resilience 194
resource
– management 175, 180, 184, 186
– sharing 175, 176
risk of flooding 69
role 142, 146, 149, 154, 236, 239, 249, 254, 256, 257, 266, 271
– shifts 135
role-playing game (RPG) 195, 198, 201, 205
RPG – *See:* role-playing game
rules of engagement 271
rural development 144

S
salient knowledge 32, 103, 139
scales 22
– linking 121
scenario 229, 236, 251
– explorations 196, 207

science
– mode 1 146
– mode 2 32, 50, 250
science of complexity 193
scientific
– posture 196
– quality 102
selection criteria 52, 99
self-organisation 154
self-referentiality 221
semantic problem 49
SES – *See:* socio-ecological systems
shared representation 204, 216
sharing of viewpoints 198
simplification 200
simulation tool 62, 73, 198
– modification 206
skill development 124
social
– actors 135
– cohesion 157
– systems 22
social learning 27, 46, 60, 149, 159, 223, 225, 226, 279, 280
societal negotiation 249, 269, 274
socio-ecological systems (SES) 193
socio-economic benefits 234
socio-political context 33
soft system thinking 26, 43, 279
South Africa 247, 260
Southeast Asia 52
spatial
– alternatives 99
– characteristics 97, 98
– development 237
– explicit choices 91
– norms 88
– structure 87
spatially explicit 87
stakeholder 76, 80, 94, 96, 134, 172
– assessment 74
– local 192

- participation 45, 77, 296
- processes 126
- regional 135, 140, 141, 145
- role 104

strategic knowledge generation 281
structure-function-value chain 87
student 135
subjectivity 90
sustainability science 21
sustainable
- development 20, 118, 122, 128, 129, 131
- farming 162
- management 187, 191

sustainable landscape
- development 17, 22, 277
- governance 17, 19

syntactic problem 49
system
- approach 154
- perspective 160
- theories 25

T

target setting 97
technical innovations 74, 75, 210
Thailand 53
theoretical framework
- fit 288
- flexible use 297

theories-in-use 288
theories of practice 136
time management 214
timing 104
trade-offs 99
training
- course 114, 116, 120, 121, 131
- process 125

transdisciplinarity 32, 135
transdisciplinary research 50, 92, 138, 277, 285, 299
transfer of technology model 19

transparency 107, 197
Trieu Duong area 65, 72

U

uncertainty 122, 298
up-scaling 207

V

validation 201
valuation method 92
value 87
- indicators 107
- judgment 260

vegetation dynamics 200, 205
viable populations 100
Vietnam 57
virtual
- landscape 209, 214
- world 213

visioning 62, 177
visualisation 100, 214
vulnerability assessment 124

W

waterlogging 67
water management 57, 71
water-related recreation 94
welfare theory 89
wet rice cultivation 58
wildlife management 171
willingness to pay (WTP) 87, 99, 102, 107
worldview 298
WTP – *See:* willingness to pay

Z

Zimbabwe 53, 169, 185, 247, 260